MICHAEL E. GLASSCOCK, Ph.D. has been associated with real estate investment consulting, teaching, lecturing on financial planning, and appraising full-time since 1963. He earned his Ph.D. at California Western University and LL.B. at Cumberland University, and his Doctor of Jurisprudence from Stamford University.

The Real Estate Investing Profit Guide

How to Successfully Finance, Purchase,
and Manage Income Property

Michael E. Glasscock, J.D., Ph.D.

A SPECTRUM BOOK

PRENTICE-HALL, INC. Englewood Cliffs, New Jersey 07632

Library of Congress Cataloging in Publication Data

Glasscock, Michael E.
  The real estate investing profit guide.

  (A Spectrum Book)
  Includes index.
  1. Real estate investment. I. Title.
HD1382.5.G57   332.63'24   81-23463
ISBN 0-13-763136-7   AACR2
ISBN 0-13-763128-6 (pbk.)

This Spectrum Book is available to businesses and organizations at a special discount when ordered in large quantities. For information, contact Prentice-Hall, Inc., General Book Division, Special Sales, Englewood Cliffs, N. J. 07632.

10 9 8 7 6 5 4 3 2 1

ISBN 0-13-763136-7

ISBN 0-13-763128-6 (PBK)

Printed in the United States of America

Editorial/production supervision and interior design by Cyndy Lyle Rymer
Manufacturing buyer: Cathie Lenard
Cover design by Jeannette Jacobs

Prentice-Hall International, Inc., *London*
Prentice-Hall of Australia Pty. Limited, *Sydney*
Prentice-Hall of Canada, Ltd., *Toronto*
Prentice-Hall of India Private Limited, *New Delhi*
Prentice-Hall of Japan, Inc., *Tokyo*
Prentice-Hall of Southeast Asia Pte. Ltd., *Singapore*
Whitehall Books Limited, *Wellington, New Zealand*

Contents

Foreword

It is always flattering to be asked to write a few lines as a foreword to a book, especially a book that is such a comprehensive work as my friend Michael Glasscock has put together from his up and down experiences in the land of real estate he describes as "the last brass ring" in his book titled *The Real Estate Investing Profit Guide*.

The writer of a foreword of a good book must read the book, and in the reading learn a great deal about the thesis, and greatly enhance his own knowledge. Dr. Glasscock's book demonstrates the basic principle that an investor must have a specific objective goal to reach. He must follow the road that leads to that goal. If he does not have a goal as to where he wants to go, it makes no difference which road he takes. He will never get there anyway.

For me, Dr. Glasscock's book is like a road map. It shows the reader what goals there are, and what roads you must take to get there. The book tells where the rough spots are, and where the road is smooth and clear.

While a book of this size covers a great number of details under its various titles, the headings make it quite easy to review any particular section, such as *Leverage,* to fit any step in your own program.

For these reasons I recommend this book for consideration to all those reaching for the "brass ring" in real estate as set forth by Dr. Glasscock.

HOWARD JARVIS

Preface

After investing in property off and on for many years, with some successes and some failures, I came to the conclusion that the failures were caused by a lack of knowledge of how to structure a transaction that was both feasible and profitable.

Throughout the years my ambition was to become a real estate investor, but with the Depression, World War II, children to raise and put through college and medical school, I was kept too busy and preoccupied to take the time to gain the necessary understanding of the complexities of real estate investing.

Finally, I said, "The hell with it." I was 50 years old and broke. I had good education, and I developed an insatiable appetite to learn more about investing in real estate. I read every book I could lay my hands on that dealt with the subject. Most were too simplified with very little substance, whereas some were too technical for the limited knowledge I had about real estate. I kept running across the word *leverage* and its importance, but I was never given a clear understanding of its principles and how to make it work for the novice. I searched the university libraries and found little material of academic value on the subject, so I enrolled in graduate school and wrote my dissertation on leverage as a creative tool in acquiring real estate. With this book, you will gain solid understanding of leverage and the other necessary tools to help you become a successful investor. In time this knowledge could bring you much wealth, depending on how well you apply the principles I have set forth.

Although I had the proper instincts and foresight, I lost a potential $7 million by the age of 35 because of lack of knowledge. This need not happen to you if you just follow the guidelines through the "pitfalls" and "quicksand" of real estate investing and climb that road to wealth.

The federal government has finally come out with something new that will aid the owners of property (real and personal) in many ways. It is called the Economic Recovery Tax Act of 1981. In the chapters which follow, I have dealt with the old method and the present method in regard to depreciation of real property; however, it behooves you to contact your C.P.A. and have him explain in detail all the ramifications of the new tax act of 1981, and how it will affect you, your property, and your business.

Owning property has always been the "American dream," but if we the people are not alert and become complacent to the status quo, private ownership of property will surely pass into oblivion.

There are some people who believe that an individual should not be allowed to own property and that it should be held strictly for the good of society as perceived by those people (the have nots and the want nots) who hold to this idea. And, in fact, at the present time, government, which includes federal, state, county, city, and village, owns approximately 53 percent of all land in the United States.

If we do not elect officials who will protect our rights, the twenty-first century will find us more like a socialistic state where only a government owns property.

Think about it. Then do something about it. The time for you to get started is now.

Dedication

This book is dedicated to my lovely wife who took dictation and was patient with me when I lost my patience, and who continued to be a loving and understanding wife during the year it took to write this book; to Betty Amo, my executive secretary, whose help in typing the draft and manuscript, making all the necessary corrections, and working long hours on weekends is greatly appreciated; to the late honorable Joe C. Carr, ex-Secretary of State of the great state of Tennessee for over thirty years, who for many years was a near and dear friend. Joe gave fully of himself, never expecting or wanting anything in return. He was the epitome of the very word "statesman." He added a new dimension to the lives of those of us who knew and loved him, and all of us were left with a void in his demise. May the Lord bless, hold and keep him. Last but not least this book is dedicated to the students I have taught in the past and those I hope to teach in the future.

Introduction

In this book you are going to learn how to (1) work up a financial statement (that is, evaluate your assets and liabilities), (2) locate property, (3) prepare a portfolio on a particular piece of property, (4) finance that property, (5) negotiate terms, and (6) negotiate the loan. You are going to learn how long you should keep the property. And how to dispose of it.

This will all be explained to you in a "hands-on" manner—this is what you should do in this situation, in that situation, and so forth. You will be led through the whole process of searching for, negotiating, purchasing, and disposing of property—with all the ramifications. When you finish this book, you will be able to deal with real estate professionals as well as independent owners. You will have become a pro. By the time you have a few transactions under your belt, you will write and tell me that this book is the best thing that's ever happened to you!

The hardest thing to do is make a decision. There have been many deals blown because of indecision. That is why there are employees and employers.

Besides making a decision, however, you must make a knowledge-able one. To me, the most fascinating thing in the world is to research, negotiate, and trade for a piece of real estate.

By way of introduction, let me tell you a story of the Great Depression. The story begins in 1929 in West Texas. There were bread lines and soup kitchens and everyone was out of work. To say that times were rough would be putting it mildly. One day during that period, on a cold morning, a young man named Bill was seeking work. He had walked more than 10 miles, stopping along the way, seeking employment at each farm house and ranch. Bill hadn't eaten for the past 24 hours, and he was getting desperate for a hot meal and sanctuary from the cold. Suddenly, he came upon what seemed the last chance for a job in his very life, for the weather had turned to freezing and he was lightly clothed.

He was so tired that he shuffled up to the farmhouse just as the sun began to peak over the horizon, and he knocked on the door. Bill was so tired, hungry, and apprehensive that he did not even hear the door open until a booming voice startled him, causing him to turn toward the door, where he saw a huge old man standing. The old man had been observing the young man, thinking how many had come before him. Even though he had been sympathetic and kind, he had been compelled to turn them all away, and this would be no exception.

"What can I do for you, young man?" the farmer asked. Bill blurted out in a shivering voice that he needed a job desperately and that he had not eaten in the past 24 hours. The old farmer said, "Son, I hate to turn you away, but I just let all my hands go except the two who have been with me so many years, and even those I can't afford. Surely, you can see my plight."

The young man replied, "Sir, I will work for nothing—all I need is a cup of coffee and hot biscuits, and I will sleep in the barn."

The farmer was a kindly soul and rather than turn the young man away, he thought he had found a way to get rid of him and ease his conscience at the same time. So, the farmer said, "I'll tell you what I'll do. You follow me to the barn and if you can complete the chore I'm going to give you, you can stay on. But remember, no pay, one meal a day, and you sleep in the barn. That's it—take it or leave it."

Bill eagerly accepted the task. The farmer told him that he was to cut a cord of wood before nightfall. Bill said, "That's fine, Sir, but what is a cord of wood?" The farmer replied that a cord of wood was eight feet long, four feet high, and four feet wide, with each log to be cut in two-foot lengths with a bucksaw. Then the farmer took off to his house where he proceeded to do his daily paper work at his desk, which was situated by a window with a view of the barn. Sometime later, the farmer saw Bill walking toward the house. The old man glanced up at the clock, noting that it had been three hours since he had given Bill his chore. Under his breath, the farmer said, "I didn't think that boy could stick it out; I guess I'd better go hear his excuse."

The old man stepped out on the porch just as Bill approached, and before the young man could say anything, the farmer said, "I thought I told you to cut a cord of wood—what's the matter, was the job to hard for you?" "Oh, no Sir," replied the boy. "I've done cut the wood just like you asked." Well, that was too much for the old man to swallow, so he says, "Okay, let's go see." When they arrived at the back of the barn, the farmer stopped in amazement and he was speechless; there was not one but three cords of wood cut! He was flabbergasted and thought there had to be some kind of trick involved, so he gave Bill another task, and damned if he didn't do that task in an unbelievable time, too.

By the end of the week, the old farmer felt guilty because Bill was worth three times his other hired hands combined and they were getting three square meals a day and pay. The farmer motioned for Bill and said, "Today is Saturday. You've worked hard; here's a dollar. I want you to go to town and enjoy yourself." And in those days, a dollar went a long way.

"But before you go," said the farmer, "I have a small task for you. It takes either of those other two hands four hours to complete this job, and you should be finished in an hour."

After walking into the barn, the farmer reached down and took out three potatoes and placed them in front of Bill. He told Bill that all he had to do was to segregate the remaining stack of potatoes into three piles—small, medium, and large. After asking if Bill understood, the farmer left.

About 10 o'clock that night, the farmer walked out on the porch, as was his custom, and began knocking the ashes from his pipe. While doing so, he glanced up toward the barn and noticed a lighted lantern. He thought the darned fool boy had forgotten to blow out the lantern that morning when he left. The farmer hurried to the barn to extinguish the lantern. When he opened the door, he was astonished to see Bill still sitting on the sack of potatoes in the same position he had left him that morning. He approached Bill, almost frightened, for the boy sat motionless and the farmer thought—my God, he's dead; I've overworked him! The farmer nervously walked over to the boy and touched him. The boy turned and looked up at the farmer startled, speechless for a moment. After he regained his composure, the farmer blurted out, partly from relief and partly from anger, "What the hell have you been doing these past 16 hours? Everything is exactly as I left you this morning at 6 o'clock. Answer me!" Bill looked up at the old man, and it seemed an eternity before he spoke a word. Finally, he said in a low and dejected voice, "Boss, I'm truly sorry, but it's them damned decisions."

Don't be like that young man of the Depression. Each time you must make a decision, it will become easier and each decision will give you the necessary confidence to become a successful real estate investor climbing that ladder of success, which will one day bring you complete financial independence. Countless others have done it, I have done it, and so will you.

This book is not written as a text, but it can serve as one. It is written so that you can integrate the multiple tasks involved in successful real estate investments and think out everything you need to sell your property before you buy it.

Make this book your handbook and reread it whenever you can. Consult it as a reference manual. You will learn more every time you do.

I wish you much happiness and goodwill on your road to prosperity and becoming a successful real estate investor.

chapter one

Developing Your Investment Strategy

The key to sound investing is informed diversification. For some investors diversification can be achieved largely through real estate; however, there are those who believe their portfolio should contain stocks, bonds, and other investments as well. Listed below are seven major advantages of investing in real estate.

1. *High yields.* Before tax, yields of from 10 to 25 percent are common in real estate.

2. *Means of building an estate.* In the case of an income-producing property, the amortization will mean that the tenants will help you pay for building your estate. As you amortize a mortgage, the value of your equity investment will steadily rise.

3. *Hedge against inflation.* Real estate is probably one of the best hedges against inflation because property values and income from properties rise to keep pace with inflation.

4. *Tax-free refinancing.* Mortgage proceeds even from refinancing are not taxable income to the owner; therefore, refinancing is an excellent way to recover your cash investment and, in some cases, you profit tax free. You might also consider using the refinance money to invest in another property.

5. *Income tax benefits.* The use of tax shelters is only one of the tax advantages gained through real estate. For instance, capital gains, made upon selling a property, are taxed at a much lower rate than ordinary income. Two more ways to use real estate to reduce your tax bill would be to use tax-free exchanges and sale lease back.

6. *Pride of ownership.* Investors often find greater personal satisfaction in owning property than stock certificates for it is something they can see,

feel, and touch, and let's not exclude the fact that they enjoy showing their property to friends and relatives.

7. *Leverage.* The use of mortgages and other financial means where you can use small amounts of your possessions or cash to gain control of large investments that earn very large returns on the amount of cash invested.

Investing for Profit and Tax Shelter

Let's look briefly at various types of real estate investments: apartments, office buildings, shopping centers, single-family homes, houses and/or duplexes, raw land, farms and ranches, hotels and motels, warehouses and industrial parks. Two things that make improved property attractive are: (1) depreciation, and (2) the tenants pay your loan payments as well as your taxes and maintenance, perhaps leaving you with a little spending money.

Apartments. Apartments are unlike some other real estate investments in that even if you hold on to the property so long that the neighborhood declines (past the usefulness of the building so far as depreciation is concerned), you can still rent those units. The rent will be cheaper, but you won't have the expensive upkeep that you had before, since in a deteriorated neighborhood tenants are more concerned with the cheapness of the rents rather than the quality of units.

The negative side to apartment owning is the human side. Some people do not like to hassle with others or leave themselves open to confrontations. However, one can get around this problem by hiring a good property management company.

Office Buildings. For quite a while office space was worth nearly zero because there was so much of it and so little demand. Now, for instance, in Los Angeles, the price has jumped from 65¢ to $1.70 per square foot per month and higher. Office space in good locations is unobtainable. Consequently, attorneys and doctors are going in together to buy or build their own offices. They find this has a lot of advantages. They can control their costs and they can deduct depreciation.

When you are considering buying a building or constructing offices, you will have to make a feasibility study to determine who you will put in there. There are nowhere near the number of persons seeking office space as there are needing apartments. Most people in the U.S. rent. Very few need office space.

Shopping Centers. Shopping centers are difficult to keep rented. A successful shopping center needs an anchor tenant to draw patrons. This may be a very large grocery store, variety store, or department store. Whatever it is, it is the magnet for the center. When an anchor tenant moves out, small shopping centers often fold.

Not far from where I live is a small shopping center that has a very large chain grocery as its anchor tenant. They have what is called a net net net lease. That grocery store will move out in two years. Actually, they will pull out before the lease is up and just pay it off.

When they move out, the draw to the shopping center will be gone. And if the owner can't find another anchor tenant fast, all the other stores will vacate and the owner will have to level the property and build something else, sell out, or go under.

Problems such as these are the reason why many of the large shopping centers are being developed by department stores. They, of course, are anchor tenants themselves. They also have the protection of picking the competitive stores for their center.

In small shopping centers, especially in ones with limited parking, you will see vacancy signs that remain for three or more years. The owner is paying taxes on that property and probably loan payments as well. But he or she is getting no revenue. If you have one vacancy out of seven stores, you have a vacancy factor of 14 percent $(1 \div 7)$. You can never recapture that rent.

Single-Family Homes. Single-family homes are usually the most significant loan that the average family will make in their lifetime. You may still be able to buy an attractive house of 2,200 square feet, with all the amenities, for $49,500, but you can bet it's out in the boonies. The factor is location.

Single-family dwellings can be a good beginning for the investor. If you can find a run-down house in a good neighborhood and buy it cheaply relative to the value of the surrounding property, do so. Fix it up, rent it, and knock off the depreciation from your income. After a year, sell it for a profit, pay your capital gains tax (if you have to), and buy another house. Keep doing this until you have enough down payment to purchase or equity to trade for a sixplex. Then you have begun your climb.

Houses and/or Duplexes. First, remember when you have a vacant house that you have a 100 percent factor, and in a duplex with only one side rented you have a 50 percent vacancy factor. Historically the duplex apartment has been a popular initial investment because at one time they were relatively inexpensive to purchase, and it can also act as a vehicle to gain experience in real estate investing. On the other hand, you can probably purchase a fourplex for very little more money down, and it is a safer investment. Most people who purchase duplexes do so because they wish to occupy one of the apartments, and in so doing they have a home and someone to help make the payments.

One basic problem with duplexes is the lack of economics of scale—physically they are somewhat inefficient. The basic costs of a building do not usually increase in direct proportion to the number of units. For example, a 14-unit building would not require a heating system seven times as expensive as that for a duplex. That same lack of economics of scale extends to management. A resident manager for two units would be ridiculous. Therefore, it would necessitate many special trips to the property to show the apartment and perform routine maintenance.

Typically, duplexes are older buildings, many built during the housing shortage of the 1940s. Their age often results in high expenses and relatively low rents, and they are usually in areas where rents cannot be raised to meet the constant repairs. With expenses and high mortgage or trust deed interest rates so high, the days of the beginning investor being able to afford to buy a duplex and live "rent free" in one unit are over.

Then there are those who believe that despite their limitations, duplexes offer possibilities for appreciation. Whereas the value of most residential income properties is determined by the income stream, the value of a duplex is influenced more by the price level of single-family homes. Thus, like single-family homes, duplexes are likely to appreciate. My personal feelings are that a duplex can be a good investment if:

1. It is well located in a good neighborhood of single-family homes.

2. The lot is large enough for expansion if the building can be made into a fourplex by raising the roof and adding a second floor. In Santa Monica, California, a small home in 1977 sold for about $35,000; it is now bringing $150,000 to $165,000. The new buyers then redesign the house, using the old structure as a foundation, and resell at $285,000 to $295,000.

3. The structure has been well maintained and is in good condition.

4. If it can be bought below market value or on unusually good terms. Duplex prices may range from $75,000 to $250,000 or more, depending on the location and the region. But duplexes, as an investment, do not appreciate as fast as do the properties with more units, and they are often troublesome to operate. A much better idea to get started in real estate investment would be to search for a home in an up-and-coming neighborhood that has deferred maintenance, but is sound otherwise, and negotiate a purchase with the owner.

After you have renovated the property but not overimproved it for the neighborhood, rent it at the highest rent possible. At the end of two years, exchange it for a fourplex or fiveplex. No capital gains will be involved, and you are then on your way to acquiring more property and building up your equity while sheltering your outside income at the same time.

Raw Land. Some people advocate the purchase of raw land, but, from first-hand experience, raw land is perhaps the worst deal of all. You are paying taxes and loan payments on it, it is bringing you no income, and the dollar you invested will be worth less (because of inflation) when you do sell the property, unless it really is in the direct line of immediate progress—not because someone told you, but if you actually know it to be a fact and plans are drawn, then go ahead.

Or you may know for a fact that there are minerals there. There is something to take out of the ground, so you can lease those mineral rights to someone. For example, we lease the zinc rights on our 200-acre farm in Tennessee, a nice addition to our income.

Farms and Ranches. That farm in Tennessee was bought over 175 years ago and everyone up until today made money farming it. But now it can't be farmed for several reasons, including the fact that there is no one locally who is willing to farm it. They prefer to work in a nearby factory. Unless you have been raised on a ranch or farm or have majored in farm or ranch management, these types of real estate investment are not for you.

Of course, there are people in California, and elsewhere, who call 3 or 4 acres a ranch. Usually such "ranches" are created as a tax shelter— which today the IRS looks at very closely. You cannot be a gentleman or lady farmer or rancher now and get away with it.

Which brings to mind an acquaintance who bought a house and 30 acres. He asked me how many cattle he could run on it. "One cow," I said. And then you're going to have to feed her." But he said, "I have 30 acres!" Said I, "Look at the typography of the land; it's like a horseshoe and there are hills all the way around it. Now if you say you wanted goats here, I can tell you you'll do better. They eat the brush, not the grass, and they won't bother you. But you'll have to have it fenced in, and you'll have to remove all the trees near the fences because the goats will climb the trees and jump over the fence. And what are you going to do with the mohair?" "Sell it," he replied, "Well, the problem is," said I, "you're not anywhere near other goats and facilities for selling the mohair. Now you could get Luken goats and milk them; that's if you wanted to go into the dairy business. Which if you do, you'll have to be licensed by the state and there are considerable health regulations to follow. Now, you could get Mexican goats, which you could use to clean the brush and for no other purpose, since where you live goat meat is not a normal marketable commodity. I think you'd better forget the whole thing."

He asked about horses, and I told him that they would destroy the land, pulling up the grass by the roots. "You won't have a blade of grass. So you can't turn them out; you'll have to feed them and keep them stalled and exercise them yourself." He didn't believe me and turned them out; eventually the rains came and the soil began to slide everywhere. So he decided to start feeding them. He eventually sold the property.

On the subject of farms and ranches, there are certain points regarding buying out in the country that are very important. I asked this same man if he had water. He told me that of course he did. And I asked how he knew. He replied that he knew because everyone around him had water. He then proceeded to drill six dry holes. There was, in fact, no water on his property except for a little spring. He was forced to put in a double filtering system to get water for the house.

His next mistake was building a house that was out of keeping, stylewise, with the surrounding property. He built a contemporary modern home in the country. He had built a home that looked like a barn, it would have sold a lot easier. But now he had to sell to someone who had the same type of taste.

Unfortunately, when he designed the house, he used a lot of glass, and not energy-efficient glass at that. So in the summer the air conditioning had to run 24 hours a day. And in the winter the house was extremely difficult and costly to keep warm.

Hotels and Motels. Hotels and motels can really be a disaster. I know of a case where a number of high-ranking military men syndicated and then built a hotel in San Diego; they promptly went broke. The hotel was sold and today is doing a flourishing business. The problem was management; the former owners knew nothing about hotel management.

Most people think that managing motels is fairly easy. What is there to it? You hire some cleaning people or do the rooms yourself. You and your husband or wife live there and rent the facilities. But it's not so simple. There is a lot more to making a motel operation successful.

Unless you run across a limited partnership, where the general partner is an experienced hotel/motel operator trained in the business, and a marketing feasibility study bears out your assumption that the area will have more than enough traffic, don't go into the hotel or motel business.

Many a chef has opened a restaurant only to fail. Why? Because he or she did not understand restaurant management. A good chef does not necessarily a good restauranteur make. On the other hand, a good restauranteur who knows nothing about cooking can be a very successful businessperson.

Warehouses and Industrial Parks. These are very special fields. Warehouses are not recommended for the average person. Industrial parks are also highly specialized, and not for the novice.

Never get into something you know nothing about, cannot learn anything about, or for which you have no natural management skills. Stay with apartments and office buildings; the percentages of success are much higher.

Converting Property to a New Use For Maximum Profit

Probably the first thing that comes to mind when you hear or see the word conversion is to think of converting apartments to condominiums or cooperatives. There are many sections of the country that have placed a moritorium on conversion from apartments to condominiums, and in some cases office buildings. This is more likely in areas where a low vacancy factor exists, leaving the rental population without adequate housing.

Therefore, there are many ways that an innovative person can do wonders with old properties by using a little imagination. Let's assume that we have found a 60-year-old building right on the borderline of a good area and the exterior is distinctive for its design of that period. The chances are greater that the building could be bought very reasonably.

Next, to what new use could that building be put? We examine the inside and find it has a two-story-high ceiling with a spiral stairway on either side. We put our imagination to work and come to the conclusion that, properly designed, the interior would be suitable for an elegant restaurant furnished in the period of its day, or a delightful woman's ready-to-wear shop, antique store, or possibly a building with individual stalls where artisans could display their works (paintings, jewelry, and the like). The upstairs could be converted into office space. These are just a few ideas of how that particular building could be put to use.

Another example would be an abandoned turn-of-the century courthouse, which when redecorated and refurbished would make excellent office space for attorneys or other professional people. Suppose we located a garden-type apartment building of perhaps 50 units, which in its day was most fashionable. The building is located in an area where there are two or three hospitals close by. This would make an ideal conversion for office space for doctors. In most cases, parking would not be a problem since many of these old apartments had ample underground parking. Or one might purchase adjacent property for parking, or perhaps it would be even more practical to get a 99-year lease, thereby making the parking lot a deductible item, as well as bringing in additional income. There are four ways in which this particular building could be purchased:

1. You as an individual.
2. Forming a limited partnership syndication.
3. Making it a co-op office building.
4. A condominium.

Since office space throughout the larger American cities is leasing for increasingly higher rents, many professional people are turning to co-ops and condominiums, which give them the advantage of adequate office space, besides being able to deduct depreciation, taxes, interest, maintenance, and janitorial services from their income, at the same time enjoying the benefit of appreciation. However, one must first check with the city and/or county zoning department to see if the area is zoned for that purpose or to peitition for a variance.

Another idea is to take an old warehouse, conveniently located and properly zoned, and build within it various-sized storage spaces with partitions that can be moved by management to suit needs for space. For example, you have two rooms 5' × 10' and someone wishes a 10' × 10' area. You merely move the partition and the renter now has the required space with two entrances. Make the aisles six feet wide and plot out the area to estimate how many enclosed storage spaces can be built. The next move would be to check similar storage space in the area to ascertain how much is being charged per square foot. I once required a space 5' × 10' for a period of 10 months and I was billed $39 per month while I had the goods in storage, making a total of $390 for the 10 months. You can see that $.78 per square foot should give one a good return on their investment. Of course, the assumption is that you bought the property for a proper price.

As a result of gasoline shortages, many filling stations have closed over the past few years. These stations can be converted into office space with adequate parking and without a lot of expense involved in the transformation. If you just sit down and start to think about it, you can come up with a dozen or more good ideas for conversions. There have been abandoned railroad stations utilized as restuarants or office buildings, or just about anything your imagination can devise.

Ingredients for Success

There are 3 important ingredients for success in this type of venture—imagination, creativity, and a thorough check before making final commitment to purchase, writing into the agreement that the conditions under which you are buying the property meet all codes and restrictions of the city or county. This will assure you that there will be no stumbling blocks to catch you unaware.

This is a proper time to point out and make clear that my reasoning and conclusions regarding different types of property for ownership are twofold:

1. I have had personal experience in the ownership and operations of the above-mentioned properties, and I have found that a person just beginning an investment program would be in a safer position following the ideas I have offered.

2. There are people who have sufficient experience to venture into the other types of property mentioned here and to be successful. My purpose in citing each type of property is to alert the reader to the dangers for the novice, not the seasoned, sophisticated investor.

chapter two

What To Look For

When looking to purchase real estate, generally you start with the newspaper. In Los Angeles, for instance, you can pick up the morning paper on a given day and find no less than eight pages of apartments for sale. You call those that look interesting, asking for the listing broker, not just anyone at the firm. The listing broker will know more about that piece of property.

Addresses are not included in ads because the selling agents don't want you dropping in. Sometimes that is because the building has an open listing, that is, the broker does not have an exclusive right to sell.

The first thing the broker will try to do is qualify you. You can visualize the problems he or she is up against. The broker doesn't want to take somebody all over town (spending precious gas and time) who really doesn't know what he or she wants or can't afford it anyway.

So you have to be ready. The broker will ask, for instance, "Is this figure within your range?" If it is or if it isn't, say that it sounds like the type of property you are interested in, and then state the price range you want. Be honest. "How much can you put down?" "Whatever is required, but I would rather only put x down, and I would like someone to carry a second." Or, better, you can say: "Well, I can put x amount down, but it would depend on the condition of the building, which I don't know, the location of the property, which I don't know, the kind of financing, which I don't know, and it certainly would depend on the expenses, gross and net income, all of which I don't know. Now, if you would be so kind as to send me a setup or proforma, whatever you happen to call it, I would appreciate it."

Then continue: "As I travel throughout the city, I will drive by the building. I will not get out, not talk to the manager, and not interview the tenants. But I will call you and tell you if I'm not interested and why. Or I will tell you I am interested and wish to go through the building and make an offer."

If brokers refuse to disclose information, it is generally because they do not have an exclusive right to sell. You can get around this by telling them that you will sign a statement that will protect the salespeople. You agree not to try to sell it or show it to someone else, that is if you are a R.E. licensee. However, if you are a buyer, state that you are a principal.

Every state publishes a journal that lists foreclosures. It explains what they are, where they are, and so forth. You can pick up distressed properties this way. Local foreclosures are posted in every courthouse. Try to crack a deal before the foreclosure takes place. This takes the burden away from the owner before he or she loses the property and financial reputation.

Of course, you can call real estate brokers who specialize in the type of property you are interested in. No matter who answers the phone, tell them basically what you're looking for. Tell them you want the toadstool among the roses, you want the worst-looking property in the area. This will give you the chance to upgrade the building. They will say, of course, everybody wants that—"You can't find that." You reply: "Maybe *you* can't, but they're out there. If you're not capable of doing it, turn me over to your broker." Then deal with him or her directly.

I have been asked many times how do I find a good reliable salesperson or broker. I really don't know. In my opinion, I don't think there are more than 10 percent who are truly professional. I became a realtor out of desperation—for my self-preservation.

Attorneys are good sources for property. Let them know that you are looking. In this light, the paper that tells of foreclosures also tells of mechanics liens, probate, and other activities that can give you a head start in looking for a piece of property.

You will be shown a lot of bad property. But some that appears to be junk is exactly what you want. It may look terrible because of the peeling paint. But if it is structurally sound and if the neighborhood is good, it is probably okay. You can capitalize some of the improvement; some you can wipe right off the top taxwise. You can raise the rents, and so forth.

REO Formula

Sometimes lenders are a good source for locating property. When an institution takes a property back because of default, it is not called a foreclosure. It is known as real estate owned property (REO). If they have something, you can ask them for 100 percent financing or better. The term *foreclosed property* causes people to conjure up two images:

the lender exercised poor judgment in making the loan, thereby losing some credibility, and some picture a large institution foreclosing on a poor, helpless widow.

You are pulling them out of a spot. If you have a good credit rating and/or good reputation, you can not only take it for 100 percent financing, you can take it for more than that in order to fix it up. If not, then you go back to the bank to get a loan to improve the property—say, in 90-day notes, which you keep renewing.

Get acquainted with some appraisers who specialize in the type of property you want and the areas you wish to be in. Take them to lunch. Find out from them what areas are hot, what the local trends are. They will tell you where to buy.

I prefer an area populated by young executives. They have money and are generally easy to deal with, reasonable people. If you are interested in apartments, you should not get involved with units that are renting for $1,000 or $1,500 a month or more. You would have to have a very large bankroll to support vacancies when they occur.

You want an average neighborhood. Stay out of areas where people move to stick together. When you have vacancies, you have a very restricted market. A more diversified area is much better from a marketing point of view.

An REO Formula Problem

An offer is made to a savings and loan company to take 15 homes at an average of $25,000 each, which would be $375,000 in land for the 15 homes.

On the part of the person trading in the land, he or she can borrow from 70 to 90 percent on the homes received and can raise considerable cash very quickly, then dispose of the equities in the homes as he or she sees fit.

The question then is what does the loan company do with the $375,000 in land it has taken for the 15 free-of-encumbrance homes? The answer is that the one who trades in the $375,000 in land subsequently, or practically concurrently, offers to buy back the land at $375,000, but on liberal terms.

What Does This Accomplish?

1. It enables the loan company to reduce its stock of real estate owned by 15 homes.

2. It enables the loan company to make new loans on these homes if it wishes.

3. It allows the loan company to immediately remove the land from its real estate owned department by selling it on liberal terms, turning it into a trust deed, contract, or mortgage, thus putting the loan company back into the loan business, where it belongs.

4. It enables the person trading in the land to raise ready cash by borrowing on the homes.

5. It allows the one who trades in the land to buy it back at liberal terms and still enjoy ready cash flow out of loan money received from 15 homes.

6. If the land owner's original book basis was, say, $120,000, by buying back this land at $375,000 on liberal terms, he or she automatically steps up the book basis on the land to $375,000.

It is not a good investment for the beginner to buy property that involves people who are in retirement. You will run up against many problems, mainly due to limited income.

As you start hunting for property, you will see advertisements that contain the phrase "pride of ownership." This probably means that you can drive your friends by your piece of property and proudly point toward it. But to have pride of ownership, one should have a well-managed, well-maintained property, and good tenants. That is not, however, the kind of building you want to buy. You want to look for the building that has absolutely no pride of ownership, period. The owner was only interested in milking it for what he or she could get out of it, and so it will have considerable deferred maintenance.

This gives you a very strong stand from which to negotiate since the building is not up to snuff. And you can point out all the things you need to do to bring the building to where it belongs.

Many owners feel that their particular building is a jewel. This pride of ownership causes them to believe their property is worth three times its value. Under these circumstances, it is sometimes impossible to negotiate.

We have been thinking about apartments primarily. For the beginner, apartments are much easier to handle. Other types, such as commercial property, are more difficult. There you are dealing with businesspeople who are renting office space or warehouse space or stores, as opposed to dealing with the average person on a month-to-month tenancy. Handle an apartment first. Then move to a small office/shop complex.

The Neighborhood

Most all neighborhoods eventually change. They will either change by going downhill, and a lot of them do, or by going uphill. But how quickly? One should anticipate these changes. You anticipate them by checking back. What was that neighborhood and that area like 20 years ago, 15 years ago, 10 years ago? Find out by talking to people who have lived there for 10 or 15 years. You may find that nothing has changed substantially in all that time. Or, they have torn down a lot of buildings, and there has been new construction. From the neighbors you can find out what changes have taken place.

If changes *have* taken place, you can determine if the area is on an upgrade. And then it stands to reason that whatever you buy will be going up in value, and should you spend a little more than you anticipated, the worse thing that can happen is that it will catch up with itself. If the neighborhood is nearly stagnant, of course that would not be true.

How To Look at
the Neighborhood

I cannot emphasize too strongly the method I use to check out a neighborhood. If it is a neighborhood where there is a school of any kind, I always drive by at the time of morning when the children are going to school. I also drive by when the children are getting out of school. In addition, I drive by that property at 8 o'clock at night to see how congested the streets are. I drive by again at midnight to see if things have settled down or if things are still popping.

I like to see how well lighted the area is, particularly the subject property. I go down one block and then another to see if there are any disturbances. I then check at 3:00 o'clock and again at 6:00 o'clock in the morning.

I check to see whether there is a pickup for garbage and whether there is a lot of noise, how many people are leaving for work, what kind of traffic situations—are there any bottlenecks? This is very important. Notice whether police cars are around. If you see no police cars during all this observation, go to the closest police or sheriff's station. Tell them that you are a prospective owner of a piece of property in their area and that you have made many rounds and have yet to see one squad car. And you would like to know why. Not because you pay your taxes or that sort of thing, but because you are an interested party buying a piece of property that is going to cost quite a bit of money and you are interested in the safety of your tenants. What is the crime rate? High? Low? What exactly is the situation? Pin them down as to whether it is a high crime area.

It may be that the area doesn't need a lot of patrols. Nevertheless, if they say that there is a shortage of manpower or the like, you say, "We should have more patrols, and if I own that building I will do my best to find out why we can't get more. We cannot take chances with our tenants, and it is likely that we will have a lot of young people as tenants and we cannot take the risk of their being in danger." Definitely check out crime rates.

Check out rents, too. Don't ask the renters of the subject building to tell you what the rates are. They may lie. What you want to know is the economic (area average) rents of the neighborhood. If you know the economic rent in the neighborhood, then you will know if the rents in the building you're interested in are high or low for the economic rents of the neighborhood. It will also give you an opportunity to project what the rents could be if the building were up to par. However, another word of caution—don't buy a piece of property on projected rents or projected gross income. Buy on the present rents, no matter what you are going to do with the property. Buy the property on the rents as they are today, not on anything else. Everyone will try to sell you a piece of property on projected rents. Don't do that.

Check out vacancies (if there are any) in the neighborhood. Ask to see the manager; say you are looking for an apartment in the area because it is close to your place of work or whatever, and you would like to see what they have. The manager may say all that is available is a one bedroom. You say you would prefer two bedrooms—will they have a two bedroom coming up later and what will it rent for? What does the one bedroom rent for?

Look at the apartment and really observe its condition. Is it clean? Check the stove and oven particularly. This will tell you something about your neighbors as well. If the manager is ready to rent the apartment and the stove is dirty, that is the type of tenant they have. That is also the way he or she manages that building, and it is going to be a deterrent as far as having the kind of people you want in your building.

Also ask to look at a two-bedroom apartment if possible, even though there is no vacancy, in case you move in and might be able to go into a two later. The manager may show it to you.

Next, go to a building that has a no vacancy sign. The manager will, of course, say they have no vacancy; didn't you see the sign? Say yes, you did, but you're curious. The building must have very low rents to have a no vacancy sign. Lead the manager into a situation where he or she will tell you how frequently vacancies occur. You might say: "You mean you have people living here 10 or 15 years? You must have very reasonable rents. How do you keep up the building? They say: "We have an excellent building and we keep it up. We don't raise the rents because these people have been with us for a long time and we know them." This tells you the rents are probably very cheap because there has been no turnover in 12 years.

When I took over one building (which I will go into later in this book), it was like a pig sty. I wondered how people could live under those conditions. They could because the rent was so cheap.

Now you have learned that these rents are way too low and that the management is not going to raise them. This would then be one aspect of the economic rents for the neighborhood. You know that the building you are interested in has lower rents than most, and you know that the building can be put in much better shape than the more expensive buildings, even though it is older. Therefore, you can come up to their level or in some cases even surpass it.

That is how you check out the area, not just within a block, but within at least six square blocks. The neighborhood is not just the street.

You can also go into the neighborhood coffee shop and talk to the help as well as the patrons. "I'm about to move into the neighborhood. What kind of neighborhood is it?" People will usually tell you.

You don't want to talk to the tenants of the building in which you are interested because you don't want them to know you are going to buy it. Make the owner verify the rents by showing you rent receipts or something conclusive. On the other hand, you are going to make sure that there arc not a bunch of relatives living there; that they are actually legal tenants.

When you walk through (perhaps under the guise of an insurance tour), you can say to a tenant: "We want to know how long you have been here. And for insurance purposes, what rent do you pay?"—right in front of the owner or manager. You watch the manager. If he or she gets nervous, you know something is wrong; this tenant is going to tell you what the real rent is for that apartment, and the numbers may not jive. Then you waltz that manager into his or her office and demand the facts; something is wrong here. Or you tell the owner that. You have to be hardnosed about it.

Use every means to pull information out of the marketplace because that is what scts the value. The owner doesn't set the value, the buyer doesn't set the value, you don't set it, I won't set it; it is set at the marketplace. And that is what that property will sell for to a prudent buyer, prudent investor, knowledgeable, by one equally so, selling on a specific day.

Go to the permit department and find out if there have been any new permits recently issued for apartment houses or condominiums. Even

Where Else To Look

though you are interested in apartment houses, you want to know all the building that is going on. In other words, the more building going on, the more upgrading going on, and the more chance for you to be successful with the property you have in mind. It is from the permit department that you find out. You might ask for information on the basis that you are doing an analysis on a piece of property and need to find out what way movement is going with apartments, or if it is stagnant. "Have you had a lot of permits for apartments, what size apartments, where in the general vicinity is the most action taking place?" This information will give you a good picture.

Here is another tip. Every big city has a company that pulls information out of the census. I have a map that will tell me, for instance, where all the older people are in Los Angeles County; the various ethnic areas, where the younger people live, the highest rents, where the most money per capita is, and so on.

All of these sources will give you an indication of income, and that is very important. You want people who can pay their bills. In higher income areas, your percentage of success or rate of appreciation will normally be higher.

Primary Data Sources Summary

Following is a list of sources from whom you can obtain pertinent information when considering purchase of property in an area.

County recorder—where title information is legally recorded.
City Hall—for zoning and land use information and data about utilities, health, and welfare laws.
Planning commissions—for zoning, planning, land uses.
Assessor—for assessed value and taxes.
Cost manuals and indexes (F.W. Dodge, Marshall Cost Calculator, Boeckh Index)—for information on replacement costs.
Physical inspection—for condition of site, improvements, and neighborhood comparables.
Land title insurance companies—sales, sale prices, terms.
Building and safety department—building codes, building permits.
Soil engineers—condition of soil and subsoil.
Water, power, and phone companies—utilities and vacancy information.
Local builders, real estate companies—construction costs.
Department of highways or streets—traffic and traffic patterns.
Multiple listing boards, local real estate boards, escrow companies—market prices and terms.
Banks—survey of business conditions and real estate markets.

More Tips

Everyone should remember that when you go to buy a piece of real estate, make sure there is plenty of parking. Let's say you are in the process of buying a building of 16 units, and it shows people paying rent on 16 units. The very first thing to do is go down to the permit department, check the records, and find out what the original permit called for. It might have called for 14 units, and it may have said that two of those units were to be storerooms, showers for workers, and so forth, and then they were converted. What happens when you go to get your loan? The bank will only loan on the 14. They will not count the other two apartments.

But you may want to rectify the situation, thinking, "Well, I'll go down and take out a permit." Let's say you have one car space for every apartment; 16 total. But the building and permit department says: "Do you have enough room for two cars for every apartment? If you take out a permit, you'll have to raise your spaces to code, two for every apartment." What does that mean? That means they will tell you to lock up those two apartments. Then you can't use them and you have just lost whatever that rent is. Assuming it's $200 apiece, that's $400 a month, $4,800 a year—$4,800 lost every year you own the building.

Sellers are liable to disclose such incongruities. Your selling price will have to be reduced accordingly, since you will have to knock out both the units. Because if and when it comes to the attention of the county, they will tell you not to rent the space. If it were a home and attached to it, they could tear it down—*make you tear it down.*

So again, when you go to invest in a piece of property, look at it upside down, sideways, through it, and in every other way. Using the inspection forms in the next chapter you will discover what you need to know about that building. The day you start managing your property is the day that you start thinking of acquiring it. What am I going to do? Do I have to do this? What's it going to cost me?

Learn To Look

Perhaps there is a piece of property where the exterior cement steps have dropped eight inches. They have been painted, outdoor carpeted, and covered up. You don't know what is underneath. And it could be that you would have to eventually cement half the building as well as tear the steps out. Whenever you see situations like that, back away. Because there is something going on you can't see, and you can't do anything about it.

I cannot stress enough that if you buy a piece of property, go in with your eyes open, knowing what you are going to buy, *all* of it, including its problems. Don't pay attention to what the brokers and owners tell you—especially as far as expenses are concerned. Check and verify, verify, verify. When you do, you will know how much it will cost you to operate the building and get it in shape for maximum profits.

Buying Out of State

If you are investing out of state, you are stepping into territory where you are really green. This goes for real estate people and appraisers, too. All the factors that make an investment dangerous are multiplied by the additional unknowns of an out-of-state situation.

For example, in December 1980, my wife and I were in Dallas looking at some property. I was talking to a broker who had been in Southern California but had moved to Texas. He relocated because he saw the Texas investment trend.

I was sitting in his office and he asked me what I wanted; I told him I didn't care, 100 or 200 units, it didn't matter, as long as it was good. He said: "I have one over here on the east side. I told him (knowing Dallas) that I didn't want a building on the east side. He mentioned another building in another less desirable area, and I said no to that.

"Well," he said, "if you're going to be choosy, I just can't help you."

I replied: "It's my money and I *am* going to be choosy. I am not going to buy just because you've got something for sale. Maybe that 50-unit building on the east side is at a price three and one-half times gross. That's not where I want to be."

A lot of Californians have invested in Texas because of that gross multiplier. Just while we sat there, three transactions were completed by phone. All were Californians and only one had seen a setup. The prices seemed right. However, the neighborhoods were really bad. Your manager would have to collect the rent with a shotgun. So, are great buys really *good* buys?

While in Dallas, I looked at a building in Richardson—a building that was really terrible. I would not have been able to make it secure. On the other hand, there was considerable construction in the immediate area, so the property would have automatically upgraded. But the area was in transition between blue and white collar, and I couldn't ascertain in what direction.

I also noticed that there was one meter for gas and one for electricity—which means the landlord pays for it.*

These are just basic examples of the danger one encounters not knowing the area or political climate. When you go out of state to invest, you have to contend with a realtor you know nothing about, in an area you know nothing about, and where you don't know where to check anything out. You have to depend on somebody. And there's nobody you can depend on. If you don't have the experience behind you, you're sunk.

If after these discouraging remarks, you are still set on investing out of your area, here is one tip. Locate at least three senior appraisers specializing in your property type, who work for different local lenders. Take them to lunch and/or dinner. Find out for what neighborhoods money is available and why. What are the hot areas? What is the normal recapture on resale? Get their real opinion on the total investment climate. Pay them a fee if necessary.

---

*In many states renters pay their own bills. In the past this has not been true in many parts of Texas. Now, however, Texas has passed a law that will require meters for every apartment. I wonder how many Californian investors feel now. Imagine a 200-unit project for which you suddenly have to shell out about $300 a meter?

chapter three

Arriving at Value

Remember that an appraisal is done on a building's fair market value—whether you would live in it has nothing to do with it. Maybe 1,000 tenants would. You have to be very objective.

There are three approaches to value—the market data, or comparative sales approach, the replacement cost approach, and the income analysis approach. There are approaches used by realtors, but not by appraisers. This is what we call the gross multiplier, which is arrived at by dividing the sales price by the annual gross. You will get a figure such as 6, 7, 8, 9, or 10, and so on.

In West Hollywood, for instance, the multiplier has gone as high as 16 times gross, which is ridiculous, but it also is a very ridiculous way of trying to appraise the value of a particular piece of property. Let us look at the correct ways.

Market Data Approach

In the comparative sales, or market data approach, you have what is called the subject property. And you find properties in the area, like for like, with which you can compare. You compare oranges with oranges and apples with apples.

In this approach you never use less than four comparables—comparables that have recently sold. Sales more than a year old are not helpful. An appraisal is made for one date, that day and that time. It is not good for tomorrow or two weeks from now. The marketplace generally moves too fast.

Do not use the asking price, hearsay, or the number of revenue stamps on the tax ticket. One can put more stamps on than necessary, which would throw you off completely.

Some of the books on real estate state that the comparables sales approach is only used on smaller properties, but that is not so. It is what we appraisers call the market data approach. It is used on all types of properties, not just small ones.

Many people who have written investment guides are under the impression that they have found some sort of formula. But usually they have had no formal training as a realtor, appraiser, developer, or mortgage banker. The money they have made has generally come from their traveling lectures. They invested that income into real estate while continuing their teaching. I know of one man who has given up buying property. He makes so much more money lecturing about his *unique* investment method.

To get back to appraising, the comparative sales approach is a very valid technique, but you have to be very careful to find out the actual sales price. You can discover this from reputable realtors or through a local multiple-listing book.

The forms on pp. 23-26 are used in making the comparative sales, or market data approach. They are reproduced more for general understanding than use, since it is unlikely that you can find an adequate number of truly comparable properties.

In its simplest form, this technique uses pluses and minuses to correct for differences between various properties. For example, one recently sold project may have two and one-half baths for every three-bedroom apartment. But the subject property has only two. You subtract the value of the extra half baths from the comparable to make it identical

---

Apartment Building Evaluation Reports: Type 1

Subject Property/Comp. #1/#2/#3/etc.

Address	Air Conditioning
Map Code	Heating
Proximity to Subject	Pool
Description:	Other Improvements
Type	
Construction	Parking
Stories	Landscaping
Year Built	Architecture
Condition	Property Appeal
Construction Quality	Neighborhood
Apartments:	Site Size
Number	Zoning
Size Singles	View
Size 1 Bedroom	
Size 2 Bedroom	Comments
Size 3 Bedroom	Expenses
Fireplaces	Price
Kitchen	Monthly or Annual Gross Income
Avg. Rent	Terms
Furnished/Unfurnished	Total Adjustment
	Comparison to Subject
Roof:	Indicated Value of Subject
Kind	
Condition	

APPRAISAL REPORT—RESIDENTIAL INCOME PROPERTY

TO BE COMPLETED BY LENDER

Borrower/Client __John W. Doe__

Property Address __1200 Genesse__

City __Hollywood__ County __Los Angeles__ State __CA__ Zip Code __90046__

File No. _____

Map Reference __33 F4__

Census Tract __.7001__

Legal Description __Lot 329 of McNair Place as per map recorded in Book 22, Page 40.__

Current Sale Price (if applicable) $ __N/A__ Date of Sale __N/A__ Loan Requested $ __N/A__

Terms of Sale __N/A__

Property Rights Appraised ☒ Fee ☐ Leasehold (attach completed Lease Analysis FHLMC Form 461)

Lender __N/A__ Lender's Address __N/A__

Instructions to Appraiser: The purpose of this Appraisal is to estimate the current Market Value of the Subject Property. The Definition of Market Value is as set forth in Certification And Statement Of Limiting Conditions (FHLMC 439).

Note: FHLMC/FNMA do not consider the racial composition of the neighborhood to be a relevant factor and it must not be considered in the appraisal.

Other Information: __N/A__

Appraisal requested from __John W. Doe__ Date __Jan. 30__ 19 __80__ By: __Jane S. Doe__

Items 1, 2, 4, 5 & 6 are required. Attach additional items and check box if items are considered appropriate for this appraisal or are requested by Lender.

1. ☒ Descriptive photographs of subject property
2. ☒ Descriptive photographs of street scene
3. ☒ Photographs of __Sale Comps/Rents__
4. ☐ Sketch or floor plan of typical units
5. ☐ Owner's current certified rent roll if existing, or pro forma if proposed or incomplete
6. ☒ Owner's income and expense statement 19 __79__, or pro forma income and expense statement

7. ☒ Map(s) _____
8. ☐ Plot plan or survey
9. ☒ Qualifications of Appraiser
10. ☐ Lease Analysis FHLMC Form 461 (required if leasehold interest appraised)
11. ☐ Summary of reciprocal agreements with other owners for use of parking, driveways, recreational facilities, private streets, (required if applicable)
12. ☐ _____
13. ☐ _____

NEIGHBORHOOD

Location: ☒ Urban ☐ Suburban ☐ Rural

Built-up: ☒ Over 75% ☐ 25% to 75% ☐ Under 25%

Present land use: __ __ % Condominiums __25__ % 1-Family __65__ % Apartments __10__ % Commercial __ __ %

Change in present land use: ☐ Not likely ☒ Likely(*) ☐ Taking Place(*) (*)From __S.F.R.__ To __Multiple Units__

Property values: ☒ Increasing ☐ Stable ☐ Declining

Housing demand/supply: ☐ In balance ☒ Shortage ☐ Oversupply

Predominant occupancy: ☐ Owner ☒ Tenant __ __ % Vacant

Condominium: Price range $ __N/A__ to $ __ __ Predominant $ __N/A__

Age __N/A__ yrs. to __ __ yrs. Predominant __N/A__ yrs

Single Family: Price range $ __110__ to $ __170__ Predominant $ __130__

Age __45__ yrs. to __50__ yrs. Predominant __45__ yrs

Typical apartment: Type __Walk-up&garden__ No. Stories __2__ No. Units __10/15__ Age __20__ yrs. Condition __Avg.__

Rent Control Rent Levels: ☒ Increasing ☐ Stable ☐ Declining

Estimated neighborhood apartment vacancy rate __2__ %, ☐ Decreasing ☐ Stable ☐ Increasing. Rent Controls ☐ No ☒ Yes (comment on page 4 if Yes)

OVERALL RATING	Good	Avg	Fair	Poor
Employment Stability	X			
Adequacy of Utilities	X			
Convenience of Schools	X			
Police and Fire Protection		X		
Recreational Facilities		X		
Property Compatibility		X		
Protection from Detrimental Conditions		X		
General Appearance of Properties		X		
Appeal to Market		X		

	Distance	Access or Convenience
Public Transportation	3 blks	X
Employment Centers	3 blks	X
Shopping Facilities	3 blks	X
Grammar Schools	6 blks	X
Freeway Access	3 miles	X

Describe any incompatible land uses and overall property appeal and maintenance level __No incompatible land used noted; Good overall appeal and maintenance level.__

Describe any oversupply of units in area by type and rental __No oversupply of units in subject property neighborhood.__

Describe any shortage of units in area by type and rental __A shortage of all types of units exists in subject property neighborhood.__

Describe potential for additional units in area considering land availability, zoning, utilities, etc. __Transition from older single family houses to multiple units.__

Is population of relevant market area of insufficient size, diversity and financial ability to support subject property and its amenities? __No__ If yes, specify.

Describe any probable changes in the economic base of neighborhood which would favorably or adversely affect apartment rentals (e.g. employment centers, zoning) __There is no change in the economic base of the neighborhood of a significant magnitude anticipated for the present time which would have an effect upon apt. rentals.__

General comments including either favorable or unfavorable elements not mentioned (e.g. public parks, view, noise, parking congestion) __None apparent.__

SITE

Dimensions __*Check from plat map.__ Area _____ Sq. Ft. or Acres

Zoning (classification, uses and densities permitted) _____

Present improvements ☒ do ☐ do not conform to zoning regulations.

Highest and best use: ☒ Present use ☐ Other (specify) _____

	Public	Comm.	Individual
Electricity	☒	☐	☐
Gas	☒	☐	☐
Water	☒	☐	☐
Sanitary Sewer	☒	☐ Sep. Tnk. ☐	

☐ Underground Electricity & Telephone

Street ☒ Public ☐ Private
Surface __Asphalt__
☒ Storm Sewer
☒ Curb & Gutter
☒ Sidewalk ☐ Alley
☒ Street Lights

Ingress and Egress (Adequacy) __Good__

Topography __Level__

View Amenity __None__

Drainage and Flood Conditions __Adequate__

Is the property located in a HUD identified Special Flood Hazard Area? __No__

COMMENTS (including any easements or encroachments or any nonconforming use(s) of present improvements) __None__

DESCRIPTION OF IMPROVEMENTS

[X] Existing Approx. Year Built 19 60 [ ] Proposed [ ] Under Construction [ ] Elevator [X] Walk-up No. of Stories 2 [ ] Row or Townhouse

No. of Bldgs. 1 No. of Units 10 No. of Rooms 34 No. of Baths 14 Parking Spaces: No. 10 Type Subterraneum

Basic Structural System Wood Frame Exterior Walls Stucco Roof Covering Composition & Gravel

Interior Walls Dry Wall Floors Cement & Vinyl Bath Floor and Walls Vinyl/Dry Wall

Insulation Walls and Ceiling Adequacy Good Adequacy of Soundproofing Avg.

Heating: [ ] Central [X] Individual Type Wall Fuel Gas Condition Avg.

Air Conditioning: [ ] Central [X] Individual Describe Wall Unit/ Min 1 Per Unit Adequacy and Condition Good

Elevator(s): Number 0 Automatic _____ Adequacy and Condition _____

Security Features None

Kitchen cabinets, drawers and counter space [X] Adequate [ ] Inadequate

[X] Range/Oven [X] Fan/Hood [ ] Dishwasher [X] Disposal

[ ] Refrigerator [ ] Washer [ ] Dryer [ ]

Hot Water Heater(s) 100 Gallon

Plumbing Fixtures Adequate

Electrical Service Adequate Sep. Meters

Recreational Facilities None

OVERALL PROPERTY RATING	Good	Avg.	Fair	Poor
General appearance of property	X			
Quality of construction (materials and finish) .		X		
Condition of improvements	X			
Rooms size and layout	X			
Closets and storage	X			
Plumbing—adequacy and condition . . .	X			
Electrical—adequacy and condition . . .	X			
Amenities and parking facilities	X			
Appeal to Market	X			

Effective Age 15 Yrs. Estimated Remaining Economic Life 20 Yrs.

COMMENTS: (Special features, functional or physical inadequacies, repairs needed, modernization, etc.) None

COST APPROACH

LAND SALES (complete ONLY if appropriate for this appraisal) Zoning Area Sales Price Date Price per Sq. Ft. or per Unit

	Zoning	Area	Sales Price	Date	Price per Sq. Ft. or per Unit
1.		∅ $			$ ___ Per
2.		∅ $			$ ___ Per
3.		∅ $			$ ___ Per

Comments & Reconciliation Land value obtained by abtraction method.

Estimated Land Value * $

APARTMENT BUILDING(S)—ESTIMATED REPRODUCTION COST NEW

x ___ = ___ sq.ft. x 2 (Stories) = 8760 sq. ft. x $ 26 $ 227,760

x ___ = ___ sq.ft. x ___ (Stories) = ___ sq. ft. x $ ___ $ ___

x ___ = ___ sq.ft. x ___ (Stories) = ___ sq. ft. x $ ___ $ ___

OTHER IMPROVEMENTS Driveway, landscaping, etc. $ 4,000

_____ $ ___

TOTAL ESTIMATED COST NEW OF IMPROVEMENTS . . . . . $ 231,760

LESS DEPRECIATION Physical 31% 70,000

DEPRECIATED VALUE OF IMPROVEMENTS . . . . . . $ 162,000

ADD—ESTIMATED LAND VALUE . . . . $ 88,000

INDICATED VALUE BY THE COST APPROACH (IN FEE SIMPLE) . . . . . $ 250,000

IF LEASEHOLD DEDUCT VALUE OF FEE INTEREST (ATTACH CALCULATIONS) . . . $ --

INDICATED VALUE BY THE COST APPROACH (LEASEHOLD) . . . . . . $ --

COMPARABLE RENTAL DATA

	COMPARABLE No. 1	COMPARABLE No. 2	COMPARABLE No. 3
	1015 N. Stanley	1213 N. Flores Street	1200 N. Harper Ave.
Proximity to subj.	1 Block	13 Blocks	9 Blocks
Rental survey date	Feb. 7, 1980	Feb. 1980	Feb. 1980
Brief description of property improvements	No. Units 12 No. Vacant 1 Age 20 yrs	No. Units 15 No. Vacant 0 Age 13 yrs	No. Units 26 No. Vacant 0 Age 19 yrs
	2 STY F/S	2 STY F/S	2 STY F/S
	Carports	Garages	Carpets

	Rm. Count			Size	Monthly Rent			Rm. Count			Size	Monthly Rent			Rm. Count			Size	Monthly Rent		
Individual unit breakdown	Tot	BR	b	Sq.Ft.	$	∉	Rm	Tot	BR	b	Sq.Ft.	$	∉	Rm	Tot	BR	b	Sq.Ft.	$	∉	Rm
	3	1	1	700	325	.46	108	3	1	1	650	300	.46	100	3	1	1	650	300	.46	100
	4	2	13/4	850	425	.50	106	4	2	2	800	425	.53	106	4	2	2	1100	425	.39	106

Utilities, furniture and amenities included in rent	Hot Water Wall A/C	Hot Water; No Wall A/C No Bltns	Hot Water Gas/ Electricity Wall A/C, Pool; no Bltns.
Comparison to subject including rental concessions, if any	Similar	Similar	Similar

MONTHLY RENT SCHEDULE SUBJECT

Utilities included in actual rents: [X] Water [ ] Gas [ ] Heat [ ] Electric [ ] Air Conditioning [ ] _____

Utilities included in forecasted rents: [X] Water [ ] Gas [ ] Heat [ ] Electric [ ] Air Conditioning [ ] _____

No. of Units	Unit Rm Count Tot. BR b			Total Rooms	Sq. Ft. Area Per Unit	No. Units Vacant	ACTUAL RENTS Per Unit Unfurnished	Furnished	Total Rents	Allowable Incr.	Per Unit Unfurnished	FORECASTED RENTS Total Rents	Per Sq. Ft. or Room
2	3	1	1	6	650	0	$ 175	$	$ 350	15%	$ 52.5	$ 402.5	.58	$67
1	3	1	1	3	650	0	170		170	18%	25.50	195.5	.30	65
1	3	1	1	3	650	0	220		220	7.5%	16.50	236.5	.36	79
1	3	1	1	3	650	0	165		165	15%	24.75	189.75	.29	63
1	3	1	1	3	650	0	120		120	15%	18.00	138.	.21	46
2	4	2	2	8	875	0	320		640	7.5%	48.00	688.	.39	86
1	4	2	2	4	875	0	230		230	15%	34.50	264.5	.30	66
1	4	2	2	4	875	0	240		240	15	36.00	276.	.32	69
10	TOTAL			34		0	$2135		$ 2135			$ 2390.75		

MARKET APPROACH

Address	910 N. Stanley	1247 N. Sycamore Ave.	6100 Fountain Ave.	7546 Norton Ave.
Proximity to subject		14 blocks	30 blocks	10 blocks
Map code	33 F4	34 B4	34 C4	34 A4
Lot size		11,600	6532	6500
Brief description of building improvements	No. Units: 10 No. Vac.: 0 Year Built: 19 60 2 STY F/S	No. Units: 16 No. Vac.: 0 Year Built: 19 59 2 STY F/S	No. Units: 13 No Vac.: 0 Year Built: 19 56 2 STY F/S	No. Units: 8 No. Vac.: 0 Year Built: 19 56 2 STY F/s
Quality	Avg.	Avg.	Avg.	Avg.
Condition	Good	Good	Good	Good
Recreational facilities	None	Pool	None	None
Parking	10 Subt. Spaces	8 carports	13 carports	4 carports
Tenant appeal	Good	Good	Good	Good

Unit breakdown

	No. of Units	Tot.	BR	b	No. of Units	Tot.	BR	b	No. of Units	Tot.	BR	b	No. of Units	Tot.	BR	b
	4	4	2	2	2	2	0	1	1	4	2	1	6	4	2	b
	6	3	1	1	8	3	1	1	11	3	1	1	2	3	1	1
					6	4	2	1	1	2	0	1				

	910 N. Stanley	1247 N. Sycamore Ave.	6100 Fountain Ave.	7546 Norton Ave.
Util. paid by owner	Hot Water	Hot Water	Hot Water	Hot Water
Data source	N/A	C.M.C. Inc.	C.M.C. Inc.	C.M.C. Inc.
Price	$ N/A XX Unf. □F	$ 430,000 X Unf. □F	$325,000 X Unf. □F	$ 275,000 X Unf. □F
Sale–Listing–Offer	N/A	Sale	Sale	Sale
Date of sale	N/A	9/79	8/79	5/79
Terms (Including conditions of sale and financing terms)	N/A	Conventional 26% cash dn 12.5 int. rate 30 years	Conventional 22% cash dn 30 years	48% cash dn 11.75% int. rate 30 years

Complete as many of the following items as possible using data effective at time of sale

	910 N. Stanley	1247 N. Sycamore Ave.	6100 Fountain Ave.	7546 Norton Ave.
Gross Annual Income	$ 25,620	$ 51,108	$ 34,332	$ 27,300
Gross Ann. Inc. Mult.(1)	N/A	8.41	9.47	10.07
Net Annual Income	$ 16,320	$ 32,709	$ 21,286	$ 17,745
Expense Percentage (2)	35%	36%	38%	35%
Overall Cap. Rate (3)	N/A	7.61 %	6.55 %	6.45 %
Price per unit	$ N/A	$ 26,875	$ 25,000	$ 34,375
Price per room	$ N/A	$ 8,269	$ 8,333	$ 9,167
Price gross bldg. area	$NA SF Bldg. Area	$ 41.34 /sq. ft. bldg. area	$ 29.74 /sq. ft. bldg. area	$ 35.03 /sq. ft. bldg. area

(1) Sale Price ÷ Gross Annual Income (2) Total Annual Expenses ÷ Total Gross Annual Income (3) Net Annual Income ÷ Price

RECONCILIATION: Most consideration has been given to price per unit and the gross annual income multiplier as they best reflect a typical investors attitude.

Price/Unit	10 Units X	$26,000	=	$260,000
GAM	10 X	25,650	=	256,000
Price Gross Bldg. Area	8760 X	$30	=	263,000

INDICATED VALUE BY MARKET APPROACH $ 256,000

INCOME APPROACH

INCOME		EXPENSES	ACTUAL	FORECASTED
Total Monthly Apartment Forecasted Rents	$ 2135*	Real Estate Taxes*	$ 2927	$ 2927
Other Monthly Income (Itemize)	0	Other taxes or licenses	35	35
	$	Insurance	756	756
Total Gross Monthly Forecasted Income Actual	$ 2135	Unsubordinated ground rent	0	0
Total Gross Annual Forecasted Income	$ 25,620	Fuel		
Less Forecasted Vacancy and Collection Loss (2 0 %)	$(512)	Gas	1207	1207
Effective Gross Annual Income	$ 25,108	Electricity		
Less Forecasted Expenses & Replacement Reserves 34%	$(8,537)	Water and sewer		
Net Annual Income from Total Property	$ 16,571	Trash removal	414	414
Less Return on and Recapture of Depreciated Value of Furnishings ($____ @ ____%)	$( ) 0	Pest control	102	102
		Maintenance and repairs	1766	1849
Net Annual Income from Real Property	$ 16,571	Interior and exterior decorating	131	0
Capitalized as follows:		Cleaning expenses and supplies	0	0
Analyzing the data presented above an OAR of 6.5% seems reasonable		Management (Off-site)	0	0
Therefore, $16,571 ÷ 6.5 = 255,000		Res. Mgr. salary & apartment	600	600
		Janitor(s) salary & apartment	0	0
		Miscellaneous	200	0
*Real Estate Taxes [X] Actual □ Est. Tax Rate Per $100 $____			0	0
Total Assessed Value $ ____		REPLACEMENT RESERVES		
Comments: Actual rents are low. Rent control in force. Actual rents used for the purpose of this appraisal.		Carpeting and drapes	47	203
		Ranges and refrigerators	0	203
		Dishwashers and disposals	0	68
		AC units (Wall)	0	100
		Hot Water Heaters		76
		TOTAL EXPENSES & REPL. RES.	$ 8,185	$ 8,537

INDICATED VALUE BY INCOME APPROACH . . . . $ 255,000

General Comments (including comments on any items rated poor or fair)   None _____

_____
_____
_____
_____
_____
_____
_____

CONDITIONS AND REQUIREMENTS OF APPRAISAL (include required repairs, replacements, painting, termite inspections, etc.): None _____

_____
_____
_____
_____
_____

RECONCILIATION AND VALUE CONCLUSION

Indicated Value by the Cost Approach . . . . $ 250,000 _____

Indicated Value by the Market Approach . . . $ 256,000 _____

Indicated Value by the Income Approach . . . $ 255,000 _____

FINAL RECONCILIATION: As an indicator of value, greatest weight and consideration has been given to market and income approaches, because they best reflect activity of the typical investor in today's uncertain market.

_____
_____
_____
_____
_____

to your subject property. Totaling all your plus and minus adjustments, you arrive at an estimate of subject's value relative to current buying habits. This evaluation can be extremely exact or merely ball park, depending on the similarity of the other projects.

Replacement Cost Approach

Appraisers usually call this valuation the residual method. This means separating the land from the improvement, arriving at a value for each separately, and adding them together. It is not a good way to analyze an investment. However, you should be familiar with the technique since the appraisal department of your bank will use it along with the market data and income approach in establishing value and, therefore, loan commitment.

The replacement cost of the improvement is somewhat indicated by the tax ticket of a comparable property. It may reveal that the county assessor has allowed 25 percent for the land and 75 percent for the improvement. Whatever the subject property's price, you can assume that 75 percent is for the improvement. Now you know what the owner thinks it is worth. Compare this with current construction costs. Contact several contractors along with the contractor's association.

When we speak of replacement costs, we are talking about the actual construction of that many square feet on that lot, not reduplicating the building. That could be exorbitant, especially if it is unique or constructed with very expensive materials. All you want to know is what a modern building of x number of feet would run.

Using the replacement cost approach will give you the upper limit of value. However, if you are not dealing with new construction, you must go one step further. You must determine the economic life of the building and other improvements, and depreciate them through physical deterioration—functional and economic obsolescence. That changes the value downward.

Once I was looking at an apartment building for which there were no comparables. It was a difficult situation. I, of course, also wanted to know if the area was going up or down. But with no recent sales to indicate demand and movement in market, I could not tell.

So I was forced to resort to the replacement cost approach to develop comparables. I went immediately to the Safety and Permit Department and asked to see the plans of the subject building. I learned the square footage, type of construction, and date. Through a general contractor, I learned what it cost to build originally. Then I checked the recorder's office to discover what the land had cost the developer. I now had an historical perspective. However, it gave me no indication as to its present value.

I returned to the permit department and said: "I am analyzing an apartment building that I wish to buy. Can you tell me if there are any new apartments under construction in the area?" I learned what was approved and what was planned, their tentative schedules plus condominium activity.

Four apartments and five condominium projects were in the works—all within three blocks of the subject property. I studied each of their plans (plans once approved are in the public domain, although you cannot photograph them). I learned their square footage, foundation type, cubic yards of cement, and feet of steel. I returned to my office and filled out my estimator's form (available to everyone). After calculating the cost of all materials that were to go into the buildings, including the pools, I arrived at their approximate cost. How close can one come? For one building I calculated $1,889,000; it sold for $1,900,000. Close enough. This is a straightforward process that you can also do. If you don't want to do it yourself, gather all the pertinent facts from the plans and turn them over to a contractor to estimate.

I then had to figure how much rental income was necessary to meet their probable financial obligations (discussed in Chapter 4). I decided that the loan was 70 percent, and knowing the rate at the time, I arrived at the monthly payment. I assumed that someone was going to take back a second* which would be at a higher rate for a shorter period of time. I then computed what each unit must rent for. I thought at the time it was high: $350 for one bedroom and $450 for two bedrooms. But I found later that I was only $10 off!

*A second trust deed can be for any amount and for any specified rate of interest (within the bounds of law of your state) or due date. It can be written for interest only, or principal and interest combined in monthly installments. It is subservient to the first T.D. backed by, or secured by, a note, and is often referred to as a "junior loan."

All of this led me to one possible conclusion. The subject building was a good buy, even though it had considerable deferred maintenance as well as a number of other problems (such as poor-risk tenants). I knew that I could raise my rents on the one hand, but lower my rents if things got bad, and still make my loan payments. I now could negotiate from strength.

How To Get the Highest Appraisal for Your Property

When an institutional lender makes a loan secured by real estate, the lenders require the property to be appraised. Typically, the lender has a policy regarding the maximum allowable loan to value ratio and that allowable may vary from one institutional lender to another. It is imperative to obtain the highest possible loan and reduce your cash outlay. In order to obtain this, you must try to have the appraiser arrive at the highest possible appraised value.

Different Loan Situations

Most real estate loans fall into one of two categories:

Those in which a buyer and seller have agreed upon a price in an arms-length transaction.

Those in which there is no sale such as an exchange or refinancing.

Usually when the buyer and seller have agreed upon a price, it is customary for the appraiser to rely generally on that fact and limit him-or herself to give the property a rough check to make sure that the buyer is not overpaying. However, the appraiser will sometimes challenge the sales price by making a sufficiently lower appraisal.

In circumstances where the owner or prospective owner of a parcel of land seeks a loan to finance the construction of a building, or when an owner seeks to refinance an existing building, the appraiser plays a much more active role. In such cases, he or she will rely heavily on the traditional approaches to appraisal.

If a sale is involved, your main purpose is to make certain nothing causes the appraiser to turn in a low appraisal. Without a sale, you have a much better chance and more opportunity to influence the appraisal upward, but it is harder to do. In a case such as this, many appraisers tend to take a more conservative stance, which can mean a lower appraised value and a smaller loan for you.

Appraisers

Some lenders employ their own salaried appraisers; others use independent appraisers known as "fee appraisers." There is little if any incentive for a salaried institutional appraiser to give liberal appraisals. It is a sure bet that his or her superiors will not offer congratulations on a great appraisal if he or she comes in with a relatively high value and proves to be right. However, if the appraiser ever overestimates the value and the lender has problems with the loan as a result, the appraiser is in "hot water." The institutional appraiser is generally more conservative, although in competitive lending markets (this has not been true since about 1976), supervisors may pressure him or her to make more competitive appraisals, in other words, raising the value of the building higher than the appraiser would under normal circumstances.

Independent appraisers tend to have a diversified clientele and consequently are less apt to be conservative. They are often more sophisticated than bank appraisers.

Appraisers have their own prejudices, likes, and dislikes, and many often work by "rules of thumb." One appraiser may deduct 10 percent or more if he is able to see the top of a roof of a house when he drives up to appraise it. This appraiser believes that the deduction reflects the public dislike of homes that are below the level of the adjacent road. It stands to reason that if you had such a house and were trying to get the highest possible appraisal, you would try to avoid that particular appraiser like the plague.

The lender selects the appraiser; however, you can influence the selection by your choice of lenders. In rare cases you can pick an independent appraiser, and if this is so, make sure that before deciding on an appraiser you discuss your property with him or her. This will help you determine whether you have personal rapport. It will give you the opportunity to learn if the appraiser has any prejudices that might adversely affect your property.

Selecting the
Appraiser

One of the best ways to learn if a particular appraiser is correct for the property is to talk to brokers with experience in your area and who are active enough that they can recommend the local lender or appraiser who is most likely to give you the highest appraisal, or at least the ones to avoid. Most real estate investors go to great pains to make a good impression on perspective renters or buyers. But for some strange reason, some investors are likely to handle an appraiser by calling the resident manager and saying that an appraiser will be arriving Thursday afternoon, so please show him around!

The intelligent way to handle the situation would be for you to personally market the property to the appraiser just as you would to a prospective buyer. Be sensible, be helpful, do his or her homework.

Find comparative sales that support your evaluation. Make certain you have all the data you can get on the property and the area, survey area, blueprints, rent rolls, and other materials. And, naturally, you should emphasize the positive and downplay or omit negative information. As for selling, spruce up the place before the appraiser arrives. If you have recently installed any new equipment, such as energy-or water-saving devices, show it to the appraiser as you would the buyer.

Before the appraiser arrives, make sure everything is ready so that the inspection is not delayed. For example, you should check and know where all of your keys are beforehand to make certain that you are not locked out of the building. Usually the appraiser will wish to look at some of the apartments, such as one of the studios, one of the one bedrooms, and one of the two bedrooms, so by all means select those apartments that are neat, tidy, clean, and preferably with the tenants off the premises.

Most appraisers appreciate it if you do some of the necessary work to dig out the information they need, and all of them appreciate it if you provide thorough information on the property and help make the inspection go smoothly and quickly. One last word of warning: some appraisers are turned off by efforts to influence them. Be careful not to alienate the appraiser involved. Play "help the appraiser" role by ear.

chapter four

The Investor's Approach

Determining Cash Flow

One necessary task in analyzing an income-producing property is to determine the pretax cash flow. When you know the cash flow, you can easily figure your return on the investment, calculate the tax shelter, and evaluate the investment in other ways. One does not need to be a real estate expert to determine property cash flow. Some uncomplicated and commonsense research will provide you with a base figure.

Following is a hypothetical example. Don Adams is considering the purchase of a new 30-unit unfurnished apartment building. He recently calculated the cash flow of the property offered to him for an investment. Let us go through his analysis step-by-step to provide an example of the process and format you can follow. Keep in mind that this is only an example; the figures vary widely from building to building and year to year.

The building in question is located in an attractive neighborhood and a prestigious suburb. The cost of the building is $500,000, and a $345,000, 25-year mortgage at 10.25 percent is anticipated. The projected figures are based on the first full year of operation of 100 percent occupancy.

The building has five singles, 15 one bedrooms, and 10 two bedrooms. To judge how much the apartments could rent for, Adams made comparisons with his prospective building to those in the area that were similar in quality, location, and construction. He questioned area real estate brokers and studied the classified section of the newspaper.

After carefully studying this information, Adams concluded that the singles (studios) would rent for $350, the one bedrooms for $450, and the two bedrooms for $550; thus, the total maximum income would be

Step 1: Figuring the Gross Income

$168,000 yearly. Additional income from laundry room fees would possibly add another $2,000, for a total of $170,000 of gross income.

Step 2: Vacancy and Bad Debt Loss To estimate the reduction in gross income caused by bad debts and vacancies, Adams looked at a publication that analyzed income and expenses for apartment buildings across the nation (see expense index page 187 this book) called a Statistical Complication and Analysis of Actual Income and Expenses experienced in apartment, condominium, and cooperative buildings. It is published by experienced exchange committee of Real Estate Management, 439 North Michigan Avenue, Chicago, Illinois 60611. I suggest that you should use caution in applying these averages. To be on the safe side Adams estimated that the vacancy and bad debt rate would be five percent of the possible total gross income of $170,000, or $8,500; although the vacancy factor in the surrounding areas was two percent. His rate was slightly higher than the recent national experience and slightly higher than the local experience with this type of building, but he took it as a precautionary measure even though he felt the building would continue to thrive and maintain a low vacancy rate.

Step 3: Operating Expenses For his initial estimate of operating expenses, Adams again used the statistical complication already mentioned together with a cost price index included in this book. After consulting both, he came to a conclusion on his own. He could have also consulted management agencies, maintenance firms, utility companies, assessors, and others to get estimates for operating expenses. However, this was not necessary due to the information given in the Expense and Cost Replacement Index, which is reproduced in the Appendix. If the building had been previously occupied, it would have been quite easy to determine the actual cost by examining the records.

Maintenance. For maintenance, Adams made a reliable assumption—and that's what it is; that the newer the building the less the maintenance—by taking the experiences of others. He estimated that the maintenance would be five percent of the total gross income, or $8,500.

Utilities. Because the cost of utilities rose substantially after the averages for his region had been completed, Adams raised the projected figure from 8 to 10 percent of the gross income, which amounted to $17,000. He was aware of the fact that this figure could fluctuate sharply.

Administrative. The building would be professionally managed, with a total administrative cost including legal, accounting, and management costs, at 8 percent of the gross income, or $13,600.

Taxes and Insurance. They would approximate the region average of 25 percent of gross income, which would be $42,500.

Step 4: Net Operating Income The projected operating expense totaled $81,600, or 48 percent of the total gross income. This left a net operating income of $79,900.

Payments at 10.25 percent on a $375,000, 25-year mortgage would be $3,673.96, monthly or $44,088 annually.

Conclusion: The estimated pretax cash flow is $35,812 on an investment of $125,000. This represents a 29 percent return on the investment of $125,000.

Table 4.1

General Format for Calculating Cash Flow

Gross Rental Income		$168,000
Plus Other Income		+ 2,000
Gross Income		170,000
Less Vacancy and Bad Debt Loss		− 8,500
Adjusted Gross Income		161,500
Less Operating Expenses		
Maintenance	8,500	
Utilities	17,000	
Administrative	13,600	
Taxes & Insurance	42,500	− 81,600
Net Operating Income		79,900
Less Mortgage Payments (Debt Service)		− 44,088
Net Pre-Tax Cash Flow		$ 35,812

Note: These are estimated figures in a hypothetical example.

The income analysis approach could be the most important and reliable method that you can use in appraising income-producing property. It should be thoroughly understood by every investor. The one thing the investor must determine is the net operating income. This is most essential. You will construct the income and expenses of the property using the form included in this chapter. Do not take anyone's word about income and expenses.

First, however, you must determine the capitalization rate for the particular area in which you are interested. Do this simply by finding the latest sale in that area. Each area has a cap rate, and the only way you are going to learn it is to find comparable sales.

Capitalization Rate

The capitalization, or cap, rate varies from neighborhood to neighborhood. First find out what has been sold and who has sold it—try the broker. Say: "I am trying to do an analysis on a piece of property. I need to know the cap rate for that area, and you just sold the building. I know what the sales price was, but could you tell me what the net income was so I can arrive at a cap rate?" If the broker doesn't want to do that, ask if he or she will just give you the cap rate. Get several cap rates, and if they are all equal, use that cap rate. Brokers may say that the cap rate is privileged information because they don't want to disclose the net income. In that case, I reply: "I am really not interested in net income . . . only from the standpoint of trying to evaluate a piece of property. I am trying to appraise something else. If you don't want to give the net, you know how to figure the cap rate, so just give me the cap rate, which is all I want. If you would do that, I would appreciate it." But first you have to ask for the person who sold the property because he or she is the one who really knows about it. And what you might do is get in touch with a broker that you know, ask to look at the multiple listing book, find out where it was listed and what the sale price was, and then look at what it sold for. In there it will indicate what the expenses are. It will give you enough information so that you can get a pretty good estimate. Then when you get the information from the broker, if it is really compatible, you can say that it is a good cap rate.

Of all the methods of evaluating income-producing property, the following are the most popular and most frequently used:

1. Income approach—the property is valued by a capitalization of net income or the potential earning power the property will and can support.

2. Cost approach—the value of the property is determined by the current cost of replacing the property less depreciation from all sources (reproduction cost is not to be confused with replacement cost, which entails duplicating a structure in every detail as it was built, possibly 70 years ago, at a relatively low cost that in today's market would be prohibitive).

3. Market approach—value is indicated by the most recent sales of comparable properties.

Although the valuation of property takes into account all the already mentioned valuation methods, the quickest way to determine the value of income-producing property is the income approach, using a given cap rate for a given property or class of properties. The following should aid in calculating the value:

$$\frac{\text{Net Operating Income}}{\text{Cap Rate}} = \text{Value} \qquad \frac{\text{Net Operating Income}}{\text{divided by Cap Rate}} = \text{Value}$$

Net Operating Income is also known as NOI. The process of capitalization is based on the assumption that the present value of the anticipated NOI available for debt service is equal to the value of the investment property. The cap rate itself is the rate of return that an investor requires. The capitalization process is a limited measure to the extent that:

• The cap rate assumes that the NOI available for debt service will continue indefinitely and without fluctuations just as an annuity in perpetuity would continue.

• As most commonly used in real estate, cap rates do not allow for residual income benefits, such as from a sale or refinancing.

Before an investor can use a cap rate to determine value, he or she must determine what an investment property's expected NOI available for debt service (mortgage payments) will be on a normalized basis.

To normalize property revenues, it is necessary for the investor to look at property performance over a period of time, as well as property performance at any given time in relation to similar properties.

For whatever reason, the inexperienced investor usually has great difficulty with the meaning of, understanding, and reasoning for the use and term *cap rate*. The following examples should help you to understand the capitalization rate and why it is used.

First, a cap rate is an individual investor's required return. Let's suppose that investor Barbara Smith is interested in property X. She concludes that 9 percent would be an acceptable rate of return on properties similar to X. She, therefore, considers that this figure should be her required rate of return for investing in property X. One useful way of figuring the cap rate would be to look at the opportunity cost; for example, what return would you expect from other investment properties in a similar risk category?

How to make calculations for the total value in this example? Given $65,000 as the NOI and 9 percent as the cap rate, the total value is determined by plugging these figures into the formula:

$$\frac{\$65,000}{9\%} = \$722,222$$

The total value of a property is very sensitive to the size of the cap rate. Let's assume that two investors have different opportunity costs and, therefore, different cap rates. The same property will then have a different value to each of them. For example, let's assume that Barbara Smith has a friend who has a cap rate of 10 percent. To that friend, the same property X would be worth $650,000.

$$\frac{\$65,000}{10\%} = \$650,000, \text{ not } \$722,222$$

In the average case, the value of a property will have two components, an equity value and a debt value. The debt value is set by the mortgage (or trust deed) that a lender will provide; the equity value is set by the difference between the mortgage (or trust deed) and total value. You can easily use the capitalization formula to calculate the equity value of a property provided a mortgage (or trust deed) already exists, meaning that a debt value has already been established.

Let's say that Bill Jones becomes interested in property Y, which has a mortgage of $400,000. Property Y, like X in the earlier example, has a normalized NOI of $65,000 available for debt service (interest and principal). Jones now wants to determine just how much equity he can justify over and above the mortgage. In order to calculate the equity value (the amount he invests), he must capitalize the cash flow after the debt service.

Example

The normalized NOI allowable for debt service	$65,000
Less debt service on $400,000 mortgage at 8 percent annual constant (total annual payment of principal and interest on mortgage with level payment amortization schedule)	$32,000
Cash flow after debt service	$33,000

Once again using a required rate of return of 9 percent as the cap rate, it calculates as follows:

$$\text{Equity Value} = \frac{\$33,000}{.09} = \$366,666$$

The total value equals:

mortgage	$400,000
equity	366,666
Total Value	$766,666

Jones concludes that he might justify investing up to $366,666 in equity.

The equity value of a property is very sensitive to the rates on the mortgage. If the annual constant were 10 instead of 8 percent, the cash flow after debt service would drop to $20,000 and the equity value to $222,222.

By taking the mortgage of	$400,000
Equity	222,222
Total Value	$622,222

Subtracting the total value of $622,222 from the previous value of $766,666 would leave a value of $144,444 less. It is well to remember that cap rates are a convenient tool to use for a quick evaluation of a property. However, they should be used and applied cautiously as they do not take into account changes in cash flow and other financial benefits that can very well result from changes in debt structure, tax consequences, and other variables.

Direct Income Capitalization

Direct income capitalization is referred to as the relationship of net income to property value. It is expressed in the formula:

$$V = \frac{I}{R}$$

Value (V) equals net income (I) divided by the capitalization rate (R). Net income is defined as operating income less all expenses, but not including the cost of mortgage(s) or debt service.

Following are examples of the use of this formula. Note that the terms *annual net income, net income, net operating income (NOI)*, and *annual verified net income* are synonymous.

To discover the current capitalization rate for the neighborhood in question, gather the prices of recent apartment building sales and their annual net income at the time of sale. You will probably have these figures handy if you have done a preliminary market data analysis. Divide the annual net income (I) by the sales price (V) to arrive at the capitalization (R).

$$R = \frac{I}{V}$$

The average of these rates is the current neighborhood capitalization rate.

Methods of Establishing Capitalization Rates

A. The method of arriving at a capitalization rate used by appraisers, both "fee" and institutional, follows:

Comparative Technique
Comparing similar properties whose net incomes and sales prices can be ascertained, computing the rate of return for each, and through averaging, adopting a rate for use in the appraisal under consideration.

Property #1 Net Income $10,000 ÷ sales price of $100,000 = 10%
Property #2 Net Income $10,450 ÷ sales price of $110,000 = 9.5%
Property #3 Net Income $10,290 ÷ sales price of $ 98,000 = 10.5%
Total of Three Properties 30%
30% total ÷ Three Properties = 10% Cap Rate

NOTE: This is an *overall* capitalization rate; that is, it includes both a provision for a return "on" the investment (pfofit) and a recapture of the depreciable portion of the investment.

B. Another method of arriving at a capitalization rate used by real estate appraisers follows:

Band of Investment Theory
A means of establishing capitalization rate by averaging the rate for available financing and owner's equity. All amounts are expressed as a percentage of total value.

Example
Financing Available   60% first @ 8%
                              20% second @ 10%

Owner's Equity
  First Trust Deed   60% × 8% = 4.80%
  Second Trust Deed   20% × 10% = 2.00%
  Equity   20% × 25% = 5.00%
                                           11.80% or 11.8% Rate

---

Example

Sales price: $480,000
Annual net income: $38,000

$$\frac{\$38,500(I)}{\$480,000\ (V)} = (R)\ 0.08$$

The capitalization (cap) rate is 8.
    The current capitalization rate (cap rate) can then be applied to the property under consideration.

Example

Asking price: $148,000
Annual verified net income: $10,800
Cap rate: 0.08

$$\frac{\$10,800\ (I)}{.08\ (R)} = \$135,000\ (V)$$

Using the direct income capitalization approach, the fair market value of this property is $135,000; $13,000 less than the asking price. This gives you a ceiling price below which you wish to negotiate. You, of course, want to pay less than the $135,000 ceiling.

The direct capitalization approach can also be used to arrive at an ideal net income at a given current cap rate. The capitalization rate (R) times the fair market value (V) equals the reasonable minimum net income (I).

$$I = VR$$

Example

Sales price: $275,000
Net income: $19,000
Cap rate: .10

$$.10 \text{ (R)} \times \$275,000 \text{ (V)} = \$27,500 \text{ (I)}$$

The proper net income for a property valued at $275,000 in a neighborhood with a cap rate of 10 is $27,500; $8,500 more than the actual net income. Properties with large irregularities in income to cap rate should generally be avoided, unless, of course, a large negative cash flow is required.

Summary

$$V = \frac{I}{R}$$
$$I = VR$$
$$R = \frac{I}{V}$$

Expenses

When you ask for a copy of the expenses, for example, from the owner's income tax return, he or she may be reluctant to show you. I personally do not think I should show my income tax return to anybody. I will show my rent receipts. I will even show my deposit receipts, which list each tenant's name and apartment number and amount of rent he or she pays. It verifies his schedule. Let the owner show you something like that if he or she doesn't want to reveal the income tax return. You can be sure that the expense sheet will be 23 or 28 percent of gross income. It should be closer to 45 percent of the effective gross income. You always want to check for reserves for replacement, such as for roof, carpeting, drapes, and so forth.

I happen not to believe in having furnished apartments. In a furnished apartment, people can move in with a suitcase and move out in the middle of the night. They are not generally as stable as tenants with furniture. Today the cost of moving is so high that people think twice about it. If you raise your rent $15, the tenant with just the suitcase might well split. But the one with the furniture will figure that moving isn't justified by $15 a month. It's going to cost them $400 minimum to move the furniture and go through the routine of finding a place.

I feel so strongly about this that I have sold the furniture out of furnished buildings as soon as I closed escrow. This is a personal choice, of course, but I have learned that in the long run, people with their own furnishings are more profitable tenants.

To err on the safe side, figure that 45 percent of your operating income will go for expenses. You want the property to carry itself in its present condition, at its present rent. Always include the 5 percent vacancy factor even if the building is 100 percent occupied. Hold 5 percent in reserve even for an unfurnished building, and estimate 5 percent for maintenance and repair. Already, you have used 15 percent of operating income. Then begin adding actual expenses—trash pickup, pool cleaning, taxes, water, gas, power, and so on. Call the water department and electric company and verify the bills for the last several years. Watch for unusual increases and investigate them.

Always include a 5 percent management fee in your calculations even if there is no manager and the state or city does not require one. You, yourself, will then have to manage the property. This takes considerable time, and your time is valuable, plus you will be using your car, gasoline, and such.

Finding Cash Flow		
Operating Income		100%
Less		
1st and 2nd Mortgage Payments (no greater than)		50%
Total Operating Expenses (no greater than)		45%
Including:		
Vacancy factor	5%	
Managerial fee	5%	
Reserve	5%	
Maintenance	5%	
Utilities*	5%	
All other expenses including taxes and insurance	20%	
Positive Cash Flow (as a percentage of gross income)		5%

* Utilities individually metered; if centrally metered would rise to 15 to 20 percent.

If, however, the neighborhood has stabilized and reached the peak of its development, total operating expenses will range from 50 to 55 percent, while declining neighborhood expenses will reach 65 to 70 percent. Of course, in these instances, due to reduced total property value, the mortgage percentage will be less—you hope!

Using these percentages as a rough guideline, we can begin to acquire data for our expense sheet. One must remember, however, to be as careful and thorough with the expense investigation as we were with the market approach.

Building Expense Sheet

1. Verified Gross Income (rent & concessions)   _____
   Less:
2. Vacancy Factor (based on historical averages of building and neighborhood)   _____
3. Total Operating Income   _____
4. Less the following stabilized annual operating expenses: _____
   - Adequate Insurance   _____
   - Electricity   _____
   - Gas   _____
   - Water   _____
   - Management   _____
   - Maintenance   _____
   - Payroll   _____
   - Trash Removal   _____
   - Pest Control   _____
   - Property Taxes   _____
   - Replacement Reserve (5 percent)   _____
   - Pool maintenance   _____
   - Other   _____
5. Total Annual Operating Expenses   _____
6. Net Cash Flow before financing costs (line 5 from line 3)   _____
7. Annual Debt Service (principal and interest) Likely Obtainable   _____
8. Net Cash Flow (line 7 from line 6)   _____

Environmental Obsolescence

Probably the most important single factor in real estate analysis is location. You can improve your property, but you cannot change the neighborhood.

You want to look long and hard so that you don't buy a piece of property that will have or has economic obsolescence. Economic obsolescence involves problems that are completely beyond the ability of the investor to change. These could be a deteriorating neighborhood, zoning changes, crime rates, high unemployment special property assessments, and so on. Look to the future. Check such things as the general income of the area, what the life-styles are, rental rates for the area, city building permits, vacancy rate, and master planning. Remember, above everything else, discover trends.

Don't rely on appearances. If it is an older property, it has many hidden expenses. You want to look at its real age, type of construction, the chronological age as well as effective age. Check for deferred maintenance, which is not bad itself (as we shall see later), but the building must be structurally sound. If you are not qualified to spot these things, hire someone to inspect them for you—the heating, the plumbing, electricity, everything.

I have a plumber who inspects properties for me, who has worked with me for the past 15 years. I have a service, which I call the Professional Home and Apartment Inspection Service. My fees, and you will probably find this similar in your area, are $1 per $1,000 sale price. As an example, I had a call from a young man. He wanted an inspection on a 50-unit building, but he thought my price was rather high. The building was a $1,000,000 structure, so the fee was $1,000. I told him that was the final price.

In about three hours he called me back. "When can you make the inspection?" he said. I told him that he had to accompany me while I did the inspection, that I would give him the report then and there, and he would pay me then and there. We made the inspection. I had my plumber there, my roofer, and my swimming pool man. We located $6,000 worth of plumbing to be done. The swimming pool looked beautiful because it had just been refinished. But I began to wonder why. Down in the basement I could see that there had been a lot of leaking, and it still was a little leaky. As to management efficiency . . . when we asked the manager to see the apartments, we found that she had over 50 keys on the board, instead of having every apartment keyed with a master.

We finished the inspection and came to an $8,000 total in repairs. The potential buyer asked what he should do and I told him that he should renegotiate his agreement. "Tell the owner that you have found through inspection, which I have signed, that there is $8,000 he is going to have to knock off the price." The owner did take that amount off.

I told the young man later, "Just think a minute. It cost you $1,000, and you saved $8,000. Do you still think that's a bad price?" He thought it was pretty reasonable.

Here was a case where someone realized that he didn't know, but he knew enough to find somebody who did. You can find professional people to do this work for you. You can also get a good contractor to inspect for you.

chapter five

Replacement Costs and Expenses

In the Appendix, you will find an Expense and Replacement Cost Index, exactly the kind that banks, appraisers, and large management companies develop for themselves. The index details major problem areas, which are the subject of this chapter.

You will have to learn replacement costs. If you are inspecting an apartment building and the refrigerators look bad, immediately get hold of a wholesaler and find out the replacement costs and what the installation charges will be. The refrigerators may have been in for seven years and the warranty is out. When you have 44 items to replace at about $400 apiece, you're talking about a great amount of money.

Apartment Checklist

Following is an apartment building checklist. A hand-held tape recorder is good to use because you can inspect quickly and yet miss nothing. Another useful device is a measuring wheel. You just walk in one direction and make a notation. Then walk in another direction. Now you know how many square feet you have. It's accurate, and it's what appraisers and county assessors use.

Apartment Checklist

Building Site

Legal description and street address

Dimensions and lot plan showing all improvements

Soil and subsoil

Drainage
  Possibility of mudslides
  Possibility of flooding
  Possibility of erosion

Topography
  How much of lot is usable
  Topographical hazards

Privacy from adjacent sites

Access to public streets

Landscaping (present and improvement potential)
  Lawn
  Trees
  Shrubs
  Garden

Ease of snow removal

Ice Hazards

Parking Areas
  Sufficient for code
  Covered, uncovered
  Heated
  How well lit
  Condition of concrete
  Improvement potential

Paved Areas
  Sidewalks
  Driveway(s)
  Improvement potential

Disutilities
  Noise pollution
  Air pollution
  Odors
  Excessive traffic (check all times of day)

View to street

Refuse removal
  Suitability of location
  Sufficient number of containers
  Health aspects
  Improvement potential

General exterior lighting
  Improvement potential
  Types of lights in use

Signage
  Type
  Suitability
  Improvement potential
  Attractiveness of name

Pool
  Usefulness
  Safety
  Attractiveness

Building Exterior

Roof
  Estimated life
  Improvement potential

Rain gutters and down spouts

Painted surfaces
  Condition
  Suitability of color
  Improvement potential

Stories

Fire escapes
  Condition
  Sufficient for code

Mailboxes
  Type
  Condition
  Improvement potential

Intercoms
  Condition
  Appearance
  Improvement potential

Electric door opener
  Condition
  Improvement potential

Exterior doors
  Condition
  Hardware
  Potential for improvement
  Exterior access to basement

Anomalies
  Major bulges along exterior walls
  Sinking steps
  Other mysterious formations

Architecture
  General appearance
  Attractiveness

Common Areas (lobby, hallway, and so on)

Walls

Ceilings

Floors

Stairways
  Sufficient for code

Elevators
  Safety
  Possibility for improvement

Fire extinguishers
  Sufficiency
  Type
  Code

Lighting
  Safety
  Attractiveness
  Possibility for improvement
  Type

Apartment Checklist (cont.)

Common Areas (cont.)

Storage areas
  Sufficiency
  Safety

Sprinklers

Garage
  Doors
  Roof
  Floor
  Safety

Special rooms
  Game or other
  Condition
  Vending machines
  Suitability

Carpeting
  Indoor
  Outdoor

Basement

Walls

Joists

Drains

Wiring
  Fuses or circuit breakers
  Gas and electric meters for every apartment
  Meter for owner

Plumbing
  Evidence of flooding

Heating system
  Age
  Fuel
  Condition
  Sufficiency

Support columns

Hot water heaters
  Capacity
  Fuel
  Sufficiency

Crawl space
  Anomalies

Tenant Interviews

Adequacy of
  Heat
  Air conditioning
  Water pressure
  Roof
  Kitchen
  Laundry facilities
  Manager

Rent
  Amount
  Suitability

Concessions

Wiring
  Reliability of circuit breakers
  Frequency of blown fuses

Disutilities
  Pests
  Other tenants
  Crime (building and neighborhood)
  Noise
  Pollution
  Traffic

Apartments

Number:

Living room
  Proportions
  Dimensions
  Fireplace
  Circulation
  Position of windows
  Light
  Adequacy of floor and wall space
  Attractiveness
  Electrical outlets
  Closet space

Dining room or area
  Proportions
  Dimensions
  Adequacy
  Usefulness
  Ease of access to kitchen
  Privacy

Bedrooms
  Adequacy of floor space
  Dimensions
  Proportions
  Attractiveness
  Light
  Position of room to bathroom
  Ventilation
  Position of doors and windows

Kitchen
  Efficiency of arrangement
  Dimensions
  Condition of refrigerator, range, sink
  Ventilation
  Light
  Condition of walls and floor
  Work surfaces
  Convenience
  Possibility of improvement

Apartment Checklist (cont.)

Closets
  Number
  Location with respect to need
Carpeting
Terraces
Bathroom(s)
  Fixtures
  Ventilation
  Lighting
  Dimensions
  Safety

Position of windows and doors
Storage space
Tile
Heating
Position of plumbing for repair
Condition of plumbing

Furniture
  Kind
  Condition
  Potential for improvement

Property Insurance Information

Insurance

First, get a good independent agent who represents a multitude of companies and will place insurance where he or she feels he is going to get the best for his clients—not necessarily in a money way, but in terms of company worth and services offered.

Commercial property is insured between 60 to 100 percent of value. This is called coinsurance. For example, you have a piece of property worth $100,000 and you have a 90 percent coinsurance policy on it. Then you agree to carry insurance for at least 90 percent of the value of the building. By doing that you get a lower rate. The higher the coinsurance, the lower the premium per $1,000 of value.

Replacement cost insurance means that the company has agreed to replace the building or give you the money, if you have that option. Sometimes it is not desirable to rebuild on the site, but some policies stipulate that you must rebuild. Replacement cost endorsement eliminates any depreciation from the reimbursement. This is the more desirable of the two. Generally, however, replacement cost is written only on buildings dated 1950 or later. Prior to that you have to go to coinsurance.

One can, however, have a stipulated value clause that is the mutually agreed value of the building—which you, of course, update. Coinsurance policies are not usually written that way, however.

It is the owner's responsibility to keep the policy up with value. Some companies do have an inflation guard endorsement you can attach. This has usually been 2 to 4 percent per quarter.

The rate of insurance is affected by many things—location, occupancy, age of building, condition. Different companies have different requirements, such as trash removal, extinguishers, and so forth. If something is not up to the code, a company will take a long and hard look before they will write a policy.

If you won't or can't measure up to the normal insurer, you will have to go through a substandard market and pay an exorbitant fee. The substandard market is made up of the surplus line carriers who deal expressly with high risk insurers. They can charge whatever they want, plus state and local taxes.

Special Multiperil Policy (SMP). The package type of coinsurance is called a Special Multiperil Policy, commonly referred to as SMP. It is written by the majority of major insurance companies on all types of commercial property. You can add different things for different parts of the country—such as earthquake for California or special crime coverages for certain urban areas. The package is quite flexible.

The SMP policy is broken into four sections. Section one covers the property, that is the buildings, the personal property. It can include loss of rents due to strikes or direct damage. Section two covers liability, which includes bodily injury and property damage liability; anybody who gets injured on the property or any property damage. Medical payments are an optional part of this section. Section three involves prime coverages. It is possible under this policy to cover apartment managers with fidelity bonds or to insure the owner's personal contents for burglary. Section four includes machinery and boiler coverage. But for boilers, it is more practical to seek out a company that specializes in them, such as Hartford Steam and Boiler. They have a package policy they offer apartment buildings that is a little more reasonable and broader in scope than the one in section four of a normal SMP.

For section one of the SMP, property coverages, two general forms are used. One is the general property form which is the less desirable of the two, what is called in the trade a "name peril," like fire, lightning, windstorm, hail, explosion, sudden and accidental damage from smoke, vehicles or aircraft, riot, riot attending a rent strike (or other), and civil disorder in general. If you have a general property form on your policy, you are limited to those perils only. To collect a loss you have to collect under one of the stipulated perils.

The other form is called a special building form. This is more desirable because it is broader. But it is only available to upgraded and/ or newer buildings. There are a few exclusions, but otherwise you are covered for all physical loss. Exclusions are mainly standard, such as earthquake (available under a separate policy) and normal wear and tear.

You can add name perils to the special building form of the general property portion. You might wish to include vandalism and malicious mischief, falling objects, weight of snow, ice or sleet, or maybe sprinkler leakage.

For section two, liability, we must stress the importance of personal injury liability. This is relatively new, since about 1976. Now personal injury liability covers injury to a person's integrity, character, and things of that nature. Basic to it are false arrest, malicious prosecution, willful detention or imprisonment, libel, slander, defamation of character, privacy, wrongful eviction, and wrongful entry. The last three are very important to commercial owners. Your exposure is very real.

You need an umbrella policy of liability. It will protect you when one of your tenants has a guest who drinks too much and injures him-or herself on the stairs. Make sure the policy is high enough that your company will protect and fight for you. We carry a $3 million umbrella policy of liability. It covers the buildings and my wife and me personally. It is also deductible.

Tenants' Property. A lot of tenants feel that if something happens to their personal property, it is the responsibility of the owner to take care of it. This is not so unless there has been negligence on the part of the owner. If a pipe breaks and water damages the apartment's contents, the personal property could be covered under negligence. But an insurance company will probably fight you on that because it might not have been your fault. You did not know the pipe was going to break. So the best way around this is to get what is called a "homeowners tenant." What this does is provide coverage for your tenants' personal property, clothing, and furniture from fire, theft, or whatever. You can buy this for your tenants and build it into their rents. It's worth it.

Workmen's Compensation Insurance. One of the most common things owners forget to do is to obtain Workmen's Compensation insurance. It could be the cheapest policy you ever bought.

Let's assume that your employee falls, breaks a leg, and suffers a concussion. He is in the hospital for six months and cannot work for a year. He sues you, and he will collect. And you will pay and pay and pay. But you are protected in this case under workmen's compensation.

Let's say you hire a man and tell him "do my gardening." All of a sudden you begin saying, "Take that plant and replace it with this plant. I want you to pull up that bed with these plants." The minute you take over the position of directing him, he has become an employee. He has lost the status of being an independent contractor.

To give another example, assume you have hired a lot of different people at low wages. One knows how to put in a washer, and you pay her or him $5 an hour instead of a plumber at $28 an hour. You hire another to do your painting, and you pay him or her $4 an hour rather than $8. These people are employees because you are telling them how to paint. You're furnishing the paint. You're telling them what to paint. But you're protected under Workmen's Compensation.

Always Get a Permit. Perhaps you want to put an extra light outside and you hire a man who is not licensed to do it. Or he may be a licensed electrician, but he may say, "You don't want a permit, do you?" You say, "Do I have to have one?" He replies, "No, not really." When you don't get that permit—which means the work is not going to be inspected—you're leaving yourself wide open. If there is a fire because this person put the light in improperly, they will trace it to that short—and they will. Then you can kiss your policy goodby. And that building for which you paid $500,000 has become only an expensive lot that you must clear of debris—which will cost you more money. And you are still going to have to continue the payments on that nonexistent improvement on your property.

That's a beautiful fix to get into, isn't it?

A minimum property insurance policy consists of fire, extended coverage (smoke, wind, hail, aircraft damage), vandalism, and malicious mischief coverage. However, the typical policy recommended for expense purposes is the "Apartment Package," which also includes a

Property Insurance

broader form of fire policy, liability, loss of rents, and other coverages. The two major exclusions to this policy are flood (a policy purchased separately from the standard policy) and earthquake (a single policy that includes the standard coverages).

The insurance premium amount is usually quoted on per $1,000 of insurable replacement cost basis, with many companies excluding the foundation and underground plumbing value. The premium quote will be given as "$X.XX per $1,000 of insurable replacement cost." In 1980 the replacement cost per square foot was typically $25-26, with a top figure of $31. In 1981 the figure changed to $45-50 with a top figure of $70. Another "jump" can be expected in 1982. For appraisal purposes, the coverage amount used to calculate the premium amount would be the highest between the loan amount, the replacement improvement value exclusive of the foundation and underground plumbing.

Unfortunately, the current coverage amount is seldom available, and the investor may have to check if the policy is sufficient. To do this, figure the number of thousands of dollars in the current replacement value of the improvement (again, exclusive of the foundation and underground plumbing) and divide this into the premium amount. This will give you the current cost per $1000 of insurable replacement value. If it is within a reasonable range of the current premium cost quotes (say, $2 to $3), use the annual figure of the existing policy. This will help avoid relying on an estimate that may be difficult to arrive at because of the differences in rate structures between companies, varieties of buildings, and other factors.

If the current policy proves not to be representative of that needed for expense calculations, a new figure will have to be calculated. This figure should be from *$2.20 to $3.00 per $1000 of insurable replacement cost depending on the Influencing Factors.*

Be sure that a Contingent Liability endorsement is placed on those properties not conforming to local zone density requirements. This endorsement provides that if the building is more than 50 percent destroyed (or whatever breaking point the municipality uses to determine whether the building must be rebuilt to code), the entire replacement cost of the building will be paid. This is so that the remainder of the building can be razed and a new structure built conforming to code. Often purchased along with this is a Demolition Endorsement, which pays for the demolition cost of the remaining improvement. In estimating the Contingent Liability expense, the investor must ascertain whether the property needs the endorsement and whether it is now carried and reflected in the owner-supplied expense statement. This may require a call to the escrow company or insurance agent. If synthesizing the Contingent Liability figure, the amount of this endorsement will be an approximate 25 percent addition to the standard premium.

Furniture endorsement cost is approximately $2.50 per $1,000 of replacement cost.

Factors Affecting Rate

AGE. Older buildings, especially brick construction, will usually cost more to insure. Among other things, this is due to open stairwells, unvented heat, fuse boxes (vs. circuit breakers), condition, and nonfireproof construction.

POOL. Some companies will charge extra for a pool, while others have the pool covered in the standard policy at no extra charge. These companies may require the pool to be fenced, however. For companies charging extra, the amount is about $75-$100. The highest quote we have heard was from a San Diego company at $250.

TENNIS COURTS AND OTHER RECREATIONAL FACILITIES.

CONDITION OF BUILDING. Buildings in good condition show a trend of less settlement and hence less premium costs.

NEIGHBORHOOD. High-crime areas will be reflected in high insurance costs.

HAZARDS. In Los Angeles, for example, one of the most common hazards is the brush area, found mostly near hillsides. It is by no means limited to this, however. We visited a property in North Hollywood, which was a standard walk-up building, but with an exceptionally high insurance expense figure. About 200 feet east of the building, with no buffer, we found an open storage yard for bottled gas, including nitrogen, oxygen, acetylene, argon, and hydrogen. Keep an eye for these hazards while inspecting for economic obsolescence.

RESIDENT MANAGER. Insurance underwriters favor on-site managers.

PROPERTY HISTORY. Previous claims will tend to raise subsequent premium accounts.

Insurance Cost Profile

1. As already noted, insurance costs will run from approximately $2.20 to $3.00 per $1000 of replacement value depending on the Influencing Factors. This replacement value is figured on a per square foot basis of $25-26, with a top figure of $31. When using the owner-supplied figure from the expense statement, *the allowable variance for appraisal purposes is $2.00-$3.50.*

2. Contingent Liability endorsements will add approximately 25 percent to the yearly premium.

3. Furniture endorsements will add approximately $2.50 per $1000 of furniture replacement cost.

4. If a particular property is carrying earthquake coverage, this may double the normal premium amount.

Flood Insurance

Flood insurance is required for properties located at sites identified by the Department of Housing and Urban Development (HUD) as Special Flood Hazard Areas. When examination of an HUD flood hazard map shows that the property is located in a zone designated A, A0, A1-A30, V1-V30, M, or E, a flood insurance policy is mandatory. Other zone designations, such as B, C, D, and P, indicate lesser degrees of hazard and do not require insurance.

When a property requires a flood insurance policy, the investor must ascertain whether the insurance figure in the Expense Statement reflects the added cost. If not, the additional premium must be calculated and added to the insurance cost.

At the present time, flood insurance policies are insured solely by HUD's Federal Insurance Administration. Prior to 1978, policies were issued by HUD and member companies of the National Flood Insurer's Association.

Emergency and Regular Programs

Premium rates and coverage requirements vary with the two phases of the National Flood Insurance Program—the Emergency Program and the Regular Program. Both require coverage *equal to the amount of the loan* if the loan amount is *less* than the "coverage required" ($100,000 in the Emergency Program, $200,000 in the Regular Program). Otherwise, if the *loan amount is equal to or greater than* the "coverage required" amount, the limit is set by the "coverage required" amount—$100,000 (Emergency Program) or $200,000 (Regular Program).

Emergency Program Coverage. Only "first layer" coverage is available for communities in the Emergency Program. These are communities for which only Flood Hazard Boundary Maps, which do not show degrees of risk, have been (or will be) published. The cost of this policy is $2.50 per $1000 of coverage. (The insurance must be written for $100,000 or the amount of the loan, whichever is less.) *A separate policy must be issued for each separate building; this applies in the Regular Program as well.*

Regular Program Requirements. A community must upgrade its building standards and flood plain management program when it is required to enter the Regular Program phase. This occurs when a complete Flood Insurance Rate Map, showing all the *degrees* of flood risk, has been drawn and published for that community; with 1981 the target date for all communities in the program to be mapped adequately for conversion from the Emergency Program to the Regular Program.

Sometimes a "special conversion" takes place when a community is determined to have no major flood-prone areas. When an entire community is zoned "C" or "B" indicating "minimal" or "moderate" flood hazards only, no insurance is required, and a special conversion to the Regular Program is allowed if flood plain management standards are adequate. Instead of publishing a Flood Insurance Rate Map, HUD sends out notice to rescind the existing Flood Hazard Boundary Map.

The flood map book in each office should indicate those communities in the Regular Program without maps (the special conversion communities). It should also indicate Emergency Program communities that do not have maps published because no flood hazard areas have been identified. These communities have yet to establish flood plain management standards that would permit conversion to the Regular Program. Insurance through the Emergency Program is available for these communities, but it is not required.

Regular Program Coverage. As already noted, flood-prone properties in the Regular Program require insurance to be written for $200,000, or the amount of the loan, whichever is less. New construction and "substantially improved" (50 percent or more newly built) buildings must be charged actuarial rates for all coverage. Existing buildings are eligible for the "subsidized rate," $2.50 per $1,000, to cover the first layer, that is, up to $100,000. If additional coverage is required by a loan amount exceeding the $100,000 first layer coverage, the property owner must pay the actuarial rate on the "second layer" (over $100,000) portion of the coverage. Note that the owner may choose to pay the actuarial rate for the first layer portion of coverage as well (if it is lower than the subsidized rate).

Since actuarial rates (that is, rates based on risk) apply when a community has entered the Regular Program, the Federal Insurance Administration's Zone Rate Tables must be consulted to estimate a flood-prone property's insurance cost (see Table 5.1). Actuarial rates based on zones not listed in the table are available from the Flood Insurance Manual. Information concerning a community's eligibility for coverage under the Emergency Program or Regular Program may be obtained from your chief appraiser or by calling the HUD Flood Insurance Program's toll-free number, 800-424-8872. Insurance-related questions should be directed to 800-638-6620, also toll-free.

Some communities with Flood Hazard Boundary Maps published have chosen not to participate in the National Flood Insurance Program. In these cases, flood insurance is not available and cannot, therefore, be deducted as an expense. Some lending institutions are required by law, however, to notify all loan applicants for properties located in Special Flood Hazard Areas whether federal assistance would or would *not* be available.

Nonparticipating Communities

TABLE 5.1 Zone Rate Table: Actuarial rates based on risk for each zone for apartment buildings in regular program (dollars per $1,000 coverage)

| | ZONE | | | | | |
Type of Structure	A	AO	B	C	D	V
One Story, No Basement	$3.00	$5.00*	$.50	$.20	$3.00	$9.00
Two or More Stories, No Basement	$3.00	$4.00*	$.40	$.20	$2.50	$7.50
Split Level, No Basement	$3.00	$4.00*	$.40	$.20	$3.50	$6.80
One Story, With Basement	$4.00	$3.30	$2.50	$2.00	$18.50	$51.00
Two or More Stories, With Basement	$4.00	$22.50	$1.50	$1.50	$11.50	$32.30
Split Level, With Basement	$4.00	$30.00	$1.50	$1.50	$12.50	$32.30
Mobile Home on Foundation	$4.00	$11.00*	$3.00	$2.50	$13.00	$34.50

*For structures without basement located in Zone AO, where the first floor is 18 inches or more above the crown (highest point) of the nearest street, use Zone B rates.

NOTE: "Basement" refers to habitable basements, not laundry, storage rooms, and so on.

chapter six
Fundamentals of Financing

When the subject is finance, leverage is important. Try to visualize that you have $150,000; with that you can buy an apartment building worth $1,000,000. There is no other investment where you can have that much leverage with such security. The loan ratio is fantastic; however, one has to be prudent.

Leverage in real estate is commonly known as OPM—Other Peoples' Money. I advocate going into debt up to your ears, as long as it is for a piece of residential income property—not going out to dinner or going to Europe. You are investing money, and that's different.

You borrow whatever the law will allow (as much as you can) for whatever you can. But you don't want to spread yourself so thin that you cannot release yourself and get out from under. You want to make sure that you have sufficient cash flow without looking at your investment for day-to-day income. Remember, there is a good chance that for a certain period of your investment, you will have a negative cash flow.

I do not recommend 100 percent leverage, except for the experienced investor, but 85 percent leverage is a good figure. That is, the loan company takes 70 percent, the owner takes back a second for 15 percent, and you put up the remaining 15 percent.

There was a time when the loan company (for example, in Los Angeles) would say that 10 percent down would be fine. Now they want 15 percent of your money in the project, which is okay, but do not get caught in the trap of being liable for debt beyond the building and the land. Do not make yourself personally liable for the debt. The building has to carry the loan itself, as far as the loan company is concerned. If you turn it back to them, they can't go after your possessions for the difference. Don't sign that type of agreement. Shop for a loan.

Lenders have a chief appraiser who usually has several appraisers under his or her supervision with various specialties. One appraises houses, one appraises apartment buildings, and so forth. Lenders depend on their appraiser to establish the market value of your potential property.

Prior to 1973, they looked primarily at the property they were loaning on, rather than the borrower, and they required a very low down payment. But in today's marketplace, with tight money, lenders are not only looking for what the value of the land is, they are also looking at the borrower. How substantial is he or she? How experienced?

On loans prior to 1973, apartment houses quite frequently got 75 and 80 percent loans. They then dropped to 70 percent. At the present time, some loan companies are committing 55 to 65 percent only. This begins to put savings and loans in the category of commercial banks, who traditionally loaned only 50 to 55 percent on a piece of property.

Savings and loan companies tend to want to lend only on properties where 55 percent or less of the gross income is going toward the debt service—that is, principal and interest. They treat each property in a different manner.

Mortgage bankers usually deal in secondary market or junior mortgages. Insurance companies go for large projects, usually over $3 million.

Mortgages and Trust Deeds

Mortgages and trust deeds (some states have one, some have both) come in various forms.

A variable interest rate mortgage is one in which the rate of interest will rise a certain percent according to law. But it has a maximum level. By the same token, it also can be lowered, but only by a specified percent. In a very high interest rate period, as today when some mortgages are 14.5 to 16 percent, this type of mortgage would be attractive. One advantage of a variable loan is that if you pay it off, there is no penalty. Some banks will make loans that do not include a prepayment penalty. Usually these are the banks or loan companies that are using the Fannie Mae forms and selling them to Freddie Mac or others, so they can get their money right back.*

*The Emergency Home Finance Act of 1970 gives the Federal National Mortgage Association (FNMA/Fannie Mae) and the Federal Home Loan Mortgage Corporation (FHLMC/Freddie Mac) authority to purchase mortgages on owner-occupied single-family residences. Freddie Mac was incorporated in 1970 as a subsidiary of the Federal Home Loan Bank. It is authorized to purchase FHA and VA mortgages from the originating lender, combine the mortgages into pools, and issue bonds secured by the mortgages and guaranteed by Fannie Mae for sale to the public. Freddie Mac has the authority to buy and sell conventional mortgages for its portfolio and can issue bonds backed by conventional mortgages, although they are not guaranteed by Government National Mortgage Association (GNMA/Ginnie Mae).

Wrap-around mortgages are very interesting. Let's say an individual has a 6 percent loan. (There are a few left which is one good reason that our rates are so high today—they are looking for recapture.) When buying this property, you could give a limited amount, wrapping it around that 6 percent loan, which the owner would keep and continue paying. But he or she would be charging you, the new owner, say, 9 percent if the current interest rates were 10 percent. You are saving 1 percent and the old owner is making 3 percent.

The advantage to the seller is that he or she can sell to someone that otherwise would not qualify with a lending institution, and at the same time the seller, in all probability, has a low interest rate, thereby allowing him or her to earn several percentage points higher (at present he or she is paying 6 percent; the seller can charge 11 percent in most cases, gaining 5 percent interest more over what he or she is paying).

Junior Mortgages

There are times when, in order to sell a piece of property, one will take back a junior mortgage or secondary mortgage, called second trust deeds (or TDs) in California. For example, I sold an apartment building and took back a second for $100,000, due in five years. Interest is 10 percent, payable monthly (at $833.33). It is written as "$833.33 or more"; "or more" means that the loan can be paid off prior to five years without penalty.

You may be approached by mortgage brokers regarding second trust deeds. I was offered $76,000 against the $140,000 my note would yield. It is not uncommon to discount a second trust deed. One must look at the current economic climate and immediate environment to decide whether discounting a note would be a good business decision.

You must keep track of property when you have a second. More building could be creating a parking problem. The type of tenants may have changed. Perhaps the person who bought the property is having a credit problem or is unable because of illness to look after the property. In such situations, it is possible that you could wind up with the property again.

When you take a second, you must notify the buyer(s) who assumed your loan, as well as who ever is holding the first (original lender), that you are to be alerted immediately of a default so that you can foreclose and take over payment on the first.

It is highly likely that if the buyer defaults, your old property will be in a deteriorated condition. If you see this kind of circumstance developing, it would be a good idea to accept an offer from a mortgage broker. When you turn over the note, you will have to endorse it "without recourse." That protects you.

If I had taken the broker's offer of $76,000 against $140,000, I would have been taking a $64,000 paper loss, but that would be wiser than taking the property back under adverse conditions. I prefer starting over on a new project involving renovating a piece of property rather than taking property back.

This is the only time I would suggest discounting a second and getting your money out of it. It is the safest thing to do, but do not forget to endorse the note so that you are not liable. That means that the first and second parties have been notified and that they cannot come to you for recourse.

Graduated Payment Mortgage. Borrowers start off with low monthly payments that are annually increased at one of five rates over five- or 10-year periods. Then the rate levels off.

Variable Rate Mortgage. Fluctuating interest rates tied to an index are reflected in the monthly payments, the term, or both.

Flexible Payment Mortgage. Payments cover only the interest for the first five years, then are escalated to begin amortization.

Flexible Loan Insurance Program Mortgage (FLIP). Part of the borrower's down payment is deposited in a pledged savings account, which is drawn from each month for five years to supplement initially reduced monthly mortgage payments.

Balloon Payment Mortgage. Essentially a leftover from pre-Depression days and largely prohibited today; entire outstanding balance is settled at loan's due date, with interest and some principal paid along the way.

Deferred Interest Mortgage. Borrower would be given a lower-than-standard initial interest rate, which would be repaid, with an additional fee, upon the sale of the home.

Dual Rate Variable Rate. Borrowers pay two interest rates—short term for the interest on the outstanding balance and long term for the monthly payments.

Reverse Annuity Mortgage. The lender makes regular payments to the retired homeowner on a fixed income, then collects the debt upon sale of the property or death of the owner.

Rollover Mortgage. Loan terms are renegotiated at regular, predetermined periods, usually every five years.

Step Rate Mortgage. Interest rates are scheduled to increase at a predetermined rate and at predetermined intervals.

Creative Financing

This is such a vast field that a book could be written on it alone. What it means is what it suggests—imagination; anything that you can come up with that is legal and to your advantage.

Allowing the lender to participate in the income property is a kicker to induce the lender to move. A lender may participate in the profits of the venture. A lender may share in the equity ownership of property or charge nonrefundable fees. These are kickers.

In the back of this book is a glossary of terms that are used in real estate sales as well as appraising. They include terms and ratios used by loan companies. Study them.

Impounded Taxes

Let me caution you: Never let your tax dollar be impounded. There may be a time when you would like to pay all your taxes off at the end of the year, since this is deductible. But if impounded, you cannot do that. Also, every month when you put that money aside for your taxes, put it in a savings account. At the end of the period, you will not only have enough money to pay your taxes, you will have earned some. But as an impound you will not, especially since usually more is impounded than should be since the bank foresees taxes going up.

Tell the bank that you are perfectly able to pay your own taxes since your credit rating is so good. And if the bank balks at this, say that you are going somewhere else to get a loan.

Closing Fees The escrow company is required to give you a list prior to closing telling you exactly the amount you have to come up with other than the down payment. Following is a typical estimated cost statement normally put out by a loan company for a condominium:

1. In connection with your loan application of $71,500 at 10 1/2 percent interest; a loan origination fee of 1 1/2 percent (often called points) plus $100.
2. Trustee fee of $10.
3. Prepaid interest based on the maximum, $20.57 per day or a total of _____ for 15 days.
4. Credit report, $20.
5. Tax service, $17.50.
6. Title insurance, $74.65 policy.
7. Recording fee, $10.
8. Escrow fee, $175.
9. Homeowner's dues (since this is a condominium, $56 (per month).

Ask in advance what the fees are going to be so you are prepared for them. It used to be that the points (loan origination fee) plus the $100 could be deducted right off the top from the loan fee; now it can't. It is now amortized over the period of the loan.

The *Thorndike Encyclopedia* is a very good volume to have in your library; it gives you all pertinent information on every type of interest there is, not only compound tables. It is something you should have if you are going to deal in real estate seriously. Of course, if you just want mortgage tables, you can get a copy of an amortization book free from your local savings and loan or bank.

Using the Amortization Tables

In the Mortgage Amortization schedules that follow, look up the term (number of years you wish to use) and the percentage rate, for example, 10 percent. On the right you will see the term, on the left you will see increments in thousands; then at the bottom of the page you will find the cross-referenced figure. Multiply that figure times 12 to give you the annual rate (interest and principal). If you want to find out how much is principal and how much interest, take the amount, for example, $200,000 at 10 percent, which would leave $20,000. Then take the multiplied figure, in this case let's assume $1,700; result, $20,400. The difference is $400, meaning that $400 only would go toward principal and $20,000 toward interest.

MORTGAGE AMORTIZATION SCHEDULES

**16.00 %
MONTHLY**

Description: This table shows how a $100 loan at 16.00% is paid off over various terms by a level monthly payment. The table shows the total of the monthly interest and principal payments made during the year and the balance outstanding at the end of the year. The heading of each schedule shows the term of the loan in Years, the level Monthly Payment, and the Annual Constant percent.

Example: A loan of $100,000 is written at 16.00% for 30 years. The level monthly payment is $ 1344.76 and the Annual Constant is 16.14%. In the first year $ 15989.49 is paid to interest, $ 147.60 is paid to principal and the outstanding balance of the loan, after 12 monthly payments, is $ 99852.40.

YEARS	MONTHLY PAYMENT	ANNUAL CONSTANT		YEARS	MONTHLY PAYMENT	ANNUAL CONSTANT		YEARS	MONTHLY PAYMENT	ANNUAL CONSTANT
23	1.368706	16.43		24	1.363391	16.37		25	1.358889	16.31
YR	ANNUAL INTEREST	ANNUAL PRINCIPAL	YEAR END BALANCE	YR	ANNUAL INTEREST	ANNUAL PRINCIPAL	YEAR END BALANCE	YR	ANNUAL INTEREST	ANNUAL PRINCIPAL	YEAR END BALANCE
1	15.967446	0.457025	99.542975	1	15.972338	0.388349	99.611651	1	15.976481	0.330186	99.669814
2	15.888714	0.535758	99.007217	2	15.905437	0.455251	99.156400	2	15.919600	0.387067	99.282747
3	15.796419	0.628053	98.379164	3	15.827010	0.533677	98.622723	3	15.852919	0.453747	98.829000
4	15.688224	0.736248	97.642916	4	15.735073	0.625614	97.997109	4	15.774752	0.531915	98.297085
5	15.561390	0.863082	96.779834	5	15.627298	0.733389	97.263721	5	15.683118	0.623548	97.673537
6	15.412706	1.011766	95.768068	6	15.500957	0.859730	96.403990	6	15.575699	0.730967	96.942570
7	15.238408	1.186064	94.582005	7	15.352851	1.007837	95.396154	7	15.449775	0.856892	96.085678
8	15.034084	1.390388	93.191617	8	15.179230	1.181458	94.214696	8	15.302158	1.004509	95.081169
9	14.794561	1.629911	91.561706	9	14.975699	1.384988	92.829708	9	15.129110	1.177557	93.903613
10	14.513775	1.910697	89.651009	10	14.737106	1.623581	91.206127	10	14.926251	1.380415	92.523197
11	14.184617	2.239854	87.411154	11	14.457410	1.903277	89.302850	11	14.688446	1.618220	90.904977
12	13.798756	2.625716	84.785438	12	14.129531	2.231156	87.071694	12	14.409674	1.896993	89.007984
13	13.346422	3.078050	81.707388	13	13.745168	2.615519	84.456175	13	14.082878	2.223789	86.784195
14	12.816163	3.608308	78.099080	14	13.294591	3.066096	81.390078	14	13.699784	2.606883	84.177313
15	12.194557	4.229914	73.869166	15	12.766392	3.594295	77.795783	15	13.250694	3.055973	81.121340
16	11.465867	4.958605	68.910561	16	12.147200	4.213487	73.582296	16	12.724239	3.582427	77.538912
17	10.611644	5.812828	63.097733	17	11.421339	4.939348	68.642947	17	12.107091	4.199575	73.339337
18	9.610263	6.814208	56.283525	18	10.570433	5.790254	62.852693	18	11.383627	4.923039	68.416298
19	8.436374	7.988097	48.295427	19	9.572942	6.787745	56.064948	19	10.535531	5.771135	62.645163
20	7.060258	9.364213	38.931214	20	8.403612	7.957076	48.107872	20	9.541333	6.765333	55.879830
21	5.447078	10.977394	27.953820	21	7.032840	9.327848	38.780025	21	8.375864	7.930803	47.949027
22	3.555993	12.868478	15.085341	22	5.425924	10.934763	27.845261	22	7.009618	9.297048	38.651979
23	1.339130	15.085341	0.000000	23	3.542184	12.818504	15.026758	23	5.408008	10.898658	27.753320
				24	1.333930	15.026758	0.000000	24	3.530488	12.776179	14.977141
								25	1.329525	14.977141	0.000000

YEARS	MONTHLY PAYMENT	ANNUAL CONSTANT		YEARS	MONTHLY PAYMENT	ANNUAL CONSTANT		YEARS	MONTHLY PAYMENT	ANNUAL CONSTANT
26	1.355072	16.27		27	1.351833	16.23		28	1.349082	16.19
YR	ANNUAL INTEREST	ANNUAL PRINCIPAL	YEAR END BALANCE	YR	ANNUAL INTEREST	ANNUAL PRINCIPAL	YEAR END BALANCE	YR	ANNUAL INTEREST	ANNUAL PRINCIPAL	YEAR END BALANCE
1	15.979994	0.280872	99.719128	1	15.982974	0.239024	99.760976	1	15.985506	0.203483	99.796517
2	15.931607	0.329258	99.389870	2	15.941798	0.280201	99.480775	2	15.950452	0.238538	99.557979
3	15.874886	0.385980	99.003890	3	15.893527	0.328471	99.152304	3	15.909359	0.279631	99.278348
4	15.808393	0.452473	98.551417	4	15.836941	0.385057	98.767247	4	15.861186	0.327803	98.950545
5	15.730445	0.530421	98.020996	5	15.770607	0.451391	98.315855	5	15.804716	0.384274	98.566272
6	15.639069	0.621797	97.399199	6	15.692845	0.529153	97.786702	6	15.738516	0.450473	98.115799
7	15.531952	0.728914	96.670285	7	15.601688	0.620311	97.166392	7	15.660913	0.528076	97.587723
8	15.406381	0.854485	95.815800	8	15.494826	0.727172	96.439220	8	15.569941	0.619048	96.968674
9	15.259178	1.001688	94.814113	9	15.369556	0.852442	95.586777	9	15.463297	0.725692	96.242982
10	15.086617	1.174249	93.639863	10	15.222705	0.999293	94.587484	10	15.338281	0.850708	95.392274
11	14.884328	1.376538	92.263325	11	15.050556	1.171442	93.416042	11	15.191729	0.997260	94.395014
12	14.647190	1.613675	90.649650	12	14.848751	1.373248	92.042794	12	15.019931	1.169059	93.225956
13	14.369201	1.891664	88.757986	13	14.612180	1.609818	90.432976	13	14.818536	1.370453	91.855502
14	14.043323	2.217543	86.540443	14	14.334855	1.887143	88.545833	14	14.582447	1.606543	90.248960
15	13.661305	2.599561	83.940882	15	14.009756	2.212242	86.333590	15	14.305686	1.883303	88.365657
16	13.213476	3.047389	80.893493	16	13.028651	2.593347	83.740243	16	13.981248	2.207741	86.157916
17	12.688500	3.572365	77.321127	17	13.181893	3.040105	80.700138	17	13.600919	2.588070	83.569846
18	12.073086	4.187780	73.133348	18	12.658172	3.563827	77.136311	18	13.155070	3.033919	80.535926
19	11.351654	4.909212	68.224136	19	12.044228	4.177770	72.958541	19	12.632414	3.556575	76.979352
20	10.505940	5.754926	62.469210	20	11.324521	4.897478	68.061064	20	12.019720	4.169269	72.810083
21	9.514534	6.746331	55.722879	21	10.480828	5.741170	62.319894	21	11.301477	4.887512	67.922571
22	8.352339	7.908527	47.814351	22	9.491792	6.730206	55.589688	22	10.459502	5.729488	62.193083
23	6.989930	9.270936	38.543416	23	8.332374	7.889624	47.700064	23	9.472478	6.716511	55.476572
24	5.392819	10.868047	27.675369	24	6.973223	9.248776	38.451288	24	8.315419	7.873570	47.603002
25	3.520572	12.740294	14.935075	25	5.379929	10.842070	27.609218	25	6.959033	9.229956	38.373046
26	1.325791	14.935075	0.000000	26	3.512157	12.709842	14.899376	26	5.368981	10.820008	27.553038
				27	1.322622	14.899376	0.000000	27	3.505010	12.683979	14.869059
								28	1.319931	14.869059	0.000000

Description: This table shows how a $100 loan at 18.00% is paid off over various terms by a level monthly payment. The table shows the total of the monthly interest and principal payments made during the year and the balance outstanding at the end of the year. The heading of each schedule shows the term of the loan in Years, the level Monthly Payment, and the Annual Constant percent.

Example: A loan of $100,000 is written at 18.00% for 30 years. The level monthly payment is $ 1507.09 and the Annual Constant is 18.09%. In the first year $ 17992.62 is paid to interest, $ 92.40 is paid to principal and the outstanding balance of the loan, after 12 monthly payments, is $ 99907.60.

YEARS 23	MONTHLY PAYMENT 1.525041	ANNUAL CONSTANT 18.31
YR		
	ANNUAL INTEREST	ANNUAL PRINCIPAL	YEAR END BALANCE

YR	ANNUAL INTEREST	ANNUAL PRINCIPAL	YEAR END BALANCE
1	17.973927	0.326567	99.673433
2	17.910045	0.390449	99.282984
3	17.833666	0.466828	98.816156
4	17.742346	0.558148	98.258008
5	17.633162	0.667332	97.590677
6	17.502619	0.797874	96.792802
7	17.346541	0.953953	95.838850
8	17.159930	1.140563	94.698286
9	16.936815	1.363678	93.334608
10	16.670055	1.630438	91.704170
11	16.351112	1.949382	89.754788
12	15.969777	2.330716	87.424072
13	15.513847	2.786647	84.637425
14	14.968728	3.331765	81.305660
15	14.316974	3.983519	77.322140
16	13.537725	4.762768	72.559372
17	12.606041	5.694452	66.864920
18	11.492103	6.808390	60.056530
19	10.160258	8.140235	51.916294
20	8.567880	9.732613	42.183681
21	6.664004	11.636489	30.547192
22	4.387696	13.912798	16.634394
23	1.666099	16.634394	0.000000

YEARS 24	MONTHLY PAYMENT 1.520887	ANNUAL CONSTANT 18.26

YR	ANNUAL INTEREST	ANNUAL PRINCIPAL	YEAR END BALANCE
1	17.978252	0.272392	99.727608
2	17.924967	0.325677	99.401931
3	17.861259	0.389385	99.012545
4	17.785088	0.465556	98.546989
5	17.694017	0.556628	97.990361
6	17.585130	0.665514	97.324847
7	17.454944	0.795701	96.529146
8	17.299290	0.951354	95.577792
9	17.113188	1.137456	94.440336
10	16.890681	1.359964	93.080372
11	16.624647	1.625997	91.454375
12	16.306573	1.944072	89.510303
13	15.926277	2.324368	87.185935
14	15.471588	2.779056	84.406879
15	14.927954	3.322690	81.084189
16	14.277976	3.972669	77.111521
17	13.500850	4.749795	72.361726
18	12.571704	5.678941	66.682785
19	11.460800	6.789845	59.892940
20	10.132583	8.118062	51.774878
21	8.544542	9.706102	42.068776
22	6.645852	11.604792	30.463984
23	4.375744	13.874901	16.589083
24	1.661561	16.589083	0.000000

YEARS 25	MONTHLY PAYMENT 1.517430	ANNUAL CONSTANT 18.21

YR	ANNUAL INTEREST	ANNUAL PRINCIPAL	YEAR END BALANCE
1	17.981852	0.227308	99.772692
2	17.937386	0.271773	99.500919
3	17.884223	0.324937	99.175983
4	17.820659	0.388500	98.787482
5	17.744661	0.464498	98.322984
6	17.653797	0.555362	97.767622
7	17.545158	0.664001	97.103620
8	17.415267	0.793892	96.309728
9	17.259968	0.949192	95.360537
10	17.074288	1.134871	94.225666
11	16.852287	1.356872	92.868793
12	16.586858	1.622301	91.246492
13	16.269507	1.939653	89.306839
14	15.890075	2.319084	86.987755
15	15.436420	2.772739	84.215016
16	14.894022	3.315137	80.899879
17	14.245521	3.963638	76.936240
18	13.470161	4.738998	72.197242
19	12.543127	5.666032	66.531210
20	11.434748	6.774411	59.756799
21	10.109550	8.099609	51.657190
22	8.525120	9.684040	41.973151
23	6.630746	11.578414	30.394737
24	4.365797	13.843362	16.551375
25	1.657784	16.551375	0.000000

YEARS 26	MONTHLY PAYMENT 1.514551	ANNUAL CONSTANT 18.18

YR	ANNUAL INTEREST	ANNUAL PRINCIPAL	YEAR END BALANCE
1	17.984850	0.189756	99.810244
2	17.947730	0.226876	99.583367
3	17.903349	0.271257	99.312110
4	17.850286	0.324320	98.987790
5	17.786843	0.387763	98.600027
6	17.710990	0.463617	98.136410
7	17.620298	0.554309	97.582101
8	17.511865	0.662741	96.919360
9	17.382221	0.792386	96.126974
10	17.227216	0.947391	95.179584
11	17.041889	1.132717	94.046866
12	16.820309	1.354298	92.692569
13	16.555383	1.619223	91.073346
14	16.238634	1.935972	89.137374
15	15.859923	2.314684	86.822690
16	15.407129	2.767478	84.055213
17	14.865760	3.308847	80.746366
18	14.218489	3.956117	76.790249
19	13.444601	4.730005	72.060243
20	12.519326	5.655281	66.404963
21	11.413050	6.761556	59.643407
22	10.090367	8.084239	51.559167
23	8.508943	9.665664	41.893504
24	6.618163	11.556443	30.337061
25	4.357513	13.817093	16.519968
26	1.654639	16.519968	0.000000

YEARS 27	MONTHLY PAYMENT 1.512151	ANNUAL CONSTANT 18.15

YR	ANNUAL INTEREST	ANNUAL PRINCIPAL	YEAR END BALANCE
1	17.987349	0.158458	99.841542
2	17.956351	0.189456	99.652086
3	17.919290	0.226517	99.425569
4	17.874980	0.270828	99.154742
5	17.822001	0.323806	98.830935
6	17.758658	0.387149	98.443787
7	17.682925	0.462882	97.980904
8	17.592377	0.553430	97.427474
9	17.484116	0.661691	96.765783
10	17.354677	0.791130	95.974653
11	17.199918	0.945889	95.028764
12	17.014885	1.130923	93.897841
13	16.793656	1.352152	92.545690
14	16.529150	1.616657	90.929033
15	16.212903	1.932904	88.996128
16	15.834791	2.311016	86.685112
17	15.382715	2.763092	83.922020
18	14.842204	3.303603	80.618417
19	14.195959	3.949848	76.668568
20	13.423297	4.722510	71.946058
21	12.499488	5.646319	66.299739
22	11.394965	6.750842	59.548897
23	10.074378	8.071429	51.477468
24	8.495460	9.650347	41.827120
25	6.607676	11.538131	30.288989
26	4.350608	13.795199	16.493790
27	1.652017	16.493790	0.000000

YEARS 28	MONTHLY PAYMENT 1.510149	ANNUAL CONSTANT 18.13

YR	ANNUAL INTEREST	ANNUAL PRINCIPAL	YEAR END BALANCE
1	17.989433	0.132357	99.867643
2	17.963541	0.158249	99.709394
3	17.932585	0.189205	99.520189
4	17.895573	0.226217	99.293972
5	17.851321	0.270469	99.023503
6	17.798412	0.323378	98.700125
7	17.735153	0.386636	98.313489
8	17.659520	0.462269	97.851220
9	17.569092	0.552698	97.298522
10	17.460974	0.660815	96.637707
11	17.331707	0.790083	95.847624
12	17.177152	0.944637	94.902986
13	16.992364	1.129426	93.773561
14	16.771428	1.350362	92.423199
15	16.507273	1.614517	90.808681
16	16.191444	1.930346	88.878335
17	15.813833	2.307957	86.570378
18	15.362355	2.759435	83.810943
19	14.822559	3.299231	80.511712
20	14.177169	3.944620	76.567092
21	13.405530	4.716260	71.850832
22	12.482944	5.638846	66.211986
23	11.379883	6.741907	59.470080
24	10.061044	8.060746	51.409333
25	8.484215	9.637575	41.771759
26	6.598931	11.522859	30.248900
27	4.344850	13.776940	16.471960
28	1.649830	16.471960	0.000000

MORTGAGE AMORTIZATION SCHEDULES

20.00 %
MONTHLY

Description: This table shows how a $100 loan at 20.00% is paid off over various terms by a level monthly payment. The table shows the total of the monthly interest and principal payments made during the year and the balance outstanding at the end of the year. The heading of each schedule shows the term of the loan in Years, the level Monthly Payment, and the Annual Constant percent.

Example: A loan of $100,000 is written at 20.00% for 30 years. The level monthly payment is $ 1671.02 and the Annual Constant is 20.06%. In the first year $ 19994.94 is paid to interest, $ 57.29 is paid to principal and the outstanding balance of the loan, after 12 monthly payments, is $ 99942.71.

YEARS	MONTHLY PAYMENT	ANNUAL CONSTANT
23	1.684251	20.22

YR	ANNUAL INTEREST	ANNUAL PRINCIPAL	YEAR END BALANCE
1	19.979542	0.231466	99.768534
2	19.928760	0.282248	99.486286
3	19.866837	0.344170	99.142115
4	19.791329	0.419678	98.722437
5	19.699256	0.511752	98.210685
6	19.586982	0.624026	97.586659
7	19.450076	0.760932	96.825727
8	19.283134	0.927873	95.897854
9	19.079567	1.131440	94.766413
10	18.831339	1.379668	93.386745
11	18.528652	1.682355	91.704390
12	18.159559	2.051449	89.652940
13	17.709489	2.501519	87.151421
14	17.160678	3.050330	84.101092
15	16.491463	3.719545	80.381547
16	15.675428	4.535580	75.845967
17	14.680362	5.530646	70.315321
18	13.466988	6.744020	63.571301
19	11.987410	8.223598	55.347703
20	10.183226	10.027782	45.319921
21	7.983220	12.227788	33.092133
22	5.300552	14.910456	18.181677
23	2.029331	18.181677	0.000000

YEARS	MONTHLY PAYMENT	ANNUAL CONSTANT
24	1.681060	20.18

YR	ANNUAL INTEREST	ANNUAL PRINCIPAL	YEAR END BALANCE
1	19.983254	0.189462	99.810538
2	19.941688	0.231028	99.579511
3	19.891003	0.281713	99.297798
4	19.829197	0.343518	98.954279
5	19.753832	0.418883	98.535396
6	19.661933	0.510783	98.024613
7	19.549872	0.622844	97.401770
8	19.413226	0.759490	96.642280
9	19.246600	0.926115	95.716164
10	19.043419	1.129297	94.586868
11	18.795661	1.377055	93.209813
12	18.493548	1.679168	91.530645
13	18.125153	2.047562	89.483083
14	17.675936	2.496779	86.986303
15	17.128165	3.044551	83.941753
16	16.460218	3.712498	80.229255
17	15.645729	4.526987	75.702268
18	14.652548	5.520167	70.182101
19	13.441473	6.731243	63.450858
20	11.964698	8.208017	55.242840
21	10.163932	10.008783	45.234057
22	7.968095	12.204621	33.029436
23	5.290510	14.882206	18.147230
24	2.025486	18.147230	0.000000

YEARS	MONTHLY PAYMENT	ANNUAL CONSTANT
25	1.678452	20.15

YR	ANNUAL INTEREST	ANNUAL PRINCIPAL	YEAR END BALANCE
1	19.986288	0.155133	99.844867
2	19.952254	0.189168	99.655700
3	19.910752	0.230669	99.425030
4	19.860145	0.281276	99.143754
5	19.798436	0.342986	98.800769
6	19.723188	0.418233	98.382535
7	19.631431	0.509990	97.872545
8	19.519544	0.621877	97.250668
9	19.383109	0.758312	96.492356
10	19.216743	0.924679	95.567677
11	19.013876	1.127545	94.440132
12	18.766503	1.374918	93.065214
13	18.464858	1.676563	91.388651
14	18.097035	2.044386	89.344265
15	17.648515	2.492906	86.851359
16	17.101594	3.039827	83.811531
17	16.434683	3.706739	80.104793
18	15.621457	4.519964	75.584829
19	14.629818	5.511604	70.073225
20	13.420621	6.720800	63.352425
21	11.946137	8.195284	55.157141
22	10.148165	9.993256	45.163884
23	7.955733	12.185688	32.978196
24	5.282302	14.859119	18.119077
25	2.022344	18.119077	0.000000

YEARS	MONTHLY PAYMENT	ANNUAL CONSTANT
26	1.676319	20.12

YR	ANNUAL INTEREST	ANNUAL PRINCIPAL	YEAR END BALANCE
1	19.988770	0.127060	99.872940
2	19.960894	0.154936	99.718004
3	19.926902	0.188927	99.529077
4	19.885453	0.230376	99.298701
5	19.834911	0.280919	99.017782
6	19.773280	0.342550	98.675233
7	19.698128	0.417702	98.257531
8	19.606487	0.509342	97.748188
9	19.494742	0.621087	97.127101
10	19.358481	0.757348	96.369753
11	19.192326	0.923504	95.446249
12	18.989717	1.126112	94.320137
13	18.742658	1.373171	92.946965
14	18.441397	1.674433	91.272533
15	18.074041	2.041788	89.230744
16	17.626091	2.489739	86.741006
17	17.079865	3.035965	83.705040
18	16.413801	3.702029	80.003012
19	15.601609	4.514221	75.488791
20	14.611229	5.504601	69.984190
21	13.403569	6.712261	63.271929
22	11.930958	8.184871	55.087058
23	10.135271	9.980559	45.106499
24	7.945625	12.170205	32.936294
25	5.275591	14.840239	18.096055
26	2.019774	18.096055	0.000000

YEARS	MONTHLY PAYMENT	ANNUAL CONSTANT
27	1.674574	20.10

YR	ANNUAL INTEREST	ANNUAL PRINCIPAL	YEAR END BALANCE
1	19.990800	0.104091	99.895909
2	19.967963	0.126928	99.768981
3	19.940116	0.154774	99.614207
4	19.906160	0.188731	99.425476
5	19.864754	0.230136	99.195340
6	19.814265	0.280626	98.914714
7	19.752698	0.342193	98.572521
8	19.677624	0.417267	98.155253
9	19.586079	0.508812	97.646441
10	19.474450	0.620441	97.026000
11	19.338331	0.756560	96.269441
12	19.172348	0.922543	95.346898
13	18.969951	1.124940	94.221968
14	18.723149	1.371742	92.850216
15	18.422201	1.672690	91.177526
16	18.055228	2.039663	89.137863
17	17.607744	2.487147	86.650716
18	17.062086	3.032805	83.617911
19	16.396716	3.698175	79.919736
20	15.585369	4.509522	75.410214
21	14.596020	5.498871	69.911343
22	13.389617	6.705274	63.206069
23	11.918539	8.176352	55.029717
24	10.124721	9.970170	45.059547
25	7.937354	12.157537	32.902011
26	5.270099	14.824792	18.077219
27	2.017672	18.077219	0.000000

YEARS	MONTHLY PAYMENT	ANNUAL CONSTANT
28	1.673146	20.08

YR	ANNUAL INTEREST	ANNUAL PRINCIPAL	YEAR END BALANCE
1	19.992462	0.085290	99.914710
2	19.973750	0.104002	99.810707
3	19.950932	0.126819	99.683888
4	19.923109	0.154642	99.529246
5	19.889182	0.188570	99.340676
6	19.847812	0.229940	99.110736
7	19.797365	0.280387	98.830349
8	19.735851	0.341901	98.488448
9	19.660840	0.416911	98.071536
10	19.569374	0.508378	97.563158
11	19.457840	0.619912	96.943247
12	19.321837	0.755915	96.187332
13	19.155996	0.921756	95.265576
14	18.953771	1.123981	94.141596
15	18.707180	1.370572	92.771024
16	18.406489	1.671263	91.099761
17	18.039828	2.037923	89.061837
18	17.592726	2.485026	86.576811
19	17.047534	3.030218	83.546593
20	16.382731	3.695021	79.851572
21	15.572076	4.505676	75.345896
22	14.583571	5.494181	69.851715
23	13.378197	6.699555	63.152160
24	11.908374	8.169378	54.982782
25	10.116085	9.961667	45.021116
26	7.930584	12.147167	32.873948
27	5.265604	14.812148	18.061801
28	2.015951	18.061801	0.000000

Amortization schedules on pp. 57-59 reprinted by permission from *The Thorndike Encyclopedia of Banking and Finance* by David Thorndike. Copyright © 1980, Warren, Gorham and Lamont, Inc., 210 South Street, Boston, MA. All rights reserved.

That figure may sound terrible. However, if you have outside income, the $20,000 in interest payments is deductible, along with your real estate taxes and maintenance.

It is wise not to rely on your real estate agent. After all, he or she is trying to make a living and may attempt to interest you in property from the standpoint of projected income. This is something you never do. Buy on present income and expenses.

Earlier I recommended that debt service on the property should never exceed 50 percent of operating income. Obviously the less it can be reduced, the greater the certainty that the project will continue to carry itself. Changes in financing terms change the cost of debt service.

Let's look at a monthly mortgage table. At 10.25 percent, $100,000 loaned for 20 years costs $981.65 a month to service. But the same $100,000 for a 30-year term, at the same interest, runs $896.11 a month—a savings of $85.54, or $1,026.48 a year (x 12).

The costs of larger loans can be arrived at by adding together the various debt amounts. Thus, a $250,000 loan at 10.25 percent for 25 years is: $100,000 (cost $926.39) plus $100,000 (cost $926.39) plus $50,000 (cost $463.20) equals $2,315.98 a month, or $27,791.76 a year.

Interest Rates and Their Effect on Cash Flow

The effect of various interest rates and financing terms can best be explained through examples. The higher the interest rate, the less can be financed for the same dollar. The following are examples based on a $100,000, 25-year loan.

$100,000 over 25 years

9%	$ 839.20/month
9 ½%	873.70/month
9 ¾%	891.14/month
10%	908.71/month
10 ¼%	926.39/month
10 ½%	944.19/month
10 ¾%	962.10/month
11%	980.12/month
11 ¼%	998.24/month
11 ½%	1016.47/month
11 ¾%	1034.80/month
12%	1053.23/month

The monthly payment ranges from 839.20 at 9 percent to $1,053.23 at 12 percent, or a monthly difference of $214.03. On a yearly basis, positive cash flow (throw off) could be reduced by $2,568.36 (214.03 × 12) because of the interest rate.

Let's look at another set of figures for the same $100,000 loan. Assume the building can afford a monthly payment of $950. The following are some examples of this amount at different interest rates and terms.

Loan Amount: $100,000

9%	20 years	$899.73/month
9 ½%	25 years	$873.70/month
10%	30 years	$877.58/month
11%	35 years	$936.96/month
11 ¾%	40 years	$988.37/month

With a monthly payment of $950 at 25-year terms, the loan size varies with the interest rate.

$108,790	at 9 ½% over 25 years	—$950/month
$104,500	at 10% over 25 years	—$950/month
$ 99,000	at 10 ¾% over 25 years	—$950/month
$ 95,000	at 11% over 25 years	—$950/month

Based on the above examples, the loan amount ranges from $108,790 at 9 1/2 percent to $95,000 at 11 1/4 percent, a difference of $13,790.

Now that we have worked with the variables of a loan—the principal amount, the interest rate, and term—we will see how these items affect the value of the property.

Apartment Building: 17 units, 10 years old
Gross Income: $34,620
Expenses (inc. vacancies, taxes, maintenance, etc.): $14,000
Fair Market Value: $220,000
Net Cash Flow: $20,620
Gross Cash Return on Market Value (annual cash flow divided by price paid): 9.4%

Example #1
Price: $220,000
Cash Down: $30,000
1st TD (trust deed): $190,000 10 ½%—25 years, 21,362.04 a year
2nd TD: $35,000 at 9% (interest only) $3,150 a year

Return
Income: $34,620.00
Expenses: $14,000.00
1st TD: $21,362.04
2nd TD: 3,150.00
Annual Cash Flow: $3,892

Example #2
Price: $220,000
Cash Down: $30,000
1st TD: $190,000 at 10%, 20 years, $17,949.72 a year
2nd TD: $35,000 at 7%, interest only, $2,450 a year

Return
Income: $34,620.00
Expenses: $14,000.00
1st TD: $14,973.00
2nd TD: $2,450.00
Annual Cash Flow: $3,197.00

Example #3

Price: $220,000
Cash Down: $30,000
1st TD: $190,000 at 10%, 20 years, $17,949.72 a year
2nd TD: $35,000 at 7%, interest only, $2450 a year

Return
Income: $34,620.00
Expenses: $14,000.00
1st TD: $17,949.72
2nd TD: $2,450.00
Annual Cash Flow: $220.28

Example #4

Price: $220,000
Cash Down: $30,000
1st TD: $155,000 at 11 ¼%, 30 years, $18,066 a year
2nd TD: $35,000 at 9%, interest only, $3,150 a year

Return
Income: $34,620.00
Expenses: $14,000.00
1st TD: $18,066.00
2nd TD: $3,150.00
Annual Cash Flow: ($596.00)

As the price, interest rate, and down payment change, so does the return. Methods to increase positive cash flow are: (1) reduce interest rate on second TD: (2) reduce price of property; and (3) increase size of second TD, respective to first TD.

Interest rates have a tremendous effect on cash flow and ultimately on total property value. This is why I will gladly spend $50,000 more for a piece of property if the building is sound and the financing excellent.

Cash Flow not Always Necessary Not long ago I bought a building that had no cash flow—$400 a year. Had I turned it down for that reason I would have made a serious mistake. The seller wanted $145,000. I appraised it for $150,000 and settled for $132,500.

If you are working and not depending on your property cash flow for income, you can take a building that is, initially, marginal. Remember, if the building is carrying itself—expenses and debt service—it will be all right since it will be appreciating. If you have chosen the correct building, you will be able to raise the rents anyway, since they will be depressed for the neighborhood.

chapter seven

Financing Innovative Exchanges
(under Federal Code 1031)

Exchange means like for like. It is tax deferred and sometimes called tax-free exchange (under Federal Code 1031). People who do these kinds of transactions generally truly work out of the backs of their cars. They go to meetings where there may be 50 people with 50 to 100 listings; not actual listings, but rather 100 copies of one listing, so they can be distributed to other people. Trades are actually completed at that meeting. They call it a pitch. They will "pitch" their piece of property and see if anyone is interested in it. It can be very exciting, in that these meetings are like auctions. Sometimes you have a tendency to bid on things that you actually would not go out and buy, and it tends to get very emotional. The disturbing thing about it is that the real estate person can work on a deal for six months trying to close it; then it falls out, and someone has to plug up the hole. If the person has a vested interest, then he or she plugs up the hole. And what the person ends up with is merely paper, or other things (in terms of barter) rather than the 6 or 5 percent commission. Exchangers take back notes and so forth in order to get the deal to fly.

Exchanging is recommended rather than selling since you pay no tax, but you must be careful how you do it. Let's look at "boot" (in terms of trader, it means something extra, the sweetener). As an example, I will buy a car from you for x dollars, which is all the cash I have, but I will throw in a cow as an extra inducement. When you take "boot" as well, you lose the element of tax-free exchange. If you exchange an apartment building and the building has furniture, and you don't make a separate deal outside of escrow for the furniture, then you don't have like for like, since yours was empty. It is then not tax free.

The best way to avoid this problem is to go to a tax attorney or C.P.A. familiar with this type of investing to make sure that you will be in a tax-free position, as opposed to winding up in a situation with a huge capital gain you could have avoided.

People are much too conservative in terms of paying for advice that may in the long run save them thousands of dollars.

Syndication

Because of the interest of a client, I recently examined every possible way of holding title. My client was particularly interested in syndication (limited and general partners), since the limited partners are protected in the same manner as stock. A limited partner is exposed only to the extent of his or her investment. The general partner (who actually operates the business) is completely responsible.

If my client were to go out into a corporation (with a 17 percent tax), he would gain all the benefits of protection, but would lose many other benefits, such as charging off the depreciation of the building from his ordinary income. So in this case I suggested syndication, with just one general partner, who was to be paid a reasonable salary for his time and was to be given ample mismanagement insurance. Then all the partners could survive.

Because of the problem of being audited, you have to be particulary careful with constructing a syndication. In the next few years, syndications surely will come under much more pressure from the IRS, which is moving toward treating syndications as a corporation. Already many advantages have been lost. The IRS is definitely trying to discourage their use, although syndications are still being formed and there is a real need for them. That is, prices being what they are (using California as a criteria), more capital is now required for investing.

Limited partnership cannot be offered to more than 25 people and can consist of no more than 10 people if it is a limited offering. Using a syndicate, you can raise the capital just among your friends, calling it a private offering (limited partnership). You can then raise enough money to make a good investment. Instead, however, of having 100 percent of the depreciation, you have only that portion you invested, but otherwise you have all of the benefits, particularly of being more liquid.

It is common after substantial growth for partners to want to split off on their own. Each partner then quit claims out, leaving title with another partner. Each then has a building from which to begin pyramiding. So the advantage of syndication is that through combined capital one can eventually become financially independent.

An outline detailing the process of syndication follows, and a facsimile case is presented in the appendix, pp. 215–232.

Workable Small Syndications*

Outline

I. Syndications in General

A. Definitions

    1. General Partnerships
      A. Liabilities of the partners

*All materials concerning syndication, including the outline, were kindly supplied with permission to reprint by Harvey Sherman.

2. Limited Partnerships
   A. Liabilities of the partners
   B. Offerings
      1. Private Offerings
      2. Public Offerings

B. Advantages of Syndications

   1. Advantages to Syndicators
      a. Own share of syndicate with little or no personal money invested
      b. Own and/or control many more properties than possible with personal money resources
      c. Satisfaction of creating and managing a successful syndicate
      d. Profit potential if successful
   2. Advantages to Partners
      a. a. All the advantages of ownership of business property
      b. No personal liability beyond initial risk capital
      c. No management responsibilities
      d. Property is managed professionally by people who have an equity interest in success

C. Disadvantages of Syndications

   1. Disadvantages to Syndicators
      a. Every limited partner is your boss
      b. Major share of the profit in your project will go to the partners
      c. Must be prepared to justify every move at all times
      d. Must make frequent periodic reports to partners
   2. Disadvantages to Partners
      a. Share of the profit goes to syndicators who have provided little or no risk capital

D. Relationships of the Parties: The Three R's of Syndication
   1. RISK
      a. Risk to the Syndicators
         1. Subject to legal action by partners even if successful
         2. May have to go back and review and justify everything at any time
      b. Risk to the partners
         1. Loss of invested capital
         2. Possible legal actions if limited partner status is not protected
   2. RESPONSIBILITY
      a. Responsibility of the Syndicators
         1. Good judgment and good business practice
         2. Full disclosures
         3. Regular periodic reporting
         4. Negotiations
         5. Competent management
         6. Success of the project
      b. Responsibility of the partners
         1. Provide initial capital
   3. REWARDS
      a. Rewards to the syndicators
         1. Share of the Profits
         2. Management fees
         3. Possible share of commission
      b. Rewards to the partners
         1. Share of profits and losses

II. Legal Documents

A. Cover Letter
1. Statement of Offering
   . Public or private offering
2. Statement whether offering registered or not registered with Securities and Exchange Commission
3. Statement whether offering qualified or not qualified by any State of California Agency
   a. Department of Corporations

B. Offering Circular

1. General Description of Offering Circular
2. Table of Contents
3. General Description of the Project Objectives
4. The General Partner
   a. Identify the General Partner(s)
   b. Statement of responsibility and authority of the general partner
   c. Capitalization
      1. Amount of capital needed
      2. Classes of shares
      3. Partnership bank accounts
      4. Termination of the Offering
5. Qualification of Limited Partners
   a. Age
   b. Net worth
   c. Residency
6. Benefits to limited partners
   a. Description of shares of profits and losses
7. Investment objectives and policy
8. Property Description
   a. Location of property
   b. Type of property
   c. Describe property
9. Property Acquisition
   a. Describe purchase contract and terms
   b. Describe financing
   c. All other relevant information
   d. Location of documents and availability to limited partners
   e. Planned improvements to the property
10. Allocation of Capital
    a. Towards purchase
    b. Towards improvements
    c. Reserves
11. Operation of the Property
    a. Operational Plan
    b. Improvement plan and scheduling
    c. Cash flow projections
    d. Projection of expenses
12. Sale/Exchange of the Property
13. Cost Projections and Operating Statement
    a. Projected cash distributions during ownership
    b. Profit projections at sale of property

14. The Limited Partnership
   a. Agreement and Certificate of Limited Partnership
      1. General reference only (detailed discussion later)
15. Risk Factors
   a. A new venture
   b. General Partner and conflicting interest
   c. Lack of guarantees and warrantees
   d. Cost projections
      1. Subject to economic conditions
   e. Changes in the marketplace
   f. Changes in local laws
16. Tax consequences
17. Personal obligations of limited partners
18. Reports to investors

C. Agreement and Certificate of Limited Partnership

   1. Name of the partnership
   2. Character of the partnership
   3. Place of business
   4. Names and residences of all partners
   5. Term of the partnership
   6. Contributions by limited partners
   7. Additional contributions by limited partners
   8. Return of contributions to limited partners
   9. Allocation of profits and compensation to limited partners.
   10. Right to assign limited partnership interests
   11. Admission of additional limited partners
   12. Priority between limited partners
   13. Dissolution of partnership
   14. Limited partner's right to property in return for contribution
   15. Other rights of limited partners
   16. General partners' power of attorney
   17. Additional terms of limited partnership agreement

III. Legal Topics

A. Federal Securities Laws

B. State Laws

C. Tax Laws

D. Fictitious Name Statements

E. I.R.S. Employer's I.D. Number

F. Partnership Bank Account

G. Hiring The Right C.P.A.

H. Partnership Progress Reports

   1. Monthly
   2. Annually

IV. Partnership Benefits and Objectives

A. Capital Gains

   1. Projected life of the partnership
   2. Sale of the Partnership Property
   3. Exchange of the Partnership Property

B. Tax Sheltering
1. Depreciation of Property
2. Improvements and Depreciation of Improvements

C. Cash Flow

1. Distributions to Partners
2. Re-Investment of Cash Flows
3. Management of Partnership Liquid Assets

D. Estate Building

1. Compatible Investors
    a. Short term holdings
    b. Long term holdings
    c. Very long term holdings

V. The Limited Partners

A. Interviewing Prospective Partners

1. Determine partner's personal objectives
2. Determine partner's financial resources
3. Determine partner's acceptable risk
4. Evaluate and qualify partners

B. Counselling the Partners

1. Describe the Program and Risks/Rewards
2. Describe similar programs and their results
    a. Establish credibility of projections of other terminated partnerships
    b. Relate other experiences to the program the client will invest in
    c. Stress all the risks of the program
3. Advise Partner of HIS BEST Interests
    a. Should he or should he not consider a syndicated investment
    b. If yes, should he consider this investment
    c. What should be his best investment objectives
    d. How much money can he risk—and—how much reserve should he maintain
    e. How should he diversify his investment program

C. Selecting a Compatible Investor Group

1. Group should have similar objectives
2. The property should fill their need

VI. Selecting the Property

A. Type of Property

1. Income Producing
    a. Apartment building
    b. Office building
    c. Commercial or shopping center
    d. Industrial
2. Non-Income Producing

VII. Evaluating the Property

A. Appraise the Property

   1. Income Approach
   2. Capitalization Approach
   3. Reproduction Cost

B. Estimate the Deferred Maintanance

   1. Attach a dollar value to the deferred maintanance
     a. Get contractor estimates if necessary

C. Establish Fair Market Value
   1. In "as is" condition
   2. After deferred maintainance cured

VIII. Evaluate Future Potential of the Property

A. Highest and Best Use
B. Property Improvements

   1. Cost Estimates—use contractors if necessary

C. Income Potential

   1. In improved condition
   2. At highest and best use

D. Appraise the Future Value of the Property

   1. Income Approach
   2. Capitalization Approach
   3. Reproduction Value

E. Future Benefits of Ownership (To Partners)

   1. Cash Flow and Income Distributions
   2. Appreciation
   3. Tax Shelter
   4. Potential For Estate Building

IX. Negotiating the Purchase

A. The Initial Offer

   1. Source of Earnest Money
   2. Protective Clauses
   3. Property Inspections and Warranties
   4. Disclosures
   5. Financing
     a. Conditions and terms
     b. Subject To's

B. The Counter-Offer

   1. Unrealistic Counter-Offers
   2. Realistic Counter-Offers
     a. Identify points of disagreement

      b. Solve Minor Problems First
      c. The Hard Bargaining Points

C. Negotiate the Differences

D. Finalizing the Purchase Contract

E. Open the Escrows

    1. The Purchase Escrow
      a. Deposit earnest money
      b. Order prelim
      c. Residential property report
      d. Time is of the essence
    2. The Holding Escrow

X. Organize

A. Form the Partnership

    1. Prepare the offering circular
    2. Prepare the Agreement and Certificate of Limited Partnership
    3. Contact and Counsel Clients
    4. Subscribe the Offering

B. Organize the Improvement Program

    1. Contact for Work to Be Done
      a. Subject to closing of escrow
    2. Schedule Improvement Plan
    3. Interview Present Manager of Property
      a. Decision: to keep or fire

C. Technical Details

    1. Partnership Bank Account
    2. Fictitious Name Statement
    3. I.R.S. Employer's I.D. #

XI. Operating the Syndicate Property

A. Initiating the Operating Plan (as outlined in offering)

B. Evaluating the Operational Plan in Action

C. Measuring Progress Towards Objectives

D. Modifications to the Operational Plan

E. Success Formula for Successful Property Operation and Management

XII. Do It Right—But Economize

A. Contractors vs Employees

XIII. Sale of the Property

A. When to Offer for Sale

    1. Goals and Objectives
    2. Additional Unrealized Potential
      a. Conflicts of interest
    3. Realistic Expectations

B. The Initial Offer

    1. The Unrealistic Offer
    2. The Realistic Offer
       a. Financing terms and conditions
       b. Disclosures
       c. Protective clauses and warranties

C. The Counter Offer

    1. When to be unrealistic
       a. Never stop negotiating
    2. Realistic Counter-Offers to Realistic Offers

D. Negotiate the Differences
E. Finalize the Purchase Contract
F. Give the Escrow Your Strict Attention

XIV. Terminating the Syndicate

A. Final Accounting
B. Distribution of Partnership Assets
C. Final Tax Returns
D. Filing Dissolution Of The Partnership

XV. Risks

A. Property Risks

    1. Errors in judgment
    2. Changing market conditions
    3. Changing economic conditions

B. Personnel Risks

    1. Death or incapacity of key personnel

Government Regulations Concerning Syndication

The following special provisions shall apply to non-specified property programs:

Non-Specified Property Programs

260.140.115.1 Minimum Capitalization. A non-specified property program shall provide for a minimum gross proceeds from the offering of not less than $1,000,000.00 after payment of all offering and organization expenses before it may commence business.

260.140.115.2 Experience of Sponsor. For non-specified property programs, the sponsor and the general partner or at least one of the principals of each must establish that he has had the equivalent of not less than five years experience in the real estate business in an executive capacity and two years experience in the management and acquisition of the type of properties to be acquired or otherwise must demonstrate to the satisfaction of the Commissioner that he has sufficient knowledge and experience to acquire and manage the type of properties proposed to be acquired by the non-specified property program. In addition, the sponsor and the general partner or their chief operating officers or an affiliate providing services to the program shall have had not less than four years relevant experience in the kind of service being rendered or otherwise must demonstrate sufficient knowledge and experience to perform the services proposed.

260.140.115.3 Statement of Investment Objectives. A non-specified property program shall state types of properties in which it proposes to invest, such as first-user apartment projects, subsequent-user apartment projects, shopping center, office buildings, unimproved land, etc., and the size and scope of such projects shall be consistent with the objectives of the program and the experience of the sponsors. As a minimum the following restrictions on investment objectives shall be observed:

(a) Unimproved or non-income producing property shall not be acquired except in amounts and upon terms which can be financed by the program's proceeds or from cash flow. Normally, investments in such property shall not exceed 10% of the gross proceeds of the offering.

(b) Investments in junior trust deeds and other similar obligations shall be limited. Normally such investments shall not exceed 10% of the gross proceeds of the program.

(c) The maximum amount of aggregate indebtedness which may be incurred by the program shall be limited. Normally this should not exceed 80% of the purchase price of all properties on a combined basis.

(d) The manner in which acquisitions will be financed, including the use of an all-inclusive note or wrap-around, and the leveraging to be employed shall all be fully set forth in the statement of investment objectives.

(e) The statement shall indicate whether the program will enter into joint venture arrangements and the projected extent thereof.

260.140.115.4 Expenditure of Proceeds. While the proceeds of an offering are awaiting investment in real property, the proceeds may be temporarily invested in short-term highly liquid investments where there is appropriate safety of principal, such as U.S. Treasury Bonds or Bills. Any proceeds of the offering of the securities not invested within two years from the date of effectiveness (except for necessary operating capital) shall be distributed pro rata to the partners as a return of capital.

260.140.115.6 Assessments. Programs calling for assessments shall not be allowed.

Rights and Obligations of Participants

260.140.116.1 Meetings. Meetings of the limited partners may be called by the general partner(s) or the limited partner(s) holding more than 10% of the then outstanding limited partnership interests, for any matters for which the partners may vote as set forth in the limited partnership agreement. A list of the names and addresses of all limited partners shall be maintained as part of the books and records of the limited partnership and shall be made available on request to any limited partner or his representative at his cost. Upon receipt of a written request either in person or by registered mail stating the purpose(s) of the meeting, the general partner shall provide all partners, within ten days after receipt of said request, written notice (either in person or by registered mail) of a meeting and the purpose of such meeting to be held on a date not less than fifteen nor more than sixty days after receipt of said request, at a time and place convenient to participants.

260.140.116.2 Voting Rights of Limited Partners. To the extent the law of the state in question is not inconsistent, the limited partnership agreement must provide that a majority of the then outstanding limited partnership interest may, without the necessity for concurrence by the general partner, vote to (1) amend the limited partnership agreement, (2) dissolve the program, (3) remove the general partner and elect a new general partner, and (4) approve or disapprove the sale of all or substantially all of the assets of the program. The agreement should provide for a method of valuation of the general partner's interest, upon removal of the general partner, that would not be unfair to the participants. The agreement should also provide for a successor general partner where the only general partner of the program is an individual.

260.140.116.6 Redemption of Program Interests. Ordinarily, the program and the sponsor may not be mandatorily obligated to redeem or repurchase any of its program interests, although the program and the sponsor may not be precluded from purchasing such outstanding interests if such purchase does not impair the capital or the operation of the program. Nothwithstanding the foregoing, a real estate program may provide for mandatory redemption rights under the following necessitous circumstances:

 (a) death or legal incapacity of the owner, or

 (b) a substantial reduction in the owner's net worth or income (defined to mean an involuntary loss of not less than 50% in income or net worth during the year in which redemption occurs) provided that (i) the program has sufficient cash to make the purchase, (ii) the purchase will not be in violation of applicable legal requirements and (iii) not more than 15% of the outstanding units are purchased in any year.

260.140.113.3 Compensation for Acquisition Services. Payment of an acquisition fee shall be reasonable and shall be payable only for services actually rendered and to be rendered directly or indirectly and subject to the following conditions:

 (a) The total of all such compensation paid to everyone involved in the transaction by the program and/or any other person shall be deemed to be presumptively reasonable if it does not exceed the lesser of such compensation customarily charged in arms' length transactions by others rendering similar services as an ongoing public activity in the same geographical location and for comparable property or an amount equal to 18% of the gross proceeds of the offering. The acquisition fee to be paid to the sponsor shall be reduced to the extent that other real estate commissions, acquisition fees, finder's fees, or other similar fees or commissions are paid by any person in connection with the transaction.

(4) The provisions of this subsection notwithstanding, the sponsor may purchase property in its own name (and assume loans in connection therewith) and temporarily hold title thereto for the purpose of facilitating the acquisition of such property or the borrowing of money or obtaining of financing for the program, or completion of construction of the property, or any other purpose related to the business of the program, provided that such property is purchased by the program for a price no greater than the cost of such property to the sponsor, and provided there is no difference in interest rates of the loans secured by the property at the time acquired by the sponsor and the time acquired by the program, nor any other benefit arising out of such transaction to the sponsor apart from compensation otherwise permitted by these Rules.

(b) Sales and Leases to Sponsor. The program will not ordinarily be permitted to sell or lease property to the sponsor except that the program may lease property to the sponsor under a lease-back arrangement made at the outset and on terms no more favorable to the sponsor than those offered other persons and fully described in the prospectus.

(c) Loans. No loans may be made by the program to the sponsor or affiliate.

(d) Dealings with Related Programs. A program shall not acquire property from a program in which the sponsor has an interest.

260.140.114.2 Exchange of Limited Partnership Interests. The program may not acquire property in exchange for limited partnership interests, except under the conditions specified herein:

(a) A provision for such exchange must be set forth in the partnership agreement, and appropriate disclosures as to tax effects of such exchange are set forth in the prospectus;

(b) The property to be acquired must come within the objectives of the program.

(c) The purchase price assigned to the property shall be no higher than the value supported by an appraisal prepared by an independent, qualified appraiser.

260.140.113.4 Program Management Fee. (a) A general partner of a program owning unimproved land shall be entitled to annual compensation not exceeding ¼ of 1% of the cost of such unimproved land for operating the program until such time as the land is sold or improvement of the land commences by the limited partnership. In no event shall this fee exceed a cumulative total of 2% of the original cost of the land regardless of the number of years held.

(b) A general partner of a program holding property in government subsidized projects shall be entitled to annual compensation not exceeding ½ of 1% of the cost of such property for operating the program until such time as the property is sold, provided the aggregate of all compensation received is consistent with the maximum allowed for nonsubsidized programs.

(c) Program management fees other than as set forth above shall be prohibited.

260.140.114.3 Exclusive Agreement. A program shall not give a sponsor an exclusive right to sell or exclusive employment to sell property for the program.

260.140.114.4 Commissions on Reinvestment. A program shall not pay, directly or indirectly, a commission or fee to a sponsor in connection with the reinvestment of the proceeds of the resale, exchange, or refinancing of program property.

260.140.114.5. Service Rendered to the Program by the Sponsor. (a) Insurance Services Prohibited. No affiliate of the sponsor may receive an insurance brokerage fee or write an insurance policy covering the sponsor or any of its property.

(b) Property Management Services. The sponsor or his affiliates may perform property management services for the program provided that the compensation to the sponsor therefor is competitive in price and terms with other non-affiliated persons rendering comparable services which could reasonably be made available to the program. All such self-dealing and the compensation paid therefor shall be fully disclosed in the prospectus or offering circular.

(c) Other Services. Any other services performed by the sponsor for the program will be allowed only in extraordinary circumstances fully justified to the Commissioner. As a minimum, self-dealing arrangements must meet the following criteria:

(1) The compensation, price or fee therefor must be comparable and competitive with the compensation, price or fee of any other person who is rendering comparable services or selling or leasing comparable goods which could reasonably be made available to the program and shall be on competitive terms, and

(2) The fees and other terms of the contract shall be fully disclosed in the prospectus, and

(3) The sponsor must be previously engaged in the business of rendering such services or selling or leasing such goods, independently of the program and as an ordinary and on-going business, and

260.102.2 Non-Public Offering And Sale. For the purposes of Subdivisions (e) and (g) of Section 25102 and Subdivision (a) of Section 25104 of the Code, an offer or sale, and for the purposes of Subdivision (f) of Section 25102, an offer or sale of any bona fide general partnership, joint venture or limited partnership interest, does not involve any public offering if offers are not made to more than 25 persons and sales are not consummated to more than 10 of such persons, and if all of the offerees either have a preexisting personal or business relationship with the offeror or its partners, officers, directors or controlling persons or by reason of their business or financial experience could be reasonably assumed to have the capacity to protect their own interests in connection with the transaction. The number of offerees and purchasers referred to above is exclusive of any described in subdivision (i) of Section 25102 of the Code and a husband and wife (together with any custodian or trustee acting for the account of their minor children) are counted as one person. This section does not create any presumption that a public offering is involved in offers not conforming to this section, and the determination of whether or not a transaction not covered by this section involves a public offering shall be made without reference to this section.

TITLE 10: Corporations—Corporate Securities
(Register 74, No. 11—3-16-74)

Subarticle 10. Real Estate Programs

Introduction

60.140.110.1 Application. (a) The guidelines rules contained in these Rules apply to qualifications of real estate programs in the form of limited partnerships (herein sometimes called "programs" or "partnerships") and will be applied by analogy to real estate programs in other forms. While applications not conforming to the standards contained herein shall be looked upon with disfavor, where good cause is shown certain guidelines may be modified or waivered by the Commissioner.

(b) Where the individual characteristics of specific programs warrant modification from these standards they will be accommodated, insofar as possible while still being consistent with the spirit of these Rules.

(c) Where these guidelines conflict with requirements of the Securities and Exchange Commission, the guidelines will not apply.

260.140.110.2 Definitions. (a) Acquisition Fee—the total of all fees and commissions paid by any party in connection with the purchase or development of property by a program, except a development fee paid to a person not affiliated with a sponsor, in connection with the actual development of a project after acquisition of the land by the program. Included in the computation of such fees or commissions shall be any real estate commission, acquisition fee, selection fee, development fee, non-recurring management fee, or any fee of a similar nature, however designated.

Requirements of Sponsors

260.140.111.1 Experience. The sponsor and the general partner or their chief operating officers shall have at least two years relevant real estate or other experience demonstrating the knowledge and experience to acquire and manage the type of properties being acquired, and they or any affiliate providing services to the program shall have had not less than four years relevant experience in the kind of service being rendered or otherwise must demonstrate sufficient knowledge and experience to perform the services proposed.

Suitability of the Participant

260.140.112.1. Standards to Be Imposed. Given the limited transferability, the relative lack of liquidity, and the specific tax orientation of many real estate programs, the sponsor and its selling representatives should be cautious concerning the persons to whom such securities are marketed. Suitability standards for investors will, therefore, be imposed which are reasonable in view of the foregoing and of the type of program to be offered. Sponsors will be required to set forth in the prospectus the investment objectives of the program, a description of the type of person who could benefit from the program and the suitability standards to be applied in marketing it. The suitability standards proposed by the sponsor will be reviewed for fairness by the Commissioner in processing an application. In determining how restrictive the standards must be, special attention will be given to the existence of such factors as high leverage, substantial prepaid interest, balloon payment financing, excessive investments in unimproved land, and uncertain or no cash flow from program property. As a general rule, programs structured to give deductible tax losses of 50% or more of the capital contribution of the participant in the year of investment should be sold only to persons in higher income tax brackets considering both state and federal income taxes. Programs which involve more than ordinary investor risk should emphasize suitability standards involving substantial net worth of the investor.

260.140.112.2. Sales to Appropriate Persons. (a) The sponsor and each person selling program interests on behalf of the sponsor or program shall make every reasonable effort to assure that those persons being offered or sold the program interests are appropriate in light or the suitability standards set forth above and are appropriate to the customers' investment objectives and financial situations.

260.140.112.4. Minimum Investment. A minimum initial cash purchase of $2,000,000 per investor shall be required.

Subsequent transfers of such interests shall be limited to no less than a minimum unit equivalent to an initial minimum purchase, except for transfer by gift, inheritance, intra-family transfers, family dissolutions, and transfers to affiliates.

260.140.112.5. Presumptive Suitability Standards. Unless the Commissioner approves a lower suitability standard, participants shall have a minimum annual gross income of $20,000 and a net worth of $20,000, or, in the alternative, a minimum net worth of $75,000. Net worth shall be determined exclusive of home, furnishings and automobiles. Under this section, the assets included in the computation of net worth may be valued at their fair market value. In high risk or principally tax oriented offerings, higher suitability standards may be required.

Rule 147: Intrastate Offerings. To qualify for this exemption from registration, securities must be *offered* and sold only to persons resident within a single state. The issuer must be resident and doing business within the state . . . The theory is that investors would be better protected both by their proximity to the issuer and by local state regulation and jurisdiction.

To rely on RULE 147, the following five factors must be present: (1) offerings must be part of a single plan of financing (2) involving the same class of security (3) made at or about the same time (4) with the same type of consideration to be received (5) for the same general purpose.

FURTHERMORE, the issuer must (1) have received at least 80% of its previous years gross revenue from within the state . . . and (2) have at least 80% of its assets within the state . . . and (3) use at least 80% of the proceeds of the offering within the state . . . and (4) have its principal office located within the state . . . and (5) resales must be restricted for at least nine months after the last sale of the securities.

There are no fixed limits on the size of the offering or the number of offerees and/or purchasers.

Rule 146: Private Offerings. This rule provides standards for avoiding classification as a 'public offering'. The rule places limitations on (1) the manner of offering (2) the nature of the offerees (3) access to or furnishing information about the issuer (4) limitations on the number of purchasers and (5) limitations on subsequent sales of securities acquired pursuant to this rule.

The rule prohibits *offering* or selling securities through any form of general advertising or solicitation, including seminars, promotional meetings, letter, circulars or other written communication. NOTE: This prohibition does not mean there can be no written communication or meetings. It means that such meeting can involve offerees and their representatives only, and there must be some pre-existing business or other relationship between the issuer and the offerees.

FURTHERMORE, the issuer must believe (and have reasonable grounds to so believe) that either: (1) the offeree and/or representative have knowledge and experience in financial and business matters to evaluate the merits and risks of the prospective investment . . . OR . . . (2) that the offeree can bear the economic risk of the investment.

THE ISSUER MUST MAKE REASONABLE INQUIRY AS TO THE OFFEREE'S QUALIFICATIONS *PRIOR TO THE SALE*!!

The rule requires that the offeree have access to the same information required by the act to the extent that the issuer possesses or can acquire it without unreasonable effort or expense, or that the offeree and/or representative by furnished such information during the transaction and prior to sale.

The issuer must provide each offeree with (1) a brief description of the securities being offered . . . (2) the intended use of the proceeds . . . and (3) any material changes not previously disclosed. The rule permits all information to be provided in one document, such as an offering circular, since such a combined document makes the information more readily understandable.

THE RULE REQUIRES THAT THERE BE NO MORE THAN 35 PURCHASERS IN ANY OFFERING!! Clients of one investment adviser are considered as separate persons . . . . . There may be an unlimited number of offerees . . . The issuer must take care to assure that none of the purchasers are underwriters.

THE SECURITIES ARE RESTRICTED AND MAY NOT BE RE-SOLD FOR AT LEAST TWO YEARS!

Rule 257: Small Offerings. This rule permits offerings not exceeding $100,000 to be made by seasoned issuers without the use of an offering circular. Seasoned issuers include issuers which have been organized or incorporated for more than one year and have had a net income from operation for one of the last two years.

The land acquisition technique is as old as real estate transactions. The land lease or leasehold is an arrangement in which the structure upon the land is sold in its entity specifically as a structure only, and the land on which it sits is leased by the owner. This practice is and has been common in industrial and commercial real estate circles, but land lease as a residential or multiresidential selling tool has been confined mainly to areas where circumstances make conventional fee simple ownership impossible, as in Hawaii, where the largest share of developable land is either under federal and state ownership or in the possession of large estates dating back to the island monarchy.

In California, this means of purchase is fast becoming an acceptable tool in the purchase of homes, particularly because the land values are so high. As an example used earlier, in Santa Monica, California, a home that sold for $36,000 to $38,000 in 1976 is now selling from $160,000 to $170,000. You can really see that by contributing 50 percent of the selling price to the land, you have a situation where an individual can purchase that house when he or she could not in the conventional manner. This method buys time for the homeowner to later convert from a leasehold status to a fee simple ownership. Although this land-lease phenomenon can be traced back to about 1979, the reason that developer interest in California has "perked up" can be traced to creative financing, which makes it possible to sell their product.

This technique can be used in the purchase of apartment buildings and office buildings in much the same way, but with more advantages. For example, an office or apartment building has a sales price of $300,000; $200,000 is contributed to the building and $100,000 to the land. In using the 125 percent declining balance on depreciation for 25 years would be 5 percent of the $200,000, or $10,000 per year. The land lease at 25 years would total $4,000 per year, thus allowing the owner an extra $4,000 to deduct from income for tax purposes.

At the time of purchase, an agreement is struck as to a total price of $300,000 for both the land and building, based on the purchase of the land at the end of the first five years. This arrangement will allow for a much smaller down payment, and at the end of the five-year period, the land is purchased at $100,000, and the whole property, which has increased at the rate of about 15 percent per year will be exchanged for a larger property on a tax-free exchange, thus avoiding any capital gains tax. It is quite possible that a higher value could be placed on the land, thereby allowing the purchaser to "put down" a lesser amount of money, which in turn would allow a larger deduction for the 25-year lease.

Another method would be to have the lease extend to just a five-year period, which would allow the purchaser to deduct $20,000 each year from income. Here again, at the end of the five-year period, the land would be bought for a predetermined price and then exchanged. It is conceivable that an agreement could be reached at purchase for the seller to credit half of the lease payments toward the purchase of the land.

Let's take another tack. Suppose the buyer needed working capital and wished a small monthly payment. The purchaser would ask for the land-lease contract to run 40 years, due in five. This method would allow the new owner a breathing spell in which to get his or her house in order. At the end of the five-year period, the buyer would have the option of refinancing to pay for the land if he or she was not in a financial position to pay for it otherwise.

How To React to High Interest Rates

In 1980, home mortgage interest rates hit 16 percent, and rates were even higher for investment real estate. Then they dropped to 11 percent, and started to move up again. Needless to say, people are in a quandary about what to do. Mortgage interest rates are at an all-time high; however, so is inflation. Current interest rates, less 1980's 13 percent inflation yield a "real" interest rate of 3 percent. This is consistent with what many observers have long contended—interest rates are usually inflation plus 2 or 3 percent. Judged by this standard, interest rates are not all that high; they are just where they always were. The sophisticated real estate investor recognizes the positive side of today's rates. Experienced real estate investors generally like the increases in the inflation rate as they apply to the value of their properties.

So, actually the real meaning of today's high interest rate is not very much different from yesterday's "high" rates of 8, 9, 11, and 12 percent, and each was shocking in its day. However, the psychological meaning is somewhat different. Many of the participants in the real estate trauma—buyers, sellers, lenders—have contracted a paralyzing state of fright from the interest rate rise. But if you can keep your head while others are losing theirs, it is quite possible to make some good sound real estate deals.

The Tactics You Should Employ When Buying

If you want to buy, you still can. If the seller demands that you get a new loan at present rates, you should demand that the price be reduced to enable you to make the payments on the debt service from the properties income. In the event that the seller refuses, merely bid him or her farewell. There is certainly nothing wrong with borrowing money at 16 percent provided that you can earn more than that on the use of the money. Therefore, if the property can be purchased cheaply enough, there is no problem.

It is more likely that you will have to search thoroughly for existing financing that you can take over from the seller. To negotiate a deal for a down payment of 10 to 20 percent, it is most likely that you will have to persuade the seller to take back a second mortgage or trust deed. For various reasons, sellers rarely demand market interest rates on loans that they take back. It is quite probable that you can get 10 percent interest only, or terms in that neighborhood. In the state of California, a seller taking back a second trust deed does not, in this instance, have to adhere to the 10 percent usury law. As a matter of fact, the seller may demand and may receive 20 percent for the second.

The seller will, probably, want a short-term note, such as two or three years on the second. Always hold out for a five-year or more second. If you remember in the case history of one of my apartment buildings, the seller was persuaded to take back a 20-year second at 8 percent with a due date in 17 years. Always stipulate that the clause that reads x amount of dollars "or more" is inserted in the agreement, which will enable you to pay off the second at anytime you wish without penalty. As today's tight money market situation has demonstrated, to obligate yourself to a balloon payment could lead to certain disaster if you have not allowed sufficient time to accumulate the money for payment or did not have dependable refinancing available.

There are other tactics you can use in today's market. For example, instead of buying a property, get an option to buy for a particular price, or get a lease option. Such an option entitles you to all the appreciation above the option price. You thereby get the benefits of appreciation without much risk and without management problems. In view of the current money market, which apparently will be with us for some time, more and more sellers are being receptive to options, because it gives the seller a feeling, in a sense, that he or she has made progress toward selling the property.

You might consider paying all cash, but only under certain conditions, such as if you raised the cash through a limited partnership you could leverage your own position, but not those of the limited partners. You could then refinance the property when the lenders go back to lending in a more beneficial manner to the purchaser. So, if you are looking for low interest loans that you can take over, states like California provide the best hunting grounds, with the exception that most properties in the desirable areas are astronomically high.

Real estate brokers who have strong connections with lending institutions can be "worth their weight in gold" in times like these. Another suggestion is to subscribe to the Crittenton Report and purchase the Crittenton book (see Bibliography), giving details as to what institutions are lending, and the amounts, interest rates, and type of property they will lend on. Although the lending institutions will rarely give you a below market interest rate, you could get loans that may be prohibited by current loan policy. An exception would be prohibition against loans on a nonowner-occupied property. Some consumer lines of credit that used to be considered high (12 to 18 percent), with mortgage rates at 16 percent and the prime at 18 percent, now they look downright advantageous. If you have an "executive line of credit," or a credit card with an unusual line of credit, you may want to use it now. However, be sure that you are in a position to make the payments on such loans. The interest rate may be relatively low, but the payments are very high. The payments on a $200,000 mortgage at 16 percent are about $32,000 a year, but the payments on $200,000 worth of short-term loan at 10 percent are about $60,000 to $80,000 per year.

It is true that high interest rates have been the cause of some paralysis in the real estate community. However, remember that since part of the problem is psychological, it should not keep you from making any sensible real estate deals so long as you can make the payments and earn more than you are paying. Borrowing under such conditions is practical and sound.

If you pay cash, you should be able to get a very favorable price, particularly in this market. In such times, cash buyers are as scarce as "hen's teeth"; those that do pay with cash are mostly not American.

Where there is an existing first loan and the seller needs cash, you might try taking over the first and getting a commercial second mortgage. It is quite possible that the commercial second may be as high as 20 or more percent interest; however, when combined with the existing first, the overall payments may be something you can live with. With terms such as these, you will be in a position to demand a lower price from the seller.

If you can buy a low rate existing first, a high rate commercial second, and a lower price, it is possible for you to come out with a sound investment and a sound positive cash flow.

One way to preserve existing financing is to invest in a state where "due on sale" laws are unenforceable. In California, for example, the state supreme court declared that such clauses, which in effect would prohibit the buyer from taking over an old favorable loan, are a violation of the state constitution. However, a word of caution: Federal Savings and Loans claim exemption from the jurisdiction of the California Supreme Court and are presently litigating that question. Most of the trust deeds (mortgages) in California, however, are "preservable," including those 11 percent loans made about 1976.

Ways To Buy Real Estate at a Discount

Two ways to make money from a real estate investment are appreciation and positive cash flow. However, there is a third way—find ways to buy at less than market value.

For Sale by Owner. One of the benefits of listing property with a real estate agent is that you get the benefit of experience in determining the value of the property. However, it is possible and more realistic to get an appraisal of the property by a qualified fee appraiser. If you intend to sell your own property, the use of a fee appraiser is most important, for most people selling their own property either overprice or underprice it. In most cases, they have a tendency to overprice; however, do-it-yourself sellers underprice their property often enough to leave many investors to pursue for-sale-by-owner bargains. Since speed is so critical, this strategy is most important for those who are self-employed. They usually get the news edition of the next day's paper late the night before, to be the first to read the classified ads, to respond to the for-sale-by-owner ads, and to be the first to arrive on the scene to make an offer.

The would-be investor will have to visit many properties to find the one that is underpriced. He or she can increase the success rate by making low offers on those properties that are not underpriced in the hopes that the owner might want a quick sale.

Buildings with Potential for Expansion. These offer still another opportunity for purchasing at a discount. For example, say you find a building with three regular-sized apartments and one extremely large apartment selling for $125,000. You calculate that the property could be turned into a fiveplex by dividing the huge apartment into two standard-sized apartments, and the conversion cost could be as little as $10,000. You estimate that the resulting fiveplex would be worth $225,000 rather than the current asking price.

The actual price at the time of completion would be $135,000 including renovation, but you would, in effect, be buying a $225,000 piece of property at a discount of more than 66 percent.

Original cost	$125,000
Renovation cost	10,000
Total cost	135,000
Present value	225,000

$225,000 market value − $135,000 cost = $90,000 profit.

$$\frac{\$\ 90,000}{\$135,000} = 66\%$$

Now, if you can get a lending institution to go along with the $225,000 value, you could obtain an institutional loan equal to 70 percent of that value, which would amount to $157,500. Out of that loan you would pay the $125,000, leaving you a balance of $32,500 tax free to use on another investment.

How and Why to Use a Delayed Closing Date. There are times when you can pursuade the seller to set the closing date long after the signing of the purchase agreement. One typical example of the delayed close: you purchase from a builder and, quite frequently, builders encounter delays and are unable to deliver the property until long after the anticipated closing date. When properties are increasing in value at a relatively rapid rate, the purchaser will get the property at a price well below market value as of the closing date. In hot markets, such as California and Texas, appreciation that occurs between the signing of the purchase agreement and the closing often result in what are known as "double escrow" deals. In one instance, a single-family dwelling sold five times while in escrow; incredible but true!

In a double escrow deal, the original buyer finds another buyer who purchases the property at the same time the initial deal closes. At closing, the builder or other seller sells the property to the original purchaser, who immediately sells it to the second buyer for a significantly higher price. In the average case, the original buyer only had $1,000 or $1,500 down as a deposit, so he or she is able to make an extremely high rate of return on the "investment."

However, it is not necessary that you sell your property in a double escrow deal to take advantage of this form of discount. It is possible to point out the increased value to a lending institution and try to obtain a mortgage that represents 80 percent of the current value, but is equal to or greater than your purchase price.

Using the Services of a Real Estate Licensee. It is common belief that when a real estate licensee makes a sale, he or she makes a fixed 6 percent commission of the sales price. This is an erroneous assumption. First, the commission is not fixed at any percent, and second, the salesperson does not get the full commission. Typically the commission is split four ways. The real estate company that listed the property gets roughly half, which is split between the agent who got the listing and the company. The real estate company that sold the listing gets the other half (approximately), which is then split between the company and the individual agent who actually found the buyer. Many investors refuse to get a real estate license themselves because they are afraid they might be declared a "dealer" for income tax purposes. This is untrue. If there is a tax question, the courts will look at the overall pattern of the investor, whether it be a licensee investor or an investor without a license. There are some disadvantages to being a broker or broker associate since there are a lot of properties listed on the market that would deal with "principals" only, the reason being that a lot of listings are open and not exclusive. (I hold licenses in Texas and California; believe me, it's true.)

Another Good Source to Pursue. While some investors specialize in for-sale-by-owner deals, others specialize in buying from out-of-state owners, since most out-of-state owners are not in touch with local property values. Quite often, they find it most difficult to manage their property and are usually very receptive to offers that will get it "off my back." To pursue this strategy, go to the tax office and scan the tax rolls for owners who receive tax bills in distant locations. Contact them by mail or by phone and ask if they would be interested in selling the property. If they are, make the offer favorable to you only after having been quoted their selling price.

No Agents Involved. When a real estate agent is involved in a transaction, he or she typically receives a commission up to 6 percent of the purchase price. By buying in a transaction where no agent is involved, you should be able to save anywhere from one-half to all of the commission in addition to any other savings you may obtain through negotiating.

There are many ways to find direct deals, such as answering for-sale-by-owner classified adds or contacting owners who have not given any indication that they plan to sell, such as out-of-state owners. It is unethical to try to cut a broker out of a transaction that he or she has brought to your attention. Of course, if there is no agent, you and the seller will have to do all the necessary work that the agent would have been required to do.

Personally, I find the use of an agent helpful in many ways when you find the right one, which we will discuss later. It is helpful to have the agent act as a buffer between buyer and seller. And with the agent doing the leg work and carrying out my instructions, it frees my time to look at other property.

When real estate investors talk about tax shelters, they are really talking about sheltering and/or excluding from income tax liability a certain amount of cash flow (throw off) from an investment, even to the point of sheltering outside income. Real Estate investors are most concerned about deductions greater than the cash flow (throw off) that created tax loss (on paper), which can be offset against other real estate income and/or against other personal income or earnings. Although equity buildup and economic appreciation is foremost for those investing, tax sheltering is an important part of the overall return on the investment. To those investors who already have a substantial income, the sheltering is more important than the actual cash flow, for in their position a negative cash flow (meaning a break-even situation) could be an advantage as a tax shelter.

In the real estate field, the primary source of tax shelter is depreciation. Expenses associated with the property can be significant. For tax purposes, depreciation is merely a paper deduction—not in anyway does it mean that the property itself (improvement) is depreciating, nor does it reduce the actual cash flow.

Depreciation in the accounting sense occurs even when the market value of a building increases. There are different types of depreciation allowed by the IRS and they can be used to allocate the building's cost over its useful life.

There are several ways of depreciating: straight line, meaning that it never varies from beginning to end, and acceleration methods that assume an asset is exhausted more rapidly in its early years. With the acceleration method, you can apply more depreciation in the first years of ownership, but less in the later years. The net result with the accelerated method is to defer taxes on income from the property until those later years. In the meantime, depreciation shelters his or her income.

On a new apartment building (first-time user only), you may use one of five types of depreciation—200 percent, 150 percent, 125 percent, Straight line, or Sum of the digits. To explain these various methods of depreciation, we will use a 25-year life. For the 200 percent method, divide the 25 years into the 200 percent, giving you 8 percent that you may deduct from the cost of the building, excluding the land (land does not depreciate) each year, thereby giving you a declining balance. Assume your building is worth $200,000; the first year you may deduct $16,000 from your income. This and all accelerated methods are called declining balance.

If you use 150 percent declining balance, divide 25 years into the 150 percent, allowing you 6 percent to be deducted as depreciation with a declining balance. If you use the 125 percent method, deduct 5 percent each year in a declining balance. Straight line would be 4 percent per year.

All tax shelters simply defer or postpone taxable income. The amount of tax shelter will decrease in time because in each succeeding year, the depreciation and interest deductions will diminish—the reason being that the depreciation deduction decreases because the very nature of accelerated depreciation is to take larger amounts of depreciation in the early years and less in the later years of useful life.

There was once an old gentleman who had two daughters; being a very wealthy man, his constant concern was how to "outfox" the IRS upon his demise. He thought long and hard, schemed, calculated, and hit upon an idea that he thought would solve his problem. Both girls had just married, so the father decided to give a party in their honor. Besides being very wealthy, he had much political influence and so he invited people from all over, including senators, governors, bankers, and others. Since he was such a powerful man, no one dared to refuse his invitation. On the night of the party the mansion had taken on a festive air, and joy and happiness were overflowing with happy guests. Besides the sumptuous dinner, there was music and dancing. During a break in the music, an announcement was made that the old gentleman wished to toast his daughters and their new husbands. The old man came forward and said, "Fill up your glasses and drink with me a toast to my two lovely daughters. I have raised these girls without the benefit of their dear mother. They have been kind, considerate, and loving daughters. They have bestowed upon me the love and affection that would make any father happy and proud. Both daughters were brilliant in college and graduated Summa Cum Laude."

After all this lavish praise, he paused a moment and said, "My only disappointment in life has been my girls' choice of husbands. For if they had searched the world over, they could not have found two men more inept and disgracefully ignorant, with the judgment of a jackass and the backbone of a jellyfish."

Everyone gasped, and there was dead silence. Finally, one of the new husbands said, "We will sue you for slander, Sir, and we will win our case for we have as witnesses some of the most reputable and respected people in our state."

The sons-in-law made their threat good—they sued and won their case, stripping the old man of all his wealth; he did not appeal the case. His wealth was divided equally between the two sons-in-law. Within two weeks the old gentleman passed on. Everyone thought it was from a broken heart. But those who came to see him for the last time as he lay in state could not understand or comprehend why he looked so peaceful, with a smile on his face. Had they only known the old man was aware that he had only a short time on earth, and he finally found a way to beat the IRS. You see, since the money and property was won in a suit for slander, it was not taxable. Had he left a will, a good portion of his estate would have gone to the federal government and the state in which he resided. Now the purpose of this story is to show that no matter how complex a problem is, with enough forethought, persistence, and imagination, one can overcome most obstacles!

However, I would not advise going to this extreme. You might find a simpler way.

Key Considerations   One must evaluate the investment as well as the shelter. A tax shelter cannot save a poor investment. It is quite possible to end up with cash losses as well as tax losses. However, on the other hand, some real estate investments, such as new residential rental property, provide large tax shelters and sometimes even tax losses together with positive cash flows because higher rates of depreciation are permitted.

Depreciation reduces the tax base in the underlying asset. Therefore, if you sell an asset for its original cost, the depreciation is recaptured as capital gains. If you sell property for which you used accelerated depreciation, some of your profit on the sale might be taxed as ordinary income. Present tax rules are complex, but basically they require that excess depreciation, that which is accelerated over what straight line would have been, be taxed as ordinary income, not as capital gains.

Depreciation Recapture

Rules on depreciation of real property have been changed drastically, particularly for residential income property; however, I must say that the changes are beneficial for those who hold that type of property. If you owned an apartment building and it wasn't placed in service after 1980 the old rules would apply. If the property was purchased in 1981 you may not use any of the old accelerated methods as previously stated. There is a published table which prescribes the percentage on an accelerated basis which takes the place of the methods of depreciation before the establishment of the Economic Recovery Act of 1981.

The Economic Recovery Act of 1981

For real estate other than low-income housing (low-income housing has a slightly different basis) we'll discuss full years since it factors down if you put something in use in the middle of the year. Under the new rules the following percentages are roughly computed as though a 175 percent declining rate was used. The formula on depreciation over the fifteen year period would be as follows:

12% for the 1st year
10% for the 2nd year
9% for the 3rd year
8% for the 4th year
7% for the 5th year
6% for the 6th, 7th, 8th, and 9th years
5% for the 10th through 15th years

You can option for a straight line depreciation, but if you don't, the above formula is the only other choice you have. The United States Treasury was given direction to come up with this table to give guidelines in a manner which will create approximately a 175 percent declining balance.

In dealing with residential income property there is no change from the old law insofar as any amount over the straight line would be treated as ordinary income, and the excess over the straight line would be subject to recapture. If one chooses to use the straight line one would not only avoid recapture but would also avoid the preference tax.

In using the straight line approach one could deduct approximately 6.7% per year. For example, on a building (excluding the land) valued at $100,000, you would deduct $6,700 per year as depreciation. In 15 years you would have deducted $100,500—$500 more than the worth of the building at the time of purchase. It is easy to see the great advantages.

If you take a mortgage on real property, you may deduct depreciation and other expenses not just on the portion of your equity investment. As an example, Jim Wright invested $30,000 and had a mortgage of $170,000; he is

Leverage

entitled to all of the deductions generated by the building, not just 25 percent of them, which represents his $30,000 investment.

It is my deep concern that too many people venture into financial areas that could be detrimental to their future. Therefore, I always emphasize "Act before and not after the fact." Seek advice to keep you out of trouble, not after you are bogged down in it. Since each one of us has different goals and needs with varied amounts of assets it stands to reason that what is good for one may be detrimental to another. Remember that tax shelters can be complicated and are subject to legislative change; therefore, you should consult a C.P.A. who is knowledgeable in these matters.

How the Bank Looks at You

The following form is a standard simplified Individual Financial Statement.* You will notice that it covers all possible categories of assets and liabilities. Banks want to know exactly what your position is. They are looking more closely now than ever. With computer credit reporting and other information systems, they can, if they wish, check you out rather thoroughly. But one element they do not and cannot know is your personal physical assets. People usually underestimate or ignore (because they are tedious to inventory) these important assets. Jewelry, paintings, heirlooms, or furniture can reinforce your credibility considerably.

It is wise to be honest with your signed statement. Willful misrepresentation involves hefty penalties. One sad example will suffice. A young man, then an Attorney General of a southern state, falsified his financial condition in order to float a loan. He reversed his assets and liabilities, that is, he placed the $300,000 he had outstanding in the assets column, and the $60,000, which were really assets, in the liabilities portion.

He was given the loan and built a horse show barn, unfortunately, not the highest and best use of the land. After considerable personal overspending and business collapse, one of his creditors foreclosed. Like dominoes the others followed, and he filed bankruptcy to protect himself. During these proceedings, his falsification was uncovered. He ultimately was sent to a federal prison.

Be straightforward.

How the Bank Looks at Your Property

There are some typical forms that the Savings and Loan and Bank people use in their analysis of the appraisal process prior to going to the review appraiser and then to the loan officer. Such forms have not been included in this book for the simple reason that they were constructed for institutional use. The forms mentioned and ascribed are for the sole purpose of giving you a more rounded picture so that you will have a better understanding of the view of the lender as compared to your view.

INDIVIDUAL FINANCIAL STATEMENT

TO   BANK:

NAME IN FULL		SOCIAL SECURITY NO.	AGE	MARITAL STATUS	☐ SINGLE ☐ WIDOWED ☐ MARRIED	☐ SEPARATED ☐ DIVORCED
SPOUSE'S NAME		SOCIAL SECURITY NO.	AGE	DEPENDENTS (NO.)		AGES

RESIDENCE ADDRESS (NO., STREET, CITY, STATE, ZIP CODE)	YRS. AT ADDRESS	PHONE NUMBER	YRS. OF EDUCATION (CHECK ONE) ☐ UNDER 12 YRS. ☐ 13-15 YRS. ☐ 12 YRS. ☐ 16 YRS. AND OVER

PREVIOUS ADDRESSES IF AT ABOVE ADDRESS LESS THAN 5 YEARS (NO. AND STREET, CITY, STATE, ZIP CODE)

(1)

(2)

EMPLOYER	ADDRESS (NO. AND STREET)	CITY	PHONE & EXTENSION
SPOUSE'S EMPLOYER	ADDRESS (NO. & STREET)	CITY	PHONE & EXTENSION

FINANCIAL CONDITION AS OF _____, 19_____

ASSETS			AMOUNT	LIABILITIES			AMOUNT
CASH	Branch			NOTES PAYABLE TO BANKS	Security Pacific National Bank	Branch	
	Other Banks				Other (Itemize, Schedule 4)		
STOCKS AND BONDS	Listed (Schedule 1)			OTHER NOTES AND ACCOUNTS PAYABLE	Real Estate Loans (Schedule 2)		
	Unlisted (Schedule 1)				Sales Contracts & Sec. Agreements (Sch. 4)		
REAL ESTATE	Improved (Schedule 2)				Loans on Life Insurance Policies (Sch. 4)		
	Unimproved (Schedule 2)			TAXES PAYABLE	Current Year's Income Taxes Unpaid		
	Trust Deeds and Mortgages (Schedule 3)				Prior Years' Income Taxes Unpaid		
LIFE INSURANCE	Cash Surrender Value				Real Estate Taxes Unpaid		
ACCOUNTS AND NOTES RECEIVABLE	Relatives and Friends (Schedule 4)			OTHER LIABILITIES	Unpaid Interest		
	Collectible (Schedule 4)				Others (Itemize, Schedule 4)		
	Doubtful (Schedule 4)						
OTHER PERSONAL PROPERTY	Automobile				TOTAL LIABILITIES		
	Other (Itemize, Schedule 4)				NET WORTH		
	TOTAL				TOTAL		

ANNUAL INCOME	(Refer to Federal Income Tax Returns for Previous Year)	ANNUAL EXPENDITURES	(Refer to Federal Income Tax Returns for Previous Year)
SALARY OR WAGES		PROPERTY TAXES AND ASSESSMENTS	
DIVIDENDS AND INTEREST		FEDERAL AND STATE INCOME TAXES	
RENTALS (GROSS)		REAL ESTATE LOAN PAYMENTS	
BUSINESS OR PROFESSIONAL INCOME (NET)		PAYMENTS ON CONTRACTS AND OTHER NOTES	
OTHER INCOME (DESCRIBE)		INSURANCE PREMIUMS	
		ESTIMATED LIVING EXPENSES	
		OTHER	
TOTAL INCOME		TOTAL EXPENDITURES	

LIFE INSURANCE	FACE AMOUNT	BENEFICIARY	COMPANY

This statement is furnished for the purpose of procuring credit, and is to be regarded as continuous until another shall be substituted for it. If the undersigned, or any endorser or guarantor of the obligations of the undersigned, at any time becomes insolvent, or commits an act of bankruptcy, or dies, or if any writ of attachment, garnishment, execution or other legal process be issued against property of the undersigned, or if any assessment for taxes against the undersigned, other than on real property, is made by the Federal or State government, or any department thereof, or if any of the representations made above prove to be untrue, or if the undersigned fails to notify you of any material change in financial condition as given above, then and in either such case, all of the obligations of the undersigned to or held by you, either as borrower or guarantor, shall immediately become due and payable, without demand or notice. In consideration of the granting or renewing of any credit to the undersigned hereafter, the undersigned hereby waives the pleading of the statute of limitations as a defense to any obligation of the undersigned to you.

I hereby certify that I have carefully read the above statement, including the reverse side, and it is a complete, true and correct statement to the best of my knowledge and belief.

Date Signed_____, 19_____. (Sign Here) _____

(Sign Here) _____

PLEASE COMPLETE THE SCHEDULES ON THE REVERSE SIDE

*Reprinted by courtesy of Security Pacific National Bank.

Give details of any contingent liability as endorser or guarantor, or on suits or judgments pending. (If necessary, use separate sheet.)

Do you do business with any other bank? _____ If so, give details _____

Have you ever gone through bankruptcy? _____ If you are married, are any of the assets described in this statement your wife's (husband's) separate property?____

If so, state which _____

Have your Income Tax Returns ever been questioned by the Internal Revenue Service? _____ If so, most recent year _____

Have you made a will? _____ Number of dependents _____ Their ages _____

SCHEDULE 1: LISTED AND UNLISTED STOCKS AND BONDS OWNED

NO. OF SHARES OR PAR VALUE	Description	Issued in Name of	Joint Tenancy?	Market Value
LISTED:				
			TOTAL LISTED	
UNLISTED:				
			TOTAL UNLISTED	

Are any of the above Securities pledged to secure a debt?

SCHEDULE 2: REAL ESTATE OWNED   (DESIGNATE: I=IMPROVED, U=UNIMPROVED.)

Location or Description	Title in Name of	Joint Tenancy?	Cost	Present Value	Trust Deeds, Mortgages or other Liens			
					Unpaid Bal.	Rate%	MONTHLY PAYMENT	Held By
		TOTAL			X X X	X X X X X	X X X X X X X X X X	

SCHEDULE 3: TRUST DEEDS AND MORTGAGES OWNED

Name of Payer	Legal Desc., Street Address, & Type of Improvements	Unpaid Bal.	Jt. Tenancy?	Terms	1st or 2nd Lien	Value of Property
	TOTAL		X X X X	X X X	X X X X	

SCHEDULE 4: DETAILS RELATIVE TO OTHER IMPORTANT ASSETS AND LIABILITIES

They will use three approaches to value, as will you: (1) the income approach; (2) the market data approach; and (3) the replacement cost approach. They weigh the results of all three and arrive at a judgement value according to the particular appraiser's experience and knowledge. Under no circumstance will they or should they "average" for a definitive answer.

They will use one form which is known as appraisal working papers when appraising 15 units or less. This form consists of the market data approach, cost approach, and income approach. Another form used is called the multiple loan card. This card will have a loan number, client's name, the person who approved, and the loan committee approval, and the property rating by the loan officer, the consultant, and the appraiser. It will have the legal description, map reference, the style and amount of units, and an opinion given as to the improvements and management. Other parts of the form that will be included are an income schedule, whether it is furnished, a list of amenities, and building details both inside and out. They will also have a card entitled "comparable rents in the area."

From this you can easily see that your appraisal analysis, if followed as laid out in this book, will be very comparable to that which institutions use, thereby giving you the opportunity to negotiate from strength.

The Use of Lease-Purchase Options to Buy

You have heard the expression "Tight-Times" and it means many things to many different people; a good time to buy-sell, a bad time to buy-sell. As we will see in one case, it meant both a bad time to sell and a bad time to buy.

Let's suppose that the two parties, buyer and seller, decide to invest in time. In this case time represents options.

Property Description. A seller initially acquired a 10,000-square-foot vacant office building for $90,000. The building was paid for in cash for two reasons: to save time and because the seller had difficulty obtaining financing. Since the building was reasonably well located, within a few blocks from the heart of downtown, and in reasonably good condition, he considered the price a bargain; it represented less than $10 per square foot, well below the replacement cost. However, there were some drawbacks; the building was completely vacant and a substantial amount of vacancies existed in the immediate neighborhood.

The seller had originally purchased the building on speculation. At the same time that he listed the space for rental, he also listed it for resale at $140,000. A buyer came along, looking for office space for his newly established business. Although not really in the market to acquire, the buyer was particularly impressed with the sales price, which, as it turned out, was negotiable. However, this created a problem for the seller since a quick turnover of the building would result in ordinary income; 50 percent of his gain would go to the government as taxes because that was the seller's tax bracket. As a result the seller wanted a substantial amount of gain over his purchase price.

With the help of a real estate consultant, the buyer sketched out the following proforma, income from the building based on fully leased space as proposed for bank financing:

Income statement

Gross income @ $7 per sq. ft. =		$70,000
Vacancy allowance 5% =	$3,500	
Operating expenses: (maintenance, management, utilities, property taxes) @ $3.50/ft =	$35,000	−38,500
Net Operating Income available for debt service and return on equity		$31,500

Even using a capitalization rate as high as 15 percent, the indicated value was over $210,000. And even presuming a bank requirement of 75 percent coverage, the $31,500 would support a mortgage of over $157,000 written for as short a term as 20 years at an interest rate of 13 percent, making the constant approximately 14 percent.

By this time both buyer and his consultant were attracted by the possibilities the proposition offered. However, both parties saw several problems standing in the way of an immediate sale.

The statement of the problem.
The buyer saw a number of obstacles, which were mostly financial.

1. Most banks would write only the very smallest mortgage, if any, on a vacant building.

2. Even if it were possible for the buyer to secure some sort of financing such as a first mortgage, with the seller financing, or a combination, the buyer will still have to have a sufficient amount of cash set aside for his other business start-up.

3. The buyer had no doubts and felt confident that he could lease all the space. However, there certainly was no guarantee of this, even if he made improvements and priced rents below market.

Now the Seller Had Other Concerns.
1. Profits from the immediate sale at $140,000 would be cut by ordinary income taxes, and in the seller's 50 percent tax bracket, a $50,000 gain would net only $25,000. However, if he could hold out for one year and one day (the capital gains holding period), the same $50,000 would net $40,000, an additional 40 percent.

2. For the seller to wait for the higher gain would mean having his $90,000 tied up for another year and generating no cash return.

The seller's alternatives look something like this:

Seller's Alternatives	Results		
1. Sell Immediately	After-Tax Returns (Excluding Selling Expenses)	—	$25,000
2. Sell After One Year	After-Tax Return	—	$40,000
3. Sell Under Option	After-Tax Return	—	$40,000
	Rents	—	$10,800
			$50,800

Note that the comparisons do not take into account adjustments for the time value of the seller's money. The first alternative (sell immediately) would probably be best if they did it using a discount rate appropriate to someone who can gain $50,000 on $90,000 in a relatively short time. However, that alternative is dependent on an available buyer willing and able to pay the full price right away, and there was no certainty that a buyer would show up in a year. With the second alternative (sell after one year), however, he could execute the third alternative (sell under option) immediately.

It is understandable under these circumstances that postponing the sale would clearly benefit both parties. Still, the buyer needed space and the seller had his cash tied up in the building.

Logical Solution. The buyer would lease the building with a 13-month option to buy at the set price of $140,000. He would pay the seller $900 per month in rent, plus $100 per month for the renewal option. It is understood by both parties that all option payments are to be credited to the final purchase price. If the buyer exercised the option, he would retain those improvements made by him; if not, and he should remain a tenant over a minimum specified time, he would retain credit for his improvements through reduced rent equal to the cost of said improvements.

What Finally Took Place. In the actual deal, the buyer took control of the building. If all goes smoothly during the 13-month period, the buyer should be able to mortgage out his purchase at $140,000 as stipulated. The projected income stream will support a mortgage greater than the purchase price, and the buyer will own the building without investing any of his own funds. If he elects not to buy, his only loss will be the rent he paid, which in any case he would have paid somewhere else.

Although the final results of the actual deal on which this is based are not in as yet, the buyer has leased almost three-fifths of the space at a rate slightly higher than projected. He is making the monthly payments to the seller on time. Most importantly, the buyer and seller are working within well-defined risk levels. The buyer can still walk away from the building if he chooses, and the seller's goal of increasing the value of the building by a large percent is nearer to being accomplished.

Although the lease-purchase option is suitable for virtually any circumstance, it is particularly appropriate when:

1. The buyer wants time to raise equity.
2. The buyer wants time to learn the building.
3. The buyer wants to speculate that interest rates and other lending terms will improve in the near future.
4. The buyer does not have sufficient funds to purchase.
5. The seller cannot afford a quick turnover due to tax disadvantages.
6. A dealer status is inferred from the seller's position because of short-term ownership.

Heed This Warning. Parties to this sort of transaction require ample legal protection. Full option terms, including terms in exercise price, must be fully spelled out in a formal option written agreement. Unspoken agreements based on assumptions can lead one into bitter and expensive litigation. *Remember,* anything pertaining to real estate transactions *must* be in writing.

The Manner in Which Options are Taxed

In this day and time as never before, investors are taking advantage of the fantastic leverage that options offer. However, the tax consequences and the use of them are understood by very few people.

As in most things, there is a basic structure. There are always at least two parties to any option, the seller who gives the option and the buyer who pays for it. It is quite possible that there may be other parties if the buyer, known as the optionee, decides to sell or assign his or her option to others.

At least two events take place during the life period of an option; its purchase by the buyer (optionee) from the seller (optionor), and its disposition. There are other events that could occur, if the option is sold or assigned before its expiration date, which could happen on several occasions.

From the Seller's Point of View There are only two events that would concern the seller (optionor): the sale to the buyer (optionee) and the buyer exercising his or her right to the option or the expiration of that option. It is quite possible that these events may be taxable.

Presuming the option is exercised, that is the buyer (optionee) exercises the right to purchase, whereby the money received for the option is to be applied against the purchase price of the property, then receipt of the money is not a taxable item or event. This would be considered an open transaction by the IRS. In other words, it is one that has begun, but is not yet completed, and so alleviates the problem of the seller (optionor) having to pay tax at this time. It is my concerted opinion that there is only one circumstance that would put the seller (optionor) in a position where he or she must immediately pay tax on the gain from the sale of the option.

This is when the seller (optionor) is certain that the gain will be ordinary income. However, it is presumed that the seller (optionor) will expect to have a long-term capital gain or at least wait to see whether the gain will be long or short term.

In the event that the optionee (or a third party to whom it has been sold or assigned) exercises his or her right to buy, it is then considered a sale for tax purposes, thereby making the original option money a part of the property's purchase price, provided the option was written in that manner.

In the event that the option is allowed to expire, the option money received will be taxed in the year that it expires as ordinary income.

Should you want to sell an option or get someone to sell one to you, a valid selling point is the seller's ability to have the use of the cash before taxes must be paid on it. In the event that the option is exercised in a year other than the year in which the option money was received, the seller (optioner) may still use the option money in any manner he or she sees fit without having to pay tax during the option period.

A Valuable Selling Point

There are three choices available to the buyer (optionee):

Buyer's Vantage Point

1. The buyer is allowed the opportunity to let the option expire. Should he or she choose that option of expiration, it would be regarded under tax law as a sale at zero dollars—a loss. The period between the date the option is bought and its expiration is the determining factor as to whether it is short or long term.

2. Picking up the option. This is merely treated as an ordinary purchase of property; therefore, it is not a taxable event.

3. Assignment or sale of the option. A taxable event would take place upon the selling of the option. Generally, options are taxed as though the buyer (optionee) had owned the property. Therefore, should the option be sold more than a year after its purchase, the buyer (optionee) will have a long-term capital gain or loss. On the other hand, should the option be sold less than a year later, it will be a short-term gain or loss.

In conclusion, to those not thoroughly familiar with tax laws, the tax consequences would seem to be complicated, but they should not obscure the main fact that an option offers the seller cash that will usually not be taxed for some time, and at the same time it gives a buyer control of a property's present value plus appreciations for as little as $200 to $2,000, depending on the circumstances involved in the negotiation.

Creative Leverage

Remember that the foremost important requirements to successful real estate investment are: financing, management, investigating, and verifying everything concerning that particular property that you intend to purchase. Follow the steps detailed in previous chapters. Refer to them often, using the checklist (see Chapters 2 to 4, pages 15–22 in particular) until all the right things become second nature.

Following are examples of the true use of leverage, both the positive and negative sides. You will learn the true meaning of leverage as it is known in real estate—the advantages as well as the disadvantages, depending on the experience and financial ability of each individual. Read this section on leverage carefully; even a most experienced and sophisticated builder and developer can get into financial difficulties due to miscalculations. Remember that you should never buy on a projected income.

Let's presume that you have found this "toadstool" apartment house among a garden of roses. Although it is unsightly, the area is good and the building is structurally sound. You have done your homework, as suggested in previous chapters. You are now ready to make your move. The place is for sale by owner, and you find that she or he wants all cash. You have one problem—you don't have the cash necessary for an outright purchase.

Now we can presume that you own your home and that you have substantial equity, but not enough to refinance to pay the cash necessary to buy the apartment. So, you make the following offer—you will give the owner of the apartment a second TD (trust deed) on your home equal to your equity as security and a note for the full amount of the apartment building, all due and payable in three years, interest only at one percent above the going rate. At this time you show the owner the type of improvements you are going to make and the approximate cost, thereby assuring her or him that in the event she or he had to take the property back at the end of the three-year period, it would be in better condition, have more amenities, and be appreciated in value with an increased gross.

After you have secured the building with nothing down (in cash), you proceed as described in previous chapters to improve the building. About six months prior to the due date, you place the property on the market, taking into consideration the new value, thereby enabling yourself to sell the property for a profit, paying off the first trust deed and cancelling the second TD on your home. Now, in less than three years, you have created a cash profit and had a period of experience in operating an apartment building in the proper fashion. You have taken before and after pictures of your improvements, all of which you put into a portfolio to show the next seller or lender your expertise in operating and upgrading apartments. Also included in your portfolio is a copy of the original and the present rent schedule. In doing your analysis, remember that every dollar increase in gross is worth $10 in value of the building. For example, your annual gross has been raised by $20,000, thereby roughly increasing the value of the property to $200,000. With the experience that you have now gained, you will be in a position to negotiate from strength plus capital that you lacked for your first venture.

Another method of buying with a small down payment is to purchase from the owner on an installment sale. For example, an individual owns a complex free and clear and it has escalated in value to the point that were he to sell it outright for cash, thereby giving him a terrific capital gain, it would cost him many dollars in taxes. The installment method of reporting income allows that income to be taxed over a period of years as it is received. This method of reporting income relieves the seller of paying tax on income that has not yet been collected, thus permitting him to report the profit only when collected.

This form of selling is also advantageous to the buyer, for he or she is able to purchase the property with a small down payment. One requirement for this type of sale is that a portion of the price be paid in two or more years. There is no requirement that any minimum be paid in the year of sale. However, if the seller took over 30 percent down, it would trigger all taxes due and payable at the time of sale. If the seller received an amount down plus monthly payments, it would exceed the 30 percent criteria and, therefore, would not qualify as an installment sale. This is no longer generally true but remains the same for California.

One legitimate and often-used method of acquiring property when one is short of cash is to form a limited partnership with you as the general partner. You put in "sweat equity"—that is, you receive an equity interest in return for organizing the venture and finding the property and putting up no cash. The tax shelter benefits of this kind of venture would not be as advantageous because of the lack of leverage. However, prospective limited partners could possibly be interested in the idea of the proceeds from tax-free refinancing at some future point.

Another way to use "sweat equity" in its truest sense is to buy a fixer-upper house where the owner has a small equity, thereby allowing you to purchase at a distressed price, giving a note to be paid off in two to three years, paying interest only based as if the loan were amortized for 30 years, but due and payable in two to three years. The steps you would follow are: (1) do all the work that you can in the evenings inside, working weekends on the outside, (2) secure a home improvement loan for new carpeting, drapes, and linoleum, and (3) when completed, rent it for two years with yearly leases, one year only with a security deposit plus first and last months' rent. During this time you will have two years' depreciation, using 125 percent declining balance, depreciation of capital improvements, right of all supplies and all labor, but your own. You then sell the property at a neat profit. Now you have money to reinvest. In the meantime, you have sheltered your regular income. You could also make a 1031 exchange.

To succeed at anything requires diligence, perserverance, and, above all else, making a commitment, a decision, prudently and with much forethought. You must make a decision, right or wrong, or you will never accomplish what you started out to do. Surely you have often heard someone say: "Why, I could have bought that land for $5 an acre," or "I could have bought that apartment building for peanuts." These people had hindsight and no foresight, and somewhere along the way they were not capable of making a decision or a commitment.

The world is full of dreamers. They are the ones who never take a chance and, therefore, never accomplish their dreams or acquire anything of great material value. On the other hand, there are those who dream and have the courage to put that dream to work—taking risks and striving to make it a reality. Show me a person who has never made a mistake, and I will show you a person who has never taken a risk.

This is an appropriate time to explain something about creative financing. The term "creative financing" is really nothing new, and people who lecture and write books stating that they can teach you to purchase property with nothing down are simply giving you "hog wash." For when it gets down to the bottom line, what they are really saying is that as long as there is no cash out of your pocket, they consider that as nothing down. They don't count the fact that there is paper involved—hard and soft money, which you very well know is something down. Taking our "toad-stool" apartment purchase as an example, it is true you would not be putting any cash down—just the equity value of your home in a second trust deed, plus a first trust deed and note on the apartment. It is a legitimate way to acquire property, but I would be absolutely wrong and irresponsible to make a statement that you were putting nothing down. Having been in this business for many years and being very realistic, knowledge of real estate finance is more important now than ever before. Therefore, please heed this advice. Don't make a fruitless search trying to find new techniques, which you hope will solve the problems of our current market. There are many articles published in newspapers, magazines, and books—and, yes, on the lecture circuit—about creative financing, which in reality are just belated discoveries by the lay people of techniques long known to the sophisticated real estate investors.

With interest rates so high, it doesn't take a doctorate degree to figure out that it pays to find existing loans you can buy "subject to," and by all means seek financing from the seller. Like you, or most any other real estate investor, whether a novice or an old-timer with years of experience, we are constantly looking for and eager to discover new ideas to cope with our present market. After having read through reams of current material on this subject, it turns out that such actions as the seller taking back a mortgage or such techniques as wrap-around mortgages, land contracts, and lease options individually or collectively may be quite creative—but new they are not. To put everything in its proper perspective and in a nutshell, one could say that most creative financing techniques are merely variations of getting the seller to take back a loan on terms that would be considered ridiculous by the standards of the institutional lenders.

chapter eight

Fundamentals of Negotiating

The price and terms for which you agree to buy a property almost always affect the eventual success of the investment. The purchase price of an investment property is not only the largest number in real estate, it is the most important.

Too often real estate investors find themselves behind the "eight ball" when trying to buy a building on their terms rather than the seller's terms. It seems that no matter how hard they try, too many end up paying far more than they had hoped and anticipated, and then they agree to terms that throw their income projections completely off. In most cases, the only thing these negotiators need is a little brushing up on technique. When you consider that a good negotiator can buy a building for as much as 15 to 25 percent lower than a poor negotiator, the value of learning and knowing negotiating skills becomes quite apparent. Although this chapter cannot make you a skilled negotiator, it may help you to become a better one by forcing you to map out your strategy before you even discuss price and terms with the seller.

How to Become a Successful Negotiator

You Decide the Price and Terms. The first thing you must decide before you even think about negotiating your strategy is the price and terms you want. You should also decide on the highest price and terms you are willing to accept. Write these down and use them as the basis on which you plan the negotiations, and only then are you ready to map out your strategy.

Know Your Seller. I know nothing about the game of chess other than that it takes skill, practice, concentration, and learning a series of moves and countermoves. Negotiating is like playing chess in that it demands a series of moves and countermoves by two participants trying to outwit each other, and like chess, negotiating demands that you figure out the opposition's moves before they are made. The more you know about the seller, the better equipped you will be to "checkmate" your opponent.

Most of what you need to know can be found in county records. Look up the seller's purchase price by checking on the seller's old deed. If the price you want to pay is close to that purchase price, the seller most probably will resist because he or she would lose money after paying the sales commission. In such a case, you might offer a higher, face-saving price, but demand excellent terms.

Find out the seller's mortgage balance by looking at the county mortgage books in those states and counties that have them. From the mortgage balance you can compute the amount of money the owner will have after settlement. You can be assured that the seller is certain to calculate this number everytime you change your offer. For you to see the seller's position, you should be prepared to do the same thing.

It is also very important to ascertain if there are any outstanding liens—you would naturally want to know this before you purchased. The county registry of deeds also contains the record of the parties with whom the seller negotiated. Look for the seller's name in both the grantee and grantor books and make note of the parties with whom the seller dealt. If it is possible for you to contact and speak to a previous owner, you may be able to find out a great deal about the strengths and weaknesses of the property, as well as the negotiating style of the seller. This may make you change your predetermined price and terms, and may even warn you of a potentially bad investment.

At this point, you might start thinking about the seller's tax situation. If you ask subtle questions and note his or her life-style and employment, it is possible to make a fairly good "educated guess" as to the seller's income level. If he or she is employed, sometimes it is possible to call the personnel office and state that you are checking an application to purchase and wish to verify employment position and salary. If properly approached, you will be amazed how often they will give you the information. It would also be wise at this time to try and calculate the amount of depreciation he or she gets on the property and the portion of the mortgage payments that is nondeductible amortization.

It is Now Time to Know Yourself. After you have calculated what will be at stake for the seller during negotiations, decide what is important to you. Make a list by taking a sheet of paper and drawing a line down the middle. On one side place those negotiating points that are most important to you, and on the other side write those that are not as important, giving you the opportunity to trade off. Keep in mind that it is important to fight over each point initially, and when you do concede a point, do it in a begrudging manner as if it were very important to you. Remember that the world exists through compromise.

Try to form a general idea of just how you will actually conduct the negotiation. There are hundreds of tactics available; however, one must remember that some are ethical and some are not. If only for defense purposes, you should make yourself well aware of both kinds.

The last step in planning your strategy is to determine what your initial offer will be. With what you have already determined, you should work backward from your target price through the most logical and probable negotiating pattern until you arrive at an appropriate offer.

Time to Keep Your Cool. While actually in the process of negotiating, remember that no matter how frustrated you get, and you will, losing your temper will only serve to possibly anger the seller, which will certainly not make your offer attractive. Be determined, yes. Be polite, yes. Be rude, never. It stands to reason, and logically so, that a friendly negotiation can better serve the both of you. But remember that behind the smile, the more prepared you are and the more you know about the seller, the more pleasant you can be, which will result in being in a better position to conclude the negotiation as planned in your favor.

The more you know about negotiating and about human behavior, the more you will control your negotiations and the more you will gain whether you are a buyer or seller. What makes some negotiators better than others is that they gain a little more than the other side with regularity. The truly skilled negotiator understands that in a successful negotiation both sides gain.

Know Yourself and Your Opponents

Although the drama may take place in the actual meeting, the outcome is often predetermined by the work you do before the negotiation begins. One of the most important factors in being a successful negotiator is to know as much as is possible about your opponent from every reliable source available, for example:

> What your opponent wants.
> Your opponents financial recourses.
> The negotiating style your opponent has used in the past.
> What kind of time pressure your opponent is under.
> If your opponent is willing or able to take a risk, and if so, how much?
> If your opponent knows, or thinks he or she knows, what your goals are.
> How much power your opponent thinks you have.
> Any and all other information that could give you a clue to your opponent's potential negotiating behavior.

You should analyze your own position just as thoroughly. Seek the same answers about yourself that you sought about the opponent. Decide with deliberation and complete understanding of what your own goals are and what you hope to achieve. One of the most common mistakes is to settle for too little. Remember, the higher your aspirations, the better chance you will have to gain in a negotiation.

The one thing to remember is that you are not concerned with an arbitrary economic value for a piece of property, but rather what it is *worth* to you or your opponent.

A horse is worth $25 assessed value as personal property in most states because there is no *set market value* on a horse, as there is for cattle, swine, sheep, goats, and such. The value of a horse is set by what a willing seller is willing to accept and a willing buyer is willing to pay. This is because most horses have always been sold by negotiating, more commonly known as "horse trading," "dickering," "palavering," or "bartering." Regardless of the term, it is negotiating for a deal.

Your preparations should lay the groundwork for the meeting itself. It has been the traditional rule for the person who desires something to go to the individual's location from whom he or she hopes to obtain it. However, there are psychological advantages to a home location; therefore, a neutral location such as a hotel or restaurant, may insure that neither party feels at a disadvantage.

Location. The choice of location and the setting (the temperature of the room, the arrangement of the chairs, the use of a conference table) must not be overlooked, for they can substantially affect the outcome. For example, a rectangular table with you at the head will tend to formalize negotiations more than a round table would.

Whenever possible I would have the negotiating take place in my office where the surroundings were very familiar to me and not to my opponent. The chair I sat in behind my desk was higher than those facing me. This gave me the psychological advantage of having opponents look up to me and me down to them. I was in an unstrained and relaxed position. There were times when I was placed on the opposite side of the desk, and in order to reverse the procedure I usually remarked that I had either been driving for a long time or had a sore back and, therefore, I would appreciate being allowed to stand, but I made certain that the other person remained seated. Now the role was reversed for I could pace around the room or stand close to the desk, forcing him or her to look up to me, and in effect, intimidating the other person and putting him or her on the defensive.

Whatever you do, do not draw up a "script" and expect to play it out. It is imperative that you be relaxed and flexible, and tailor your strategy to the situation as it develops. It is a foregone conclusion that the more techniques you have in your repertoire, the better you will cope with any developments that might occur.

Negotiation Techniques. There are literally hundreds of techniques and maneuvers that you can use. Some are ethical and some are not, however, you should be familiar with both kinds if only for defensive purposes. Useful reference books in this area are Gerald T. Nierenberg's *Fundamentals of Negotiating* and *Winning Through Intimidation* by Robert J. Ringer (see Bibliography).

Some general negotiating guidelines are:

Ask questions.
Be more of a listener than a talker.
Be sensitive to the meaning of nonverbal as well as verbal communications.
Set a businesslike tone in a congenial manner.
Avoid personal bickering by dealing only with the issues, never personalities.

When you have reached agreement, immediately write down the terms as agreed upon and have both sides initial the paper until a formal agreement can be drawn. This will avoid any differences later about what terms were actually set.

I cannot stress too strongly the necessity of committing everything to the written word. A small tape recorder is invaluable; it eliminates the chance of misinterpretation or misunderstanding. From the tape recording, the formal agreement can then be written.

It is quite possible that you might make an extra thousand dollars or so on your next investment or avoid a damaging deal by investing a small amount of time and money in developing your negotiating skills, which offer a very high return.

First, find out what is motivating the individual to sell. Is he or she being transferred, needs the money, being foreclosed—what? If the seller is being transferred and has limited time, he or she might be more anxious. Very often, what the seller tells you is not the true motive.

Using a Middleman. Let's say that you find a piece of property on your own, without a realtor, and are going to negotiate directly with the individual. This can be hazardous. Sometimes when you make a lower offer than the owner is asking, the owner is infuriated. He may love his building and you have insulted him! It is then very difficult to get back into negotiation.

Take the same situation (a low offer) using a buffer, or someone in the middle. You request that the agent present the offer, and if the agent is reluctant, require that he or she show you some proof that the offer was presented to the seller. (If an agent refuses to present an offer, he or she should be reported to the Dept. of Real Estate.)

The agent can present the offer and if the seller says it is ridiculous, the agent can agree and suggest a counter offer. The agent is put in the position of wanting the commission (paid by the seller), so the fiduciary relationship is with the seller and not the buyer (but an agent still has to treat the buyer and seller equally by law). Then you can go back and forth with counter offers from each party. This would never be accomplished if you tried to negotiate on your own. You can't lowball somebody like that and expect someone to enjoy it, particularly if pride is involved.

When you are dealing with realtors, you must make sure that they know what you want. You lay down in the beginning the specifics of what you want—the location, size, and other requirements.

Offers. Now you have found a piece of property that you like. Don't hesitate to contact the individual who has the listing and ask to look at the property. He or she may say, "You can't look at it until you make an offer." This happens quite frequently, and, in other words, you are buying a pig in a poke. So you say that you will make an offer, and in that offer you spell out, for instance, that you have to inspect each and every apartment. Next, you have to approve of each and every apartment, and if you disapprove, that negates the whole situation. Put in these various escape clauses to protect yourself. Give the seller two or three working days to answer your offer. In the meantime, you start checking on the property. Go to county planning, look at the plans, and see what they call for. For example, if the plans call for 14 units and the owner is advertising 15 units, there is something wrong. You have a bootleg. You will have a problem then when you go to get the loan. The bank will only loan on 14, not 15. Check on how many garages are legitimate. See if there are any liens against the property, including tax liens.

You must insert into the offer that the "title is free of liens, easements, restrictions, rights, and any other conditions known to the seller," as well as a statement that the property meets all present code standards, and that "all improvements and amenities are in the same condition as when the offer is made and accepted with reasonable wear and tear to be expected." Also include "at buyer's election this offer is null and void if any part of the property is damaged or destroyed, removed or materially damaged."

Protect Yourself. It is suggested that you take pictures of the property from all angles, and that you use two cameras. Use a regular camera that will provide dates on the developed film; also use a polaroid so that you can write on the back of the photograph the date, time of day, and compass degrees from which the picture was taken (be sure to take a picture of the address itself). These pictures serve many purposes, for instance, when you take over the property, and find something missing—such as all of the plants or the beautiful outside light fixtures—you have proof that these items existed during the negotiation.

You cannot overlook anything; you cannot assume that everyone is going to be straightforward. You have to protect yourself.

Later when you wish to sell or trade your property, you can show what it looked like when you took over. These photos will document that you did upgrade. These pictures also substantiate your ability and business ethics for your bank. They show that you did not milk the property, that you increased its value. This, of course, makes it much easier for you to get a larger loan at a better rate.

For the protection of both the seller and the buyer, the insurance policy in force should be amended to protect both parties the moment the sales agreement is signed. Usually this can be accomplished by telephone.

One must be particularly careful to see if the owner, manager, or both live on the property. If this is the case, you would be wise to specifically fix the date that you will take possession—"possession to be given at close of escrow" or "possession to be given immediately on close of escrow." To further protect yourself, you should insert that a portion of the sales money be held in escrow until the owner, manager, or both comply. Otherwise, they could occupy an apartment until they decide to leave at their leisure, which could be very costly since then you would become involved in a court action.

Be sure to insert that "expenses and income statements are to be provided and are to be certified by the seller, approved by the buyer before the close of escrow, and become part of the escrow instructions." Ninety-nine percent of the setups you see will say that "the above information is believed to be from a reliable source, but we do not guarantee this to be a fact," or some equivalent statement. In other words, they are making a disclaimer. If something turns out to be wrong, they are off the hook.

You must also insert that "the sale is subject to inspection by a competent, licensed, bonded pest control company," which will make sure there is no dry rot infestation, fungus, termites, or other such things. In addition, insert "any such damage to be repaired by the seller."

When making an offer, be sure that it is to be accepted within a minimum of five or seven days. (I sometimes use three days.) This is to force the seller to make a decision. Never make an offer "to be good at any time" or "until accepted."

Always give a good-sized deposit in the form of a check to assure the seller that you are very serious. This is impressive. However, you should endorse your check to read "this check is to be deposited into escrow at the opening of escrow, as it is a deposit of earnest money to purchase." When you do this, you are not allowing the seller to deposit the check if the deal falls through; he or she has to return the check. You can merely say that this check "is not to be deposited until the opening of escrow."

You want to impress the seller. When the seller sees the check and knows it will be his or hers if, in three, five, or seven days he or she accepts the offer and opens escrow, it helps to push the seller into a decision. At the same time it helps protect you.

After the Offer. If the offer is accepted, go in for the inspection. My offers depend on a lot of contingencies, how much deferred maintenance, and so forth. I carry a little recorder and take down the information on each apartment—"This is apartment 110, a two-bedroom apartment, the color of the walls, approximate size of rooms, and so on." This saves time. Then I go over the outside of the building. I write out all this information, figure the deferred maintenance, what ways I could improve the looks of the building, and what that would cost, how I could cut down on expenses, such as lights being used in the halls, and so on. See if there are timers. Look at the meters. One of the best ways of checking the age of a place is to take the lid off the toilet tank, turn it over, and look at the date (although sometimes lids will be replaced). But check each one. You can also verify this at the hall of records. If the owner tells you that the building is only 15 years old, and you know it's really 24, but really has an effective age (looks 15 but is really 24 years old) of only 15 years, that's fine.

You have escape clauses if you want to pull out. If so, use them. You say: "After examining the building, I find that it is going to cost me $15,000 to put it in proper shape to rent. Therefore, I will offer $15,000 less than I agreed to, because of these conditions. I just cannot come out-of-pocket for $15,000." The salesperson will be very disappointed, thinking he or she has lost the deal. Assure the salesperson that you still want the building and the only thing he or she has to do is convince the owner that what you are saying represents the real situation, and you know it is true. Point out again all the particulars that need to be worked on or are problems.

The salesperson has spent a lot of time on the deal and does not want to see it go down the tube. Ninety-nine times out of 100, the salesperson will sit down with the seller and convince him or her that the buyer is absolutely correct about the condition of the building and the amount of money needed to put it in proper shape. In your dealings with the salesperson, you have said that actually it will take $20,000 to restore the building, but you are willing to go down only $15,000, and he or she will use this point when talking with the seller. Or the salesperson may come back with a counter offer—but you are going to save a minimum out of that deal of $10,000. And you will use that for the purpose of enhancing the building, which will in turn increase the value of the property. For every dollar that you have spent, you will have to get two in return to make it worthwhile. You should not overimprove property by doing something just because it suits your fancy and doesn't do anything for the building. Avoid doing unnecessary work—period.

How to Buy

Having been a salesman for many years, I appreciate a great buyer. I vividly remember an incident in Tulsa when I was selling a prestigious line of dresses. The cheapest one wholesaled for $29.75 (that was over 25 years ago).

I had a buyer in my hotel room. I carefully explained every detail of every dress. But my client never changed her expression. I thought she had died and forgot to close her eyes. I couldn't even tell if she was breathing.

Finally, I said, "Madam, may I ask you a question? Do you play poker? You know, you should take it up professionally. I have watched you all through this, and I don't know whether you think this is a bunch of garbage or what."

With that she got up and took four dresses and hung them on the end of the rack. "Now we write on those," she said.

I thought, I've spent an hour and a half with this woman. She's driven me crazy and now she's going to buy four lousy dresses. So I said, "Which one of these four do you want to start with?"

She replied, "Not those, the others." So she was going to write on 41 dresses. I thought I was really in trouble then; her credit probably wasn't worth a damn.

Finally she left, and instead of being elated, I was depressed because I knew damn well that I had wasted my time. It ruined my whole weekend. On Monday I learned that her credit was AAA.

The object of this story is that you cannot tell by looking what someone is worth and you cannot always tell whether someone likes something or they don't. When you are buying, act like that dress buyer. Show no emotion, no expression. You will make people awfully nervous. They in turn may become talkative. The hardest person to sell is one who won't say anything.

Then as now salespeople have a technique to overcome this problem. They begin asking simple questions that have a positive answer. "Do you like where you live?" "Yes." "Do you enjoy your car?" "Yes." "Do you like this property?" "Yes."

chapter nine
Management

The extreme importance of proper management for whatever piece of property you purchase will be the extremely important key to your success. More businesses "go broke" due to poor management than any other single factor. When purchasing stock from a stock broker, the first thing a prudent and knowledgeable buyer will want to ascertain is who is management, what is management's background, and what has management's track record been since taking over control of the company?

Some companies have been in business for decades and have shown little progress. They are basically in the same financial condition with very little expansion, if any. Others in like businesses have within a span of five years, starting from a very minor position, outgrown the old companies. Think back on how many stores, restaurants, or gas stations you know about that were unsuccessful and were forced to close. Some may have had several owners over a period of time, each in turn being as unsuccessful as the predecessor. Then one day you notice that one or more of these businesses are back in operation, and not only are they successful, they are expanding.

Because a person is an excellent chef does not make that person a restauranteur. Because a person opens and operates a business does not necessarily make or qualify that person to become a businessman or woman. There is a fine distinction between those people who own and operate a business and those who own and operate a business with knowledge and perception.

All of this also holds true for the apartment owner. Unfortunately, too many apartment owners do not treat the operation of their apartments as a business, and too many that do are poor managers. The key to any successful business, regardless of its nature, is good, sound management practices.

Many people despise paper work. However, it is a very essential part of operating any business. Everyone knows that apartment owners must keep the apartments occupied and collect the rents on time. However, management does not stop there; there is much more to the overall management process.

Most people have some good and some bad personal habits, so it holds true that most businesspeople have some good and some bad business habits. It is very difficult for a person to analyze his or her own mistakes; it's human nature not to find fault with oneself. However, it is essential that your business practices are analyzed to locate the weak spots so that they may be corrected.

One of the most frequent omissions in the business structure is the keeping of good and accurate records. Another is not using the proper legal procedure when it is necessary to do so. It is a good practice to commit everything to the written word. It is also convenient and a good practice to keep a file on each tenant by apartment number, keeping all correspondence with that tenant, all copies of change of terms notices, rent receipts, rental agreement, and form showing expenditures made for improvements and repairs contributed to that particular apartment as well as all other pertinent data.

You and Your Tenants

One particularly bad practice is to allow a tenant to be late or to get behind in rent payments. You may excuse yourself by thinking that you are just being a compassionate person by allowing a tenant to slide by a week or more before paying the rent. But your gesture will not make a friend of that tenant, nor, probably, will that tenant be on time again—and eventually you will be forced to issue a three-day notice to pay rent or quit! You, as a businessperson, are expected to meet your obligations when due, and this you cannot do on empty promises.

Most tenant problems can be avoided if you select the proper tenant and have a firm understanding with him or her at the very beginning of the tenancy. Listed below are a few suggestions to help you avoid tenant problems.

1. Join the apartment association.* They will have all the necessary forms you will need to operate your apartment business in an efficient manner. They can also offer you expert advice.

2. Have all prospective tenants fill out an Application to Rent form. Get a deposit and give a deposit receipt. Do a thorough checking via a credit check through your apartment association; check the prospective tenant's employment record, social security number, all references (credit and personal), and the apartment manager of not his or her present address, but the previous address.

3. Establish a set of written rules that are reasonable and that you and your tenants can live with. Read these rules to the prospective tenant,

---

*These associations can usually be located in the phone book.

answer any questions, and make sure that he or she clearly understands them. Have the prospective tenant sign them, along with your signature, and give him or her a copy. Keep one for your file for that particular apartment.

4. After the prospective tenant has met all your standards, has agreed to rent and you have agreed to accept, and has paid you the required amount of money, have the tenant sign the rental agreement after he or she has read it and you have answered all questions. Such forms are available at your apartment association office.

5. Before turning over the keys, ask the tenant to accompany you on an inspection tour of the now rented apartment. Take along an inspection sheet in duplicate on which you will make notations in the appropriate places indicating damage, faded carpet, torn drapes, and such. After the inspection is complete, each of you signs in the spaces provided. Put the date and time on the document, give the tenant a copy, and keep the other for your file. This will be of great benefit to you when that tenant leaves and you have to make your inspection to ascertain if there has been any damage and, if so, to what extent. This will also have an effect on the tenant's security deposit.

6. Take care of any complaints immediately, if possible.

7. Use the "Golden Rule."

8. Always be polite but firm in making any decision.

If you are still having problems after following these rules, you should receive professional help by seeking a Real Estate Consultant to set up a proficiency program. Once you are properly organized, you will have better and happier tenants and a lower vacancy factor, but best of all, peace of mind and a profitable business.

Managing the Apartment

Now you have the building. What is the first thing you do? When do you start managing? You started the day of the offer. You did that by checking all those expenses and gathering all that information. You have found out what the water bill was last year, the electric bill, the gas. Now you know what the costs were, so you can evaluate where you can cut expenses. You have already begun to manage.

This is what is meant by premanagement, managing the property before you acquire it. You start immediately by hunting sources of supplies if you don't already have them. If you are new to the business, you don't have them. Where can you get a good grade of carpet the cheapest? Where can you find people to install carpet? Where can you find reliable painters? Where can you make the best deal on good quality paint? Where do you find welders?

The first thing to do is paint the outside of the building (and the exterior trim) because that is what people see first. Do all of the necessary things to make the exterior more attractive. Change the lighting fixtures, put up awnings and/or drapes. If the entrance is concrete, install some attractive

Changes that Increase Rental Income and Resale Value

tile. If the building has a plain door, you can dress it up with "plant ons," wood or composition plaques that you attach with screws or glue. They change a plain door into an eye-catching one. Then paint the hallways. At this point, do not disturb or do one thing to the interior of any apartment. Replace all of the carpet and all the light fixtures in the common areas. Make the entrance and lobby very attractive. When you have a building that is attractive, if somebody leaves, you will have no problem finding a new tenant. When the first person leaves, redo that apartment. All of these are capital improvements. Painting comes right off the top, as well as carpentry or electrical work.

You will find that most of your expenses will have to do with plumbing. So, solve the problem at the beginning—get a good plumber. For instance, if you have pipes that are concealed in the ceiling of the garage, you will want to drop them down with nipples so that all the pipes are exposed. Then you don't have to keep breaking the plaster if the pipes need more work.

Furnished or Unfurnished?

Should an apartment building be furnished or unfurnished? Some people say that all you need to do to improve a building is to unfurnish the furnished apartments or furnish the unfurnished apartments. But, as stated in an earlier chapter, when you have furnished apartments, you tend to attract transients. They come in with a suitcase and leave with a suitcase. It is too easy for them to move, but is costly for you to be constantly changing tenants. The first thing I do when I buy a place that is furnished is to get rid of the worst tenants; second is to remove all of the furniture by giving it to the Salvation Army or Goodwill, and then charge it off my income taxes.

Remodeling Tips

If you have any appliances that do not have good colors, have them refinished. Popular kitchen colors are harvest gold, almond, and avocado. Use pleasing combinations and replace any necessary parts so that the appliance is like new. You can charge off these expenses also. The only thing you will have to replace later should be the refrigerator. It probably will not pay you to fix a refrigerator (see Replacement Cost Approach in Chapter 3). Give it to the Salvation Army, put a figure on it, and take it off your income tax.

For carpets, I don't recommend Hi-Lo. It has been over done. Heavy shag also isn't good. Get something that wears well—pay a little more. Get the more closely woven, nylon heat-set, which lasts much longer than most. With this type of carpet, you can patch holes very easily. Try to use colors that go with most everything. Avoid beige. Coco or bronze are nice and cause few problems. Don't use multi-color carpets such as two-tone green.

If possible, replace drapes that go to the ceiling with standard sizes. Drapes to the ceiling get dirtier, are harder to clean, and may have to be custom made. Also, use cotton rather than acetates; cotton holds up better. If you use a standard size throughout a building, you can also have an extra pair so that if any are down for cleaning, you will have a spare.

Never allow tenants to use your storage space, no matter how much empty storage space you have. It only creates headaches. Whenever I buy a building, one of the first things I do is send a notice to all tenants asking if they have anything stored in the building and if so, where it is located. When I determine where everything is, I send another notice advising that all things stored must be removed within 24 hours or else I will give it to the Salvation Army or Goodwill. Of course, there are phone calls galore from the tenants, but I do this for good reason.

Once I had a pipe break in a building and could not get to it because a tenant had things stored in that area and had it padlocked. Fortunately, I was able to take the door off and get in that way. I repaired the leak and then put the door back on. Of course, the owner claimed damage because the pipe broke and his property got wet. It was a big hassle. This is another reason for not allowing tenants to store things—they can then claim damages. They will generally put a price tag on their damaged property that is unbelievable.

Many beginning investors think they are handy and try to fix things themselves. Problem number one is that you cannot charge the labor off—only the parts. Second, you will find that eventually your investment in time and inconvenience will make an improvement very costly. A professional will take less time to do anything.

One of the things we stipulate is that the tenants cannot paper, paint, or repair. We will do it. I have bought buildings with the most outlandish paper done in a horrible manner. Tenants are not generally paper hangers. We absolutely will not allow anyone to do any of this. We do the painting and use an off-white so that anybody's furniture will go with it. Now if you are getting very high rents and the tenants have a lease for say five years, and you have built into the rental agreement percentage raises each year, you can say yes to tenant repairs. You then stipulate in your agreement that they must put it back in the same condition it was when they got there. In other words, plain walls, paper off, repainted the same color, and so forth.

Set aside reserves in case you find yourself in an emergency situation. For example, you have four units vacant all at once for eight months. That once happened to me. Just visualize losing all that income and still paying your mortgage and all the other things you have to pay. So you can see the necessity of having reserves.

Let's assume that you do get into a bind financially. Never, never get delinquent on a note. If you are going to be late, call up immediately and say, "Look, I've got a problem. All of a sudden I have four vacancies due to this problem we have with the building. I want to know if you can make some arrangements for me for some penalty later down the line, or let me have a month's breather so I can get these things rented." You would be surprised how often people will go along with this. They will help you out because they don't want that property back. They want you to keep it, and they will help you to keep it if you go to them in the proper way. But if you just ignore them and don't say anything, they will keep after you once you are delinquent. You finally may push them into a position where they have no choice but to foreclose. But you can eliminate that situation if you speak to your lenders and explain the problem. And don't just tell them the problem, tell them how you are going to solve it. Have it all written out clearly. Go down and talk to them. Here is the problem, this is the way it is going to be resolved, and this is how long it is going to take; now what can we do to work it out? Most times they will work it out with you. Just don't ignore it, hoping something will happen, because it won't unless you make it happen.

An apartment building is a business. If it's not treated as such, you are not going to make it.

Being Audited

If you have never been audited by the IRS, rest assured that you will be. As an income property owner, you will be taking deductions on your tax return that are different from the norm.

I have been audited many times, and I have never had to make an adjustment. Each time I have received a written clean bill of health. Through it all, I have learned to:

1. Have a receipt and cancelled check for everything.
2. Stamp with date and time both the bill and the check.
3. Write the check number on the bill.
4. Attach the cancelled check to the bill.

If you do these things, you will impress upon the auditor that you are thorough and above board.

The people who are auditing your return are merely doing their job. As long as you are not attempting to evade paying your taxes, you will have no problems. There is no reason to be frightened.

Tenant Inspection Sheets

Once when we were building a house, we were forced to take an apartment. When we moved in, I insisted on an inspection. The manager kept saying, "Don't worry about that." I said, "I do. I want an inspection because I see a flaw here and there." Sure enough, when we moved out, there had been three different managers, and there was no inspection sheet. I got a call from the property company that ran the building. They told me there were stains on the cabinet and some worn-out places on the floor. I said that worn-out places would indicate an awful lot of traffic, and there were just the two of us. I told him I had insurance, but that I was not going to have the insurance company pay for something that I did not do. He was holding my security deposit, and, in California, it must be returned in two weeks. But they have to show you a copy of the bill and so forth. So my company has designed a regular form stating what was deducted, where the money went. Make photostatic copies and enclose the bill to the tenant so they are protected. If we treat people like we like to be treated, we can eliminate a lot of management problems.

Previous Owner's Suppliers

Know who the previous owner's suppliers are, but don't use them, no matter how cheap they seem. If there is a handyman involved, don't use him, because you don't know what kind of work he does. You really don't know if there have been any kickbacks or what. Start with a clean slate.

You will learn when taking over a piece of property that the tenants have probably asked the landlord for many things, many times. He or she ignored them, and they have become used to living in the building in that condition. Their first impulse immediately upon a change of ownership is to find out how much they can get out of you. "I want my place painted. It hasn't been painted since I moved here. We need new carpets." One of the biggest mistakes I think most new owners make is to go around and introduce themselves. "I am the new owner, anything I can do for you, let me know." And believe me, they will. Then if you don't do what they want, they get upset and will pester you to the point that you wish you had never been in the apartment building business. All the problems with operating apartments are caused by the owner. He or she is the one who puts in the tenants, who makes the policies, who makes or doesn't make the improvements.

A better way to handle new ownership is to say, "I am the manager of this building and anything you have to say or do, you do through me."

They will, of course tell you everything they want just as they would the owner. You can then say, "Well, it sounds plausible, but I really don't know if they want to do that. I will have to consult with the owners, and if they agree, I will be more than happy to meet your request. I will get right back to you." They ask you today and you tell them the next day—yes or no. "I discussed it with them and they said yes, they would be glad to do it," or "No, not at this time. Maybe at a later date but not at this time. I am sorry, but there is nothing I can do. You know, after all I don't own this place." This keeps you from being pushed into a corner—into saying yes or no immediately. And they will push for an immediate answer.

If you are new in the business, handling it this way gives you a chance to learn how to manage. And if you make a mistake, you can go back and say, "You know, I did this on my own and I got my tail eaten out, and they told me that I had to change this. And, therefore, here is a written letter from the owners." You have said they could do something and all of a sudden you realize you made a mistake. You can backtrack. But if you own the building and you say you are the owner and you make a mistake, well, you said yes, and there is no way you can back out of it.

On the other hand, if you want to deal directly with people and you are strong enough to say no and mean it, and stand by it, fine. Handle it yourself.

I learned a very valuable lesson in the Navy. As a senior lieutenant, I had just taken over the job of operations officer for a carrier service unit. The chief petty officer asked, "Lieutenant, how do you want me to handle this?" "How long have you been a chief?" I asked. He said, "I've been a chief for 25 years." "Well, "I said, "if you don't know how to do it by now, then you shouldn't be a chief. You do your job and I'll look at it. If it isn't done correctly, you will be so notified. If it's done incorrectly the second time, I think we'll put you back without stripes." Needless to say, he never bothered me again. Don't get backed into a corner. Don't let them test you.

To hire a resident manager you should run a blind ad, only a box number. Briefly describe the job and ask for a resume that includes age. If you have a building with middle-aged people, you don't want a young person. You want someone near your average tenant's age.

After reviewing the resumes, pay a visit to the candidates unannounced one *morning*. Identify yourself and talk about the position. In whatever condition you see that person and his or her home, rest assured that is the way you are going to see the person in your apartment.

If you let them visit you they will appear looking beautiful. But a month after they move in you may find your place a pig sty.

We like to furnish the apartment for our managers. If we want them out, it's easier to get them out. Then, too, we can furnish their unit so it is consistent with the building's image.

Resident Manager Supervision

A brief story will illustrate the need for proper supervision of a resident manager. Through an attorney I learned of a Los Angeles resident who owned, among other property, a 35-unit building in Orange County. He was having a terrible time finding good management. Finally he found a capable attractive woman. She proved to be perfect beyond his wildest dreams. All the rents were collected on time. She periodically raised the rents on her own. Maintenance became minimal. Her bookkeeping was exceptional. Her apartment was always immaculate. There was never a problem.

Eventually she suggested that he needn't come around at all. She would continue to deposit as she had been doing. Her management had been expert and it was a long drive for nothing, so he agreed.

Late one night he was awakened by the police. They showed him a warrant and then arrested him for operating a house of prostitution. He shortly learned that his fabulous manager was a madame who placed her 34 girls in his building so she could keep an eye on them.

The owner did clear himself. But he now had an empty 35-unit building, one he couldn't rent. He told me that he was getting out of the real estate business all together. I advised him to convert to condominiums. He did and made a handsome profit.

This story is not meant as a criticism of women managers—there are many, many good ones—but only as a warning that, as an owner, you should be aware of what is happening on your property at all times, and that includes knowing what your manager is doing. For you as owner of property are responsible for any illegal use of or by your tenants.

Security Deposit

You may find that the previous owners have allowed the tenants to use their security deposits or last month's rent to pay a current month. When you take over, you must solve that problem immediately. Use the Notice to Change Terms of Tenancy form at the end of this chapter.

Check thoroughly, because experience has shown that when you take over a building, there will be a number of tenants who have already used up last month's rent. Often they could not come up with the money, so there was no choice but to evict them.

In one instance I was forced to evict six tenants, which created a hefty vacancy rate for a 14-unit building. But I bought new carpeting for the vacant apartments (saving money because I bought in quantity) and I quickly repaired and refurbished in assembly-line fashion. I then had six new units at a much higher rent. What could have been a difficult situation became increased income.

Do not use oral contracts for painting or any other bids. Have everything written into the contract specifically—down to the number of coats of paint. The time the job is to be finished must be stipulated. You should require the contractor to put up a bond for completion at the specified time. If the job is not completed, the bond is forfeited. If you don't do this, your contractor may work on several jobs at once, dragging yours out.

When you hire a professional, ask for references. Call those people. If the job involves exterior work, go look at previous jobs. Find out when they were done.

Always get a detailed contract that specifies no charges for overruns. If contractors underbid a job, that's their problem.

An additional advantage of using an independent contractor is that he or she will have a resale number and will be able to get materials wholesale. Negotiate so that you won't pay the retail price for things the contractor provides.

Never pay for a job until it is completed. Contractors will try for one-third in front, one-third in the middle, and one-third when finished. Your response should be—if you haven't got enough money to support the job, I don't want you working on it. I will pay you when the job is finished and I am satisfied. But so you can make sure you are paid, I will put the money in escrow, and when you prove to the escrow company that you have completed the contract and they have inspected the work, you will collect your money.

Having been in the construction business and being a professional estimator, I never have things done by the job; I have them done on an hourly basis.

You want to make sure that contractors have a license, but also get the license number and call to find out if it is in their name. There are lots of plumbers today, for instance, who don't have a license personally, but operate under someone else's license. This is illegal under some circumstances. In California the licensee stands responsible for work done under his or her license. Check your city and state regulations. If you think you are hiring someone who says he or she is licensed but isn't, report the incident to the proper bureau and make a formal complaint.

Make sure that material and labor releases are from the actual suppliers and the workers. If the contractor is going to furnish the materials, make sure they are paid for, the labor is paid for, and that you know this for a fact. You could pay for the job and the contractor could skip, not paying the suppliers or laborers. They can then get a mechanics lien and you have to pay for all of it. I sit down with the contractor, go over the job, and find exactly what is needed. Then I order it myself from my own suppliers. That way the contractor is just working for me by the hour. I also am able to get the quality of material that I want.

If you are doing something that requires a permit or plans filed, make sure this is done according to specification so that the inspection is approved—and can be approved when the job is completed. The permit doesn't cost that much. Many people don't want to get a permit because it is a hassle. They have to go down to the Permit and Safety Dept.; they must have plans, a sketch, and have them approved. So, many contractors will try to get around this by saying to owners: "Look, it's a simple job, and if you get a permit, you'll have to have plans and they have to be approved. You may have to make a change, and that will delay the job—which will cost you money because I'm sitting around not able to do the work. So, it's up to you. Do you want to do it without a permit or with a permit?" And the owner says to do it without a permit—that person has been taken. The property owner is wide open to all kinds of problems.

There is a lot of "bootleg" construction (something done without a permit). If you have built something without a permit and this is discovered by an inspector, you can be required to tear it down. And there is very little recourse in this kind of situation because the people who do the bootleg work are usually fly-by-night.

If a contractor has been a real flake and has done things very badly, you should contact the Contractor's License Bureau and report it.

Remember—make the contractor sign a completion form. Make the laborers sign that they have been paid. Find the suppliers and make them sign the form, and then turn that over to the escrow with the list of all the suppliers the contractor said were used. You now have a release from the contractor and everybody else. You post the sign of nonresponsibility. Then if the contractor doesn't pay somebody, it's not your problem.

Raising Rents We have found that if we fixed something or made an improvement and then raised the rent, the tenants felt that they were paying for that improvement, and they didn't like it. So we don't do it that way. The correct way is to raise rents when necessary. After the rent is raised, we write the tenants a letter explaining what improvements we intend to make and we compliment them on the way they have kept the premises; how nice they were about being quiet and considerate of their neighbors—whether they were or not. That is one way of telling tenants that if they aren't quiet, they should be.

You should also test the market concerning rents. For example, you find that in the same neighborhood a very nice one bedroom is going for $300. You ask the highest price, but don't put out a for-rent sign. Use a newspaper ad instead to screen prospective tenants (see the forms at the end of this chapter). But remember, *never* show an apartment until it is vacant and completely done over, so that prospective tenants can smell that freshness. There is nothing worse than showing an apartment that is a mess.

Management Forms

On the following pages are examples of the forms necessary for proper apartment management. Some of them have been discussed throughout the chapter. Additional forms follow the Bibliography.

Confidential Rental Application
Please fill in completely for rental

Name _____ Husband or Wife _____
        First   Middle   Last   Age

Present Address _____
                     Street   City   State   Zip Code

Social Security No.   /   /   /   Spouse   /   /   /   Phone _____

Names & Ages of all persons residing in apt. _____

Employment History (Last five years)—Use Reverse Side if Necessary

Present Employer _____ Phone (   ) _____

Address _____
             Street   City   State   Zip Code

Salary _____ Job Title _____ Date Employed _____

Former Employer _____

Address _____
             Street   City   State   Zip Code

Salary _____ Job Title _____ Date Employed _____

Spouse's Employer _____ Phone (   ) _____

Address _____
             Street   City   State   Zip Code

Salary _____ Job Title _____ Date Employed _____

Other Income _____

Automobile: Year _____ Make _____ License _____

                Year _____ Make _____ License _____

Do You Have Any Pets? _____ How Many? _____

RENT	
SECURITY	
CLEAN	
KEY	
PETS	
OTHER	
TOTAL CHARGE	
TOTAL LESS DEPOSIT	
FN/UNF	
REFRIG.	

LAST THREE PLACES OF RESIDENCE

Name of
Apt. Bldg.   Manager's   Dates
and Manager   Address   Phone No.   From/To

1. _____

2. _____

3. _____

CREDIT REFERENCES

    Name   Address   Acct. No.   Payments

                                              Checking

BANK _____ BRANCH _____ Acct. No. _____

                                              Savings

BANK _____ BRANCH _____ Acct. No. _____

In consideration of the sum of $ _____ Management agrees to reserve Apartment No. _____ for Applicant until _____. Should Applicant rent said apartment said sum shall be applied to the first month's rent. If this application is not accepted by Managment within seven (7) days from the date of this application, said amount shall be refunded. Should this application be accepted and Applicant fail to rent said apartment, the amount received hereunder shall be retained by Management in consideration for removing said apartment unit from the market for said period. In the event the premises are not ready for occupancy by said date, Management shall refund the money paid by Applicant hereunder or Applicant shall have the option of extending the reservation until such time as the premises are ready for occupancy.

Applicant agrees that Management shall not be liable for any delay in the date said apartment unit is ready for occupancy.

ACCEPTED BY MANAGEMENT:

BY _____   APPLICANT_____

DATE _____   APPLICANT_____

DEPOSIT RECEIPT

Subject to approval by the undersigned operator of the application to rent Apartment No. _____, located at

_____ St., _____, Calif.,

and to vacation thereof by the present occupants, the undersigned hereby accepts from Applicant the sum of $_____,

as a deposit on the rental of said premises for occupancy by_____adults and_____children only beginning _____,

19___, at the rental of $_____per month, payable monthly in advance on the_____day of each month. In event of such approval and vacation, said sum shall be applied on the first month's rent, but if the balance thereof is not paid when due, all rights of Applicant hereunder shall terminate, and the sum so deposited shall be retained by the undersigned operator as liquidated damages. Such tenancy shall be subject to all the covenants contained in the rent or lease agreement hereto attached, which Applicant agrees to execute on demand. If such application is rejected, or if possession of said premises cannot be delivered to Applicant on the date specified, the sum so deposited shall be returned to Applicant and Applicant shall not acquire any right in or to said premises by reason hereof.

Dated_____, 19___ .   _____

Accepted and Agreed to:

_____   _____
                                             Operator/Agent

_____
          Applicant

Telephone Log for Response to Rental Ad

Company Name _____ Apartment _____

Apt. Number _____ Address _____

_____ Apartments

Copy:

Cost $ _____ Lines _____

Media: _____ Date Ad Started _____ Period of Time _____

Calls/	Name	/Phone Number/	Appointment/	single couple	/Type of Work

1. _____
   Comment: _____

2. _____
   Comment: _____

3. _____
   Comment: _____

4. _____
   Comment: _____

5. _____
   Comment: _____

6. _____
   Comment: _____

7. _____
   Comment: _____

8. _____
   Comment: _____

9. _____
   Comment: _____

10. _____
    Comment: _____

APARTMENT LEASE

THIS LEASE, is made this_____day of_____BY AND

BETWEEN_____, herein

called "LESSOR" and_____, herein
called "LESSEE."

For and in consideration of the prompt payment of the rents by LESSEE and the exact performance of the covenants hereinafter set forth by LESSEE, LESSOR does hereby lease to LESSEE, and LESSEE hereby hires from LESSOR, that certain apartment No._____, together with

parking area No._____, situated at_____, in the

city of_____, California, for the term of_____, commencing on the_____day

of_____, 19____, and ending on the_____day of_____, 19____, at the total

rent of_____Dollars ($_____),

payable at_____, California, in installments of_____Dollars

($_____), each due and payable in advance on the_____day of each and every month during said term, which rent LESSEE

agrees to pay promptly in the manner set forth herein. LESSOR hereby acknowledges receipt from LESSEE of the sum of_____

_____Dollars ($_____) in payment of the first installment of rent.

This lease is made by LESSOR and is accepted by LESSEE upon the following conditions, and it is agreed that each of the terms hereinafter specified shall be conditions as well as covenants. The breach, default, failure or violation of any one or more thereof shall, without limitation of his other rights, entitle LESSOR, after the giving of proper notice, to terminate this lease, re-enter and take over possession forthwith.

1. As a further consideration for the execution of this lease by LESSOR, and in addition to the rent agreed to be paid herein, LESSEE agrees to pay LESSOR the sum of $_____as a Security Deposit upon the execution of this lease, the receipt of which is hereby acknowledged. Upon termination of the tenancy, LESSOR may use, apply or retain such portion of the Security Deposit according to law. Any remaining portion of the Security Deposit will be returned to LESSEE upon the termination of his tenancy and after the surrender of possession of the leased premises.

2. LESSEE shall pay LESSOR the rent hereinabove provided at any place specified by LESSOR and, in addition thereto, shall pay when due all utility charges accruing or payable in connection with the use of said leased premises during said tenancy, except LESSOR shall pay all charges for water.

3. LESSEE has examined and knows the condition of said premises, and has received the same in good order and repair, and hereby agrees (a) to use said premises for living rooms and as a private residence only (b) not to sell or assign this lease nor sublet said premises, or any part thereof without the written consent of LESSOR first had and obtained, (c) to surrender possession of said premises at the expiration of this lease without further notice to quit, in as good condition as reasonable and careful use will permit, (d) that said premises will be occupied by no more than the following named adults

_____

and the following named children_____
either as guest, lodger, roomer, boarder, licensee, or any other status, without, in each instance first obtaining the written consent of LESSOR, and (e) to keep said premises in good condition and repair at his own expense.

4. LESSOR shall not be liable to LESSEE nor his invitees, except as provided for by law, for any loss or injury to persons or property caused by or resulting from the act or neglect of LESSEE, other tenants, or other persons upon the demised premises.

5. The occurrence of any one or more of the following events shall constitute a default and breach of this lease by LESSEE: (a) vacating or abandonment of the premises, (b) the failure by LESSEE to make any payment of rent or any other payment required to be made by LESSEE hereunder as and when due, (c) the failure by LESSEE to observe or perform any of the covenants, conditions or provisions of this lease to be observed or performed by LESSEE.

6. Upon termination of this lease in any manner. LESSOR may, after giving proper notice, re-enter the leased premises in the manner allowed by law and, to the extend allowed by law, remove any and all persons and property therefrom, and repossess and enjoy said premises again as of his first and former state. All remedies of LESSOR under this lease are cumulative and are given without impairing any other rights or remedies of LESSOR as provided by law.

7. In the event of any default or breach by LESSEE, LESSOR may at any time thereafter, after first giving notice as required by law, and without limiting LESSOR in the exercise of any right or remedy which LESSOR may have by reason of such default or breach: (a) terminate LESSEE's right to possession of the leased premises by any lawful means in which case this lease shall terminate and LESSEE shall immediately surrender possession of the leased premises to LESSOR. In such event, LESSOR shall be entitled to recover from LESSEE all amounts set forth in Section 1951.2 of the California Civil Code as well as the worth at the time of the award by the Court having jurisdiction thereof of the amount by which the unpaid rent for the balance of the term after the time of such award exceeds the amount of such rental loss for the same period that LESSEE proves could be reasonably avoided. The prevailing party shall be entitled to recover all damages, including, but not limited to, the cost of recovering possession of the premises, expenses of reletting, and reasonable attorney's fees; (b) maintain LESSEE's right to possession, in which case this lease shall continue in effect whether or not LESSEE shall have abandoned the leased premises. In such event, LESSOR shall be entitled to enforce all LESSOR's rights and remedies under this lease, including the right to recover the rent as it becomes due hereunder. LESSOR agrees not to unreasonably withhold consent should LESSEE desire to sublet the leased premises, assign his interest in the lease, or both; and (c) in addition, to pursue any other right or remedy now or hereafter available to LESSOR under the laws or judicial decisions of the State of California.

8. If, upon failure of LESSEE to pay the rent as aforesaid, or to comply with any of the other covenants, conditions, rules and regulations of this lease, action shall be brought or notice served on account thereof to enforce the payment of rent herein, or to recover possession of the premises, or to enforce any provision of this lease, or to obtain damages, the prevailing party shall be entitled to recover reasonable costs and expenses in said action or for said notice, including attorney's fees, whether or not any such action proceeds to judgment.

9. LESSOR shall have the right by himself or agent or with others, to enter the premises in the manner provided by California Civil Code Section 1954.

10. LESSEE shall pay (a) for any expense, damage or repair occasioned by the stopping of waste pipes or overflow from bathtubs, closets, wash basins or sinks which are caused by LESSEE and (b) for damage to window panes, window shades, curtain rods, wallpaper or any other damage to the interior of the leased premises which are caused by LESSEE and LESSEE shall commit and suffer no waste to be committed therein and no change or alterations of the premises shall be made or partitions erected nor wall papered without the consent in writing of the LESSOR first had and obtained.

11. LESSOR shall not be liable, except as provided for by law, for any damage occasioned by failure to keep the premises in repair, for any damage done or occasioned by or from plumbing, gas, water, steam or other pipes or sewerage, or the bursting, leaking or running of any pipe, tank, washstand, water closet or waste pipe, in, above, upon or about said building or premises, or for damage occasioned by water, snow or ice being upon or coming through the roof, skylight, trapdoor or or otherwise, or for any damage arising from the acts or neglects of co-tenants, or other occupants of the same building, or any owners or occupants of adjacent or contiguous property.

12. LESSEE agrees that said premises shall be used only for the purpose set forth above, and for no other purpose, and none of the rooms shall be offered for lease by placing notices on any door, window or wall of the building, nor by advertising the same directly or indirectly in any newspaper, or otherwise, save and except with the written consent of the LESSOR first had and obtained. There shall be no lounging, sitting upon, or unnecessary tarrying in or upon the front steps, the sidewalks, railings, stairways, halls, landings or other public places of the building by LESSEE, members of his family, or other persons connected with the occupancy of the leased premises, and no provisions, milk, marketing, groceries or like merchandise shall be delivered into the premises through the front entrance of said building.

13. If said premises shall be wrecked or destroyed by fire or the elements or by an Act of God so as to render them unfit for occupancy, or if the furnishings provided by LESSOR be so damaged or destroyed as to render them unfit for use, and are not speedily repaired or replaced, and should the damage be so extensive as to render the premises untenantable, provided said damage or destruction was not caused by LESSEE, this lease may be thereupon terminated. In such event LESSOR shall not be liable for any damage on account of such destruction, nor shall the LESSOR be liable for damage occasioned by the termination of the lease, provided that such destruction or wreckage was not caused by LESSOR.

14. If LESSEE shall hold over after the expiration of the term of this lease with the consent of LESSOR, express or implied, such tenancy shall be from month to month only, and shall not be a renewal hereof, and LESSEE agrees to pay rent and all other charges as hereinabove provided and also to comply with all the terms and covenants of this lease for the time LESSEE holds over.

15. The within lease constitutes the entire agreement between the parties and recites the entire consideration given and accepted by the parties, and no representations not expressed herein or endorsed hereon have been made by either party or their agents.

16. Each and all of the provisions hereof shall be binding upon and inure to the benefit of the heirs, executors, administrators, successors or assigns of LESSOR, and the heirs, executors and administarators of LESSEE, and upon the assigns of LESSEE, if any assignment has been made with the consent in writing of LESSOR.

17. Waiver by LESSOR of any breach of any term or conditions of this lease, shall not constitute a waiver of subsequent breaches. Time is expressly made of the essence in connection with the payment of the rent called for herein and the performance of any of the terms and conditions of this lease by LESSEE.

18. The following items of furnishings are included herein:

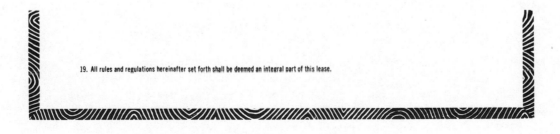

19. All rules and regulations hereinafter set forth shall be deemed an integral part of this lease.

RULES AND REGULATIONS GOVERNING TENANCY IN THE APARTMENT BUILDING

1. Dogs, cats, parrots and other birds or dumb animals are not permitted on or in the premises without the prior written approval of LESSOR.

2. Children are not to play or be unnecessarily in the halls, entrances or on stairways.

3. In consideration of others, tenants or their guests are not to make any disturbing noise at any time before 9:00 A.M. or after 10:30 P.M. Singing, playing on a musical instrument or loud operation of a television set or radio is not permitted, if disturbing to other tenants.

4. No loud talking, unnecessary noises or boisterous conduct is permitted at any time.

5. Television antennae may not be placed on the roof without the written consent of LESSOR and must be installed and removed only by a licensed television installer. Upon removal of television antenna, tenant will be held liable for any damage to the roof.

6. No sign, advertisement, notice, door-plate or other similar device shall be inscribed, painted, engraved or affixed to any part of the outside or inside of said premises.

7. Nails, tacks, brads, or screws shall not be driven into the woodwork, walls or floors of said premises, nor shall there be any boring or marring of the woodwork or plastering, without the prior written consent of LESSOR.

8. The use of gasoline and/or other similar combustibles for cleaning or for other purposes is strictly prohibited. LESSEE shall so use the premises so as not to cause any increase in the insurance rates.

9. Garbage cans, milk bottles, brooms, mops, and similar articles must be kept inside and out of view. Hang nothing on fences or hedges.

10. Use separate container for combustible rubbish and separate container for tin cans. Upon inquiry, the management will be glad to inform you of collection days.

11. The work of the custodian, janitor, or employee shall not be interfered with by tenants. The heating apparatus, heat controlling apparatus, elevators, or any portion of the building shall not be tampered with.

12. No right of storage is given by the lease. Upon request a limited amount of storage space may be provided by the LESSOR at LESSEE's risk.

13. LESSEE shall pay for broken, damaged or missing articles furnished by LESSOR and for damages caused by them, their guests or family to the building, its fixtures, furniture or equipment.

14. LESSOR will not be responsible for loss of property of LESSEE, their guests, or families through theft or otherwise.

15. Any drape or curtain rod bracket or track or any blind or venetian blind, or any other article, affixed by LESSEE to the premises shall become part of the realty of LESSOR and shall not be removed by LESSEE without the prior written consent of LESSOR.

RULES AND REGULATIONS GOVERNING USE OF APARTMENT SWIMMING POOL

1. Children will not be permitted to use the pool.

2. Persons not able to swim well, shall use the shallow end only and notice is hereby given that there is a limited shallow area which drops off abruptly.

3. Care shall be exercised in the use of the pool ladders.

4. No running around the pool or playing upon the ladders or sides thereof is allowed.

5. There shall be no diving from balconies or other elevated places.

6. The pool is to be used only between the hours of 8:00 A.M. and 9:00 P.M. on weekdays, and 10:00 A.M. to 9:00 P.M. on Sundays.

7. No intoxicated person, or persons having an infectious disease, shall use the pool.

8. There shall be no loud or boisterous conduct, or "horseplay" in and about the pool.

9. There shall be no throwing of foreign matter or debris into the pool, and all tables, chairs and other furniture and equipment used about the pool shall be left clean and free of debris.

10. All persons swim in, and use, the pool at their own risk.

11. The management reserves the right to exclude any and all undesirable, non-conforming, and ineligible persons from the use of the pool.

12. No person shall remove any of the posts or unlink any of the chains or guard rails surrounding the pool.

13. The pool is reserved for the exclusive use by tenants of LESSOR and shall not be used by guests of tenants without express prior permission from the management.

14. Bobby pins and hairpins shall be removed from hair and suntan oils shall be removed from body before using pool. Women must wear bathing caps.

15. Bathers shall bathe or shower thoroughly before using pool.

16. The pool may not be used while it is being serviced or is in the process of repair.

IN WITNESS WHEREOF the parties hereto have executed this lease the day and year first above written.

_____
Lessor

_____
Address

_____
Lessee

_____
Lessee

_____
Address

Apartment Inspection Sheet

Company Name _____ Apartment Name _____

Apt. Number _____ Address _____

Date: _____

LIVING ROOM

Carpet _____

Drapes _____

Fireplace _____

Guest Closet _____

Entry Floor _____

Entry Light _____

Front Door _____

Front Door Light _____

Condition of Walls _____

Color of Walls _____

Powder Room _____

Stairway and Landing _____

FAMILY ROOM

Carpet _____

Drapes _____

Patio Door _____

Patio Screen _____

KITCHEN

Counter Tops _____

Cabinets _____

Floor _____

Sink _____

Kitchen Window _____

Dishwasher _____

Disposal _____

STOVE

Top Oven _____

Lower Oven _____

Broiler _____

Range _____

Pantry _____

Washer _____

Dryer _____

Kitchen Lights _____

MASTER BEDROOM

Carpet _____

Drapes _____

Wash Basin _____

Medicine Cabinet _____

Mirror _____

Vanity Cabinet _____

Vanity Top _____

Shower _____

Comode _____

Bath Door _____

Triple Closet Doors _____

Window Screens _____

HALL

Carpet _____

Linen Cabinets _____

BATHROOM _____

Bath tub _____

Commode _____

Mirror _____

Vanity Top _____

Vanity Cabinet _____

Medicine Cabinet _____

Light Fixtures _____

Fan _____

SOUTH BEDROOM

Carpet _____

Drapes _____

Window Screens _____

Closet Doors _____

NORTH BEDROOM

Carpet _____

Drapes _____

Window Screens _____

Closet Doors _____

Notice To Change Terms of Tenancy

To: _____

_____ ,tenants in possession.

     YOU AND EACH OF you are hereby notified that effective and commencing _____ , or thirty (30) days after service of this notice upon you, whichever is the *later* in time, the terms of your month to month tenancy of the premises you now occupy will be changed as follows:

     You are required to deposit with the owner no later than the effective date of this notice the sum of _____ Dollars ($ _____) as and for a *security deposit.* Said deposit will *not* be considered a "last months rent" deposit.

     If you contend that you have made a security deposit, please confirm this fact with the owner.

     Said premises concerned are located at:

Apartment _____ , North Weatherly Drive, Los Angeles, California.

By: _____

Change of Terms

Company Name _____   Apartment Name_____

                                           Apt. Number _____

To: _____

You and each of you will please take notice that the terms of the agreement under which you hold possession of the premises known as _____

_____

California, will be and the same hereby are changed effective the _____ day of _____ , 19_____ , as follows: From and after said date the rent for said premises will be $_____ per month, payable in advance on the day of each calendar month.

Dated this _____ Day of_____ 19 ____ , _____ ,

                                                         City

_____ .

     State

The other terms of said tenancy will remain as before.

SERVED: _____ 19_____

OWNER/OPERATOR

Log of Warnings and Complaints

Apartment Name _____ Address _____

NOTICE TO PAY RENT OR QUIT   CHANGE OF TERMS   NOTICE TO QUIT _____

Tenant: _____ Apartment Number: _____

Name of Apartment Building _____

Street Address: _____

City: _____ State _____ Zip _____

Tenant's Home Phone: _____ Office Phone _____ Ext. _____

DATE	TIME	

AGENT——MANAGER

Expense Distribution
(Short Form)

For the Period _____ 19 ___ to ___ 19 ___   Apartments

Date	Check No.	IN ACCOUNT WITH	Guest Advances	Pay Roll	Utilities	MISCELLANEOUS		Maintenance Repairs	Repairs & Replacements	Fixed Charges	TOTALS
						Laundry	Supplies				
TOTALS											

TIME SHEET
RECORD OF HOURS WORKED

EMPLOYEE _____

ADDRESS _____

CITY _____ CITY OF _____

ADDRESS OF EMPLOYMENT _____

DATE		DETAIL OF TIME SPENT ON APARTMENT BUSINESS (Show fractions, thus: 8:30-9:30, 2:15-5:45)	TOTAL HOURS
MO.	DAY		

Total hours worked during period - - - - - - - - - - - - - - -

NOTE: Explain reason for any hours worked over and above those agreed upon in contract; - - - - - - - - - -

This will certify the above time record is complete and accurate.

Signed _____
                    Employee

Employee NOT to use space below this line

Salary or wages for period (including allowance for use of apartment) - - - - - - - - - - - - - $ _____

Deductions: Federal Old Age Insurance - - $ _____
                Unemployment Insurance - - $ _____
                Other (_____) - - $ _____

NET Salary Paid - - - - - - - - - - $ _____

Refunds and Forfeiture of Deposits

PROJECT NAME _____ NUMBER _____

ADDRESS _____ CITY _____ STATE _____ ZIP _____

TENANT NAME _____ BLDG. NO. _____ UNIT NO. _____ UNIT CODE _____

ADDRESS _____ CITY _____ STATE _____ ZIP _____

FORWARDING ADDRESS _____

CITY _____ STATE _____ ZIP _____

CURRENT REFUNDABLE DEPOSITS

SECURITY............ $ _____

KEY.................. $ _____

.... $ _____

.... $ _____

.... $ _____

TOTAL REFUNDABLE DEPOSITS . . . $ _____

LESS: CHARGES OR FORFEITURES (IF ANY)

.... $ _____

.... $ _____

.... $ _____

.... $ _____

TOTAL CHARGES OR DEDUCTIONS . . . $ _____

AMOUNT TO BE REFUNDED TO TENANT . . . $ _____

DATE OF REFUND: _____ CHECK NO. _____ VERIFIED BY _____

X _____ X _____
MANAGER'S SIGNATURE

THIRTY DAY NOTICE TO QUIT

_____

To

Tenant   in Possession.

TAKE NOTICE, that you are hereby required to quit, and deliver up to the undersigned the possession of the premises now held and occupied by you, being the premises known as

at the expiration of the rental period ending on_____, 19____.

This Notice to Quit specifically terminates any oral/written agreement you may have with respect to the said premises at the date specified above.

THIS IS INTENDED as a thirty (30) day notice to quit, for the purpose of terminating your tenancy aforesaid.

DATED this _____ day of _____, 19____.

_____
Landlord.

_____

_____

THIRTY DAY NOTICE TO QUIT – Wolcotts Form 1004. Rev. 12-79   **WOLCOTTS INC., 1979**

NOTICE TO PAY RENT OR QUIT

(C. C. P., Sec. 1161)

TO _____

_____

_____

Tenant—in Possession

Within THREE DAYS, after the service on you of this notice, you are hereby required to PAY THE RENT of the premises hereinafter

described, of which you now hold possession, amounting to the sum of _____

_____ Dollars ($_____)

at the rental rate of _____ Dollars ($_____)

per month (or week), being the _____ rent due from the _____ day of

_____, 19____, to the _____ day of _____, 19____,

or you are hereby required to DELIVER UP POSSESSION of the hereinafter described premises, within THREE DAYS after service on you

of this notice, to the undersigned, or _____ agent, who is

authorized to receive the same or the undersigned will institute legal proceedings against you to recover possession of said premises

with ALL RENTS DUE and DAMAGES. The undersigned, as a landlord, declares and gives notice that, if the said rent is not paid within

three days after service on you of this notice, I do hereby elect to declare a forfeiture of the lease and agreement under which you occupy

the hereinbelow-described property:

The premises herein referred to are situated in the _____ of

_____ County of _____

STATE OF CALIFORNIA, designated by the number and street as _____

_____ and more particularly

described as follows: _____

_____

_____

_____

_____

Dated this _____ day of _____, 19____.

_____

_____

Penal Code Section No. 594 reads: "Any person or persons who wilfully or maliciously destroys or damages any Real or Personal Property
not their own will be punished by Fine or Imprisonment or both."

NOTICE TO PAY RENT OR QUIT
WOLCOTTS FORM 1006—REV. 12-79

This standard form covers most usual problems in the field indicated. Before you sign, read it, fill in all blanks,
and make changes proper to your transaction. Consult a lawyer if you doubt the form's fitness for your purpose.

© 1979 WOLCOTTS, INC.

Maintenance Record

Tenant _____ Apartment Number _____

Took Possession: _____ Vacated _____

DATE	COST	PLUMBER	PAINTER	ELECTRICIAN	CARPENTER	CARPET	DRAPES	FIXTURES

REMINDER
YOUR RENT IS PAST DUE

To: _____

This is a reminder that your rent was due on

_____ 19 ___, in the amount of $ _____

We will appreciate your prompt payment.

Thank you!

_____

By: _____

Record Keeping Form

Company Name

Apartment Name

Address

TENANT	ADDRESS APT.	RENT MONTH	PAID FROM	PAID TO	CHANGE TERMS	AMOUNT	CHANGE TERMS	AMOUNT	CHANGE TERMS	AMOUNT	CHANGE TERMS	AMOUNT
	# 1											
	# 2											
	# 3											
	# 4											
	# 5											
	# 6											
	# 7											
	# 8											
	# 9											
	#10											
	#11											
	#12											
	#13											
	#14											
	#15											
	#16											

Rent Receipt

Company Name

Apartment Name

Address

APARTMENT NUMBER: DATE: 19   RECEIPT NUMBER:

RECEIVED FROM:

                                                                                                    DOLLARS

FOR RENT AT

FROM: TO   19

$

KEY DEPOSIT: $

CLEANING FEE: $ BY:

SECURITY DEPOSIT: $ MANAGER:

MONTHLY OPERATIONS REPORT

FOR MONTH OF_____DATE_____19___

RENTS RECEIVED					VACANT	RENT PAST DUE			CASH REPORT		
NAME	APT. NO.	RENT	EXTRAS	TOTAL	APT. NO.	APT. NO.	AMOUNT		CASH ON HAND....		
									CASH RECEIVED....		
									TOTAL.....		
									LESS PETTY CASH PAID OUT		
									ITEM	AMOUNT	
									TOTAL CASH ACCOUNTED FOR		
									DEDUCT CASH PAID OUT		
TOTAL									CASH TURNED IN		

REMARKS AND REQUISITIONS FOR SUPPLIES_____

_____

_____

_____

SIGNED_____

chapter ten

Disposing of Your Property – Profitably

When is the right time to sell? When is the right time to buy? The right time to buy is when you have the money. But the right time to sell is a different story if you have been paying attention to what you are doing; that is, you have checked out comparable properties every week (or at least twice a month) and have checked the neighborhood, sales, and rents. If the rents have been going up, you are in good shape. The neighborhood is improving.

Let's assume, however, that the opposite is happening and you have not been paying attention. All of a sudden rents start going down. Different people are moving into the neighborhood, low salaried, and you find your apartments are overpriced for them.

Five years have passed and it is time for you to get rid of this turkey. Suddenly you find out all the things that you should have known, and had you known you would have sold out two years before. That is why I say hold property from three to five years; a lot can happen in three years, but it is usually a gradual process. Over a period of five years, drastic changes can and do take place.

Selling and Brokers

You wear two hats. When you are buying, it is one thing, and when you are selling, it is another. You should be two different personalities.

You have gone out into the field and checked comparables. You know what your property is worth. You don't have to ask an appraiser; you know.

Anybody who has been in this business for any length of time, investor or realtor, does not regret spending money in order to sell property properly and quickly. When I am ready to sell, I use the services of another realtor even though I am one myself. In that way I get more exposure. But more importantly, I do not have to have a face-to-face confrontation with a potential buyer.

For example, you have a piece of property that you have improved. You see many things that the buyer doesn't notice. On the other hand, the buyer sees things in your project that you don't. Now imagine that this person approaches you with a figure of $200,000, when you are thinking one-half million. You say "forget it," because even if you would reconsider, you would not want to lose face. You may sell it at that price, but not to that buyer.

When you begin negotiating with the broker or realtor, you will find that he or she wants an exclusive. The broker will want 120 days; but give 90 days. If the broker can't turn it in 90 days, you have the wrong person. So you say: "If you want an exclusive on this, you can only have it for so many days and I will cut back your commission. I will only offer so much." Or, you might say: "I will also have the right to sell. If I sell it to someone you haven't shown it to, then you don't get a percentage. It will be an open listing." You can negotiate in any way you so choose. You want to stand hard and fast, but be realistic about price.

Don't fall in love with your building. You have worked hard and improved it greatly, but it is still just a building to someone else. If you get too protective of your property you will overprice.

Of course, most real estate people are guilty of encouraging astronomical figures. They want your listing, so they will claim that they can get you, say, $350,000 for your project—which in reality is not worth over $220,000. After they have the exclusive and have tried to sell it for 120 days, they will come to you and say that the property is not moving. "I've had hundreds of people call, but it is just overpriced. We are going to have to lower the price." They will try to lower the boom on you. This is what you don't want. So go into it realistically; then you won't have a problem.

Commissions, Disclaimers, Disclosures

Remember that there is no such thing as a set commission of 5 or 6 percent. You can offer 3 percent. You can negotiate perhaps 2 percent or 1 ½ percent depending on how big the project is and how much money is involved. The more money involved, the more negotiable the terms.

Normally, a realtor or broker will, on the listing, state: "This information we deem to be accurate, but we are not responsible," and so on. Even in cases where I have asked the square footage of something, they just did not want to give me the figure, because there have been lawsuits where square footage was incorrect. The lawsuits were successful and the realtor or broker was held liable. But the one thing you must do, by all means, is the very thing that you would want if you were buying. That is, be very accurate and truthful about what you have and what you are trying to sell. First of all, it is in your best interests to be that way because actually you are supposed to make disclosures.

In one of my buildings we had an underpinning problem due to some cracked foundations. This was brought to the attention of the buyer. The buyer was told that we had had a lawsuit, we won the suit, the problem had been inspected, and we had the finished report. We included everything. We showed that the building was approved by the county engineer. We showed the reports of the engineers, the soil report, everything. We did so because if the buyer found out that the building had an underpinning job and we had not told him, we could be sued for misrepresentation. So you must make a disclosure. When you do that, you are on safe ground. And you should expect that of other people when you go to buy. Unfortunately, that is not always the case.

Making the Prospectus

The first thing to do is to take last year's bills and photocopy them—in color. They then look like the bills themselves. On the front page put what you have to sell. Describe the property in detail. Follow that with a disclaimer (a sample appears at the close of the final chapter).

Show all the gross revenue, where it originates, and all of the expenses. Present an analysis that shows the value of the property (realistically) for a particular bracket of taxes, 50 percent, 40 percent, or whatever. Bind it attractively. It should look very professional.

You will also have to include photographs. When you photograph or have photographed the property, concentrate on noticeable improvements. Stress attractive features and overall quality.

Keep It in Escrow

The difference between going into escrow and going out is that when you are going in, you want to be able to fall out. But when you are selling out, you want out—period. When you sell, make sure there is as little added literature to the purchase agreement as possible.

If a piece of property goes back onto market because it fell out of escrow, it will automatically lose value, not in a true sense, but because real estate people will think that there must be a problem with that property. So, once you're in there, try to stay in.

Many things can cause it to fall out. The agreement could be written improperly. Information was not disclosed. There were numerous escape clauses.

As a buyer and seller, you wear different hats. When you buy, you want to put as much in for your protection as possible. However, when you sell, you want to keep as much out as possible.

Auctions

Another way to sell is at auction. There are many occasions where people have paid incredible prices. They can get carried away. But auctions have many variables, such as the time of year that you sell. A nice spring day is a lot better to auction a piece of property in Chicago or anywhere in the

Midwest than it would be in November or December. When it is cold and icy, who wants to think about buying?

As stated earlier, selling property by public auction is becoming more popular each year. Statistics prove that in many cases the prices received for properties sold at public and private auctions are higher than nonauction sales. Some auctions publish lavish brochures that are mailed to a select clientele. Some merely run ads in public papers. The practice of auctioneering real estate property differs from state to state. In Tennessee, for example, all auctioneers must be real estate brokers and have an auctioneer's license. There is no special license required by the state of California other than a real estate license.

Since there are many ways in which the purchaser at an auction signifies to the auctioneer that he or she is "upping" the price or buying at the last price, if you attend an auction to buy or just out of curiosity, be aware of your "body English"; it is possible for you to purchase something you "can't eat"!

In the 1930s, my brother and I owned and operated a horse and mule barn. We put in a false front, cleaned and painted the place, and installed a new auction ring shaped in a three-quarter circle. The bleachers were in tiers as in a sports stadium. Everyone was in a position to see the animals, but most importantly the auctioneer could easily see the buyers.

We had had "commission men" traveling throughout the country buying horses and mules. All animals had a large number applied to their left shoulder. Our barn was overflowing with livestock. My brother was to stay in the bleachers, and my job was to see that the animals went out in sequence. The auctioneer was instructed to look at my brother before the final gravel; if the price wasn't right, he was to bid them in.

At the end of the day we had sold every head of livestock. Then I was astounded to find that we had bought every head ourselves! It had slipped my mind that when my brother became nervous or excited, he would twitch his head to the left and nod up and down. The auctioneer took my brother's action to mean that he wanted to buy it in. The more animals that were sold, the more nervous he became, and he nodded his head more often, thereby giving no one a chance to buy anything. Needless to say, never again was he allowed in the ring where the auctioneer could see him!

Refinancing

There will be a time when you think that instead of selling you would like to refinance. Your loan will be, at that point, way down. If you refinance, you can take that money and simply put it into your pocket, perhaps with no income taxes. This would be, of course, the time to check with your tax attorney or C.P.A.

Trading on Equity

Refinancing is expensive. A bank will ask, perhaps, 1½ points and $200. If you are currently paying 10 percent and they want to charge you 11¾ percent, you have a 1¾ percent increase. This will result in an annual percentage rate much higher than you could have imagined.

There is a better way—trading on your equity. Let's assume your equity is $140,000. You find a project that requires $100,000 down. Make the owner this offer: "I have a building worth X dollars and the amount I owe is nominal. I will give you a note for $100,000 secured by my equity. I will pay you whatever percent you wish. The note will serve as my down payment."

If the owner agrees, you insert into the purchase agreement that sale depends on getting a specified loan amount at a specific rate. You are still in control of your mortgage payments.

But don't get too excited over the possibilities of equity trading. Find a building where that $140,000 equity will fit, that is, a $500,000 building, since a 70 percent loan is normal. Then you need very little cash, just $10,000 in this example. Of course, you now have more mortgage payments, but you still have your original property and it is increasing in value.

The Market

During the hot market, no one really had to know much about the business. Any idiot could go out and buy at the asking price and sell for a profit. Inexperienced investors bought, repainted, and sold. Dynamic residential areas developed fantastic prices for homes. Eager speculators slept out all night just to get a lottery number, which, if they were lucky enough to win, would entitle them to buy a $200,000 house.

Those days are over, at least temporarily. The residential income property owners are increasingly locked into a negative cash flow. They paid a greatly inflated price more than the rents could bear, expecting that the next investor/speculator would make up the deficit and pay them a handsome profit. Many foreclosed. More are going thousands of dollars out-of-pocket every month just to keep a project afloat.

We have come to a situation where people are saying that the bubble is going to burst. But there is no bubble to burst. Inflation will keep climbing; prices will keep going up, but at a slower rate. They certainly won't go down, particularly through any sun belt area. It was natural for Southern California to boom as it did, but other areas will do so in turn.

In California, particularly the south, there is a very low vacancy factor, between 0 to 2 percent. As long as that is in effect and as long as inflation continues, the less places there are for people to rent, so the higher the rents. Some cities have panicked and enacted rent control, which, in turn, throws the burden on everybody since they lose a lot of their tax base. Californians are investing millions of dollars out of state, particularly in Texas and Oklahoma, because of rent control. Due to rent control, apartment owners have been converting to condominiums in order to sell them. Where they have been stopped from converting to condominiums, they have put in co-ops.

Around Rent Control | As it now stands under Los Angeles rent control, few apartments are being sold. The time to buy is when the situation gets desperate. Forget upgrading because you cannot afford it. At the end of the first year, raise rents 7 ½ percent. Do the same in the following two years until you have about a 22.5 percent increase in rent, and you haven't done anything.

In the meantime the value of the property will have gone up about 36 percent. So you have increased the rents 22.5 percent. Every dollar increase you gross means $10 more in sales value. So, assuming that $12,300 was your original gross, 22.5 percent times 12,300 would be $2,767.50. That would mean that the building would be worth 10 times that $2,767.50, which would be a $27,675 increase just due to the gross income. That is not even counting what has happened to the value of the property because of inflation and appreciation.

The effect of rent control is to destroy exactly what it was supposed to protect. In trying to protect renters, rental property is destroyed. This has happened all over the country where there is rent control—look at New York City. There are probably 500 cities in the nation that have some form of rent control, and everywhere it has been instituted, it has proved a disaster. Many people, instead, would be willing to pay a head tax so that people can have proper housing. I'm not ready to have someone tell me what to do with my property. We already have too much control.

Real estate is the last stronghold. If we lose here, we lose everything. No one will want to own anything anymore. We all got our start in the soil, and it would be sad to see our demise in our beginning.

The Necessity of Choosing a Good Broker

Most real estate investors depend heavily on the services provided by brokers. However, too often the selection is based on inadequate understanding of the investor's needs and usually an incomplete, if any, investigation of the broker's qualifications. You can improve your ability to identify the broker most suitable to your needs if you keep in mind some basic points.

In real estate as in other professions, there are many services provided by specialists who respond to different needs with varying degrees of success. Quite often, such services become confused for they often overlap. You must be aware of and understand the distinctions so that you may properly select those services that would be most appropriate to your particular situation. Some real estate brokers offer free appraisals in order to secure an exclusive listing. However, you should be aware that the type of appraisal they would undertake would be of little use because a broker's opinion of property value cannot be considered a true appraisal unless the broker complies with the professional standards of either the American Institute of Appraisers, the Society of Real Estate Appraisers, or the American Association of Certified Appraisers and other recognized organizations.

Real Estate Consulting is another advisory service in which the practitioner works for a predetermined fee. The real estate consultant will provide an unbiased professional service on a broad range of real estate matters, such as financing, marketing, and other arrangements. To avoid any conflict of interest, the consulting services should not be tied into the use of a brokerage service that the consultant or counsler may also provide.

The primary business of the real estate broker is to facilitate real estate transactions between interested parties. As a client's agent, the broker acts as a source of information, a problem solver, and a negotiator to bring about the desired transaction as quicky and efficiently as possible. The fee for such services is negotiable as to what percentage of the transaction amount the broker will receive.

Some brokerage houses are competent and adequately staffed by the proper personnel to give relevant appraisals, counseling, and brokerage services, as well as property management, escrow services, and property insurance. Most brokers are more limited in the services they are qualified to perform, since approximately 90 percent of those in business devote their time to listing and selling single-family dwellings and/or condominiums. Be sure to understand what type of service you require; then make sure the firms you investigate can provide that need. Once you have determined that you need the services of a broker, you must focus on the specific type of brokerage service. *Sales brokerage* is the most common, since it facilitates the transfer of property ownership from seller to buyer. Some are highly specialized, such as farm and undeveloped land, industrial, commercial, and investment brokerage. Since each specialty requires its own expertise you must be certain that the broker you ultimately select is sufficiently knowledgeable in the types of property that most interest you.

Mortgage brokers assist borrowers in placing loans by helping with the loan application, obtaining an appraisal of the property's current value, and finding a willing lender at the most reasonable rate obtainable.

Lease brokers handle transactions between tenants and property owners. Brokers who are proficient in lease transactions can be particularly valuable in handling long-term leases due to their complexity.

Exchange brokers assist investors who, because of tax or other reasons, would be better served by exchanging one property for another rather than going through the regular sales-purchase routine. Exchange brokers are of the highest order and must be very knowledgeable since the exchange transactions can be most complicated, and if not handled properly the exchange can result in a capital gain tax situation rather than the intended tax-deferred exchange. Keep foremost in your mind that the quality of brokerage service you receive is important in determining your investment success. Under no circumstances should you make your selection for the services of a broker before adequately considering your needs and the broker's ability to perform.

Protecting Yourself from the Broker

Brokers are going to try many methods on you. To protect yourself, give absolutely no information—nothing about your finances and nothing about anything except that piece of property. You ask the questions. You want the broker on the defensive.

The one asking the questions is the one in control. When the broker starts, you become silent. When the broker gets exhausted, you start. The broker will be so relieved to hear you speak that he or she will tell you things he or she never intended to.

If the Deal Fails

My father told me years ago: "There's never a deal so good that another will come along as good or better." I have found this to be true. There never was a deal you could not live without. Don't get so eager to act that you do not check things out. And never let your false pride stand in your way. When something is wrong, drop it if you cannot correct it. Take the loss and forget it.

chapter eleven

From Personal Experience

After reading this book, you may definitely decide to use the suggestions that have been detailed on how to select and buy a piece of property. And suppose you do decide to invest in real estate? What then? You do all the necessary research and come up with a description, price, and terms of the property you want. You set forth the following:

1. You want the "thorn in a garden of roses," the property that needs cosmetic maintenance, but is structurally sound, in a good section of town, and in a good neighborhood.
2. You wish to make as low a down payment as possible, as little as 10 percent and no more than 15 percent.
3. You want some positive cash flow; however, if the building can carry itself on the terms you are purchasing, you would be reasonably satisfied.

So what happens? When you talk to a real estate agent and go into detail describing just what you want, you are immediately told that "the property you want doesn't exist." The agent tells you that you must be realistic and if you are really serious about investing in today's market, you will have to make a larger down payment and no way can you expect anything other than to accept a negative cash flow.

The agent speaks with authority and conviction and is able to back up his (or her) statements with dozens of examples. What do you do now? Do you get depressed and believe everything the agent told you? No! Keep your cool and remember that there are other people selling real estate who are willing and capable of seeking the type of property that meets your requirements. Now what do you do? First, be assured that the property you want is out there. Agents and other people have been giving me that same line for 30 years. The action plan you have is sound. What no one may have told you is that it is not easy to find properties that meet your price; it's not easy to meet your terms; it's not easy, period. However, it certainly is possible. I, among others, am proof of that.

The key is patience, perserverance, persistence, and hard work. The truly hardest part in today's investment climate is finding the property.

It is not unusual for a sophisticated, experienced professional investor to look at as many as 15 to 150 properties to find one that is truly worth investing in. The professionals have the edge over the novice in that they realize that the deals are rarely presented in a form in which they will eventually take a closing. You are not the only one to run into these obstacles; the professional investor encounters the same stubborn sellers, ridiculous asking prices, and people unwilling to take back mortgages. But here is the difference between the professional and the novice—the professional pays absolutely no attention to any of that.

The professional has found through taking his or her "lumps" in lessons of experience that properties can be bought for better terms, often at drastically better terms than those advertised. Furthermore, the pro knows that even those sellers who swear that under no circumstances will they take back a mortgage, in fact, often will and at surprisingly favorable terms. The difference is that the professional speaks from experience, authority, self-assurance, and strength in knowing that he or she has set the maximum commitment with such forcefulness that the seller begins to show weakness.

The key to the professional investor's success is continually searching for those properties that he or she wants. The pro never expects property to be offered on the terms he or she wants and needs, but rather makes an offer that fits his or her needs regardless of the asking price. The pro asks for the desired terms, ignoring the terms offered and knowing full well that all the seller can do is to say no.

An advantage that the professional investor has over the novice or the seller is that the pro has taken the time and effort to sharpen his or her negotiating skills. The pro has become extremely adept at realizing the true needs and desires of the seller and at structuring a deal to meet the objectives of both buyer and seller. The professional has obtained the skills of a good salesperson, which enables him or her to sell the seller on making the deal that the buyer needs. Keep in mind that you will often "change hats"; one time you will be the buyer, the next you may be the seller. The advice you get from most books or articles as to what property, price, and terms to get is generally correct; however, these books often fail to convey the persistece required to get through the difficulties of the search and the final negotiations that follow.

The rest of this chapter is a true personal story. It illustrates what one should do to buy and run residential income property successfully. It also illustrates how you can get into trouble even if you know what you are doing.

Locating the Building

In 1973 I was interested in finding a run-down apartment building in a good part of Los Angeles. After much searching, I thought I found one. To determine if the building was in a good area—and an area on the way up—I went to the Department of Permits and Safety, Los Angeles

County. I found out when the building was built and what portions had been built first. Then I discovered what was happening in terms of condos and apartment construction in the immediate area. I learned the construction cost of each new building and what their rents had to be.

I then checked the average rents in the area: studios; one, two, and three bedrooms; furnished and unfurnished. I visited all the apartment buildings in the neighborhood. As you recall, these actual rental figures are called contract rents in that they are what tenants are really paying. I was looking for a building with rents about 25 percent below the neighborhood market. I had found one.

Knowing what the new apartment building rents had to be gave me even more confidence. I could undercut them no matter what happened. I had an excellent deal. I looked further and noted the vacancy rate—extremely low.

I then proceeded to find the cap rate for that area. I compared that with the cash flow and expenses given me on the building. It indicated that 48 percent of the effective gross income was close to the truth, quite a bit higher than the proforma indicated.

Now I wanted 90 percent leverage. I knew I could get a first TD (trust deed) for 70 percent of the price, for 25 years at 8 percent interest. I intended to have the owner take back a second for the remaining 20 percent of the purchase price, or more, also at 8 percent.

Therefore, based on the rental income they had given me ($17,600/year), less 48 percent expenses ($8,467/year), less my probable mortgage payments ($11,000/year), I knew that I would have a negative cash flow of $1,867/per year.

We settled on a price of $132,500 with the provision that the owner would take back a second for $29,000 at 8 percent. Then I told him (through my broker) that I wanted the second amortized over 20 years with a 17-year due date. I wanted the 20-year amortization in order to cut my costs per month. I had the provision worded "$200 a month or more," meaning I could pay it off without penalty. He screamed—"That's ridiculous!"—but he eventually agreed.

During the time the deal was in escrow, federal rent control hit. All rents were frozen. Increases were limited to 2 1/2 percent annually. At that point the owner attempted to raise one apartment $10 a month. I exploded and wrote him a check for the $10. Before I had taken possession, he could have lost me a tenant. I was going to decide for myself what I was to do.

Throughout the two-month negotiation, I never met the owner or talked with him over the phone. Everything was handled by my broker.

Verifying Expenses

While my offer was being considered, I contacted each individual or company the owner used. I said: "I have just purchased the building. It is not closed yet, and I would like some information. Could you tell me please what your rate is, how much an hour? Also, would you tell me what were the expenditures on the plumbing (or whatever) last year? In your opinion, what would you suggest should be changed? What bad pipe is in there? What should be replaced?"

I called the electrician and asked: "How is the wiring in this building? Has it been recently rewired? Do you think it should be rewired? Is it up to code or what?"

I talked to the gardener, garbage disposal people, washing machine company—everyone. I asked about anticipated raises, verified expenses, and deferred maintenance. But I still wasn't sure.

There was, however, one person who would tell all—readily, gladly, no problems—and that was the manager.

At the first opportunity I talked to the manager. "I am contemplating buying this property," I said, "and I was wondering if you would care to continue as manager if I bought it?" She said, "Yes." And I said, "Well, that's marvelous."

I later called her back and mentioned some of the apartments that I had been through. "Are there any apartments renting below the rents I've been given?" I asked. "Let's go over the apartments, shall we? Apartment one—what is the actual rent and how long has it been occupied by that person?" I asked. "Were there any special concessions made to entice these people to rent, like free rent or anything? Did they have a security deposit, plus a first and last month's rent?" Now, of course, she did not want to lie because she knew I would fire her.

Remember, the owner will tell you as little as possible. But the manager who thinks he or she is going to work for you will tell you what you want to know.

With these facts, I went back to the owner and said, "I've discovered that there is $5,000 worth of plumbing to be done and that the building is in a certain state of disrepair; proper maintenance that should have been made wasn't." I explained that we were going to have to renegotiate a little bit first, and that I was not going to pay for all that plumbing.

Premanagement

We were now at the stage that we had negotiated the settlement and were actually opening escrow. We had 45 days before we took over the building. During that time I kept in touch with the manager by phone and in person, made an appointment, and took her to lunch again. I made her feel at home and reassured her that she was in a secure position and that she now knew that the building was sold.

Then I said, "I know you've been under terrible stress not knowing whether you have a job, not knowing what to tell me and what not to tell me. But now that I have taken over the building, or will in a few days, this is the time, I think, if we are going to have a rapport with each other, that you must tell me the things that you forgot to tell me before." With that I opened my briefcase and pulled out the pad on which I had written what she had already told me, saying, "Just to refresh your mind, these are the things that you have told me." I checked them off.

I had left myself contingencies so that I could get out of the deal while it was still in escrow. If you find something wrong, make sure you can kick it out.

If you do as I had done, you will have an accurate record of what your expenses actually are. Then, when you go to negotiate with a supplier, you really have an idea of what you should be paying. One immediate change I made was with the washer-dryer. I insisted on having one that had a set meter, one that was changeable, so that when you or they enter that machine for some reason, perhaps to empty it, you have the number of units written down. Then you can tell whether they are cheating.

Restoration

I had all the plumbing done first, which by the way, is the one thing that many owners will not do. They let the pipes go; they will do everything but replace the pipes. I also immediately put a time clock on the circulating pump so that I could cut down on the amount of time the motor runs. In this way you can cut down on the heat loss due to the water circulating all night. You cut down on the amount of gas that you are using and you immediately make a savings.

I called in the electrician and where possible replaced all the incandescent lights with a fluorescent circular type, which will last five years. They are good fixtures; 23 watts will burn like a 100-watt incandescent bulb. I cut back the electricity bill. Remember, when you buy fixtures they are a capital improvement. When you hire an electrician to put them up, that is labor and it is taken off your income tax that year.

Now, we had repainted the inside and outside of the building, and the plumbing and electricity were taken care of. Yet, we still had some things to do. We improved security by putting on door closers. We tried to get the people to cooperate by keeping the outside doors closed and locked.

The tenants' first reaction was negative because they had to go and let their guests in. They protested to keeping the doors shut. I then picked the four worst tenants and evicted them; notified them all at exactly the same time so they would leave at the same time. Then we could work on all four vacant apartments at once.

The other tenants stopped screaming about the locked doors. Having just seen four tenants evicted, they assumed the evictions were due to complaints about the door being locked.

We eventually put in a communications system that went directly to the tenants' telephones. This worked nicely; expensive but well worth it. It satisfied them and it certainly satisfied me for security reasons. I did not have to worry about security of the tenants.

This was a 25-year-old building we had now rejuvenated and upgraded. We even had small touches done like regrouting tile, repairing chips in tubs, or if the tub was really bad, having it reporcelained. Of course, you can buy a tub for almost as much, but you have the added costs of taking it in and out. And we put on attractive new faucets.

When we were ready to rent the apartments, we furnished one as a model, kept moving the model furniture from apartment to apartment, and rented them all very quickly in this way. It helped people to visualize what could be done with an apartment.

Because of all the renovation work, we were able to increase the rents from approximately $115 to $350, on the average. But, remember, if you are going to raise rents, make sure it is just before you are going to do something. Raise the rents on the apartments that you have not fixed. You may get people to get out without having to evict them.

In the beginning, the building was an awful mess. When I showed it to my wife, she said, "This is the worst-looking place I have ever seen." I said, "Well, it will be nice when we get through with it." And it was.

Vacancies and New Tenants

Although this has already been mentioned, let me reemphasize it. Many owners just cannot stand to see a vacancy. So what do they do? They throw all the rules out the window. They will rent to anybody, or they won't put somebody out that they should put out because they are afraid of a vacancy. They don't really run the building; they let the tenants run it.

Each time we ran across problem tenants, we got rid of them. We had no problem with any tenant we put in because we checked them out very thoroughly, using a credit application form. It is very thorough and we take the trouble to make a credit check. We also check the previous places that applicants have lived. You may hear that the manager at the place they just left was sorry to have them go because they were marvelous tenants. But it may be that actually he or she is glad to be rid of them. If you check a couple of places back, if possible, the manager may say, "Do I ever remember them! They tore my place up; it was filthy!" So check the references carefully. Check and verify salaries and employment. And if they don't check out, don't rent to them. We require deposits when they come for the ad; we number everything and do not allow them to take the application with them.

We also give them a deposit receipt on which we state the amount of money. If the apartment for some reason would not be available we would give them their money back. Or in the event we find that they did not qualify, they would be refunded.

Sometimes I would have five or six people applying and the first two did not check out. The third one did and the third one got it. We would notify the other two immediately that we had taken their checks and marked them void and were mailing them back. We would then void them and make a photocopy of the checks, marked "void," and put them in the file with their application. They could never claim that the check was cashed.

When a new tenant came in, we used our inspection sheet (shown in Chapter 9) and inspected every room with them. If there was a defect that could not be fixed, it was so noted. If the defect could be fixed, we said that it would be and so specified in writing. We gave them a copy signed by them and signed by management. When they moved out we would go through the process again and we could just put forms side by side and tell if there was any problem.

Everything was going well with the apartment building. Then the nightmare hit. While the property was still in escrow and I was out of town, excavation began for a 66-unit apartment building on the adjacent lot. The law reads that prior to excavation the developer is required to notify all adjacent property owners, in writing. This was not done.

When I returned, they asked me if they could tear down a division wall they would later replace. I agreed. But before I agreed, I checked their plans to find out how they were excavating. They were to slot-cut along my driveway and rear building area. This is normal and would give me lateral support. A slot-cut is one in which they alternate excavation, leaving fingers of earth to support the adjacent structure. They then put in footing with Raybar steel and concrete block and fill with steel and cement. After the concrete has cured, the contractor removes the remaining dirt and builds the rest of the footing. This results in a solid retaining wall.

Unfortunately, they did not follow their approved plans, but instead shear-cut the earth next to my property. I immediately began taking pictures of each step, making notes of the time of day, date, and compass heading. I contacted my attorney to seek an injunction to stop excavation to prevent further damage. The injunction was not allowed. We, therefore, began litigation.

The developer attempted to placate me by shoring up the earth alongside my property with 4' × 8' plywood and soil. This did not stop the loss of 36 inches of dirt under my slab or the growing cracks throughout my patio and driveway. Then they attempted to solve the problem by driving soldier piles (steel and casing) down 30 feet. But they were excavating to a depth of 25 feet, so this only resulted in kicking action, creating more cracks in my foundation.

We hired one of the best local structual engineering firms to give us a report. Next we located a top soil engineer to take samples (to a depth of 30 feet) on our land and the adjacent property.

At the direction of the engineering firm, we tore out one patio and the floors of four apartments to get at the underpinning. We excavated by hand eight feet below the subfloor. Then we dug squares 18" × 18" × 4', skipping every four feet in which we placed Raybar steel and used the recommended L-shaped 2' × 18" blocks. Layer by layer we filled with cement and at the end we dry-packed it with Emblico (like concrete but stronger and with no shrinkage).

During this period we were notified that thousands of gallons of water were leaking from one of our pipes. This was also due to the neighboring construction. We had to remove part of the floor of another apartment to correct that.

Since the rear building had developed many cracks, we were forced to refinish all the walls. We than added stained and leaded glass windows to the bedrooms, all new kitchen appliances, new carpeting, linoleum, and bath fixtures, astro turf to the patios, redwood fencing, and potted trees.

Unfortunately these apartments were of such configuration that it was difficult for people to visualize how they could decorate them. When this became apparent, we rented attractive furniture and decorated an exceptional model complete with accessories. On the day we ran the ad, we rented the model apartment. We moved the furniture across the hall and rented that apartment also. The following day we rented the other two. All four were rented for $300 a month in 1974. They had originally rented for $115 a month. However, it had taken eight months before we could rent them.

The cost of the reconstruction was $64,000. Legal fees, lost rent, and renovation were extra. It took us four years to come to trial. We requested a tough settlement judge. The case was resolved on the first day, and I agreed to be paid in cash on the first Friday following the settlement. As you might have expected, the settlement by no means recovered all the expenses, much less the loss in revenue.

Selling Out

I do not buy property to hold on to. When I sold this building, all my losses were deductible and the other expenditures were capital improvements. Deducting these from my outside income, I was able to limit my taxes. I had, over the course of time, raised my rents substantially and thereby achieved a much higher net income than I could otherwise have had.

At that point, the building's income was netting $26,000 a year after expenses and amortization. I had refinanced the property for $250,000, with which I had paid off the original loans, taking the balance tax free.

I had gone through hell to take a piece of bad property to the point where it was returning a good income. I asked myself, do I keep it and reap the benefits? Or do I sell out? I chose to sell. I had had the property long enough and it was time to get on with another project.

I put it on the market (see the Figure 11.1) and within two days had a satisfactory offer, $600,000. We closed escrow in 30 days. Today that property is yielding a 19.5 return on the invested dollar. And this is because I did not raise the rents to their possible level. It gave the new owner room to grow.

Selecting an Agent

The selection of a real estate agent is an extremely important part of selling real estate. Although you may consider the commission a large amount of money to pay, perhaps 5 to 6 percent of a property's sale price, the seller more often than not selects an agent with very little thought. In the state of California, there are approximately 450,000 real estate brokers or salespeople so it is possible that many people in the state have relatives with a real estate license. Relatives generally let it be known that they would welcome a listing from you. However, whatever you do don't feel obligated to "keep it in the family." On the street where I live in Santa Monica, there were six new houses built and there are seven real estate people living in them, which assured each of us that we had made a proper choice. Now, your neighbor may be entitled to an occasional libation or invited to one of your barbeques but not listing real estate worth thousands of dollars.

If for example you were selling a $250,000 property, you are probably going to be paying $15,000 for brokerage service, and the cost of an agent could rise much higher as the result of selecting a poor agent in a sale on terms relatively unfavorable to you, the seller. Since securing the best real estate service possible for your money is so important, we will first describe the ideal agent, then discuss just how to systematically find one. In my opinion, the ideal agent *specializes* both in the type of property you want to sell as well as in your desired location. You should never list a property with an agent who does not have a successful track record in these areas. The ideal agent works full time; to list with a part-time agent is almost always bad judgment.

You can ascertain the agent's seriousness about his or her profession by any membership he or she holds in professional organizations, subscriptions to professional journals, and frequency of attendance at professional courses and seminars. Also important is that the agent is a seasoned, experienced salesperson.

Novice agents, as a rule, are generally ineffective, and the so-called supersalesperson, on the other hand, may not be the best choice either. The agent who is experienced and does not avoid the tough properties is probably the best person to list with. This agent has many satisfied clients who have owned property of the same type and similar locations to the property you wish to sell. He or she should rank in not less than the upper middle in sales in the office and should enjoy a good reputation within the industry. The agent should be a property owner, a person with whom you can establish a rapport, and should have a sincere attitude toward your property. Often you may find an agent who will look ideal on paper, but you feel uncomfortable with him or her, for some reason the agent may have a hang-up about your property—don't engage his or her services.

The ideal agent's company is strong and is a member of all the pertinent multiple listing services and other property exchanges. If you are selling commercial or residential income property, the broker should have a strong marketing program and be first in marketing properties of the same type and location as yours. The company should be well established and respected in the community. The firm should have attractive, easily accessible offices. Hours should be set for a time that will not exclude any buyers. And although income property brokers seem to get lost on weekends, make certain that your company is available at all times. The agents should have excellent contacts and relationships with sources of financing, for financing income property can be most difficult. A real estate agency with loyal and reputable sources can be invaluable.

The best place to start looking for an agent is with property owners who have had good experience with a particular agent concerning similar property type and location. Again, experience with a similar location and property type is most important. Another good source is the classified ads. Which companies offer properties similar to yours? Are the prices quoted in line with what you think your property is worth?

How Not to Boost the Selling Price

Under no circumstances do you want to overimprove your property for the neighborhood and area. For example, your house is situated in a mixed neighborhood of blue and white collar workers, or incomes are average to a little below for that type of neighborhood; basically the houses all have about equal amount of square feet, three bedrooms, two baths, living room, family room off the kitchen. Since all the houses are tract houses, they were built at practically the same time. One had recently sold for $42,500 and another for $45,000. All houses have average amenities and there are no houses with swimming pools in the neighborhood. The house that sold for $45,000 had new carpeting and drapes two years prior to sale; the one that sold for $42,500 had new carpeting and drapes six years prior to sale.

Now you decide to upgrade your house so you can get the best selling price possible. You decide that a swimming pool would be a nice touch, and you are almost envious of the prospected buyer. After thinking it over, you decide that you can also put in a jacuzzi for very little more money, so after shopping around you finally contract with a firm to build both, and by the time that is done, adding the extras such as a diving board, heating for the pool, decking, and tile, the contract totals $16,000. You also decide your property needs new landscaping, at an additional cost of $4,000. Then you realize that you need a fence around the property to prevent children from swimming in the pool unsupervised (in case of accident you could be held liable) and that adds another $3,500. So you have made improvements in the amount of $23,500. Since the highest house on the street sold for $45,000, you would have to get $68,500 just to break even, and that house needed new carpeting and new drapes. The next step is $5,000 for new carpeting and drapes. Now you have to sell your home for $73,500 to break even, provided you sell it youself without the aid of a real estate agent. If you use the services of a real estate broker at 6 percent, that will cost you $4,410 and would give you a return of $69,090, which throws you $4,410 in the hole, not counting what your closing costs will be. All you succeeded in doing was to keep your backyard torn up for seven months, and you have improved all the houses around you, but your own. Your only solution and hope is that everyone else will be as foolish as you—all your neighbors should build swimming pools—thereby creating uniformity. In that case, although you won't make a profit, you will most probably break even. Of course, your property will be reassessed and your taxes will go up. You may, however, have the enjoyment of the pool for a short while without, perhaps, the thought of wanting to drown yourself.

Getting the Highest Selling Price

Let us assume that you have a house, recently bought, and you are wondering how to bring in top dollar. The first thing to do is inspect all the open houses for sale in the neighborhood, for more than likely you will find a licensee who will show you throughout the house pointing out all its good features. Usually the real estate agent will have what is known as a pro forma, which is a set-up giving such pertinent information as the price of the house, how many bedrooms and bath, approximate age, and the amount of taxes, and if it is written properly, it will also show all the amenities. After having gone through several of these inspections, you will have something with which to compare your house. You should then have a good idea of what your house would be worth if it were in the same condition and had the same amenities.

The most important thing at this point is to make sure the house is immaculate, with everything neatly stored, including closets (people will look in your closets), and if the closets happen to be the large walk-in type, you want to encourage people to inspect them. If the wood trim on the outside of the house is flaking, scrape and paint.

Be certain that the yards, front and back, are free of any kind of debris. Replace dead plants or shrubs. If your carpeting is relatively new, have it steam cleaned and tinted. Have your draperies cleaned; if they cannot be cleaned, replace them with ready-made, off-white drapes. These few inexpensive things can add thousands of dollars to your property's worth.

Remember, buyers like attractive properties. "Pride of ownership" (an almost overused phrase by real estate brokers) is one of the most powerful motivations; therefore, you should give buyers as appealing a building and grounds as possible. Concentrate on the exterior; that is the first thing the buyer sees and what the buyer's friends will see.

Now let's look at an apartment complex.

Again, concentrate on the exterior. Most investors are tough-minded businesspeople; however, many have one fault in common—most fall in love with a pretty building, and they will rationalize and wear out their calculators trying to justify buying it. All of us have a touch of ego; just ask yourself, "Would I be proud to own this building?"

There are some common "rules of thumb" in purchasing income-producing property. They include:

> Price per unit.
> Gross month multipliers.
> Capitalization of net income.
> Cash on cash return.
> Net operating income.
> Pride of ownership.

If any particular rule seems to be used more often in your area, play to it in the way that you would improve the building and manage it. Keep foremost in your mind that income is the key and, therefore, is the most important number; push it to the maximum. This does not mean that you need the maximum rent on each and every apartment. All you really need to get credit for the income in your selling price is to prove that it can be obtained.

Too many investors tend to adopt rigid percentages on such items as vacancy losses, repairs, and management. Many tend to accept the most recent calendar receipts on such items as insurance, taxes, utilities, and payroll. It is quite common for the average investor to overlook such important items as workmen's compensation insurance, payroll taxes, turnover costs, contractors' services, equipment service contracts, leasing costs, reserve for replacements, advertising, and administrative expenses. Because of the carelessness of buyers, you can maximize your selling price at minimum cost by working hard on those things that buyers focus on, such as income, taxes, utilities, payroll, and insurance. If you spend more money than usual on repairs, turnover renovation, management, marketing, contract service, and other similar items, it is possible for you to improve income and reduce expenses such as utilities and payroll.

Some might suggest that this amounts to deceiving the buyer, but such arguments are based on the notion that income property ownership is solely a mechanical matter and that the buyer is purchasing an "income stream." As a matter of fact, income property is bought by people and as anyone should know, people are certainly more complex than the mechanics of the income stream. The seller who prepares his or her building for sale as I have suggested is a person who understands why buyers really buy and gives them what they want.

In 1932 during the Depression, when I was in law school, I was in a position to acquire several houses—some by adverse possession and some had been abandoned and were up for taxes, which amounted to only a few dollars. All were sound wooden frame houses with one bath, large kitchen with an eating area, living room, and two bedrooms. The actual cost to me was taking title, and my cost averaged $25 a house. These houses were not located in a very desirable part of town, but I was able to rent them for $6 a week paid on a weekly basis. I hired a "big guy" to go by every Saturday to collect the rent. No one ever missed a payment, with the exception of one woman, who had several children.

A year later a man wrote me a letter offering to buy my houses, which totaled 19 at the time, for $300 each. I thought the man had lost his mind or was "pulling my leg," and I started to investigate, thinking that maybe something was going on, such as the fact that 30 miles away from the property was an oil field called Summerset, where my father had begun his oil career in 1921. After checking all my sources, I came to the conclusion that the buyer must have had something else in mind. It was too good a deal to pass up, so I wrote him a letter that I would sell at $400 per house and retain the mineral rights. He replied that I could retain the mineral rights, but his top figure was $350 per house. I accepted the offer, but in so doing I told the man (I felt duty bound to tell him) that one tenant had not paid a penny's rent since the day I had taken over the property. I enclosed a statement to the fact that I had made him aware of this condition and requested that he sign the paper, acknowledging the condition.

I thought this buyer was "nuts" and I had really pulled off a big "coup." Since it was vacation time, I went home and immediately went to the property. I noticed that several of the houses had been moved or demolished. I was not able to reach the buyer, but I went to the area a week later very early in the morning. As I neared the place I saw a house on wheels being moved; it took nearly the whole day to follow it. It finally arrived in a very good neighborhood where the buyer had been taking the homes I sold him, painting them, putting in new plumbing, and selling them for what at that time was a high price. I went back to the original site and found that all the houses had been moved.

When I was finally able to talk to the buyer, I asked how in the world he was able to evict the woman and all her children. His reply was: "Very simple. I had my rig up there and the day she and her family left the house, my men moved in, removed all her furnishings, put them in the yard covered with a tarpaulin, disconnected all the wires and pipes, jacked it up, and drove it off."

Can you imagine the expression on that woman's face and her thoughts when she returned to an empty lot where once stood her home? Can you imagine what would happen to that buyer today under those same circumstances? I learned two very important things here: *one*, due to the location the houses were worth only $350, and *two*, the land that was left was turned into an industrial site, so the original buyer made even more money, which proves that with a little foresight, thought, and imagination, one can come up with many ways to profit on a purchase.

FIGURE 11.1

(Date)

STAR APARTMENTS

Dear realtor/realtor associate:

I am placing this most desirable apartment complex on the market as of this day.

We are cooperating with those realtors and realtor associates who cooperate with others.

The commission will be a 50–50 split on 6 percent of the sales price. As listing realtor, I will retain 3 percent, the other 3 percent going to the one that sells the property, if that person that makes the sale is other than myself. There is a complete description of the property in this enclosed packet.

The apartment will be shown by appointment only. Our tenants do not know of this proposed sale; therefore it will be appreciated if you do not attempt to talk to or bother the tenants.

We thank you for your cooperation.

Sincerely,

_____

Michael E. Glasscock LL.B., C.R.A., A.A.C.A.

PLEASE NOTE: I take this means and opportunity to advise you and your client that on the next two pages there is an analysis of the investment regarding this property located at_____, and such analysis is subjective.

It is suggested that you advise your buyer client to consult with his or her tax attorney and/or his or her C.P.A. in order to ascertain if this offering is suited to his or her needs. I, as a realtor, owner, and seller do not offer or suggest financial, tax, or legal advice and take no responsibility in this regard. The seller makes no warranties to any of the terms or conditions set forth herein.*

_____

Michael E. Glasscock

*This is a disclaimer.

FIGURE 11.1 (continued)

This is a thirteen (13) complex consisting of five (5) singles and eight (8) one-bedroom apartments. There are two (2) buildings, one building has nine (9) units and the other building has four (4) one-bedroom apartments. Both buildings are located on the same lot.

BUILDING # _____

New carpet in all apartments, stairs, and landings. New linoleum in all the kitchens. All bathrooms have vinyl wallcovering, new shower doors, and new water fixtures.

Each apartment has new:

    Receptical Outlets and Face Plates
    Draperies in Living Room and Bedroom
    Door Locks and Door Knobs
    Light Fixtures Throughout the Building
    Permanent Built-ins (range, broiler, and oven) have been reporcelained
    New Disposals
    Dishwashers in all One-bedroom Apartments

- Smoke alert detectors at each level, front and back levels.
- Each apartment freshly painted, interior and exterior.
- New central antenna system with connections in each apartment.
- Latest telephone intercom system for security.
- All outside doors double locked.
- Automatic fire sprinkler over trash bin.
- Lower level interior carpeted including the laundry room.
- Laundry has new automatic bronze sump pump.
- Hot water circulating pump is on a timer.
- Each apartment has separate gas and electric meters.
- All the one-bedroom apartments have three (3) closets, a linen closet, and a large wardrobe with mirrored doors.
- All one bedrooms have hand-made leaded stained glass windows for light and privacy.
- All apartments have wall air-conditioning units less than six (6) months old.
- All the singles have three (3) lighted closets, a dressing table with mirrors, and formica or marble top.
- All singles have full kitchens with bar and overhead cabinet with glass sliding doors and dining area.
- The exterior has been freshly painted and has new canvas drapes and valances, new light fixtures, and fluorescent lighting in each garage area.
- There are malibu lights on top of the block and cement fence and also in all of the flower beds. There is a closed tool room with a working desk and a telephone outlet.

FIGURE 11.1 (continued)

BUILDING # _____

This rear building consists of four (4) one-bedroom apartments. The two lower apartments have ten (10) by eighteen (18) foot patios, enclosed for privacy by a seven (7) foot redwood fence. The patios are covered with astroturf, large trees in two (2) corners of the patios. Both have an outside light to light the patios and each has an electrical outlet and a water faucet with attached hose.

This building was completely stripped and a one (1) by four (4) by eight (8) reinforced concrete underpinning was constructed eight (8) feet below the old foundation footing, completely around the east, south, and west side of the building. The voids were filled with sand and cement mixture. New floors were installed in all four (4) apartments.

Each apartment has new carpet, drapes, and all new electric outlets. Each apartment has new air-conditioners, ceiling to floor, wall-to-wall mirrored wardrobes, crystal chandeliers, and stained-glass leaded windows in each bedroom.

Each bathroom has ceramic tile, new vanity, new medicine cabinets, new shower doors, new light fixtures, new low-boy toilets, vinyl wallcovering, all new water fixtures, new thirty (30) gallon water tanks heated with gas and all bathtubs reporcelained.

New linoleum in the kitchens, new double stainless steel sinks with new formica drain boards (butcher style), new disposals, new dishwashers, new standing range consisting of eye-level oven, dark glass, four (4) burner gas top and lower oven and broiler. Vented gas chest with new thermostats.

New decorative kitchen shades for privacy. New light fixtures in all the kitchens. All of the apartments have been freshly painted. There is a smoke alert detector on each landing. The exterior of the apartment has been freshly painted as well as the interior.

Both buildings have new roofs.

Michael E. Glasscock

TABLE 11.1: Month-to-Month Tenancy (Sales Price $600,000)

Income Schedule (Monthly)			Expense Schedule	
1 bedroom	@ $340.00	$ 680.00	Taxes 80/81	$ 3,684.78
1 bedroom	@ 350.00	700.00	Insurance	505.00
1 bedroom	@ 315.00	630.00	Water	356.28
1 bedroom	@ 300.00	300.00	Gas	471.74
1 bedroom	@ 285.00	285.00	Electric	291.10
Singles	@ 250.00	1,250.00	Trash Pick-up	360.00
			Management 5%	2,301.00
Laundry		$ 10.00	Maintenance 5%	2,301.00
Monthly		3,855.00	Health License	35.00
Annual Gross		46,260.00	Gardener	300.00
Vacancy 3%		1,388.00	Total Expenses	$10,605.90
Adjusted Income		44,872.00	Rounded to $10,606.00	

Financing	Amount	Interest Percent	Term	Annual Payment	Principal Paid	Interest Paid
Existing	$250,000.00	9.5%	30	$25,236.00	$1,486.00	$23,750.00
1st trust deed						
2nd trust deed						
Proposed:						
Down Payment	$250,000.00					
2nd trust deed	100,000.00	10%	5	10,000.00	Int. only	10,000.00
Total	350,000.00					

Depreciation	Value	Percent	Amount	Method of Depreciation		
Land	$150,000.00	25				
Building	450,000.00	75	$22,500.00	25 years 12.5%	5%/year	
Carpets	5,740.00	20	1,148.00	Five years		
Drapes	2,700.00	33	900.00	Three years		
Appliances	6,807.00	14	972.00	Seven years		
Built-ins	7,700.00	14	1,100.00	Seven years		
Water Heaters	1,800.00	10	180.00	Ten years		
Total	624,747.00		26,800.00			

Summary		Depreciation		
Adjusted Income	$44,872.00	Taxable Income		$ 516.00
Exp. and Int.	44,356.00	Depreciation		26,800.00
Taxable Income	516.00	Tax Gain/Loss		26,284.00 × Tax
		50%		13,142.00 Bracket

Cash Flow

Taxable Income	$ 516.00
Equity Growth	1,486.00
Net Operating Income	34,266.00
Tax Saving 50%	13,142.00
Projected Total Returns	$48,894.00

chapter twelve

Leverage

What Is Leverage?

Real estate investment as a vehicle for top earnings entered a dynamic period of growth in the 1970s as the price of real property—and the dollar return to investors who anticipated the boom—soared and became front page news throughout the United States.

   Leverage is used in the real estate industry to mean the ability to control a large investment with only a small amount of one's own money as a down payment, known as outlay of equity capital. At first glance, this is a relatively simple concept. A prospective buyer who desires to purchase a property valued at $1 million, but who has only $200,000 in cash, may negotiate a loan for the remaining $800,000, thereby allowing him- or herself to purchase the property. The buyer now controls $1 million dollars worth of property, but has only invested $200,000 of personal funds. This is leverage—using borrowed funds with a minimum of personal funds to enable oneself to control property. The concept is not quite as simple as it sounds, however, and because a number of investors have not delved thoroughly into the concept, many have seen their leveraged investments turn sour.

   Mass consumer investment texts do not give the potential investor enough of a grounding in the financial principles of real estate to steer him or her around the pitfalls that dot the field. The advice (often from get-rich-quick authors of controversial merit) to use as little of your own money as possible, as much borrowed money as you can, but to be sure that the income from the property will cover the payments on the debt, is often the extent of the aid given. Most texts on the subject tend to stress the importance of borrowing as much as possible to finance the property, but they tend to play down a major part of their own advice—to insure that the income from the property is adequate to pay the mortgage and amortization payments. A miscalculation of as little as 5 percent with respect to the income generated from a particular property can easily negate any advantage that the owner gained by leveraging the property. As an example, using the property worth $1 million purchased for $200,000 down and $800,000 financed, if a rate of 9.75 percent for 30 years is assumed, the mortgage and amortization payments come to $6,873 per month.

If the monthly cash flow from this building is estimated at $7,000, but for one reason or another falls to $6,650, the buyer is $223 per month short on income to pay the mortgage and amortization, and will most likely have to invest more personal money to make up the difference. The reason for the 5 percent drop in anticipated cash flow could stem from a simple vacancy to unanticipated construction, to legislated rent rollbacks, or virtually anything else.

Realistically speaking, the $127 per month in anticipated income ($7,000 less $6,873 in payments each month) from this property would not be enough for a person to live on, but the loss of this expected income could easily tip the balance of a person's investment budget into the red. For this reason, a person who invests in income property should exercise the same caution that applies to one investing in speculative securities: do not invest what you cannot afford to lose.

The concept of leverage, as applied to the real estate industry, goes back decades. Those who have made wise investments using low leverage tend to praise its principles; on the other hand, those whose investments have been at best marginal tend to think that the concept is overrated. Nonprofessional real estate investors generally give little, if any, thought as to whether the concept of leverage as applied to their investment is in harmony with the reason that the investment was made. This is a crucial point to leverage, and yet it is not well understood by those who would use it.

In a typical situation involving the purchase of an apartment building, while it is true that the less the buyer invests of personal money, the more he or she makes on the invested dollar, it is also true that the less the person puts down, the less cash flow is generated. Using the same example, a substitution of figures easily reveals this. On a $1 million purchase price, $800,000 of which was financed, the net cash flow after mortgage and amortization costs are paid amounts to $127 per month ($7000 less $6873 equals $127). The yearly rate of return would be $7,000 times 12, divided by $200,000, or 42 percent. Substituting a leverage rate of 75 percent instead of 80 percent in this example, the investor would pay $250,000 of personal money and borrow $750,000 at 9.75 percent for 30 years. Monthly mortgage and amortization payments would amount to $6,444, leaving a net cash flow of $556 per month ($7,000 less $6,444 equals $556). Further, the rate of return would be 33.6 percent ($7,000 times 12 equals $250,000). If one were to substitute another set of figures wherein the investor puts in less personal money, the following situation could evolve. Leveraging 85 percent of the cost, the investor would put up $150,000 of personal funds and borrow $850,000 at 9.75 percent for 30 years. The monthly mortgage and amortization payments would be

$7,303, for a net negative cash flow of $303. The rate of return, however, would be 56 percent, but the investor would have to invest an additional $3,636 in the building each year simply to pay off the mortgage and amortization costs.

The following principle applies to leverage. If the investor is interested in the maximum cash flow from the building, he or she should seek a leverage percentage somewhere between 60 and 80 percent of the price of the building. Conversely, if the investor is looking for a high yield, without reference to the cash flow, he or she should seek the highest leverage level obtainable, generally between 80 and 90 percent of the cost of the property. In the continuing example, a 60 percent leverage rate would give the following set of figures:

Cost of property	$1,000,000
Investor's funds	400,000
Borrowed funds	600,000
Monthly cash flow	7,000
Monthly mortgage and amortization	5,155
Net monthly cash flow	1,845
Yearly cash flow	22,140
Yearly rate of return	5.53%

By contrast, a leverage rate of 90 percent would yield these figures:

Cost of property	$1,000,000
Investor's funds	100,000
Borrowed funds	900,000
Monthly cash flow	7,000
Monthly mortgage and amortization	7,732
Net monthly cash flow	(732)
Yearly cash flow	(8,784)
Yearly rate of return	0

Assume a rate of 9.75 percent for 30 years. A buyer in a high equity position, whose cash flow minus mortgage and amortization payments is marginal, is in financial trouble. Virtually anything unexpected that affects the property could move the net cash flow from the plus to the minus area and require an infusion of additional funds simply to keep up the monthly payments. One of the potential traps that could well affect cash flow is slow deterioration of the neighborhood. Neighborhoods are generally classified as being in one of three categories; integration, equilibrium, or disintegration.

Determining which state a neighborhood is in requires a fairly good knowledge of the geographic area in which one is investing.

A prospective purchaser should thoroughly acquaint him- or herself with the neighborhood before investing in it. This can be accomplished simply by taking a walking tour and conversing with the residents. A surprising amount of information can be obtained in this manner, especially information concerning negative trends that may beset the area. Further, the prospective purchaser can see new construction or signs of impending abandonment. The presence of children or pets is usually indicative of decline of one sort or another. In the absence of prohibitive legislation, most owners prefer not to have children or pets on their properties because of the amount of damage that both can inflict. The prospective buyer can also check other rental rates in the area in an effort to determine whether he or she can, as a practical matter, raise the rents in the buildings under consideration should building expenses increase. Comparable rents usually indicate that such a raise would be hard to administer, since rents in most other buildings in the neighborhood would then be lower.

The prospective purchaser should also keep one other thing in mind. The building is to be bought as an investment. This means that regardless of how attractive it is, or how nice the tenants, when the appropriate time occurs, the property should be disposed of without delay. Far too many investors hold properties that have started declining in yield, only to find themselves unable to dispose of the properties when they choose to. The timing of investments is something that must be learned through practice; no amount of reading will instill it in a person.

Mass-oriented investment texts do not adequately explore the subject of real property investment. The readers of these texts are generally not expected to require a thorough analysis of the subject, however, and a more cursory examination of the field is really all that is needed. Other texts do delve into this subject on a professional level; yet most still do not make an adequate connection between the reason for the investment and the type of financing used. This is a very crucial point as it affects the return on an investment initially. In the years 1967 through 1977, investments in real estate appreciated more than 20 percent, when figures are adjusted for inflation. Investments in corporate bonds rose slightly under 20 percent; savings accounts depreciated nearly 6 percent; common stocks depreciated a full 20 percent; and cash itself depreciated almost 45 percent. These figures allow for interest on bonds and savings accounts, and the common stock figure reflects the Dow Jones Industrial Average with dividends reinvested. Nevertheless, performance such as this attracts potential investors, be they amateur or professional, and guidance to one degree or another is needed that correlates the immediate requirements of the invested capital with the method of financing used in the transaction.

A leading Los Angeles newspaper quotes a senior vice president of a large savings and loan association as saying that most properties since about 1980 have been sold at prices where there is a negative cash flow. The article says that buyers are lured into purchasing properties yielding negative cash flows because they feel the properties will, in time, reverse themselves and generate positive cash flows. The buyers also feel that a property carrying a negative cash flow will appreciate substantially on a sale, once the flow has turned positive.

None of the major texts on real estate investment deals with this phenomenon, whereby buyers deliberately purchase properties with negative cash flows.

Negative cash flow may well be in the interests of the buyer for any number of reasons. An investment made solely for purposes of tax sheltering requires a negative cash flow to be effective. In a property that should be producing a positive cash flow, a negative cash flow can be induced through the proper application of leverage. Higher mortgage and amortization costs generated through a higher percentage of leverage can produce a negative cash flow. As an example, a 90 percent leverage produced a negative cash flow of $732 per month, or $8,784 per year, compared to a positive cash flow of $42,756 generated on the same property using a leverage rate of 60 percent. This difference of $51,540 in cash flow was the sole result of differing degrees of leverage. The impact of this $51,840 on an investor's income taxes could be very significant, yet most texts consider negative cash flows as something to avoid. This is not, obviously, always the case.

One of the more prestigious books on the subject of leverage and taxes is the *Real Estate Tax Shelter Desk Book* (see Bibliography) published by the Institute for Business Planning. In its discussion of the effects of leverage on the investor, it points out that leverage can work for the investor if the property rises in value, but can work against the investor if the property declines in value. It does not address itself to the situation where a negative cash flow is induced by the investor solely on the premise that the property will rise in value in time. This rise in value can give an investor a substantial profit on the property, especially when coupled with a rapid depreciation rate during the holding period, which gives the investor substantial tax advantages. When the negative cash flow is also included in the tax overview, the investor, depending on the tax bracket, may net more than if the property had provided a healthy cash flow during its holding period. The *Desk Book* does mention refinancing a property immediately before selling it so as to gain a tax advantage from the amortization payments, but, again, it does not discuss the use of leverage in the determination of an advantageous refinancing rate.

Double Leverage

Double leverage occurs when not only a major portion of the buying price of the property is borrowed, but the down payment is borrowed as well. This is actually 100 percent leverage, since none of the investor's own funds are involved in the purchase, and it has very advantageous tax benefits. However, this is generally accomplished through two different lending sources, one lending against the property and the other against the borrower's own assets. Dissimilar rates of interest are apt to be charged, and the borrower must have sufficient credit to negotiate the two separate loans. The total of mortgage/amortization and the payback of the personal loan are apt to be very high, but the substantial interest charges can be deducted from the investor's income taxes.

Provided the investor does not become severely overextended financially from double leverage, this is an extremely desirable tax shelter for an investor who wants large deductable interest payments. If the investment appreciates over a number of years, the investor can reap a windfall provided he or she disposes of the property via a method generating the least taxes.

The risk in a venture of this type is substantially more than in a "normal" leverage situation, because if the property declines in value, not only does the investor have to provide extra funds to pay the mortgage and amortization, but the personal loan as well. Further, even if the property is foreclosed, the personal loan still has to be paid. As a result, this type of leverage should not be recommended for any but professional investors with sufficient assets to withstand a default in both loans.

As we know, financial leverage is the use of debt to increase the return on investments. In real estate, the debt is almost always secured by the property itself in the form of a mortgage or trust deed. Leverage does not guarantee an increased return on investment; however, as discussed earlier, you can frequently earn a very much higher return on investment by using as much of other people's money as possible and as little of your own, allowing you to realize more than if you were using your money alone.

When you speak of investment in property, you are speaking of your down payment, whether it be in cash, a note, or personal property. Consider the following example.

Mr. A owns an apartment building for which he wants $100,000 full price. You wish to purchase it for $80,000. Mr. A agrees to $90,000 and wants a cash out. At the time the interest rate is 10 percent. You persuade Mr. A to sell to you on an installment sale with 10 percent down ($9,000) and interest only for four years, all due and payable at the end of the four-year period at the rate of 12 per cent annually (2 percent higher than the going rate, a kick in). The interest is based on a 30-year loan. By completing a transaction in this manner, you have accomplished three important factors. One, you have used "creative financing"; two, your actual investment on a $90,000 building is only $9,000, not $90,000 (in essence you are controlling a piece of property worth 10 times your actual investment); and three, you have depreciation, expenses, and interest, which can be deducted from your total income.

Prior to the due date on your obligation, you exchange this property for another under rule 1031 of the Internal Revenue Code (deferred tax exchange), thereby trading into a more productive property without paying any taxes on your capital gain, and you have accomplished all of this with only a $9,000 original investment.

Remember, when people speak of their investments, they are speaking of that outlay of cash, note, or personal property as a down payment, not the market value of said property.

How well leverage works to increase your return depends on how much the debt or leverage costs. The annual cost of the debt in real estate is considered to include both principal and interest payments. The cost of the debt is determined by the rate of interest charged, the length of the term (years, months), and the percentage the mortgage or trust deed is of the investment.

In order for leverage (debt) to increase your return, its cost must be less than the return on the assets without any debt; that is, there must be a spread between the cost of the debt on the return that can be earned on the property. Although it is true as an investor that you cannot always control the mortgage or trust deed interest rates or terms, which are set in the capital markets, you should shop and should be able to calculate how different rates and terms will affect your investments. Note the following example of a possible investment:

Investor John Hitchcock was seriously considering the purchase of an income-producing property costing a total of $500,000. After investigating, it was concluded that by deducting all operating expenses, the property would provide a net cash flow of $50,000 before the payment of the debt service and income taxes. Had Mr. H been willing or able to purchase the property for $500,000 in cash, the $50,000 cash flow would have provided a pretax return on his investment of 10 percent ($50,000 ÷ $500,000). But Mr. H wanted a larger return and, besides, did not have $500,000 to tie up in a single property. His hope was that leverage would increase his return and would also enable him to gain ownership of the property. Mr. H calculated how various interest rates could affect his return on his investment if he took out a 30-year mortgage or trust deed for $450,000, leaving him with an equity (down payment) investment of $50,000. The relationship between the interest rates and the return on his equity investment showed that the higher the interest rate, the lower the return. With an interest rate of 9.5 percent, he actually would earn a lower return than the 10 percent he earned with no debt—he would be suffering negative leverage.

The return on investment is calculated simply by subtracting the annual mortgage (trust deed) payments (both interest and principal) from the cash flow and dividing the remainder by the equity (down payment) investment of $50,000. In this example, at 9.5 percent, the annual mortgage or trust deed payments are $45,406 (paid monthly). So, $50,000 less $45,406 equals $4,594, and $4,594 divided by $50,000 equals 9.2 percent. This return does not include the increase in equity (down payment) interest through mortgage or trust deed payments.

In evaluating this property, Mr. H should consider capital appreciation and tax-sheltering benefits as well as return on investment.

Other factors being equal, higher interest rates mean lower returns on investment. However, sometimes paying a higher interest can increase your return on investment if you can get a larger or longer mortgage or trust deed together with the higher interest rate.

For example, Mr. H's banker suggested a mortgage or trust deed for 80 percent of the total cost at an interest rate of 8.5 percent for a term of 30 years. This mortgage gave Mr. H a projected 13.1 percent on his investment. But his banker was also receptive to a mortgage or trust deed for 90 percent of the total cost of an interest rate of 9 percent and a term of 35 years. Despite the higher interest rate of the alternative mortgage or trust deed, Mr. H would increase his projected return from 13.1 percent to 15 percent because the mortgage or trust deed would be larger and longer.

Mr. H figured how varying from 10 years up to 40 years would affect the return on his investment. He assumed that he took out a $450,000 mortgage or trust deed and that he paid an 8.5 percent interest rate. He learned that the longer the length of the mortgage or trust deed, the higher the return on the investment. This relationship occurs because the monthly mortgage payments will be substantially larger with a shorter mortgage, even though the interest rate remains constant.

Mr. H then determined the effect of varying the size of the mortgage or trust deed, while holding constant the interest rate and length of the mortgage or trust deed at 8.5 percent and 30 years. As already indicated, the larger the mortgage or trust deed, the higher the return on equity (down payment) investment. This occurs because the larger the mortgage or trust deed, the smaller Mr. H's equity (down payment) investment has to be.

A significant advantage of leveraging your investment is that while you borrow in today's dollars, you will be repaying in tomorrow's dollars, which will be less valuable due to inflation. Although many borrowers believe that today's high interest rates reflect an expectation of continued high inflation, others do not. Many borrowers have actually been able to profit from the inflation rates of recent years, but there is no guarantee that high inflation will continue, and if it does, for how long. If inflation slows appreciably, the interest rate on mortgages negotiated today will not be lowered to reflect that change. However, it is often possible to refinance at lower rates.

Leverage and Tax Shelters

Depreciation is figured on the total cost of the building (improvement), not the size of the equity (down payment) investment. If Mr. H, for instance, had taken out a $450,000 mortgage or trust deed and thus made a $50,000 equity (down payment) investment, he would be entitled to all of the depreciation on the entire property (improvement), not just 10 percent of it.

Interest payments are tax deductible. In the early years of a mortgage, a large percentage of the payments will be for interest, and thus will be tax deductible. However, in later years, an increasing percentage of the payments will be for the amortization or reduction of the principal, allowing less deductions for interest.

The Risks of Using Leverage

In contrast to mortgage payments, which are fixed for the life of the mortgage in most cases, the net cash flow of the income-producing property available to pay the mortgage or trust deed is not guaranteed. The cash flow could decline if any number of unpredictable events occurred, such as the deterioration of the neighborhood or an increase in property taxes. As the owner, you might have to add additional cash to hold on to the property.

In some cases when the cash flow declines, foreclosures can occur. Foreclosures sometimes result not only in the loss of the equity (down payment) investment, but also in a tax liability. With a foreclosure, the unamortized amount of the mortgage is considered to be the sales price. In some cases, this sales price can be higher than the book value of the property, and a capital gain is considered to have been made on the difference, even though no cash is generated to pay the tax. As you can see, leverage, when properly used, has enabled many individuals to make fortunes in real estate. Leverage can make a sound investment better and a poor investment worse. This is an example of my contention that most people are safer using 70 to 85 percent leverage, as opposed to 100 percent financing. I must further state that when purchasing with leverage, one must not look upon that property for a livelihood, but rather what it really is—an investment in your future.

I strongly urge you read an article in *New York Magazine,* authored by Peter Hellman, entitled "Towering Fiasco," which appeared in the July issue, 1978.

The above mentioned article will further illustrate what can go wrong in using too much leverage at the wrong time, in the wrong circumstances, predicated upon an assumption of what the future worth will be, based on future income, as opposed to purchasing or building at present income and value.

After reading this article, you will be amazed to find the high business caliber of the people involved in this project and it will strongly enforce my reasoning for that which I have stated prior to this point. *Never* buy on projected income.

It can safely be concluded, as a result of this literary review, that successful execution and appropriate application of leverage to real estate investments "all depends." It depends on whether one is a firm or an individual (or group of individuals acting as one); whether one requires a tax shelter (and if so what kind and when); whether one requires a cash flow and to what extent; and whether one is an analyst in real estate; and whether one is a superior "seat of his pants" analyst and/or just plain lucky.

Therefore, it must be a foregone conclusion that it is absolutely necessary to correlate purposes with financing and construct a solid guideline for the prudent investor.

Other Views of Leverage

To present a wider viewpoint of the use of leverage, I made an informal inquiry among my peers of Realtors, investors, people in loan institutions, and others connected in one way or another with real estate. In exchange for complete anonymity, I was provided with information. A simple numbering system from 01 to 50 was used to identify the participants, and they are referred to in this way. However, where appropriate, some details of clarification are provided, such as the field of expertise of the individual (broker, real estate developer, or other). The bulk of the information pertained to specific experiences in the use of leverage in real estate investments, including details of positive and negative aspects and financial outcomes.

As a result of the interviews, it was found that most of the sample group had used leverage to at least some extent. About 20 percent of the group heavily depended on leverage in creating real estate investment deals; the remainder ranged from essentially minor use to frequent use as an adjunct to other investment programs and policies. As expected, the subgroups of people who make real estate investments utilizing the concept of leverage are small, middle-range, and large investors. In discussing the findings from the interviews, the small investor will be examined first.

Interviewee 09 is a real estate broker with a fairly typical story of small investor experiences with leverage. She pointed out that a typical small investor real estate program might involve purchase of an apartment building of about 10 units. Often the investor will live in one of the units and take care of the building and ground maintenance. The broker notes that this can adversely affect cash flow, since the apartment that might otherwise be rented and producing income is instead occupied by a nonpaying person. In her example, the investor was a businessman who sold his home in 1971, purchasing a West Los Angeles apartment building with 11 units. He and his family moved into the largest apartment, three bedrooms in a prime noise-free location above the carports and utility area. He had been paying a total of $171 a month for mortgage, taxes, and insurance on his house, but he used the money from the house as a down payment on the apartment building. His apartment at the investment site had been continually rented for the three years since the units had been built and was renting for $345 at the time.

This investor was able to use leverage because the previous owner of the building was leaving the state and was willing to take back a second mortgage if necessary to push through a sale quickly. The property, in an attractive neighborhood, was a good value at $277,500. A 10 percent down payment was made, with a first and second mortgage making up the balance.

Payments were high, as was upkeep, and the new purchaser had some very rough months, which were compounded by the fact that he was losing $345 a month (at least) on the three-bedroom apartment he and his family occupied, and this trade-off was made to get the down payment money, so there were not a lot of alternatives available to him. He had to live somewhere, and for reasons of maintaining the place and the cost of living in alternative housing, it made logical sense to live on the property. However, two-bedroom units, which were fairly well soundproofed and about the same size, with the exception of the third bedroom, were available. The investor's family consisted of himself, his wife, and one teenage daughter. The third bedroom was used as a catchall and was not really needed. Had he moved into the two-bedroom unit after selling his house, he would have lost only $215 a month in cash flow instead of $345. Also, the two bedroom apartments were more frequently vacant than the three bedroom since the building was comprised of the one three bedroom plus ten two bedroom units. The loss per annum was at least $2,000, and this was money he could have used to meet mortgage and maintenance costs.

There were other grave concerns facing the investor. Although the vacancy factor in the West Los Angeles area is one of the lowest in the city and county, the early 1970s were not good years for many who wished to rent, and the rates, while quite reasonable, were still above the ability of some potential dwellers to pay. Some of those who saw rents going up began lobbying for rent controls, which would have meant the small investor was stuck with the income he had in 1971 with almost no increases, while inflation was beginning to nibble at his savings and income.

New York City is a prime example of the potential difficulties in rent control. To counter soaring rent rises, ceilings were put on apartment rentals. This had the effect of creating a financial pressure cooker, wherein costs to maintain the building continued to escalate, but rentals could not be raised to cover the costs. Landlords were forced by this financial pressure to put more and more of their own money into the properties, with resulting negative cash flows. The final result in many instances was that the landlords, caught in the income-cost squeeze, abandoned their buildings to recoup whatever they could by eliminating losses. As more and more buildings were abandoned in such areas as the South Bronx, where profits were slim from the onset of rent control, New York City collected far fewer tax dollars. Residents of the areas, faced with all the problems that can occur from blights like abandoned buildings, moved away and were replaced by still poorer families. The tax base was eroded, complicating an already difficult problem.

New York City's 1942 rent control law was replaced by a rent stabilization law in 1965, which permitted increases in percentage scales when apartment leases were renewed. Otherwise, the fixed ceilings remained. The New York Urban Coalition reported in early 1978 that, in actual fact, the percentage rise in typical landlord expenses was 6 to 8 percent lower than the permitted rent increases. In a move that could conceivably start a new round of abandoned buildings in New York City, the City Council lowered the legal rent increases to bring them more in line with the actual landlord expenses.

The fear of some similar experience faced the investor represented by Interviewee 09, but the result did not, in fact, materialize. Other problems were also faced, like a plumbing leak in an upstairs apartment that caused damage in the downstairs unit and required cleaning up plus repairs. The costs included roof repair, plumbing repair, replacing paint and carpeting, and losing a month's rent in the downstairs unit. In this particular situation, the plumbing broke in the ceiling and ruptured the roof with its explosion of water.

The investor tried to be particularly careful about screening tenants, but when one apartment was empty and not producing rent for over a month, he took a chance on renting it to someone with no references that could be checked easily. The tenant paid for the first and last month, plus a security and cleaning deposit, and signed a one-year lease. No payment was received after that time despite frequent requests from the investor-manager. Finally, a legal action was initiated, but six months elapsed before eviction was completed. The investor had a court order awarding him damages, but the tenant had no job and no assets, and the money could not be recovered. Four months lost rent plus attorney and court costs amounted to more than $1,350—money that put a further drain on the investor's assets. Another $280 was needed to repair damages to the apartment (not including the investor's time and that of his wife, since they did the extensive painting and cleaning themselves). After refurbishing, the apartment was rented at $30 a month more than it had been priced, but recovery of losses would take a very long time at that rate. Certainly the investor did not need or want additional tax write-offs, since the taxes and interest (for mortgage) on the place put him almost in a nontaxable bracket.

This all occurred in the early 1970s, which was a key reason for the final happy outcome. Many investors considered as small investors, as was this man, would have gone under with the heavy financial burden of maintaining the mortgage payments, repairs, ordinary maintenance costs, and so on for this 11-unit apartment. However, this investor had a substantial amount of savings. He could have used that money for a down payment instead of selling his house, but he wanted to have the money to draw on for emergencies, even though he hoped such emergencies would not materialize. He could also have made a much larger down payment, but again elected not to do so, preferring instead to use leverage—to use the mortgage holder's money rather than his own to the extent possible. It was a calculated gamble on his part, and because of rising rents and property values, he did very well.

Interviewee 09 reports that the investor began to reach good equilibrium between income and costs for the property after a few years, and when rents began to move higher and higher in his area of the county in 1974, he began to make a profit despite high mortgage payments. He still had the advantage of the high interest and other tax write-offs, but he also began to see more and more each month as income almost doubled and outgo remained approximately the same. In 1977 this investor sold the apartment building for $685,000, a total of $407,500 more than he had paid, and he had also enjoyed profits for a number of years prior to the sale.

As noted, this is a fairly typical story of small investor use of leverage, and Interviewee 47 had a very similar story. He, too, was a broker who had sold an apartment building to a small investor. It was a 16-unit group of one-bedroom apartments, unfurnished, located in the mid-Wilshire area of Los Angeles, an area in transition, which for a while in the mid-1970s was experiencing a high vacancy rate, but which began to fill up as rents for apartments in more western areas went beyond many people's ability to pay.

Interviewee 47's investor did not live on the property, but did buy on leverage and get a second mortgage to make up the difference. The investor, an unmarried woman with a career who needed a good tax write-off, did not have substantial funds to draw on. At first she was achieving her goal of maintaining a reasonable balance and having tax deduction advantages. Then she had an experience similar to the previous investor; a tenant moved in and did not pay any rent after the first month. The investor here was less aware of her legal rights and was slow in reacting. She also did not have a resident manager alert to the proper procedures. By the time the tenant was finally evicted, the apartment itself had been turned into a shambles, with even plumbing removed or cracked. The estimated cost of refurbishing was in excess of $6,000, and rent losses were over $1,200. It was more than she could handle, and she was forced to sell the apartment building. Although she sold at some profit, it did not solve her tax write-off problem on the one hand, or provide enough profit to make the tax write-off absence a good trade-off.

Interviewee 47 expressed the belief that while the initial purchase seemed sound to the investor, especially through use of leverage, she simply did not have the ability to withstand such a loss and was thus put in the position of having the decision to sell the property made *for* her rather than being done at her own selected time.

An even more damaging story was noted by Interviewee 19, whose own experience with the unexpected in New York was firsthand. He has been a real estate investor for 15 years despite a financially painful first-time experience. He had purchased a small apartment house, with 10 one- and two-bedroom units, and rented one of the apartments to an Asian couple whose credit application checked out very well. And, in fact, he never experienced any problem with getting payments promptly each month.

This dwelling was a two-story building, with the five apartments on each story identical top and bottom—a single two bedroom on each floor, and the rest, one-bedroom units. The couple lived in a two-bedroom unit. The problem first came to the attention of the owner from a neighbor on the kitchen side of the couple's apartment. The complaint was that there was an infestation of cockroaches and that efforts to get rid of them were fruitless. The tenant suggested that they must be coming from another apartment. Not long after that other tenants voiced the same complaint. The owner made a thorough investigation, finally reducing it to the probability that the infestation was from the couple's home. He had not been able to reach them to ask, but he did reach the other tenants, who by then were increasingly irate.

The owner's efforts to eliminate the roaches by sprays and individual apartment bug bombs failed, and several tenants moved out since they did not have leases and could leave on 30 days' notice. The problem continued until finally the owner determined that the apartment occupied by the couple was, in fact, the source of the cockroach infestation; it was by then an advanced problem. The owner also learned that the Asian couple's religious beliefs prevented them from killing any living thing, which included cockroaches!

When the owner sought the services of an exterminator, the couple politely declined to leave their place so that the exterminators could take care of the whole building. In effect, the wife, staying in her apartment, was the protector of the bugs. The owner, in the meantime, got several more notices of intent to move and was spending hours of time and energy trying to right the problem. Only when the husband and wife were convinced that they would not be responsible for the death of the bugs, but rather must vacate the premises since the exterminator's spray would harm them also, did they leave long enough to permit the owner to get the job done. By then it took three visits from the exterminators to clean up the building, and three apartments were empty, with three others threatening to follow. The other three tenants were not happy, but had not yet given actual notice, although they had been vocal about the problem.

The owner had an enormous public relations job to do with his existing tenants, had to rerent the vacancies, and also had a big bill from the exterminators. All of this put him into serious financial straits, and he lost the building within six months because he could not sufficiently recoup his losses to make the big mortgage payments and other expenses of operation.

Interviewee 19, speaking in part from his own strange but true experience and in part from expertise gained from 15 years in real estate investing, cautioned against leverage use by small investors unless they are prepared to take the same kind of loss he did. That is, they should stay in more conventional investment patterns unless they are prepared to lose everything they invested. Interviewee 19, for example, had been prepared for the possibility that he would lose it all. He did not believe he would lose, but when it happened he was not caught totally by surprise since he knew he was operating on a very fine cash flow line.

He stated that there are many potential pitfalls that are felt more heavily in most instances by small investors than by those with more irons in the real estate fire. Such things as rent control legislation possibilities were also noted by him, and he said that in areas where legislation prohibits discrimination against children, expenses will escalate since children almost always increase maintenance costs. The presence of children and/or pets also creates tenant problems on occasion, as one or another react to the other tenant's child or pet. This means a strong resident manager is important, to keep an eye on the property and to help settle disputes amicably. Such a manager is added expense. The investor who lives on the property is not always free to spend time on such concerns, and in those instances, a resident manager is still needed at least for the people-to-people aspects of apartment management even if maintenance is handled by the investor-owner.

Interviewee 19 suggested that potential small investors, and especially those considering the gamble of leverage use, should be sure they understand all legal restrictions existing at the site of the potential investment, whether it be an apartment or business building or some other form of real estate investment. Such things as trash disposal regulations, retroactive fire regulations, safety regulations, insurance regulations, and others can affect the cash flow significantly.

Also, an awareness of potential hazards and problems should be considered. The real property with a building constructed on fill land can suffer bad cracks and other settling damage. An apartment or office building fronting on a busy and/or charming street with great "rentability" potential may have a retaining wall in back that could easily give with heavy rains.

Interviewee 07 provided an illustration of how yields at the time of sale can be changed through the use of leverage. The example for the following constants:

Cost of building	$500,000
(11 times gross yearly rentals)	
Monthly rentals	3,788
Monthly expenses	2,000
(excluding mortgage/amortization)	

With a 65 percent leverage rate, using the constants supplied, the investor uses 35 percent of the total as a down payment, which is paid from his or her own funds. Interviewee 07, a real estate developer, drew up these figures for a real situation and shared them for inclusion in this report. The figures with the first set of percentages thus become:

35 percent down payment	$175,000
Amount financed (30 years at 9.25 percent)	325,000
Monthly mortgage/amortization	2,674

This interview was conducted before the mortgage rate moved above 10 percent, when the developer predicted a downward climb in interest to 9.25 percent. This would alter the cost figures, but they are included as provided during the interview.

With these computations, the addition of the mortgage and amortization payments of $2,674, plus the monthly expenses (excluding mortgage and amortization) of $2,000, gives a total for monthly expenses of $4,674. When monthly rentals are deducted, this leaves a net monthly negative cash flow of $886. Multiplied over 12 months, the buyer here would have to invest an additional $10,632 per year just to keep the investment from defaulting.

Assuming a five-year holding period for this investor, a sales price of $553,160 would be required just to break even on the investment. This also assumes no major crisis will erupt to pitch the expenses to an even higher level. That sales price represents a 10 percent increase in property values over five years, which appears realistic as a minimum level in the current real estate market.

If the property appreciates 15 percent instead of 10 percent, and sells for $575,000, the buyer would have a net profit of $21,840 (a 12 1/2 percent yield) on the $175,000 over five years. A 20 percent appreciation would bring a sales price of $600,000 and a net profit of $46,840, or 26.8 percent, on the initial down payment. No profit appears until the building is sold, however, since there is a projected negative cash flow of $10,632 each year.

If the buyer's investment is less, 30 percent as down payment and 70 percent financed (a 70 percent leverage rate), then the following occurs:

30% down payment	$150,000
Amount financed	350,000
(30 years at 9.25%)	
Monthly mortgage/amortization	2,879

With total monthly expenses of $4,879, including mortgage and amortization, the negative cash flow each month is accelerated to $1,091, or a loss of $13,092 for the year in actual cash income versus outgo. The loss that would be encountered over a five-year period would be $65,460, and a 10 percent appreciation of the property would net $550,000 with losses at a level where they would not be recouped in full by a 10 percent increase in value. There would still remain a $15,460 loss. Fifteen percent appreciation would net $9,540 in profit (6.36 percent yield) over the five years, while 20 percent appreciation would net $34,540, or 23.02 percent yield on the $150,000 invested. Thus, for an additional $25,000 initial investment, the owner receives $12,300 more at the end of the five-year term, as presented by Interviewee 07. Projecting this into a 25 percent down, 75 percent leverage rate, the property must appreciate by 15.56 percent if the owner is to break even after five years, and the net yield from 20 percent appreciation would be 17.7 percent ($22,180) after five years.

This example of what figures emerge from various computations of leverage is typical of the responses, experiences, and demonstrations secured from those interviewed. Although the interest rate changes will alter these figures significantly, the basic format is identical in that a certain amount will be lost when using leverage; it usually cannot be recouped for many years; and even then is speculative.

There are tax advantages to substantial losses, and some small investors may find it equitable to suffer large losses over the five years or so involved. Others, however, say the great majority of those interviewed, could find use of leverage too big a gamble for the small investor.

In summary, the interviews in this research that addressed the question of the suitability of leverage use in actual practice by small investors today across the board found that it is not recommended for anyone except the small investor who is willing and financially able to lose every cent invested and sometimes even more. The degree of success attained through using leverage is not sufficient at the small investor level to make it a suggested plan except in those instances where tax write-offs are important and recovery of funds is not.

That was not, however, the finding at a more advanced level of real estate investment. Although some of the same problems existed for the middle-range investor, for the most part those interviewed felt that leverage was potentially an outstanding way of gaining exceptional returns on investment dollars for those beyond the small investor level.

Interviewee 23, an investor who is also a tax accountant, stressed the tax benefit aspects of leverage use. He stated that, of course, profit made on the sale is subject to taxation as a capital gain (most investors would not qualify for any new federal capital tax one-time exemption). He pointed out that a big sum of profit could be a plus to one investor, but a negative factor to another, depending on their respective tax brackets. This reflects the original reason for the investment.

If the original reason for the investment was to secure a tax shelter, and the seller wishes to keep taxable profit at a minimum, he or she might choose to borrow as much as possible initially and have more to write off. This, in effect, puts the mortgage and amortization figures at a high level, which is maintained through the holding period and keeps net profit at a minimum when the property is sold.

Interviewee 23 specified that this presupposes the investor is able to forecast the anticipated appreciation of the property over a period of years with some accuracy, and says he has been able to do so with a good rate of success during his 25 years as a real estate investor and tax accountant, although recent years have been more difficult to forecast or understand economically.

If the initial reason for the investment was profit and the market is such that a positive cash flow is virtually impossible to achieve on the property, the investor might decide to make a higher down payment and finance less of the purchase price. Thus, the mortgage/amortization payments will be less, the tax write-off will be less, and if a sufficient down payment is made, a profit may be realized during the holding period. In any event, using these alternatives of higher down payment and thus lower monthly payments, a reasonable return or investment at the time of sale could in most instances be expected. The gamble is greatly reduced when leverage is smaller.

The question that must, therefore, be confronted is whether, in fact, leverage is worth the gamble. Are the benefits sufficient to outweigh deficits? If so, under what conditions should leverage be used?

The answers to these questions were supplied during the personal interviews with the fifty sample group population. It should be noted that, although the criteria for selection of the sample group was that they be experienced (minimum of five years) professionals in the real estate field as investors, brokers, and/or developers, many have other professions or a combination of professions. Several have retired from active business, but continue to keep in touch and tend to "dabble" in it despite their "retirement" status. Real estate has no age limitation and is an ideal way to keep mind and body alert as the industry goes through the dramatic changes that began back in 1970. Other interviewees are working full time (plus) in real estate as multiple careerists, such as developer-investor, broker-accountant-investor, developer-financial consultant, or broker-appraiser. There are, in fact, so many different groups that it was considered inappropriate to try to classify the respondents, and instead they are referred to by their major area of professional career.

Just as there were basic similarities in the experiences of small investors using leverage, so there are basic similarities in the experiences of middle-range or large investors who utilize leverage.

Interviewee 38 had a fairly typical experience in leverage use. He has used leverage extensively and is a large-scale investor involved in many real estate negotiations at any given time. One of the examples he selected as typical concerned the purchase of an office building and land in Thousand Oaks, Ventura County, California. His primary business is as a real estate investor. He contracted for the construction of the building to his specifications, then took over its management upon completion. His firm continues to handle the property management. He originally took out a construction loan, then converted it to a mortgage when the building was completed and ready for occupancy.

Thousand Oaks is a fast-growing community, once entirely separate from the Los Angeles area, but now considered a suburb. It is about 50 miles from downtown Los Angeles and adjoins the western end of the San Fernando Valley, which is also a growing business, industrial, and residential area. The trend toward rapid growth was noted by Interviewee 38, who perceived that the influx of people into Thousand Oaks would mean more services would be needed there. Accordingly, he built an office complex suitable for professionals such as doctors, dentists, lawyers, and insurance agencies. It is a one-story, Spanish-style building with some street-front offices for those seeking access to the public and courtyards with offices facing scenic areas for those who do not need or particularly want street-front locations.

The total package at the time of conversion from a construction loan was valued at $1,200,000. He financed it with a 10 percent down payment and 90 percent on interest-bearing mortgage. The 90 percent leverage was the highest he could get, as he preferred to put in the minimum amount of cash. The facts and figures of this experience are:

Property value	$1,200,000
Original equity (10% × $1,200,000)	120,000
Amount of loan (90% × $1,200,000)	1,080,000
Financed at 9.5% for 20 years	
Debt service (yearly payments)—	
.11856 × $1,080,000	120,805

Cash flow (annual net income of $129,100 less debt service $120,805)	8,295
Debt coverage ratio (net income divided by debt service)	1.06
Rate of current yield on equity (cash flow divided by original equity of $120,000)	.06
Loan balance at the end of a 10-year holding period (72,0362% unpaid × principal)	777,991
Resale value as percent of original value, at 10% minimum estimated appreciation (110%)	
Resale value as a dollar amount (110% × original value)	1,320,000
Net reversion (terminal equity) (resale value less loan balance)	542,009
Deferred yield amount (reversion net less down payment)	422,009
Terminal equity ratio (reversion net divided by resale value)	.410613

The net reversion refers to the estimated profit from sale to a new purchaser at the conclusion of the 10-year holding period for which this investor kept the property. Additionally, he realized a cash flow of $8,295 per annum beginning with the first year, despite the fact that he had a 90 percent leverage.

This investor is now in this third holding year on this property and is finding that his computations, as shown above, are in line with his experiences with respect to debt service, cash flow, and rate of current yield. He also expects to realize a higher cash flow in two more years when some of the present leases will run out and rents can be increased. It is still too early, he believes, to guess at whether he will, in fact, realize more than 10 percent resale appreciation, although already the property appears to have appreciated by that much by today's standards. He is willing to further his gamble by holding on to the property to see if real property prices continue to escalate and give him an even stronger position.

This interviewee is a staunch advocate of leverage, saying it has brought him profits far in excess of what he might have made through conventional financing. He contends that the only reason he has had the substantial success and the high standard of living and financial security that he now enjoys is because he has used "the other guy's money" in investment dealings. He has consistently kept his equity very low in going into real estate deals and has consistently financed the bulk of the property at the interest rate then going to good customers.

Asked about his reaction and experiences in light of a rising mortgage interest rate, this interviewee stated that it is not having a major effect on his operations. He said that although he has at times gone with 100 percent financing, and frequently with 90 percent, he now finds the banks prefer 80 to 85 percent funding as a maximum. He believes that, nevertheless, if a deal sounds good enough, he could still get 90 percent bank funding in view of his record of continued success in this business.

As with small investor experiences, there were many duplications (approximately) of the findings and experiences of Interviewee 38. Almost without exception, the individuals interviewed expressed the opinion that the major fortunes in real estate have been made by those who employ leverage, getting the full benefit of property value increases even though they had put up only part of the price in cash.

Some dramatic figures appeared as a result of the rapid rise of California property values in the mid-1970s, which is only now slowing.

Interviewee 35 supplied an example of her experience with using leverage in purchasing an income property in the city of Fresno, in the agricultural belt of central California, which is a fast-growing business center as well. She purchased property valued at $500,000 in 1973, incurring a debt of $425,000 and an equity of $75,000. By 1975 the property had appreciated to $1,000,000, while the debt remained at $425,000, less the small amount of principal paid during the two-year period. Her equity at the same time rose to $575,000 (all this in just two years). She sold the property for $1,000,000, reinvesting the money in numerous other real estate ventures and continuing to utilize the leverage concept. She advises that the property continued to appreciate and the new owner, who also bought on leverage, has also realized a substantial profit from the same piece of property.

Such stories are not infrequent. Of the 50 people interviewed, 40 knew from personal experience or other firsthand knowledge that such profits had been made by themselves or others.

Interviewee 49 had a similar experience with property, buying a block of apartment houses in Oakland, California, in 1973 and doubling his equity in four years. He, too, reinvested the money in properties and used leverage in each of those investments. As he put it: "It isn't like real money. Suddenly you find yourself with an extra $700,000 that you didn't work for. It just happened by escalating property values. Maintenance costs didn't come close to eating it up. It was like play money. I put it back into some other deals and now they have appreciated too, and the money just keeps rolling in. My costs are high, but I can get out from under the debts overnight and still be a millionaire. It is hard to believe, but it's true."

This interviewee, a developer turned investor, says he thinks his success was due in large part to timing. The property he first invested in was a business section near the Oakland ghetto area. Right after he bought it, the redevelopment agency decided to direct its energy toward downtown Oakland, and the building he owned was in an area adjoining the redevelopment site, so as new, modern construction was completed, his own property appreciated. He used that profit to purchase the apartment houses. As rentals soared in San Francisco, more and more potential customers for apartments across the Bay in Oakland were available, and the value of the apartment complex went up at the same time the vacancy rate dropped to less than one percent annualized basis. Despite inflation, which increased costs across the board, the income and equity both jumped upward. The interviewee here said that in both of the examples cited the timing was right—first, because he purchased the business property prior to the decision of the redevelopment agency, and so paid preredevelopment prices for the property, but netted postredevelopment profits, and second, while Oakland's property values did not rise per se, the property he owned did escalate in value since he was able to supply what was very much in demand—quality apartments at lower prices than were being asked in neighboring San Francisco.

Interviewee 08 was one of the few who experienced depreciation of property in California during the 1970s. He is an investor who bought land in Petaluma, California, in 1971 and went into partnership with a developer to construct condominiums on it. He had intended to build 50 units at first and, after selling them, construct a second block of 50. The land was purchased with a five percent down payment and 95 percent financing. The mortgage payments were high, but the potential profit was considered to be an almost assured doubling of value. Petaluma is a northern community that was getting more and more residents who worked in the Bay Area towns and were willing to make a long commute to enjoy a country-like atmosphere.

Interviewee 08 used leverage to keep his tax write-off high and also to keep as much of his cash available as possible for the actual construction. As with the other investors advocating leverage use, he had high financing levels because he elected to use his available funds for more investments—also using leverage.

Just as construction was in its early stages of getting plans together and obtaining the necessary permits, the Petaluma city officials passed a law prohibiting new building. Their no-growth policy was immediately challenged in the courts, but in the meantime it was operative and meant that the investor and developer were prevented from using their land as they had intended.

They had an option on land for the second group of 50 units, which, if not exercised, would mean a $5,000 loss. An effort to get out from under the debt for the purchased land by selling it produced a not unexpected result: the property depreciated in value as soon as the no-growth ruling went into effect. Land that had been purchased for $100,000 with a $95,000 debt became worth $80,000 on resale at that time. Not only did this mean a total loss of the $5,000 equity, but, additionally, a $15,000 loss on the portion that was not paid for, but was being financed. A sale for $80,000 would leave the investor $15,000 in debt, with no chance for recovery. He did not need that big a tax write-off, and although the mortgage payments were a heavy burden with no income to offset them, he found that this was the best alternative. In this way he did have some tax write-off without losing all possibility of recovering from the land purchase. Finally, in 1977, he sold the land at a profit, making up for the losses and netting about 6 percent profit from his total investment.

Interviewee 26 provided another point of view on how to best take advantage of the tax savings aspect of leverage use, which by its nature leaves the investor with high interest payments annually until the conclusion of the holding period. This interviewee generally elects not to sell the property at the conclusion of a holding period, but rather to exchange it and thus continue to save on taxes. He is a developer and investor who reported a pattern he had used throughout the first six years of the 1970s.

Under Section 1031 of the Internal Revenue Code, he was able to exchange property under certain conditions without being required to pay on "gains." The IRS Code section stipulates that no gain or loss is to be recognized if certain business or investment property is exchanged solely for property of a like kind that is also to be held for use in business or as an investment.

The criteria established by the government for qualification for nonrecognition or nontaxation were:

1. The property received and the property traded must be held either for productive use in a trade or business or held for investment. (Stock in trade or other property primarily held for sale, stocks, bonds, notes, choses in action, certificates of trust or beneficial interest, and other securities or evidence of indebtedness or interest are specifically excluded from the kinds of property that benefit by this section.)

2. To qualify, both properties must be of like kind to each other. The nature and character of both properties must be alike.

3. The properties must, in fact, actually be exchanged for each other.

The interviewee says that although the first element was cut and dried and relatively simple, the second has been interpreted to relate to the nature of the property rather than its grade or quality. Improved real estate is considered to be of the same nature as unimproved real estate, and the fact of improvement or nonimprovement relates only to the grade or quality, not to the nature. The third stipulation means simply that care must be taken to avoid a sale and buy-back agreement where an exchange is intended.

In one exchange deal, the interviewee had property with a market value of $500,000 and a mortgage blance of $220,000, leaving an equity of $280,000. This was used in an across-the-board exchange on a property valued at $280,000, which was free and clear. Thus, at the conclusion of the holding period on the leveraged property, he was able to make a tax-free conversion to another property, using no cash at all.

In other exchanges, he has had a greater equity than was needed to meet the purchase price of an exchange property. In those instances, the difference between purchase and exchange equity was considered capital gain. Wherever possible he reinvested the gain in other leverage purchases to avoid taxes.

He has also been party to a three-way exchange, exchanging his property for that of someone who does not want what he has to offer, but will trade with a third person who, in turn, wants what Inverviewee 26 wants to exchange.

In all exchanges, time is a factor that must be considered since exchange negotiations often take longer than standard buy-and-sell deals. Another investor must be found, usually by brokers who specialize in such transactions, and must be tied into the exchange. A greater time factor is usually required for multiple party exchanges, which take even more extensive negotiations.

Exchanges represent the kind of tax benefits that leverage can lead to, since it is a tool often used not only as a means of making money while operating on someone else's funds (the lender's money), but also as a means of having high write-offs to avoid high tax brackets.

Although the results of interviews with 50 people are not listed one by one, the foregoing is generally a good representation of what was discovered. There seemed to be like reactions to leverage, with a basic split between those involving small investors and those involving middle-range or large investors. The small investor was generally identified as one who has just one investment or at most two operating at one time. The middle-range investor tended to be identified in dollars and cents, being one who had less than $1 million in investments. The large investor was the person or company with more than $1 million invested.

Among the comments written at the conclusion of the questionnaire were: "Leverage is like shooting craps. If you can't afford to lose, you shouldn't play," and "Anyone who is inexperienced and intends to use leverage should be sure to get an expert in the field to guide them through the process."

In summary, these trained realty people relied on leverage as an effective tool in their investment package. Further, they believed that the potential far outweighed the risks, that it was extremely useful to accrue maximum tax advantages, that inflation does not substantially affect leverage's usefulness, that it offers the greatest potential, and that they themselves were successful at using it.

To these trained real estate people, leverage offers investors the opportunity to use other people's money to make money for themselves. These results would support the widespread belief (used by marketers of get-rich-quick books) that leverage has been and will continue to be a highly successful actual practice, provided the investor is in a financial position to withstand total loss and/or to maintain payments for debt services.

It is surprising how different these findings are—the difference in experience of these California realty investors and their more conservative counterparts on the East Coast (as represented by the review of literature). There it was discovered that a very conservative approach should be taken with the use of leverage, that one had to be extremely skillful analytically and be extremely lucky as well. But the California sample suggests that working without a formula was almost universally successful! This is probably due to the fact that California, and Southern California, have far outdistanced the rest of the nation in appreciation of real property.

The entire field of real estate investment is marked by fluidity and change. There are, however, certain constants that have made it an attractive arena for investment dollars. Although the changes have included extreme market highs and lows, losses and gains, strengths and weaknesses, the constants have been tangible. Real estate investment by its very nature implies solidity—land and buildings—rather than alternative investments such as stocks and bonds, which can leave investors holding worthless paper. Historically, land ownership and property ownership have meant a certain amount of built-in security. There is always some residual value.

The counterfactor here, of course, is that there is residual value only to the extent that value exceeds debt. Leverage puts the investor in a somewhat vulnerable position in the respect, since the tangible—land and buildings—may be there, but the equity in such land and buildings is often very, very minor. In fact, the mortgage holder is the one with the tangible, while the investor holds paper and has liens to meet.

What draws investors to leverage? Essentially it is one thing—the opportunity to use the other person's (company, bank, whatever) money to make money for the investor. If leverage is used, and is used effectively, the investor may use his or her equity funds for multiple rather than single investments. With, for instance, 90 percent funding for a property and 10 percent equity holding, rather than making a 30 percent down payment on the same property, the investor has the additional 20 percent of the money to move into other ventures, each with the purpose of making profit without maximum risk of equity dollars in one holding. The risk is spread out among a number of investments, which in turn can mean that the risk is lessened.

Unless the leverage use is wisely made, however, the risk can be escalated. Debt service can be so high that the investor is crippled by efforts to repay costs and stay ahead of the property. The result can be a loss of the total investment. In some cases, if debt service were lower, this loss would not occur because the operating costs would be manageable to the investor.

After probing the available literature on leverage use in real estate investment and exploring journals, treatises, and other publications for validated studies on the subject, it became apparent that there was an absence of substantiated fact surrounding leverage. Its use is popular and well recognized, but the extent of usage and the results of its use have not been chronicled. This study is an effort to effectively correct this lack to the extent possible.

The need for more academic comprehension of the subject of leverage is becoming increasingly apparent during this volatile period of financial change. In a period that has seen promises of halted inflation, but no results, the federal government and its agencies have taken steps to preclude double-digit inflation. So far these efforts have been relatively ineffective, but it is nevertheless correct that the efforts have been and are being made.

Primary among these efforts, from the viewpoint of the potential real estate investor, is the pressure from the Federal Reserve Board to raise the interest rate to a level that will inhibit borrowing. One of the first areas to be the focus of these efforts was the real estate market. Mortgage rates have now gone above 14 percent in most of the United States, and in some areas is higher by as much as one or two points.

It was expected that the net result would be a slowing of construction, and that did, in fact, occur. At the time of the Board's decision, however, home buying continued to flourish—especially in California—and this in turn lifted real estate values to ever-increasing highs for the state, not only with respect to single-family housing, but also for investment income-producing properties.

A study by the nation's largest bank, Bank of America, showed that in April of 1974, prices for homes in California and in the rest of the United States had the same average: $37,800. By April 1978, that balance had radically changed; the average for the Southern California home had reached a level of $27,100 *above* that of the average home in the United States as a whole. The totals were $56,100 average in the nation, compared to $83,200 in Southern California. By October 1978, there was an even greater gap—an estimated $60,000 for the United States at large, versus $91,500 in Southern California, for a gap of $31,500. The Southern California region in the survey included a seven-county area, led by Los Angeles where the county average was $100,200 because of extremely high single-family home prices in Beverly Hills, San Marino, and West Los Angeles.

These changes are attributed in part to the energy crisis and a whole string of cold winters in other areas, which made Southern California more desirable, but there is also an acceleration prompted by a high level of demand and low level of supply of fine homes in choice areas. As the price rose, the real estate market itself rose. The investor was faced with higher prices to be paid for investments, which meant higher equity returns from sales, but at the same time meant that more equity dollars were needed for investments whether on leverage or not.

Real estate developers and investors were seen as slowing their investment involvements as a result of this and other considerations, such as higher interest rates. These responses were beginning to appear throughout the nation.

From January to November of 1978, the prime rate—the rate offered to the banks' best customers—rose from 7 1/2 percent to 11 percent, and construction loans usually require another 1 1/2 to 4 1/2 percentage points above the prime. Before a developer will consider making 15 percent or higher interest payments on a loan, he or she is going to do some second thinking in most instances. Construction forecasts for 1981 are, therefore, showing only moderate gains even in those instances where there is a demand for construction.

Leverage is simply the use of borrowed funds to complete an investment transaction. One hundred percent leverage means 100 percent financing of the real estate purchased, which is the opposite of 100 percent equity purchase. Generally speaking, leverage is in the area of 70 to 90 percent. That is, the larger the proportion of borrowed funds used to make the investment, the higher the leverage is, and conversely, the lower the proportion of equity funds will be.

Another term for leverage is "trading on the equity," and it refers to the use of borrowed funds to acquire an income-producing asset based on expectations of producing a higher rate of return on the equity investment. The core of the idea is that money can be borrowed at a lower rate than the rate produced by the property. To the extent that this return on investment is achieved at a higher rate than the interest rate on the mortgage interest, the portion of the investment covered by the mortgage fund loans makes money for the investor. This surplus increases the yield on the equity investment.

Thus, where a $400,000 property produces $40,000 a year after capital recovery allowance is deducted, the rate of return is 10 percent. The investor who buys the property outright has an equity dividend rate of 10 percent and cannot possibly make more since he or she owns the property 100 percent and is not paying mortgage interest. For the investor who purchased the same property with a 70 percent leverage at 8.5 percent interest, debt service of $23,800 is deducted for mortgage payments. The mortgage of 70 percent ($280,000) yielding $40,000 is going to leave $16,200 after debt service payment, which is for simplification here considered the only debt service. The property has to earn 5.95

percent on the total investment to cover mortgage interest, and the balance of $16,200 is a return on the 30 percent equity investment in the property. This means the equity dividend rate is 13.5 percent, made possible because leverage was used appropriately and successfully. In this example, the total investment was 10 percent, with mortgage interest of 5.95 percent and a resulting return on equity of 4.05 percent times three, or 13.5 percent.

The key to leverage is that the greater the leverage and the variance of the property income, the greater the variability in equity returns and equity dividend rates will be. The investor accepts the mortgage liability in the expectancy of earning a higher equity return from leverage, but at the same time takes the risk that it may, in fact, be lower. If the rate of return on the entire investment falls below the mortgage rate, the impact falls on the equity investor and the greater the leverage, the greater this negative impact will be on the equity dividend rate. This risk is precisely the chance the leverage user accepts by agreeing to pay fixed mortgage interest on borrowed funds.

Some conclusions can be reached. For example, a change in mortgage interest rates can mean significant differences in the computations of whether leverage is appropriate in a given situation. Generally speaking, the higher the interest rate, the lower the equity dividend rate, and the lower the value of both the equity investment and the entire property itself. (This assumes the other loan terms remain the same.) In the sample given above, had interest on the mortgage been 9 percent (with no other changes), the return on equity would have dropped to 12.33 percent (30 percent equity times the difference between the total investment and mortgage interest). The half-point increase in the mortgage interest rate led to a 1.17 percent decrease in equity dividend rate. Considering that mortgage interest has risen to 11 percent plus or minus, the change is easily recognizable as a force of great impact.

Another common real estate practice—discounting a mortgage loan and charging points—results in a reduction of value of the equity investment, both because it increases the effective mortgage interest rate and further increases the amount of equity investment and percentage of total investment represented by equity that are required. While the return on equity is the same, the amount of equity required is lower and the equity dividend rate drops.

Variable mortgage interest rates are not common practice and are seldom available as a consideration for leverage financing in real estate for investors.

There are many tools available in real estate for analyzing property. One area of particular concern to many potential investors is the after-tax cash flow that can be gained from a given investment. Tax considerations are important factors to many investors, regardless of leverage. That is, the potential for tax savings is a consideration separate from whether to use leverage, but where leverage can add to tax savings, then it is a double benefit.

In calculating after-tax cash flow, the present worth is of little value in investing analysis. The importance of such calculations is in providing the investor with indications of how much net cash flow can be anticipated in each of the individual years of the projected investment holding period.

There are two areas of concern in after-tax cash flow: it should be maximized annually and it should be positioned to keep for the investor as much of the net proceeds as possible at the time of reversion from sale.

Judicious use of leverage plus good management can lead to optimum net operating income, which, in turn, leads to optimum before-tax cash flows, which in turn lead to maximizing after-tax cash flow for the investor.

Tax liability is calculated against net operating income, and deductible items include mortgage interest charges and depreciation. This is where leverage is representative of potential large tax savings since leverage means high mortgage percentage and resulting interest charges. The interest payments are actual cash output from the investor and are a totally unquestioned deduction from net operating income. Amortization payments are more complex. They are included in the debt service computations, which constitute equity build-up for the investor rather than being deductible from net operating income in calculating taxable net income. Annual interest payments must be segregated from amortization of principal to determine the actual amount deductible from the net operating income figures.

Although depreciation is not a cash outlay, it is a charge that provides for recovery of anticipated capital loss. There is a predetermined formula for depreciation. To the extent that such annual depreciation and interest charges are increased, the base of taxable income and tax liability are decreased, and to this extent the investor has a tax shelter for his or her cash inflow. Thus, the larger the depreciation and interest charges, within the bounds of prudent investing and return on investment, the greater the tax shelter benefit. Lower taxes mean higher after-tax cash flow for the investor.

Deferring tax liability is also considered a good and valid money-saving tool since the dollar not paid out today has an expected higher value than the dollar ultimately paid out for taxes later. The inflation-reduced dollar used in deferred tax payments is the basis for this method of handling investment taxes. Partially amortized mortgages with balloon payments at maturity have the effect of increasing cash flow to the investor in the first years of the investment holding period, both through reducing actual total annual debt service over the term of the loan and increasing cash throw-off, and through moving a larger proportion of the annual debt service to a tax-deductible interest payment.

Tax liability avoidance can also be achieved through conversion of the net proceeds of reversion into long-term capital gain rather than ordinary income to the extent possible, since long-term capital gains are taxed at a lower rate than is ordinary income. Net savings in taxes through taxation as a long-term capital gain lead to net cash proceeds retention at a higher level than would be achieved through taxing as ordinary income the same proceeds.

The implementation of these tools for maximization of tax deductible charges, minimization of taxable income over the preliminary years of the holding period for the investment, and through obtaining capital gains taxation levels rather than ordinary income will add strength to the present worth of a given income, making such an investment significantly more attractive to an investor than would be true if such tools were not utilized in keeping tax liability as low as legally possible. The chain of movement is the net operating income less mortgage interest and depreciation charges equals taxable income, so that taxable income times tax rate equals income tax liability.

This study concentrated much of its energy on the development of a profile of the typical investor who uses leverage. The 50 men and women elicited the information that, almost without exception, these real estate brokers, investors, and developers were fully familiar with leverage, but did not have valid formulas developed for its analysis. It was agreed by all but one respondent that most of the substantial fortunes made in real estate during this period by investors were the result of using leverage to get involved in investments with low cash equity and high return as a result of escalating property value, income cash flows, and reversion profits at the time of sale or exchange.

This does not mean that leverage is a tool for speculation and speculators, or that those who made the high profits were, in fact, speculators more than they were investors. Rather it was a case of reputable investors seeing opportunities to spread their available cash into numerous directions rather than concentrating it all for equity in one venture. The opportunities were there at a time of unprecedented real estate growth in real dollars, and through careful evaluation of the market, the investors were able to move in and out of investment real estate packages to their considerable advantage. They accomplished this both through tax savings efforts and through insightful investing. But, as the *Wall Street Journal* article cited earlier pointed out, the opportunities for investors are narrowing as more and more people enter the field of real estate investing, including those with petrodollars and other inflationary dollars such as those generated by the trade deficit with Japan. For this reason, which was acknowledged by the large majority of the sample population, additional tools are valuable for the investor no matter what the size of the investment—small, medium, or large.

Leverage is considered a thoroughly effective and valid tool for real estate investors, according to the interviews and results of the questionnaires, and most agreed that wise investors at least try to incorporate leverage into their investment packages. The tendency on the part of the investors was to see that leverage was a better way to make a profit than by investing the same funds in other types of enterprises, while some of the brokers believed that second trust deeds were either equally or more advantageous from a pure investment standpoint. Many stated that investing in real estate was the most exciting and involving way to take investment risks and had the most provocative payoffs since they could be dramatically successful, while investments such as second trust deeds were far more predictable.

The classic, typical investor who should use leverage, according to an analysis of the answers received both during the interviews and from the questionnaires, should have financial strength and size so that one or more losses would not sink his financial ship. The size of the typical investor would, therefore, be middle or large, and it was generally agreed that the small investor who had just one or two operations at a time stood the greatest risk and was atypical in many instances and inappropriately involved in leverage financing in at least half the cases in which such an investment tool was used.

Ideally, the investor who uses leverage should, according to those surveyed, have at least three or four concurrent investments. As previously discussed, this could mean greater loss if the risk taken proved to be a bad one, but on the other hand the spread across numerous endeavors usually meant protection for the leverage investor, provided the investments were detailed and analyzed carefully before any commitments were made and cash and contractual agreements rendered.

Because of its popularity among the larger dollar investors, leverage was seen to be generally useful in major real estate transactions. The interviews showed that those who viewed this differently often did so because they believed that major real estate transactions were, by their nature, likely to involve leverage and should not be singled out and separated from other-than-major real estate transactions.

The respondents tended to agree essentially that a poor situation is magnified by leverage, but so is a good one, saying that the good ones are less visible in this respect. Leverage permits strong equity dividend rates on successful deals, but the losses that develop from poor situations are amplified by word of mouth within the industry itself. Generally, the respondents felt that inexperienced investors should use leverage only if they can be guided through the steps and stages by someone who has "been there." There was general agreement that the degree of success attained through the use of leverage was, in fact, quite high, in that it accomplished the goal for which it was used in the first place—to provide additional income beyond what would be achieved with higher equity involvement.

Conclusion

I would like to suggest that you follow the procedures set forth in this book in a certain way. Prior to going to sleep each night, take a pad and, in the order of their importance, write down those things that you intend to accomplish the following day. You should develop your checklist that you will be using in your search for property; keep it with you always.

Remember what was said in this book: "Those who do not take a risk will not have anything of worth." Also remember that "the hardest part of a long journey is the first step." Search for that particular piece of property. Start with a house if that is all you realistically can afford at the time—seek out the owner, negotiate as you were taught, and make the best deal possible using leverage. Perhaps you are in a financial position to start with a sixplex using the same tactics.

To illustrate the importance of following a guideline as explained in this book, let me relate an event that happened early in my life; it made a believer out of me. Before World War II, I had an appointment in Longview, Texas, and I flew my Sky Ranger there and landed in a small sandy field with high lines and pine trees surrounding the area. I went into town to keep my appointment, which took longer than I anticipated. I left the meeting and returned to the airplane as quickly as possible, jumped in, and after warming it up for a few minutes, headed the plane into the light wind, giving it full throttle to take off.

The sand was creating drag, and for some reason I was not getting full power although the engine was not misfiring. The runway kept getting shorter and shorter, and the plane still wasn't off the ground. I quickly glanced at the instrument panel and found the carburetor heater switch in the "on" position. I immediately turned it off—the engines roared into full power and we were off the ground, but not in time to gain enough altitude to clear the high lines. I was forced to fly under them and dodge pine trees for what seemed an eternity before reaching a safe altitude.

The experience made a lasting impression on me. Never again did I take off in an airplane without first reading the checklist and checking each item, nor did I land before reading the landing checklist and checking each item. I have never since failed to read my checklist first, and I have carried that practice over into my everyday business life. I have saved thousands of dollars by not overlooking anything or leaving things to chance.

May you have good fortune on your road to becoming a professional investor, aided by the knowledge you have acquired in this book. Remember, you can be and do anything you wish if you want to badly enough. Many others have become successful. I have and so can you. Think positive. Out there are thousands of untapped opportunities. All you need do is seek them out and act.

I believe this is the time to tell you a short story about a young man who applied for a job as a pilot in 1945. I was released from the Navy in 1945, and since there was an abundance of qualified pilots, a flying job was hard to come by. So we bought a cub aircraft and eventually started a G.I. flying school. We were seeking qualified instructors, and a young pilot applied.

During the interview, to ascertain his qualifications one of the questions asked of him was, "Have you ever been lost in an airplane?" Without hesitation, the young man replied, "Never." My reply was that he was either a damn liar or hadn't been flying very long. Which was it? His answer was, "I don't lie and I never was lost. I might have been confused for three or four hours, but lost, never." He was a good pilot and he was honest. He just couldn't differentiate betwen being lost and being confused. There are times when you are going to be in doubt and confused—just don't get lost. Keep both feet on the ground, think positive, and don't lose sight of your destination.

Appendix

Expense and Replacement Cost Index

The following material was gathered with the courtesy of various savings and loan institutions, banks, certified property management companies, appraisers, wholesalers, contractors, and real estate brokers.

The figures are as close as could be ascertained for 1981, and as each of us know, prices never stand still. Therefore, these figures are to be taken as indicators, not hard, fast rules or fixed prices. To update the arithmetic, use the Cost of Living Index, Consumer Index, Gross National Product, and check with the same type of sources I used. Part of the information was compiled from my own experience and records with the aid of a computer. This data is intended as a guideline for your future use. Remember that everything in this business of investing involves checking, double checking, and then checking again.

Expenses and replacement costs for various items or areas are listed in the following order:

Utilities	Elevator maintenance
Laundry	Air conditioning maintenance
Gas	Reserves
Electricity	Appliances
Water	Furniture
Repairs, maintenance, and decorating	Roof
Gardening	Carpeting and drapes
Trash	Other equipment
Pool maintenance and equipment	Management
Jacuzzi maintenance	Property taxes

Utilities

Emphasis must be placed on the history of utility expenses for the building as shown in the owner's Expense Statement records. Even utility companies themselves have no forecasting guidelines due to variables.

Consumption for each building will vary relatively little from year to year or ownership to ownership. This is because utilities are a mostly fixed function of either tenant consumption (such as hot water) or improvement (such as house lights). *Important:* Due to seasonal fluctuations, Expense Statement figures should reflect 12 consecutive months' billings. Also, watch for rate increases.

Laundry

Find your type of building (according to tenancy) in the following yearly tables and multiply the average dollar consumption (far right column) by the number of units. Subtract this amount from the utility expense amounts to obtain the adjusted expense figure. Water cost (approximately two cents per load) is negligible and can be omitted from computation.

GAS

Tenancy	Avg. Number Loads Per Unit Per Year	Gas Cost Per Load	Avg. Gas Cost Per Unit Per Year
Older tenants	36	6.5¢	$2.34
Singles	48	6.5¢	$3.12
Married couples	84	6.5¢	$5.46
Married couples w/children	108	6.5¢	$7.02

ELECTRIC (using gas heat)

Tenancy	Avg. Number Loads Per Unit Per Year		Avg. Elec. Cost Per Unit Per Year
Older tenants	36	3.0¢	$1.08
Singles	48	3.0¢	$1.44
Married couples	84	3.0¢	$2.52
Married couples w/children	108	3.0¢	$3.24

ALL ELECTRIC

Tenancy	Avg. Number Loads Per Unit Per Year	Elec. Cost Per Load	Avg. Elec. Cost Per Unit Per Year
Older tenants	36	21.0¢	$ 7.56
Singles	48	21.0¢	$10.08
Married couples	84	21.0¢	$17.64
Married couples w/children	108	21.0¢	$22.68

Most buildings will have individual gas meters, but will have central hot water systems, meaning that management pays for hot water. Often, hot water and the laundry room are the only gas consumption items paid for by management. Smaller units with individual 20- or 30-gallon water heaters and no laundry facilities may not have any gas expense.

Rate structure

1 Billing Unit = 1 Therm

1 Therm = 100 cubic feet of gas

1 cubic foot of gas = 1075 BTUs

1 BTU = the amount of heat required to raise the heat of 1 lb. of water by 1° Fahrenheit.

Let's calculate the cost of running a 100-gallon, 220,000 BTU hot water heater for one day. We will use a six-hour operating time (approximately the amount of time per day a heater may operate).

Consumption Example

220,000	BTUs	
× 6	hours per day	
1,320,000	BTUs consumed per day	
+ 1,075	to find cubic foot consumption	
1,228	cubic feet of gas per day	
+ 100	as 100 cubic feet = 1 Therm	
12.28	Therms consumption	
+ $1.88	using current Los Angeles billing rate (local rate)	
$2.31	operating cost per day	

Factors to note

Type tenancy and number of tenants: family units are the biggest consumers.

No circulating pump on water heater: in a demand system, much hot water will be wasted as the water travels the lengths of the pipes before it hits the faucets.

Varying billing rates and structures of different municipalities.

Appliance efficiency: includes BTU ratings, water heater, insulation, gas pilot vs. electric ignition, and efficiency of laundry room appliances.

Amount of gas service paid by tenants.

Inaccurate meters.

Temperature setting of water heater.

Plumbing leaks: includes pipes in slab foundations.

Gas service cost

$10–$16 per room per year for central hot water and laundry facilities.

For buildings with gas service included in the rent, the cost will be approximately $50–$70 per unit per year.

For a pool, add $30 per month for pool heat for six summer months; $65 per month for heating during six winter months (if applicable); $5 per month for recreation room with kitchen.

Electricity

Rate Structure The standard billing unit is the kilowatt hour, or KWH. One KWH = 1,000 hourly watts, or the equivalent sum of 10 100-watt bulbs burning for one hour.

Consumption Example A common item on which the management will be paying electrical costs is the hot water circulating pump. This may be a one-eighth horsepower unit consuming 125 hourly watts. In this exercise we find the monthly KWH consumption and multiply it by the billing factor (using current Los Angeles rates). We assume the water pump is on a timer and/or demand system and is running 12 hours per day.

$$
\begin{array}{rl}
125 & \text{watts} \\
\times\ 12 & \text{hours per day use} \\
\hline
1.5 & \text{KWH per day consumption} \\
\times\ 30 & \text{days per month} \\
\hline
45 & \text{KWH per month consumption} \\
\times\ \$.04480 & \text{billing factor per KWH} \\
\hline
\$20.16 & \text{or, the cost of running } our \text{ circulating}
\end{array}
$$

pump will be about $20 per month. Remember, this is a sample problem and may not be reliable for your property.

Factors to note

Billing rates and structures: basic rates and surcharges vary from community to community.

Number of fixtures: entails the number of house lights, whether there is a circulating pump, pool equipment, security system, central A/C, sauna, jacuzzi, and so on; an elevator will be a major consumer.

Types of fixtures: fluorescent lighting will be more economic than incandescent; also, on smaller buildings the absence of a circulating pump will further reduce electric expenditures.

Type of tenancy: not of much importance on individually metered buildings, but plays greater significance in master metered buildings.

Timers: simple and inexpensive tools that can save on consumption.

A FINAL NOTE: Some buildings will have the exterior lights wired to the adjacent units and may not even have a house electrical account. While inspecting the building, try to note which fixtures are billed to the house account and which are paid for by the individual tenants.

Electricity Costs

5,000–10,000 sq. ft. 2¢ to 3¢ per year per sq. ft.

Over 10,000 sq. ft. . . . . 3¢ to 6¢ per year per sq. ft.

Add $35 per month (for all 12 months) for pool pump.

MULTIPLIER: For example, when using the previous twelve months billings in areas served by the Los Angeles Department of Water and Power, use the following multipiers:

Yearly bill	Multiplier
0–$100	$.85
$101–201	.78
$201–300	.76
$301–400	.75
$401–500	.74
$600 and up	.74

Water

Almost all apartment buildings have a master meter for water, which means management pays for all consumption.

Billing unit

1 billing unit = 100 cu. ft. of water = 748 gal.

Factors to note

Number of tenants: usually the most important factor.

Tenancy type: family buildings will consume the most amount of water per tenant.

Landscape requirements: factors include size of a lot, type of landscaping, soil conditions, and sprinkler equipment.

Building efficiency: newer buildings will have toilets, showers, and other appliances requiring less water to operate; approximately 75 percent of a typical apartment's water consumption is attributed to bathroom use; dishwashers (large consumers) will use up to 200 gallons of water per cycle.

Leaks: often in slabs or in the underground main; a small shower drip will waste approximately 2,000 cubic feet of water per year.

Meter inaccuracy: due to worn meter bearings and generally gives the advantage to the building owner, this condition is found more commonly in water meters than in electric or gas meters.

Added surcharges: includes the "purchased water adjustment" or other charges to cover the supplier's price fluctuations; this amount would be contingent upon the amount of water purchased from outside suppliers, for instance, the effect would be much more pronounced in San Diego, where 90 percent of the water is purchased from the Metropolitan Water District, than in Los Angeles, where only 5 percent is purchased from this same outside supplier. The bill may also include sewer service charges, tap size charges, and fire service charges.

Pool consumption is negligible as only about six cubic feet of water evaporate per year for every square foot of surface area.

Water cost

$10–$18 per room per year.

Repairs, Maintenance, and Decorating

Repairs, maintenance, and decorating include all redecorating and building upkeep as outlined below. The estimate used should be adequate to maintain the subject property at a level where the adjusted rents used in the rent schedule will be obtainable over a period of time.

This is one expense that the investor should arrive at without the help of the Expense Statement. This is due to: (1) owners frequently making improper distinctions between capital improvements, reserves, and the repairs and maintenance; (2) omission of repair expenses; (3) nonuniformity of accounting systems; (4) Expense Statement reflecting a year of exceptional costs; and (5) the owner "milking" the building while performing inadequate upkeep.

Items to remember

Painting of interior and exterior.

Preparation of units for rental.

All repairs, including those to the roof, driveway, diato, and plumbing and electrical systems.

Factors to note

Age of building: as with reserves, the older building will require a greater outlay to keep competitive on the rental market; items with a medium-term life-span will start needing repair, such as doors, screens, and light fixtures, as the building reaches midlife.

Tenancy type: family units and pet-allowed buildings will require more frequent repairs and maintenance; an all-singles building may follow close behind.

Area: buildings in high-income areas will require more maintenance and decorating to keep competitive in the rental market.

Turnover: buildings with furnished single units and catering to a more transient group will require more redecoration.

Building quality: better quality buildings will require less maintenance work.

Condition: if the appraisal is for a sale and the building is in poor or fair condition, the new owner will probably have to make numerous expenditures over the initial part of the holding period.

Maintenance figures are shown in two different forms: Dollars Per Square Foot and Percentage of Gross Possible Total Income.

• *Dollars per square foot.* This method represents maintenance as a function of building size. However, no regard is given to the target rental market or type of tenancy.

• *Percentage of gross possible total income.* This method recognizes that maintenance is a function of tenants' demands according to various rent levels; the same building would have a wide range of maintenance expenses if physically placed into different markets. This method takes size into account, but only so far as the rents increase because of unit size. This is a good method, but may distort where unusually high or low rents are encountered.

Maintenance figures are further subclassified into "high," "median," and "low" maintenance. The "low" and "high" values are chosen so that the bottom 25 percent of the sample falls below the "low" and the top 25 percent is above the "high." The amount chosen for expense projection must be sufficient to maintain the building in the appraised condition and to sustain the projected rents. Following are some rough guidelines for choosing between the alternatives:

High

Children or younger tenants.
High turnover such as smaller furnished units.
Poor building quality.
Physical deterioration that cannot be deferred.

Median

Effective management.
Typical building.
History of continued maintenance.

Low

Typical owner-managed property.
Few mechanical items not accounted for in reserves.
Good condition; however, consider amount of maintenance investment necessary to sustain the building in the appraised condition.

Expense Figures
5 – 24 Units
Percentage of Gross Possible Total Income

	1945 & prior	1946–1960	1961–1968	1969–1974	1975–1980
Maintenance/repairs	5.9%	6.1%	5.4%	3.5%	2.0%
Painting/decorating	3.7	2.3	2.7	2.2	2.0
Supplies	.7	.3	.6	.7	.7
Total (median)	10.3%	8.7%	8.7%	6.4%	4.7%
Low	5.9	5.0	5.0	3.4	2.5
Median	10.3	8.7	8.7	6.4	4.7
High	18.1	15.3	15.3	11.3	6.7

Dollars Per Square Foot*

	1945 & prior	1946–1960	1961–1968	1968–1974	1975–present
Maintenance/repairs	.17	.23	.18	.11	.07
Painting/decorating	.10	.08	.08	.06	.04
Supplies	.08	.01	.02	.04	.02
Total (median)	.35	.32	.28	.21	.13
Low	.19	.17	.15	.11	.07
Median	.35	.32	.28	.21	.13
High	.68	.62	.54	.41	.25

* Square footage for purposes of maintenance, repair, and decorating expense projections can be computed by measuring *inside finish* of permanent outer building walls (assume 6″ walls). Rentable area shall include all area within outside walls less stairs and stairways, center halls, elevator shafts, janitor closets, laundry rooms, electrical closets, water heater rooms, balconies, and such other rooms not actually available to the tenant for furnishings and personnel, and their enclosing walls. No deductions made for columns and projections unnecessary to the building.

Expense Figures
25 and More Units
Percentage of Gross Possible Total Income

	1960 & prior	1961– 1968	1969– 1974	1975 to 1980
Maintenance/repairs	6.2%	7.4%	5.9%	3.5%
Painting/decorating	4.0	2.9	1.9	1.2
Supplies	.8	.4	.3	.2
Total (median)	11.0%	10.7%	8.1%	4.9%
Low	6.5	6.3	4.8	2.9
Median	11.0	10.7	8.1	4.9
High	17.6	17.2	13.0	7.9

Dollars Per Square Foot

	1960 & prior	1961– 1968	1969– 1974	1975 to present
Maintenance/repairs	.17	.20	.18	.13
Painting/decorating	.07	.07	.07	.04
Supplies	.04	.02	.01	.01
Total (median)	.28	.29	.26	.18
Low	.19	.19	.17	.12
Median	.28	.29	.26	.18
High	.46	.47	.42	.29

Gardening

Gardening and grounds care will generally be the task of both the resident manager and the gardener. The manager will most likely have the responsibility for watering and cleaning the public areas; this is covered under Management Expenses. The gardener may make one or two visits per week to mow the lawn, edge borders, care for flowers, trees, and shrubs, and generally clean up.

Factors to note

Amount of landscaping: may have little to do with the size of the building; some duplexes have more landscaping than some 60-unit centercourt buildings.

Type of landscaping: some plants and shrubs, obviously, require less care for the area than others.

Amount of difficult work: extra lawn is a minor problem, but edging along the building and fencing can mean considerable extra time and money.

Rental market: as rent levels increase, tenants expect better looking grounds.

Existing landscape improvements: such improvements as brick and wood planters can reduce work; however, the plantings in these improvements may require more care than if the area were seeded with grass or another low-maintenance item.

New landscape work may reflect a high figure in the Expense Statement. One building analyzed for this guideline indicated an especially high figure for gardening; a visit to the property found four new trees and a number of new planter boxes. The gardening expense would be adjusted to reflect a more typical year.

Gardening services begin at about $300 per year (or $25 per month). This is considered the least amount a gardener will require to make a once-a-week visit. Following are the results of a survey to ascertain monthly gardening costs for two typical types of buildings:

Typical 10-unit walk-up building with 200 sq. ft. of lawn, 100 sq. ft. of planted area, and several trees—$30 per month.

Typical 20-unit center-court with pool, landscaping around court, and minimal front lawn—$70 per month.

For larger units and those properties that present extra difficulty in estimating gardening costs, the Income and Expense Statement should be referenced for an actual figure. Again, the investor must draw on his or her own resources and experience to decide whether the owner has submitted a reasonable cost.

Trash

Some cities provide for trash disposal and some do not. City services may be practical only for smaller units, as the trucks may not be equipped to handle bins. City collection may also necessitate the owner or manager setting the trash out on the proper day. A typical one-bedroom unit with a single tenant will produce enough trash in one week to fill one 32-gallon can, so more than six or seven units may make collection in smaller containers rather cumbersome. Assuming an owner will go with free or low-cost city collection if possible, a look at the Expense Statement will help determine the most feasible practice. Also, some communities have a limit on the amount of trash they will collect.

Commercial trash collectors generally use three-cubic-yard bins in conjunction with their front hydraulic lift disposal trucks. One of these bins will typically accommodate up to 12 units with a once-a-week pickup.

Factors to note

Tenancy of the building: of paramount importance; family buildings can easily produce two or three times the rubbish of an all-singles building with an equal number of units.

Bin accessibility and amount of push-out to truck: truck operators must get the bin to the truck, and a bin with difficult access will cost more to service.

Elevation of the container: a container that must be pushed uphill will cost the owner more than one that will roll along level ground; something to consider when the bin is located in a subterranean parking area.

Street accessibility: takes into account the topography, turnaround, parking, amount of traffic, and width.

Custom applications: includes containers specially designed for chute-type garbage disposal.

Time element: higher rent area buildings often prefer service after a certain time of the day to avoid disrupting the tenants; this may cost more due to traffic and routing problems.

Distance from dump site.

<u>Cost of commercial collection service</u>

$7 – $9 per room per year for 10 – 40 rooms.

$6 – $8 per room per year for 41 – 60 rooms.

$5 – $7 per room per year for over 60 rooms.

or

No. of 3 Cu Yd. Bins*	No. Pickups Per Week	Cost Per Month
1	3	$30
1	2	$50
1	3	$70
2	2	$92

* This table is for a building with easy truck access and a 10-ft. bin roll-out.
Each 3 cu. yd. bin with one pickup per week will accommodate 6–12 units.

Pool Maintenance and Equipment

Costs presented here are for an average apartment-sized pool measuring 15′ × 30′ with a 20,000-gallon capacity. This size pool is most commonly serviced twice a week, but could be serviced as little as once a week or as often as three times a week. Sometimes, during frequent summer use, an additional call each week must be made.

<u>Pool maintenance contract charges</u>

Twice-a-week service for average pool .... $55 per month.

Twice-a-week service for smaller pool .... $50 per month.

Three-times-a-week service for larger pool .... $80 per month.

<u>Services to be rendered</u>

Chemicals twice weekly.

Scrub tile once a week.

Vacuum once a week.

Backwash filter once or twice a month.

<u>Equipment</u>

Pool filter: Life expectancy for a filter is five to seven years, with a replacement cost of $200 for the unit and another $125 to install (for a typical 38- to 48-square-foot, earth-type filter).

Pool pump: These run an average of five to eight hours per day all year and need replacing every three to four years; cost of a 1 ½ horsepower pump is about $150 installed.

Pool heater: The normal apartment house pool heater is a 175,000-250,000 BTU unit with a life of eight to ten years based on six months a year use. Repairs are generally restricted to thermostat replacement about once every two years; cost is minimal. Cost of a new heating unit runs about $450 to $500, plus another $125 to install.

Combined pool equipment costs: For quick calculation of reserves, pool equipment may be combined into one cost utilizing a weighted and combined life expectancy:

Total pool equipment—$1,100

Weighted and combined life expectancy—7 years

Contract charges for jacuzzi maintenance may be:

Jacuzzi
Maintenance

Twice a week with accompanying pool service ...... $20 per month.
Twice a week without pool service .... $40 per month.

Factors to note
Pool size.
Number of people in apartment complex: family building pools receive much more use than other types.
Adequacy and condition of filtering unit.
Amount and type of landscaping around pool: deciduous trees and bushes can create large amounts of debris that will collect in the pool.
Jacuzzi pump has life expectancy of five years; installed cost of about $250.

Elevator Maintenance

Costs for elevator maintenance have been figured for a typical lo-rise apartment elevator: a 2,000-pound capacity, four-stop hydraulic unit. Service contracts are offered by most elevator manufacturing companies, as well as the many independent elevator maintenance firms. Service contracts of the manufacturers generally carry a considerably higher price tag than those of the independents. Suggested figures listed below are based on quotes from independents, as this would be the approach most reasonably taken by the prudent investor. However, manufacturers' quotes have been included separately.

The two types of elevators are the hydraulic and the electric. The hydraulic unit is operated by oil being pumped into and out of a plunger unit (much the same as in a service station bay). The mechanics are located at the bottom of the cab shaft. The electric unit is operated by a traction system with cables. The mechanics are located at the top of shaft. An electric unit is more suited to a building higher than 60 feet requiring five or more stops. The cab, controls, and doors can be identical on both applications. Two types of contracts are offered: preventative maintenance and full service. The preventative maintenance contract consists of periodic oil and grease; the full service contract covers that as well as all parts and labor for repairs. Following are price quotations and influencing factors.

Examples of maintenance
contract charges by manufacturer

Oliver and Williams (Los Angeles)
Preventative maintenance .... $32 per month
Full service .... $85 per month
Otis (Los Angeles)
Preventative maintenance .... $100 per month
Full service .... $140 per month
Westinghouse (Burbank)
Preventative maintenance .... $127 per month
Full service .... $200 per month

Charges by independent contractors

Preventative maintenance .... $35 per month
Full service .... $65 per month

Appendix **197**

Again, these costs are for the typical apartment elevator as described earlier. For appraisal expense purposes, use of the full service contract is recommended; it automatically accounts for repair expenses, which would otherwise have to be accounted for in the repairs, maintenance, and decorating section.

Similar electric installations will run the same for a preventative maintenance contract, but will run from $100 to $125 for the full service contract. As a further example, a 10-stop, hi-rise full service contract will cost about $225 per month.

Factors to note

Age and condition of equipment.

Number of stops and elevator capacity.

Type of mechanical system (hydraulic vs. electric).

Type of tenancy: buildings with children will subject elevators to much extra usage.

For a building with two elevators, deduct 15 percent from the cost of two maintenance contracts. However, if the elevators are adjacent to each other, the costs may be somewhat higher due to complications in the mechanical system.

Air Conditioning Maintenance Contracts

This section contains information pertaining to individual roof-mounted units and central air conditioning systems. Wall units are generally maintained as needed or even replaced upon breakage due to their relatively low cost. Roof-mounted systems with individual mechanical units for each separate dwelling are usually gas and electric units, which supply both heat and air conditioning. The typical unit is a three-ton size requiring service every two months. Although the two-month servicing periods are most common, it is not unusual to find contracts that call for one-month or three-month servicing periods, depending on the influencing factors. Servicing generally requires 15-30 minutes per unit and includes checking the electrics, replacing the filter, lubrication, cleaning condensers, inspection for leaks, and inspection of the bearings, compression switch, and compressor motor. This type of unit is typically found on buildings of less than 10 years of age and almost always have service contracts due to the expense and intricacies of the systems.

Cost of contract for three-ton system

Per visit per unit .... $15–$20.

For large central units, the price will vary with the system and special attention should be paid to the owner's Expense Statement. Variables include whether water is used, cooling towers, size of unit, and the like. These units are usually inspected every two months.

Cost of contract for 50-ton central system

One visit every two months .... $100.

A split system is one with the forced air heating unit located in a closet and the air conditioning compressor located above in the attic or on the roof. Maintenance contracts may or may not be used in conjunction with this type of system. One of the main reasons for this is the often difficult access arrangements. If no contract is utilized, costs for maintenance and repairs would be included in the repairs, maintenance, and decorating category. If a contract is used, it will most often call for servicing every three months with a service charge of $15–$30 per unit. Most typically, the charge will run $20 per unit.

Factors to note

Climate: areas with warmer temperatures and longer summers will require more frequent servicing as air conditioning creates more stress on the unit than does heating; humidity is also a big factor.

Unit exposure to the elements: includes proximity to the ocean, exposure to winds, sun, and rain; dust is also a big factor, with buildings on major streets requiring more servicing due to air movement and added pollution.

Type of tenancy: buildings housing senior citizens or others at home a good portion of the day will carry higher demands on the system; same applies to family units.

Age of equipment: older equipment will cost more to maintain.

Quality of the system.

Adequacy of system for size of dwelling unit: undersized systems are subject to increased demands and maintenance.

Reserves

Reserves for replacements is an allowance to replace those short-lived items necessary to sustain an income appropriate to the building. They include furniture, carpets, drapes, appliances, machinery, and equipment. The amount required for reserves is calculated by dividing the replacement cost of a specific item by its useful life expectancy. Little weight must be given to the owner's Expense Statement figures due to improper distinctions between capital improvements, repairs, and maintenance and the reserves, and also a nonuniformity of accounting systems.

Factors to note

Quality of the building: owners will most likely choose replacement with a quality similar to the original item; in a good quality building, this will tend to set both the life expectancy and the cost at the top of the range; therefore, you will find furnishings separated into different quality categories.

Property age: property with the least reserve requirements will be the new building. Considering a probable holding period of 10 years on the part of the initial investor, the appraiser will use reserves for carpets, drapes, water heaters, disposals, and only those other items with a life expectancy of 10 years or less. At the far end of the scale is the older, poorly maintained building. The very reason the owner is selling or refinancing may be that the building is due for refurbishing. But don't let the older building fool you—some are well maintained, especially those "fixers" renovated by professionals who make a living at this. Here, the purchaser would most probably buy under the assumption that there will be little additional investment over the initial holding period. This philosophy would probably be reflected by the appraiser in his or her evaluation.

Type of tenancy: buildings attempting to hold down a spot in the higher rental market will need more frequent replacements of interior and decorative appointments to be competitive, and, obviously, components in family or pet-allowed buildings will receive a great deal more wear than those in buildings catering to the adults-only market; hence, will have a shorter life expectancy. Senior citizen buildings will require special analysis as the tenants may be home for most of the day, but they will also tend to lead a more sedentary life-style.

Calculating Reserve Amounts

Set up a reserve account for any component with a remaining life expectancy of 10 years or less (that is, reserve account required for any roof with a 10-year or less life expectancy, not required for a roof that has a remaining life expectancy exceeding 10 years. See the owner's Income and Expense Statement for date of last roof replacement).

Use a 10-year holding period for reserve calculation of components with a total life expectancy of over 10 years. Use actual life expectancy for calculating reserve amounts for components with a total life expectancy of less than 10 years.

Appliances

Free-standing appliances

Bachelor refrigerator: typical, 6.6 cu. ft., estimated life expectancy 10 years, $160.

12-cu.-ft. refrigerator: manual defrost, single door, life expectancy 10 years, $300.

18-cu.-ft. refrigerator: frost-free, top-mount freezer with single door, life expectancy 10 years, $450.

20″ stove: four burners, nonwindowed, separate broiler, life expectancy 15 years, $210.

30″ stove: four burners, nonwindowed, separate broiler, no timer, life expectancy 15 years, $240.

30″ stove: trim, clock with signal timer, windowed door, separate broiler, life expectancy 15 years, $325.

BUILT-IN APPLIANCES

Item	Life Expectancy (years)	Part Cost w/Tax*	Installation	Total
Built-in range and oven	15	$265	$60	$325
Drop-in range and oven	15	$210–265	$60	$270–315
Disposal	5–6	$ 35	$20	$55
Dishwasher	5–7	$210	$40	$250
A/C, wall 9,000 BTU	6–8	$265		$265

Water Heaters				
30 gal.	5–10	$ 90	$ 40	$130
40 gal.	5–10	$105	$ 50	$155
50 gal.	5–10	$135	$ 60	$195
*80 gal.	5–8	$350	$100	$450
†100 gal.	5–8	$530	$100	$630

*For 80-gal. electric unit, use total cost of $410.
†For 100-gal. electric unit, use total cost of $450.

Item	Life Expectancy (years)	Part Cost w/Tax*	Installation	Total
A/C, individual roof mount with combined heating and cooling	5–10	(cost installed)		$1,260
54" combination unit with stove, oven, sink, refrigerator	15	$750	$100	$850

*All costs include 6% sales tax

Since the greatest percentage of the furnished or partially furnished operations are two or three story, frame and stucco, average or good quality conventional or side walk-up buildings, these were used as the subject of inquiry. The number of units was not found to be of significant importance. The owner in this example would be the "typical" investor, perhaps owning one or two other buildings, but having no special or unusual connections for purchasing furnishings. We have specifically excluded the large developer and/or operator of a large number of units, since these corporations usually have a special "in" with a manufacturer or are in a position to warehouse in large quantities for future use. These buildings will require special consideration and are often rented unfurnished.

Three general classes of furniture are discussed here—"fair," "average," and "good" quality. Which grade is best suited to the subject will depend on the present grade of furniture, rent levels, the desired rental market, tenancy type, and location. The following cost estimates are based on units of average size and design. Typical apartments would be:

Single & Bachelor . . 1–2 rooms . . . . 300–500 sq. ft.
One bedroom . . . . 3-1/2 rooms . . . . 500–700 sq. ft.
Two bedroom . . . . 4-1/2 rooms . . . . 650–900 sq. ft.
Three bedroom . . . 5-1/2 rooms . . . . 1,100-1,600 sq. ft.

Furniture quality should be self-evident to the appraiser, but here is a short list of quality attributes:

Fair

Sofas and chairs without removable cushions.
No leaf in dinette table.
Low back on dinette chairs.
End tables with lightweight, screw-in legs.
No padding on rear of sofa.
Wood frame easily felt through the upholstery on the lower front side of sofa or padded chair.
Six-drawer dresser with or without small mirror.

Removable chair and sofa cushions with wrapped upholstery.
High-back dinette chairs.
Stylish pictures and frames.
Nine-drawer dresser with mirror.
Upholstered arms on occasional chairs.

Good

Better quality materials and workmanship.
Larger lamps.
Pictures framed with glass.
Coffee tables with legs attached to side aprons (not screwed to base).
Dinette set with leaf and high-back chairs.
Heavier and more sturdy construction.
Upgraded accessories.
Upholstered furniture more heavily padded.

Roof

The cost of roof coverings is continually updated in the Yard Costs/Unit in Place Section (Section C, p. C-16) of the *Marshall and Swift Residential Cost Handbook*. As an example, the following table includes these costs along with life expectancy figures obtained from California roofing contractors.

Type Roof	Life Expectancy	Cost Per Sq. Ft. of Roof Area
Asphalt Shingle, 235 lb.	15 yrs.	$ .46
Asphalt Shingle, 300 lb.	20 yrs.	$ .57
Built-up, 3-ply, and gravel	17 yrs.	$ .61
Cedar shingles	18 yrs.	$ .83
Shakes, Medium	20 yrs.	$1.01
Mineral surface cap sheet, 3-ply (flat roof with sealed seams)	12 yrs.	$ .38

Carpeting and Drapes

Carpeting   Nylon is used in more than 70 percent of the carpets produced today and is a favorite of apartment owners, as it is strong, resilient, and long wearing. Other types of carpeting include wool, acrylic, polyester, and polypropylene, or blends of any two or more fibers. Carpeting is often referred to by the manufacturer's brand name, such as Zefram (acrylic); Antron (nylon); and Herculon (polypropylene). Specifications for nylon carpeting as typically found in apartment buildings is as follows:

Quality	Life Expectancy	Cost
Fair	3–5 years	$3.50–$4.50 sq. yd.
Average	5–7 years	$5.25–$6.50 sq. yd.
Good	7–10 years	$8.50–$12.00 sq. yd.

Jute and one-half-inch rebound are the most popular. Jute, 100 percent animal hair or an animal hair-fiber combination, is graded by weight, with 40 to 50 ounces per yard being standard. Rebound is made from sponge rubber or foam rubber with either a smooth or waffled surface. The weight for this type of pad would typically be 40 to 50 ounces per yard. Other types of padding incude urethane and pneumatic cellular pad.

Some owners or managers prefer to lay the new carpeting over the old without using any padding. However, this is not suggested as the new carpeting will tend to "walk" with the direction of the sweep of the underlying carpet. This necessitates periodic relaying. Many times, especially with jute, the owner will retain the old padding when recarpeting, maybe replacing the padding with every other carpet replacement. For this reason, our installed carpeting costs reflect a "double life" for the padding. Actual costs for padding are as follows:

Jute .... $1.25 sq. yd.
1/2" rebound .... $1.50 sq. yd.

Average cost of labor is between $1.25 and $1.50 per square yard for installation. This service is often supplied by the retailer and charged as an extra item.

Carpeting Costs Basis

Unit	No. Yards Carpeting
Single	38
One bedroom	54
Two bedroom	81
Three bedroom	108

Carpeting Costs

Quality	Carpet Cost	Pad Cost*	Sales Tax	Labor Cost	Total Per Yard
Fair	$3.70	$.65	$.26	$1.25	$ 5.86
Average	$5.60	$.65	$.37	$1.25	$ 7.77
Good	$9.00	$.65	$.57	$1.25	$10.97

*Actual cost divided by two: reflects pad replacement only once for each two carpeting replacements.

Most apartments will be using self-lined fabric for drapes. Typically, the same quality drape will be used for both fair and average quality units, while good quality units will use a somewhat heavier drape with possibly a better weave. Specifications used for this report are shown in the table below.

Size Drape	Type of Window	Fair to Avg. Quality	Good Quality
44" × 46"	Kitchen	$12.50	$14.75
84" × 56"	LR or BR	$22.50	$25.50
120" × 96"	Sliding door	$43.50	$47.74

Note: Above costs do not include sales tax.

Life expectancy for drapes is from three to five years. For purposes of calculating reserve amounts, the drapes will be grouped together with the carpets and both will be figured according to carpeting life expectancy.

Preparation and/or installation costs for draperies average $3 per window for double-pull drapes. Costs listed below assume the hardware is already in place.

Per unit requirements

Drape costs are based on the following per-unit requirements:

Single .... 1(84″ × 56″)
One bedroom .... 2(84″ × 56″), 1(44″ × 46″)
Two bedroom .... 3(84″ × 56″), 1(44″ × 46″)
Three bedroom .... 4(84″ × 56″), 1(44″ × 46″)
1(120″ × 96″)

Combined Costs for Carpets and Drapes (6% sales tax included)

Quality	Single or Bachelor	One Bedroom	Two Bedroom	Three Bedroom	Item
Fair	$223	$317	$475	$633	Carpets
Fair	$ 27	$ 70	$ 97	$155	Drapes
	$250	$390	$570	$790	Total
Average	$299	$425	$638	$851	Carpets
Average	$ 27	$ 70	$ 97	$155	Drapes
	$325	$495	$735	$1005	Total
Good	$436	$620	$ 930	$1240	Carpets
Good	$ 28	$ 78	$ 109	$ 192	Drapes
	$465	$700	$1040	$1430	Total

Other Equipment

Most buildings are now using a one-twelfth to one-sixth horsepower B&G circulating pump for their hot water systems. These units are produced in two materials: bronze and iron. Bronze pumps are almost always used due to the iron pump's inability to stand up to hot water. Bronze pumps will last between 10 and 15 years, but with some minor repairs required over this expectancy. These repairs are covered under maintenance, repairs, and decorating expenses and consist of impeller replacement, seal replacement, and bearing replacement. The cost of a one-twelfth B&G pump is about $130 (without installation). The purpose of the pump is to save on gas and water consumption—the continuously circulating hot water will be right at the tap when a tenant on the far end of the building pours a cup of hot water or takes a shower.

Pumps may be controlled by an aquastat, which turns off the pump when the water temperature gets below a predetermined level (usually around 100°F). However, this on-off operation is the worst enemy of the pump's life expectancy. A setting of about 165°F should keep the pump running continuously.

A pump now gaining popularity is the Grundfos—a Danish-built, stainless steel unit that is somewhat less expensive than the B&G (about

$95 for a one-twelfth horsepower unit). However, it is not suited to repairs. Life expectancy is from seven to 15 years. This is the same pump which is utilized with most solar water heating application.

Management

The first thing to ascertain is whether the building should have a resident manager. Buildings in California are required to have one for 16 or more units—for a lesser number it will remain a judgmental decision. Reasons for utilizing a resident manager revolve around the amount of day-to-day work required to operate the building. These factors include the neighborhood (a resident manager is more common in a low-income neighborhood), amount of clean-up work, watering, trash removal, turnover, and the like. Factors influencing the particular owner will be his or her own time schedule and traveling time to and from the property. However, these two factors cannot be taken into account, as we are estimating expenses under typical ownership. For this same reasons, management fees must be included for owner-occupied properties.

Resident manager duties

Liaison between tenant and owner or management company.
Clean and water public areas.
Collect rents.
Show and rent units.
Notify owner or management company of needed repairs.
Ready trash for removal.
Direct maintenance and service workers.

Occasionally, duties may also include gardening, bookkeeping, pool maintenance, and from light to medium plumbing and electrical repairs.

Professional management duties

Direct resident manager or perform those functions.
Hire resident manager and other employees.
Decisions on when and how to upgrade to remain competitive in the rental market.
Perform accounting work.
Make purchases at the most beneficial prices; includes supplies, furnishings, equipment, licenses, services, and service contracts.
Make sure the property is operated in accordance with the applicable rules and regulations.
Otherwise keep the property in an acceptable condition, run it efficiently as possible, and make sure it is providing an acceptable cash flow for the investor.

Factors to note

Turnover: much time is spent in preparation and rental of the unit.
Condition: the poorer the condition of the property, the more work required on the part of the management; this is especially true for high-rent buildings, where tenants expect better property condition.

Rental market: small furnished apartments catering to transients would require the most management work, while buildings with established tenants would require the least.

Amount of work in common areas: generally the resident manager's responsibility to care for exterior clean-up, watering, and the trash area.

Management
Fees

Resident Manager. A fee for the resident manager is to be included if one or both of the following situations exist:

The subject property has 16 or more units.
The building currently utilizes the services of a resident manager.

Fee is $100 to $150 per unit per year (represents monetary reimbursement and/or portion of all of free apartment).

Professional Management. A fee for professional management is to be included if one or both of the following conditions exist:

The subject property has 24 or more units.
The building currently utilizes the services of a professional management company.

The following fee schedule does not include the cost of the resident manager.

Number of Units	Fee as Percentage of Effective Gross Economic Income
5–15	5 1/2% – 7%
16–100	5% – 6 1/2%
over 100	4 1/2% – 6%

Owner/
Manager

In the case of a smaller building that utilizes an owner/manager arrangement, a fee of three to four percent of the effective gross economic income will be charged for management.

Property Taxes

Check with the county assessor. In California, following Proposition 13, *to compute the tax amount, divide the sales price by four to obtain an estimate of assessed value. Multiply each $100 of assessed value by the applicable tax rate to obtain the yearly property tax estimate.* If no tax rate is available, an alternate method would be to multiply the sales price by 1.25 percent. This figure covers the maximum tax burden as mandated by Proposition 13 (1 percent) plus an additional .25 percent for bonded indebtedness.

If the appraised property is a refinance, not a sale, the appraiser will use the value approximated by the market approach as the basis for the new tax estimate. Since we do not have the final value, this method will serve only as a reasonable approximation of the new tax level, and it is likely that once the final value is estimated, the tax estimate used in the income approach will not be precisely the same as if we initially had the final value.

Practical Math for Real Estate

Regardless of the extent of one's education, most people seem to have a problem with real estate arithmetic. However, there is a simple method to learn it, which we will call the "T" method—"T" stands for "think." The following examples will help you to work and understand the math problems that you will confront as a real estate investor. Understanding them will enable you to rely on your own judgment and analysis of a real estate investment. If you understand real estate or math, the battle is half won; if you understand both, you have conquered real estate math. We will attempt to integrate the two and simplify all types of real estate problems.

To begin, look at Figure A.1. The box represents the property, which is divided into parts A, B, and C by two lines that form a "T"—for "think—and the parts will be filled in by arithmetic terminology.

FIGURE A.1

(A)	
(B)	(C)

The product is the numerical result of a multiplication. The product of two numbers is not affected by reversing the order. Expressed in simple terms: $B \times C = A$ or $C \times B = A$. For every problem presented, there is a way that a solution can be found.

Remember that to solve a problem you must have the facts; with any two known facts, the unknown can be found. The biggest problem most people have with real estate math is determining when to use which formula. You know how to multiply, subtract, add, and divide, but you don't know when to use which one. Problems will arise that will not be stated in terms that are familiar to you. As one example, you may have memorized the formula that states: the rate divided into the return will give you the investment. Words such as *rate* and *return* may not be expressed in that manner. It might state how much did he or she invest or it might say how much did he or she pay or what did it cost? The return could be called several things, such as *earned, made, profit,* or *gain.* There are many words that mean the same as *rate, return,* or *investment.* To be a good real estate mathematician, one must be a good mathematical mechanic. If you were asked to find out what the investment is, the rule says "divide the rate into the return." The tools needed in this case are rate (percentage) and return. The following words in a problem will often be a key as to what arithmetic symbols will be used:

> *Of* frequently stands for multiply ($\times$).
> *Is* frequently stands for equals ($=$).
> *And* frequently stands for add ($+$).
> *What* frequently stands for divide ($\div$).

Study carefully how a formula really works. The reverse of addition is subtraction and vice versa. Multiplication is a shortcut to addition. Division is a shortcut to subtraction. The reverse of division is multiplication and the reverse of multiplication is division.

$$3 \times 4 = 12$$

To inverse the formula, divide the 3 back out.

$$12 \div 3 = 4.$$

Note Figure A.2. The horizontal line of the "T" means to divide; the vertical line means to multiply. Use any two factors to compute this example:

$$3 \times 4 = 12$$
$$12 \div 3 = 4$$
$$12 \div 4 = 3$$

FIGURE A.2

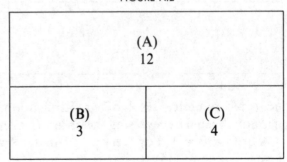

The same formula will work for any combination of numbers. In algebra it is expressed in the following way:

$$BC = A \text{ (B times C = A)}.$$
$$\frac{A}{B} = C \text{ (B divided into A = C)}.$$
$$\frac{A}{C} = B \text{ (C divided into A = B)}.$$

If any number must be multiplied against another to get a result, put the formula into the box and you can see the other two formulas. If any number must be divided into a number to get the result, put it into the box and you can see the other two formulas. This basic formula can be applied to dozens of real estate problems.

FIGURE A.3: Land Measurements (Square or Rectangular Lots)

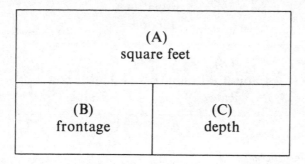

Land Measurements

Rule 1. Frontage times depth equals square feet (BC = A).

Rule 2. Frontage divided into square feet equals depth (B into A = C).

Rule 3. Depth divided into square feet equals frontage (C into A = B).

FIGURE A.4: Investments

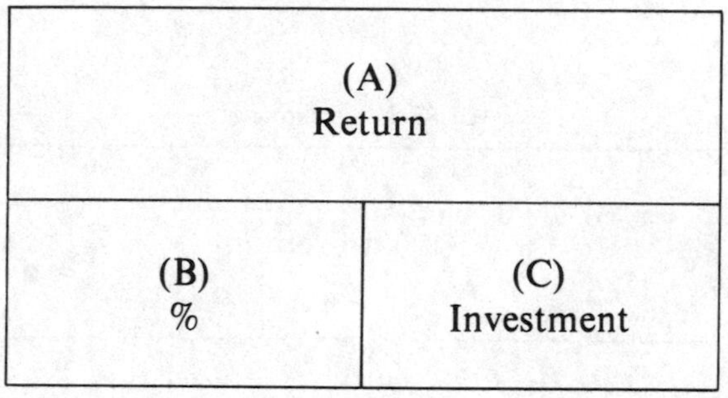

Investments

Rule 1. Percentage (%) times investment equals returns (BC = A).

Rule 2. Percentage (%) divided into returns equals investment (B into A = C).

Rule 3. Investment divided into return equals percentage (C into A = B).

FIGURE A.5: Finance

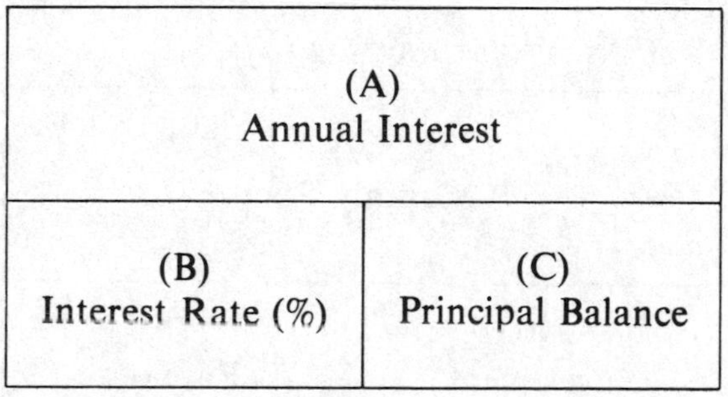

Finance

Rule 1. Interest rate times principal balance equals annual interest B into A = C.

Rule 2. Interest rate divided into annual interest equals principal balance (B into A = C).

Rule 3. Principal balance into annual interest equals interest rate (C into A = B).

FIGURE A-6: Appraising

(A) Annual Net Income	
(B) Capitalization Rate	(C) Fair Market Value

Appraising
(Net Operating Income)

Rule 1. Capitalization rate times the fair market value (price paid) equals annual net income (BC = A).

Rule 2. Capitalization rate into the annual net income equals the fair market value (B into A = C).

Rule 3. Fair market value into the annual net income equals the capitalization rate (C into A = B).

Taxation
(Property tax)

FIGURE A.7: Taxation

(A) Ad Valorem Tax	
(B) Tax Rate (%)	(C) Assessed Value

Rule 1. Tax rate times assessed value equals the amount of the tax (BC = A).
Rule 2. Tax rate into the tax equals the assessed value (B into A = C).
Rule 3. Assessed value into the tax equals the tax rate (C into A = B).

FIGURE A.8: Rental Formula

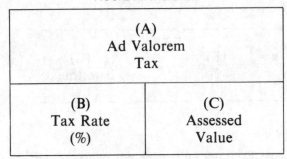

(A) Monthly Rent	
(B) Investment	(C) Rate of Return

FIGURE A.9: Investment Formula

(A) (earned)	
(B) Investment Purchase Price	(C) Rate of Return (%)

FIGURE A.10: Gross Multiplier Formula

(A) Comparable (sales prices)	
(B) Gross Multiplier	(C) Gross Rent

FIGURE A.11: Acreage Conversion Formula

(A) Number of acres × 43,560	
(B) Frontage	(C) Depth

FIGURE A.12: Basic Capitalization Formula

(A) Annual Income	
(B) Price (FMV) (Fair Market Value)	(C) Cap Rate

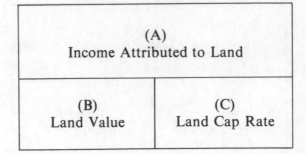

FIGURE A.13: Land Residual Technique

(A)
Income Attributed to Land

| **(B)** Land Value | **(C)** Land Cap Rate |

FIGURE A.14: Depreciation Formula

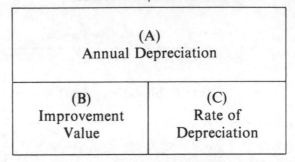

(A)
Annual Depreciation

| **(B)** Improvement Value | **(C)** Rate of Depreciation |

FIGURE A.15: Loan Balance Formula

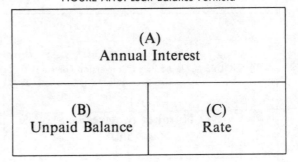

(A)
Annual Interest

| **(B)** Unpaid Balance | **(C)** Rate |

FIGURE A.16: Interest = Principal × Rate × Time:

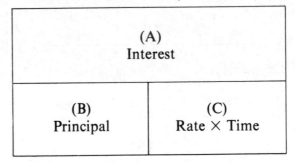

(A)
Interest

| **(B)** Principal | **(C)** Rate × Time |

Steps in working a problem

1. Learn the formula.
2. Practice on each type of problem.
3. Read the problem to find out what the question part of the question is.
4. Translate the terms used in the problem into your language as you learned it, and select the correct formula needed to work the problem.
5. Find the factors in the problem needed to work the formula.
6. Work the problem (add, subtract, multiply, or divide).

Mortgage and Appraisal Ratios and Terms

Mortgage (loan) Constant: annual debt service divided by original loan amount.

Annual Debt Service: loan amount multiplied by the loan constant.

Amortization Rate: annual constant minus interest rate.

Interest Rate: constant minus amortization rate.

Loan Rate: loan amount divided by the appraised value.

Loan Ratio: loan amount divided by the sales price.

Breakeven (default ratio): debt service plus total expenses divided by potential income (revenue).

Debt (loan) Coverage Ratio: net income before recapture (NIBR) divided by debt service.

Percentage of Loan Paid Off (balloon loan): full term constant minus interest rate divided by projected term constant minus interest rate.

Minimum Rent Per Apartment: breakeven divided by 12 months divided by total number of apartments.

Minimum Rent Per Room: breakeven divided by 12 months (equals monthly breakeven) divided by total number of rooms.

Minimum Rent Per Square Foot = Gross Building Area (GBA): (annual monthly breakeven divided by square footage (GBA).

Minimum Rent Per Square Foot - Net Rentable Area (NRA): monthly (or annual) breakeven divided by square footage (NRA).

Loan Amount Per Apartment: loan amount divided by total number of apartments.

Loan Amount Per Room: loan amount divided by total number of rooms.

Loan Amount Per Square Foot: loan amount divided by the square footage (GBA).

Loan Amount Per Square Foot: net rentable area: loan amount divided by square footage (NRA).

Loan Gross Multiplier (potential): loan amount divided by gross revenue (potential).

Loan Gross Multiplier (effective): loan amount divided by effective gross revenue.

Leased Space Coverage: actual lease rent divided by breakeven.

Twenty Year Plus Major Coverage: actual lease rents from major tenants with lease terms of 20 years or longer, divided by breakeven.

Major Tenants Coverage of Breakeven: major tenants coverage divided by breakeven.

Minimum Rent Per Square Foot of Remaining Space: breakeven minus actual rents from 20 years or longer major tenants divided by total NRA minus total NRA of tenants with 20 years or longer leases.

Shortage: breakeven minus actual lease rentals.

Rental Achievement: amount of rent required by lender to be generated from property before lender will disburse full loan.

Full Loan: maximum amount lender agreed to lend.

Floor Loan: initial loan amount to be disbursed by lender on the loan.

Appraisal Ratio and Terms

Potential Gross Income (PGI): income produced with 100 percent occupancy.

Effective Gross Income (EGI): PGI less allowance for vacancy and rental collection loss plus other applicable income.

Net Income Before Recapture (NIBR): EGI less expenses (fixed) and reserves for replacements and miscellaneous.

Overall Rate (OAR): NIBR divided by value and/or sales price (SP).

OAR: net income ratio divided by gross rent multiplier.

Net Income (NI) Ratio: NIBR divided by PGI.

Gross Rent (income) Multiplier—Potential: value and/or sales price divided by potential gross income.

Gross Rent (income) Multiplier—Effective: value and/or sales price divided by effective gross income.

Gross Income Rate: PGI divided by value and/or sales price (reciprocal of GRM).

Sales Price or Value: gross income multiplied by gross income multiplier.

Annual Gross Rental Needed to Support Sales Price or Value: value or sales price divided by gross rent multiplier.

Rate of Net Annual Return Needed to Satisfy Mortgage and Equity: net income rate (OAR) multiplied by net income ratio.

Appraised Value: NIBR divided by OAR.

Expense Ratio: Expenses (excluding real estate taxes) divided by potential gross income (PGI).

Total Expense Ratio: total expenses (including real estate taxes) divided by PGI.

Tax Ratio: real estate taxes divided by potential gross income.

Categorical Expense Ratio: operating expense (fixed, operating, and so on) divided by potential gross income.

Individual Expense Ratio: each individual expense divided by PGI.

Average Monthly Apartment Rental: monthly gross rental divided by total number of apartments.

Average Monthly Room Rental: monthly gross rental divided by total number of apartments.

Operating Cost Per Apartment Per Annum: total expenses divided by number of apartments.

Operating Cost Per Room Per Annum: total expenses divided by total number of rooms.

Individual Expense Per Room and/or Per Apartment Per Annum: individual expenses divided by total number of rooms and/or apartments.

Appraised Value Divided by Assessed Value (AV).

Land AV Divided by Total AV (used in land abstraction, extraction method).

Efficiency Ratio: square footage NRA divided by square footage GBA.

Original Equity Ratio: 100 percent minus loan ratio.

Original Equity Ratio: down payment (equity) divided by sales price.

Cash Flow: NIBR minus debt service (also known as net cash flow, equity dividend, cash on cash, and others).

Cash Flow Rate: cash flow divided by down payment (equity), also known as equity dividend rate, equity return to investor.

Owner's Appraised Equity (equity reversion): appraised value less loan amount (balance).

Return on Owner's Appraised Equity: net cash flow divided by appraised equity.

Terminal Equity Ratio: net reversion divided by resale price or value at end of holding period.

Recapture Rate: one divided by remaining economic life or 100 divided by remaining economic life.

A Facsimile Case of Syndication

1012 Zulu Ave.
Los Angeles, California 90000

Re: A Real Estate Investment Opportunity

XYZ ASSOCIATES

A California Limited Partnership

Dear Investor,

I am enclosing for your careful review and consideration the following:

1) Offering Circular
2) Agreement and Certificate of Limited Partnership
3) Additional Copy of the signature page of the Agreement and Certificate of Limited Partnership
4) Two copies of the Subscription Agreement

Please be aware that the limited partnership interests herein have not been registered with the Securities and Exchange Commission (SEC) nor qualified by the Department of Corporations nor any other agency of the State of California, and no permit of any kind has been sought in offering this investment opportunity.

If, after you review and consider this investment opportunity you wish to subscribe to a limited partnership interest in XYZ Associates, please execute (and have your signature acknowledged by a notary public) and promptly return one copy of the signature page of the Agreement and Certificate of Limited Partnership, and one completely filled-in copy of the Subscription Agreement. The remaining enclosed documents are to be kept for your files.

After the purchase escrow closes, and upon the recording of the Agreement and Certificate of Limited Partnership in the County Recorder's Office, you will be sent a copy of the appropriate schedules indicating the names of all the limited partners with their respective participation interests, as well as a copy of the first page of the recorded Agreement and Certificate of Limited Partnership.

If you have any questions concerning this project, contact me at (555) 661-1194. You are invited to examine all papers and documents pertinent to the acquisition of the Partnership property, as well as the Limited Partnership itself, at the office of the General Partner.

If you wish to participate in this investment opportunity, return the following:

1) One copy of the completed Subscription Agreement;
2) Signed and notarized Signature Page of the Agreement and Certificate of Limited Partnership,
3) Check made payable to XYZ Associates.

Sincerely,

APEX, INC.
A California Corporation

XYZ Associates

By _____

OFFERING CIRCULAR
XYZ Associates

Presented By:

APEX, INC., A California Corporation
1012 Zulu Ave.
Los Angeles, California 90000

$110,000 Offering

22 Investment (Class "A") Units

At $5,000.00 Per Unit

THIS OFFERING IS LIMITED TO CALIFORNIA RESIDENTS WHO MEET CERTAIN QUALIFICATIONS DESCRIBED HEREIN.

IMPORTANT NOTE: This offering has not been qualified nor registered with any governmental agency and no permits of any kind have been sought or received prior to making this offering. This offering is made only to people who have a close personal or business relationship to the general partners and who meet certain financial and residence requirements.

THESE SECURITIES INVOLVE A DEGREE OF RISK
(See Section XVII., Risk Factors)

The Partnership is newly organized and has no operating history. It has negotiated the purchase of certain real property in the City of Carthage, California. On this real property the Partnership will refurbish and lease offices. A description of that operation is identified in Section XI (Operation of the Property).

The limited partnership interests offered have not been registered with the Securities and Exchange Commission (SEC), nor qualified by the Department of Corporations, nor any other agency of the State of California. Such registration is not required for private offerings such as this. Public offerings registered with the SEC must be qualified under 10 California Administrative Code, Chapter 3, Sections 260.110, 260.113, 260.114.110.1 through 260.140.119.1. BUT, to repeat, such registration and qualification is not required for this offering.

The units offered may be subscribed to only by California residents, all of whom shall have had a pre-existing personal or business relationship with any General Partner, or be sufficiently well informed in real estate investment to independently discern the risks inherent in this offering; and each having a personal net worth consistent with the provisions of Section IV of this offering.

The material set forth in this offering circular is a solicitation and presentation of this offering. It is an accumulation of material facts and data for the General Partner to present to prospective purchasers of this offering.

This investment involves risk factors and is speculative (see Section XVII, Risk Factors); contains restrictions on transferability of interests (Section X of the Partnership Agreement), and may be difficult to market or resell, as is more fully set forth in this offering circular.

The Partnership has not applied for a ruling from the Treasury Department that it will be treated as a Partnership and not as an association taxable as a corporation for Federal Income Tax purposes. There can be no assurance that this Partnership will not at some later time be found to be an association taxable as a corporation (see Section XVII G. Tax Consequences).

The General Partner has the absolute right in his sole discretion to accept or reject any subscription submitted to him and shall incur no liability for such rejection.

In the event that the transaction for the acquisition of the property or the subscription of sufficient investors fails of consummation for any reason, the subscriber's funds will be returned in full without diminution and with any interest earned thereon (see Section III—Capitalization).

TABLE OF CONTENTS

XYZ Associates

A Limited Partnership Formed for the Group Acquisition of the Property Commonly Known as Cynthia Professional Building, 415 Hope St.

I. SUMMARY OF THE OFFERING

XYZ Associates (hereafter called "The Partnership") will be a California Limited Partnership located at 1012 Zulu Avenue, Los Angeles, California 90039. It will be formed to acquire fee ownership of the land and building located at 415 Hope St., Carthage, California (hereafter called "The Property"). The Partnership will make appropriate improvements in the property and lease the various suites to maximize the net income and the market value of the Property, and thereafter operate the Property for profit, and finally sell the Property for profit OR exchange the Property, if a potentially profitable tax-deferred exchange is available, OR refinance the Property if the following two conditions are met: (1) 100% of invested capital is returned to all investors and (2) potential for great future profit exists.

II. THE GENERAL PARTNER

The General Partner of XYZ ASSOCIATES will be APEX, INC., a California Corporation, whose address is 1012 Zulu, Los Angeles, California 90000. The principal stockholders of APEX, INC. are JOE BLOW, and DAVE SMITH. DAVE SMITH is a licensed real estate broker, and JOE BLOW holds a valid California real estate salesperson's license.

The General Partner will have general responsibility for supervising the partnership's operations, including the supervising of compliance with legal and regulatory requirements and preparation and transmission of periodic and annual reports to the Limited Partners. The General Partner has the ultimate authority in all matters affecting the business and affairs of the Partnership, and in the formation of guidelines and limitations with respect to the Partnership's investments, and has unlimited liability for the Partnership's obligations.

III. CAPITALIZATION

The amount of capital to be raised by cash contributions from the Limited Partners will be $111,100.00, as follows: 22 Class "A" units at $5,000.00 per unit, and 22 Class "B" units at $50.00 per unit. The General Partner will not make a cash contribution.

All funds contributed by the Limited Partners will be deposited into a partnership checking account opened at Taylor National Bank, 5560 Dale Boulevard, Los Angeles, California, and will be applied toward the consummation of the contemplated transaction and subsequent improvement and leasing of the property. In the event that the total amount to be raised, namely $111,100.00 is not raised on or before Oct. 15, 1979, or the purchase escrow is not consummated by that date, all funds shall be returned in full to the contributing parties. Such refund checks will be drawn on the Partnership checking account of XYZ ASSOCIATES.

The 22 Class "B" units will be sold to JOE BLOW and DAVE SMITH at the nominal price of $50.00 per unit. These are sold to BLOW and SMITH in consideration for time, effort, expertise and ingenuity in locating, negotiating and forming the transaction described in this offering circular. Thus, DAVE SMITH and JOE BLOW will own eleven Class "B" Limited Partnership units each, in addition to being employed by APEX, INC. the General Partner.

This offering relates to the 22 Class "A" units of Limited Partnership interest in the Partnership. The offering price is $5,000.00 per unit with a minimum purchase of one unit, and a maximum subscription of 22 units. At the discretion of the General Partner, fractional units may be sold. Subscriptions must be accompanied by full payment. Funds received from the sale of units will be deposited in the Partnership XYZ ASSOCIATES checking account, located at Taylor Bank, 5560 Dale Boulevard, Los Angeles, California, which will act as the depository for the Partnership's funds. Unless the full amount of $111,100.00 is received prior to November 20, 19xx, the offering will terminate and all funds received for the purchase of such units will be returned promptly to investors with interest, if any, earned thereon. Any interest earned on deposited funds shall be placed in a reserve fund. This offering will terminate on November 20, 19xx, unless sooner terminated by the General Partner.

IV. QUALIFICATION OF CLASS "A" LIMITED PARTNERS

This offering is limited to persons who reside in the State of California, are 21 year of age or over and are purchasing for their own account (or for the account of a minor child or ward of such person, providing they are California residents) with the intention to hold the units for a long term capital gain investment.

The General Partner's acceptance of an offer to purchase a share (or fraction of a share) of Partnership interest is subject to a determination of the offeror's suitability as an investor. Investors will be required to meet minimum financial standards of either:

(1) The combination of (a) projected adjusted gross income of $25,000.00 for the taxable year and (b) an existing net worth(exclusive of home, furnishings, and automobile) of $25,000.00, or two times the aggregate of the investment, whichever is greater; or

(2) A net worth (exclusive of home, furnishings, and automobile of $50,000.00, or four times the aggregate investment, whichever is greater.

V. BENEFITS TO LIMITED PARTNERS

In exchange for their capital contributions, the Limited Partners shall be entitled to the following:

(1) Class A Limited Partners: fifty percent of the Partnership gain or loss upon the sale or exchange of the property AND, in the event of a tax-deferred exchange, fifty percent (50%) of the gain or loss upon the sale of the successor property.

(2) Class B Limited Partners: fifty percent (50%) of the Partnerhip gain or loss upon the sale or exchange of the Property AND, in the event of a tax deferred exchange, fifty percent (50%) of the gain or loss upon the sale of the successor property.

VI. INVESTMENT OBJECTIVES AND POLICIES

The Partnership will buy, renovate, own and operate the professional building located at 415 Hope Street, Carthage, California.

The objectives of the Partnership are to provide the Limited Partners with:

1. Cash flow;
2. Long term capital appreciation;
3. An increase of net worth through equity build-up (loan payoff);
4. Shelter from taxation; and
5. Resale or exchange for other investment property.

There can be no assurance that these objectives can be attained, but it is the belief of the General Partner that conditions will allow the Partnership to attain these objectives.

The General Partner will direct the acquisition of the real property and the construction, renovation and leasing of the office suites purchased by the Partnership. Profits and earnings of the Partnership will be the result of the rental of the office suites and the ultimate refinancing or resale of the office suites to the public at large. The General Partner will manage the day-to-day operation of the Partnership in order to achieve the investment objectives.

The investment objectives and policies of the Partnership described above may not be changed by the General Partner without the consent of a majority in interest of the Limited Partners.

Information presented in the Offering Circular is intended to provide a prospective investor with the facts concerning the proposed investment which may affect his decision to invest. Projections of costs, profits and cash returns to the Partnership must of necessity be based on the best estimates of the General Partner, however, and are not intended as guarantees, warranties, or representations to be relied upon by an investor. Because any investment is speculative in nature and includes some risk, it is suggested that a prospective investor consult his attorney, accountant, or other investment advisor for advice concerning his own personal investment considerations.

VII. PROPERTY DESCRIPTION

The property to be acquired is the land and improvements at 415 Hope Street, Carthage, California.

The property consists of two adjacent parcels. Parcel One (Lot 1) contains a modern one-story office building with 4,500 square feet of leasable space with parking at the rear of the building. Parcel Two (Lot 2) contains a two-story frame and stucco three-unit apartment building located at the rear of the lot. The front of the lot is an asphalt parking area. Total parking for both parcels is 42 spaces (more than required by city code). The apartment building is presently vacant (city ordinances forbid residential use in a commercial zone).

VIII. PROPERTY ACQUISITION

A. XYZ ASSOCIATES has entered into a contract to purchase the subject properties from H.B. WELLS and KAREN WELLS for a purchase price of $200,000, and, as part of the consideration, the current tenant, ZIGLER AND ASSOCIATES, a California corporation owned by H. B. ZIGLER has agreed to lease-back both properties. The lease-back is secured by the assets of ZIGLER, INC., and by the personal guarantees of the sellers.

B. The terms of the purchase are as follows:

$63,000 cash down payment and XYZ ASSOCIATES will assume an all-inclusive note and deed of trust in the amount of $122,000, payable $1,500 or more per month, including interest at 10% per year, all due and payable October 1, 1986;

AND

XYZ ASSOCIATES will execute in favor of the sellers a note (purchase money) secured by a trust deed, in the amount of $15,000, payable $144 or more per month, including interest of 10% per year, all due and payable November 1, 1986.

C. The terms of the leases are as follows:

1. The Cynthia I property will be leased for 48 months at $2,250 per month for 36 months and $2,520 per month for the remaining 12 months.

2. The Cynthia II property will be leased for 48 months at $1,000 per month for 36 months and $1,120 per month for the remaining 12 months.

3. The two leases are triple net leases whereby the lessee and the guarantors assume full responsibility for maintaining and servicing the leased premises, including but not limited to payment of all taxes and assessments that may arise during the lease terms and will also maintain and pay for suitable hazard and liability insurance acceptable to XYZ ASSOCIATES.

4. XYZ ASSOCIATES has agreed to make certain improvements to the leased properties as consideration for the leases:

a. The Cynthia I property will be improved by removing certain existing partitions, decorating certain interior areas of the building and installing new carpeting in certain areas of the building.

b. The Cynthia II property will be refurbished and modified as necessary to create suitable office space according to building plans to be approved by the city of Carthage.

D. All papers and documents pertinent to the acquisition of the Partnership Property and to the Partnership itself may be examined in the office of the General Partner.

The records of the partnership checking account may also be examined at any time at the same place.

IX. ALLOCATION OF CAPITAL

A. The cash proceeds in the amount of $111,100.00 will be applied towards the purchase price and subsequent improvements as follows: approximately $74,350 for the down payment, acquisition fee, Partnership set-up, legal fees, escrow and miscellaneous costs (see Exhibit "B"). $5,000 will reimburse the General Partner for the advance purchase escrow deposit, and the balance of approximately $36,750 will remain in the Partnership bank account to be used for working capital (see Exhibit "B").

B. If the Partnership is dissolved at any time before the sale of all its assets, title to the Partnership Property may vest in the Limited Partners as tenants in common. Prospective investors should be aware that certain difficulties may be encountered in managing and disposing of property held by persons as tenants in common.

X. ACQUISITION FEE

At the close of the purchase escrow, EMPRISE, Inc. will receive an acquisition fee of $10,000 from ASSOCIATES. At the close of the sale (or exchange) escrow, will receive a second $10,000 installment of the total acquisition fee of $20,000.

XI. OPERATION OF THE PROPERTY

A. The Partnership Property consists of two parcels: Cynthia I and Cynthia II on 415 Hope St., Carthage, California.

B. The building at Cynthia I has been occupied by ZIGLER & ASSOCIATES, Inc. for approximately 8 years. The building at Cynthia II has been vacant, boarded by order of the city Carthage, but is in basically sound condition.

C. ZIGLER & ASSOCIATES, Inc. will continue to occupy Cynthia I and will pay rent under the lease described in Section VIII C; $2,250 per month starting with the date of the close of the purchase escrow. The initial rental rate is $0.50 per square foot per month.

D. Once the renovation of Cynthia II is completed, ZIGLER & ASSOCIATES, Inc. will occupy and will pay rent under the lease described in Section VIII C; $1,000 per month starting with the date the city of Carthage issues a Certificate of Occupancy. The initial rental rate is $0.50 per square foot per month.

E. The Gross Scheduled Income (GSI) will be $3,250 per month or $39,000 per year. As the leases are Triple Net, our expenses will be small.

F. With these leases, the properties will look extremely attractive to prospective purchasers at a price of about 10 times the annual income ($390,000). With a sale at $390,000, the Partnership would realize a net profit of $111,400 (see Exhibit "A"); or a return of 50% to each limited partner. We anticipate selling the Property at the end of one year of ownership.

G. *Cash Flow Projection*

There will be cash flow to the Partnership from the very first month of ownership. The following table summarizes the cash flow position of XYZ ASSOCIATES during the first year:

INCOME	First 2 months @ $2,250/mo	=	$ 4,500*
	Next 10 months @ $3,250/mo	=	32,500
	Total Income	=	$37,000
EXPENSES	Twelve months debt service	@	$ 1,644/mo
		=	19,728
	Management/miscellaneous	=	3,700
	Total Expenses	=	$23,428
FIRST YEAR CASH FLOW		=	$13,572

*Assume 60 days required to renovate Cynthia II.

Cash flow distributions made during the first year will represent a return of approximately 6% to the limited partners. This is over and above the anticipated return upon the sale of the Property (see Exhibit "A").

XII. SALE OR EXCHANGE OF THE PROPERTY

A. At the end of a holding period of at least one year, the Partnership will attempt to sell the improved Property at a profit. The General Partner may, however, at his sole discretion, exchange the improved Partnership Property for like property. It is contemplated that the like property to be received in exchange will be a commercial property whose market value is equal to or greater than the improved Partnership Property, but which has been mismanaged or neglected. The like property received in exchange would then be improved, operated, and an attempt made to sell it at a profit. The General Partner's decision to exchange the improved Partnership Property for like property will depend upon the availability of suitable like property for such an exchange. Under no conditions would the Property, or like property, be sold if the cash proceeds were not sufficient to return to the Limited Partners the amount of their capital accounts, less the amounts of any prior cash distributions to the Limited Partners.

B. The contemplated exchange of the Partnership Property for like property to be improved, held and sold at a profit will be either a tax-deferred exchange under Section 1031(a) of the Internal Revenue Code (hereafter called "The Code"); or a partially tax-deferred exchange under Section 1031(b) of the Code. In the case of an exchange pursuant to Section 1031(a), the Partnership Property will be exchanged solely for like property with no recognition of gain at the time of the exchange. Taxes on the gain are deferred until the time when the like property received in the exchange is itself sold. The adjusted basis of the Partnership Property is substituted for the unadjusted basis of the like property acquired in the exchange. At the time the like property is sold, the gains realized from the sale will be determined by subtracting the substituted basis and any expenses from the selling price. A partially tax-deferred exchange under Section 1031(b) will result if the seller (exchanger) of the like property acquires said Partnership Property subject to any liability (loans or encumbrances) which is greater than the liability on the like property. The difference in the amount of the liabilities is considered money received in exchange, and gain will be taxed to the extent of money received.

C. The Limited Partners will not be assessed any further cash contributions to be used for the improvement of any like property received in exchange for the improved Partnership Property, or for any other purpose. Expenses of renovating and improving such property will be met by financing the like property.

D. Should the General Partner exercise his discretion to exchange the improved Partnership Property for like property, the Agreement and Certificate of Limited Partnership provides for continued existence of the Partnership until the property received in exchange is improved, held and sold and the Partnership assets are distributed.

E. If at any time during the holding of the Property it becomes apparent to the General Partner that the potential for future increase in value of the Property is great enough that the Property should *not* be sold, then the General Partner may attempt to refinance the Property in such a manner as to generate cash in the account of **XYZ ASSOCIATES** sufficient to return to each Limited Partner an amount equal to or greater than the initial cash contribution made by said partner, less any prior cash distribution received by said partner. Proceeds from any refinancing meeting the above requirements would be distributed immediately following the conclusion of the transaction.

F. It is suggested that a prospective investor consult his attorney, accountant, or investment counselor concerning possible tax consequences for the investor resulting from a sale of the Partnership Property, or from an exchange of the Partnership Property for like property which will be improved, operated and sold.

XIII. MANAGEMENT OF THE PROPERTY

A. During the period the Partnership operates the Property, or like property, property management services will be performed by APEX, INC. For those property management services, APEX, INC. will be paid a management fee equal to six percent (6%) of the gross collected rents. The management fee will be discontinued upon the General Partner's resignation or removal as General Partner.

XIV. COSTS PROJECTION AND OPERATING STATEMENT

A. All costs associated with the formation of the Partnership will be paid for by the Partnership. These costs will include, but may not be limited to, preparation of documents, legal services, filing fees, etc.

B. In the event the Partnership elects to sell or exchange the Property, or the like property in the event of an exchange, a licensed real estate broker may be retained. A maximum commission of five percent (5%) of the gross sales price will be paid to the broker subject to a satisfactory sale or exchange. In the event DAVE SMITH or JOE BLOW should be the procuring cause of the buyer of the subject property, they shall be entitled to receive the sum of five percent (5%) of the gross sales price. In any sale or exchange, the General Partner will attempt to maximize the profit to the Partnership, consistent with prevailing market conditions. Nothing herein should be construed to constitute an exclusive sales or exchange listing agreement with SMITH REALTY.

C. There is a good possibility that when the Property, or the like property in the event of an exchange is sold, the Partnership may have to accept the buyer's promissory note as a part of the purchase price. However, any promissory note taken in order to consummate a sale will be secured by a deed of trust, and the promissory note will be due and payable in not more than five (5) years and will bear interest at a rate not less than 10%. Upon the sale of the Property, or like property, the General Partner will attempt to sell at the best price available any promissory note taken by the Partnership. Under no condition would the Property be sold if the cash proceeds were not sufficient to return to the limited partners the balance of their capital accounts.

D. The percentage participation of the profits and losses resulting from the sale of the Property is as follows:

    Class A Limited Partners—50%
    Class B Limited Partners—50%

We project that if the property is sold at the end of one year, the net profit from the sale will be at least $111,400 (see Exhibit "A"); thus, each Class A Limited Partner holding one unit of Partnership interest could expect a profit of about $2,500, plus his $5,000.00 investment. Each Class B Limited Partnership share will receive a profit of about $2,500, plus the $50.00 investment.

The General Partner will exclusively determine when and if any distributions of Partnership profits shall be made, and the Limited Partners shall have no right to any other compensation by reason of their contributions.

XV. EXHIBIT "A"

Profit Projections

Buy Costs:		
Acquisition Fee ($10,000 @ purchase and $10,000 @ sale)	$20,000	
Escrow	350	
Set-up and legal	500	
Miscellaneous	500	
	$21,350	
Improvements:	35,000	35,000
Sell Costs:		
5% Commission	19,500	
Escrow	700	
Transfer Tax	500	
Miscellaneous	3,500	
	$24,200	24,200

TOTAL COSTS 80,550
BUY PRICE 200,000
SELL PRICE 390,000
NET PROFIT TO PARTNERSHIP FROM SALE $109,450
CASH FLOW DISTRIBUTION DURING ONE YEAR 13,500
TOTAL PROFIT TO PARTNERSHIP $122,950

XV. EXHIBIT "B"

<u>Cash Requirement Breakdown</u>

Down payment	$ 63,000
P-ship set-up, 1/2 acquisition fee, etc.	11,350
Improvements	35,000
Reserves	1,750
TOTAL CASH REQUIREMENT	$111,100
Class A Limited Partners	110,000
Class B Limited Partners	1,100

XVI. THE LIMITED PARTNERSHIP

A. The terms of the Partnership are set forth in the Agreement and Certificate of Limited Partnership which has been provided for the information of the prospective investor, along with this Offering Circular.

B. If the Partnership is dissolved at any time before the sale of all its assets, title to the Partnership Property may vest in the Limited Partners as tenants in common. Prospective investors should be aware that certain difficulties may be encountered in managing and disposing of property held by persons as tenants in common.

C. The Partnership will not purchase any property from, nor sell any property to, the General Partner, nor any employees thereof. The Partnership will not purchase or sell property to another partnership in which the General Partner is serving as general partner. With the exception of compensation set forth in this Offering Circular, the General Partner shall enter into no contracts on behalf of this Partnership which involve transactions in which the General Partner or any employee thereof has a conflict of interest.

D. The Limited Partners, as such, will not be entitled to participate in the management or control of the Partnership, which is vested exclusively in the General Partner, except as otherwise provided in the Partnership Agreement.

XVII. RISK FACTORS

An investment in the units offered hereby involves a high degree of risk, and potential investors should consider carefully, among other factors, the following:

Construction
and Operations

A. The partnership is newly organized and has no operational history.

B. The General Partner and his agents will devote to the Partnership's affairs only such time as they, in their sole discretion, deem necessary.

C. Information presented in the Offering Circular is intended to provide a prospective investor with the facts concerning the proposed investment which may affect his decision to invest. Projections of costs, profits and cash returns to the partnership must be based on the best estimates of the General Partner, however, and are not intended as guarantees, warranties or representations to be relied upon by an investor.

D. The renovation costs will depend on the availability of supplies and man-power and the general condition prevailing at the time. Any predictions of construction and development costs are subject to these conditions. Similarly, the Partnership cannot predict its cost of operation. Reserves for repair, replacements and continuing operations will be established for the Partnership by the General Partner in amounts deemed reasonably adequate by him. There can be no assurance that such reserves will be adequate to cover the expenses and costs of the Partnership in connection with repairs, replacements and continuing operations.

E. Investments in the type of real estate in which the Partnership proposes to invest are speculative and involve a high degree of risk. Many of the factors which may affect the partnership and its affairs are subject to change, or are not within the control of the Partnership. The extent to which such factors could restrict the activities or adversely affect the value of the Partnership is not currently ascertainable. Factors which may affect the Partnership may include environmental controls and other governmentally imposed restrictions, adverse use of adjacent or neighboring real estate by its owners and changes in the demand or supply of competing properties, changes in state or local tax rates and assessments, rapid depreciation in the value of property, unexpected expenditures for repairs and maintenance, changes in general or local economic conditions, shortages or reductions in available sources of energy, acts of God or other calamities. The Partnership will not be able to obtain insurance against most of such factors.

F. Should the Partnership's revenues be insufficient to service its debt and pay taxes and other operating costs, the Partnership will be required to utilize reserve funds, and in the event reserves are not sufficient, the Partnership will seek additional funds in the form of loans.

Leverage

G. The availability to the Limited Partners of many of the deductions intended to be claimed by the Partnership, and the period in which they may be deducted, involve complex issues which should be considered by a prospective limited partner. You are therefore urged to consult your tax accountant or tax counsel with respect to the California State Franchise and Federal Income Tax consequences of such an investment. An opinion of counsel has been obtained to the effect that the Partnership will be treated for Federal Income Tax purposes as a partnership and not as an association taxable as a corporation, and as to certain other matters. The Internal Revenue Service is not, however, bound by an opinion of counsel and the Partnership has not, and will not, apply for a ruling from the Service. Accordingly, the Service could challenge the Partnership's status on audit.

Tax Consequences

H. Limited Partners will not be personally liable for Partnership obligations in excess of their capital contributions and undistributed profits. The amount of the full capital contribution required to be paid by purchasers of the units offered hereby is $5,000.00 per unit.

The Partners and the Partnership

I. The General Partners and his employees have numerous other business responsibilities and ownerships in real property interests now existing and will in the future take on or reduce their responsibilities and ownership in real property. Some of the existing projects are, and in the future acquisition of these individuals may include, ownership of projects like or comparable to the project in this transaction.

Conflicts of Interest

XVIII. REPORTS TO INVESTORS

The General Partner shall be responsible for maintaining adequate books and records of the Partnership income and disbursements, and shall employ a competent accounting firm for this purpose. This accounting firm shall, in addition, make spot checks as necessary, to verify the various items of income and disbursement.

A monthly report shall be issued to all partners. These reports shall be completed and mailed to all partners together with any cash distribution on or before the 15th of the month.

A Public Accountant shall be employed to prepare the annual statement and income tax return for the Partnership.

An annual report shall be sent to each partner along with an individual summary of his individual taxable position in regards to the Partnership.

The taxable period for this partnership shall be on a calendar year.

All expenses for accounting and reporting shall be expenses of the Partnership.

AGREEMENT AND CERTIFICATE
OF LIMITED PARTNERSHIP

XYZ Associates

I. NAME OF PARTNERSHIP

The name of this Limited Partnership shall be XYZ Associates.

II. CHARACTER OF PARTNERSHIP BUSINESS

The business of the Partnership shall be the acquisition, improvement and operation of the real property and improvements commonly described as Cynthia I and Cynthia II, Carthage, CA. (hereafter said "property").

III. PLACE OF BUSINESS

The principal place of business of the Partnership shall be 1012 Zulu Ave., Los Angeles, California 90000.

IV. NAMES AND PLACES OF RESIDENCE OF PARTNERS

A. General Partner

APEX, INC.
1012 Zulu Ave.
Los Angeles, CA 90000

B. Limited Partners

Class "A" Limited Partners	22 units
Class "B" Limited Partners	22 units
JOE BLOW 3030 Fisher Ave. Los Angeles, CA 90048	11 units
DAVE SMITH 2622 Olive St. Santa Monica, CA 90403	11 units

V. TERM OF PARTNERSHIP

The Partnership shall exist from the date the last partner signs this Agreement and Certificate of Limited Partnership to the date that the Partnership assets are distributed after the sale of said Property, except that if a promissory note is received by the Limited Partnership as part of the consideration paid for the purchase of said Property, the Limited Partnership shall continue until the Limited Partners receive all payments to which they are entitled on said promissory note, or until said promissory note is sold by the Partnership; or to November 20, 1986, in the event that said Property is not acquired by said date.

In the event that said Property is exchanged solely for property of like kind (hereinafter "said like property") pursuant to Section 1031(a) of the Internal Revenue Code of 1954 (hereinafter "the Code"), or is exchanged for said like property and money pursuant to Section 1031(b) of the Code, the Partnership shall continue in existence to the date that the Partnership assets are distributed after the sale of said like property, except that if a promissory note is received by the Limited Partnership as a part of the consideration paid for the purchase of said like property, then the Limited Partnership shall continue until the Limited Partners receive all payments to which they are entitled on said promissory note or until said promissory note is sold by the Partnership.

VI. CONTRIBUTIONS BY LIMITED PARTNERS

The Limited Partners shall contribute only cash to the Partnership in the amounts indicated below and said sums shall be paid by each party not later than the date this Agreement and Certificate of Limited Partnership is executed by said party:

CLASS A LIMITED PARTNERS

NAME	CONTRIBUTIONS	NO. CLASS B UNITS

(amounts would appear here)

| | $110,000.00 | 22 @ $5,000.00 |

CLASS B LIMITED PARTNERS

NAME	CONTRIBUTIONS	NO. CLASS B UNITS
JOE BLOW	$ 550.00	11
DAVE SMITH	$ 550.00	11
	$1,100.00	22

The General Partner shall not contribute any cash to the Partnership.

VII. ADDITIONAL CONTRIBUTIONS BY LIMITED PARTNERS

Except for the contributions provided in paragraph VI, the Limited Partners shall not be required to make any additional contributions to the Partnership.

VIII. RETURN OF CONTRIBUTIONS OF LIMITED PARTNERS

The contributions of the Limited Partners shall be returned upon the expiration of the term of the Partnership, provided that the assets are sufficient to return said contributions.

IX. ALLOCATION OF PROFITS AND COMPENSATION TO LIMITED PARTNERS

The Limited Partners shall receive that share of the Partnership's operating profits and losses and that share of the gain or loss realized on a sale or exchange of said Property, and on said like property in the event of an exchange, in the percentages indicated below:

CLASS A LIMITED PARTNER	SHARE OF PARTNERSHIP'S GAIN OR LOSS ON SALE OR EXCHANGE

50%

CLASS B LIMITED PARTNER	SHARE OF PARTNERSHIP'S GAIN OR LOSS ON SALE OR EXCHANGE
DAVE SMITH	25%
JOE BLOW	25%
	50%

The General Partners shall exclusively determine when and if any distributions of Partnership profits shall be made, and the Limited Partners shall have no right to any other compensation by reason of their contributions.

X. RIGHT TO ASSIGN LIMITED PARTNERSHIP INTERESTS

The Limited Partners shall have no right to substitute an assignee as contributor in his place, or to sell, transfer, assign, hypothecate, or in any way alienate his interest in the Partnership.

XI. ADMISSION OF ADDITIONAL LIMITED PARTNERS

The partners shall have no right to admit additional Limited Partners to this Partnership.

XII. PRIORITY BETWEEN LIMITED PARTNERS

No Class A Limited Partner shall have priority over any other Class A Limited Partner as to contributions or as to compensation by way of income, but Class A Limited Partners shall have priority over Class B Limited Partners as to return of capital contribution.

XIII. DISSOLUTION OF THE PARTNERSHIP

Upon the resignation or removal of the General Partners, the Partnership shall dissolve.

XIV. LIMITED PARTNERS' RIGHT TO PROPERTY IN RETURN FOR CONTRIBUTION

The Limited Partners shall have the right to demand the Property for their contributions.

XV. OTHER RIGHTS OF LIMITED PARTNERS

A. The Class A Limited Partners, by majority in interest, shall have the right to:

1. Elect any other General Partners;
2. Terminate the Partnership;
3. Amend the Partnership Agreement;
4. Require the sale or exchange of all or substantially all of the assets of the Partnership.

B. The Class A Limited Partners by majority of interest vote may remove the General Partners.

C. The Limited Partners may inspect the Partnership books and records at the office of the General Partners during reasonable business hours.

XVI. GENERAL PARTNERS' POWER OF ATTORNEY

Each Limited Partner appoints the General Partners as his attorney-in-fact to make, execute, acknowledge, and file the original and any modification or amendment to the Agreement and Certificate of Limited Partnership, or any other instrument that may be required to be recorded or filed by the Partnership, and all documents that may be required to effectuate the dissolution and termination of the Partnership.

XVII. ADDITIONAL TERMS OF LIMITED PARTNERSHIP AGREEMENT

A. *Property Management Fee and Expenses.*

1. The General Partners shall be entitled to receive six percent (6%) of the gross rental receipts collected from the operation of said Property or, in the event of an exchange from the operation of said like property, for management services to be provided in connection with said Property, and, in the event of an exchange, with said like property, shall include rentals, rent collection, record keeping (but not preparation of Partnership tax returns), maintenance, co-ordination and supervision of improvements of said Property, and of said like property, and other activities that are necessary for the smooth and efficient operation of said Property and of said like property.

2. The expenses incurred by the General Partner in the formation of this Partnership and preparation of this Agreement and Certificate of Limited Partnership shall be paid by the Partnership.

B. *Sale of Said Property.*

1. The General Partner shall exclusively determine the terms on which said Property shall be sold; except that the sale shall neither be made:

(a) to: (i) any General Partner, (ii) any partner of the General Partners, (iii) any stockholder of the General Partners, (iv) any member of the family of a stockholder of the General Partners or, (v) any Limited Partner or Partners; nor

(b) unless the assets which shall be distributed immediately after the sale of said Property are sufficient to return to each Limited Partner cash in an amount equal to his initial contribution less any prior cash distribution received by him.

2. In the event that the sale of said Property results in the partnership's taking a promissory note secured by a deed of trust on the Property, said promissory note shall be due and payable in not more than five (5) years from the date of said sale and shall bear interest at a rate at least equal to ten percent. Further, in the event that the sale of said Property results in the Partnership's taking a promissory note secured by a deed of trust on the Property, the General Partner shall attempt to sell said promissory note at the best cash price obtainable; except that the sale shall not be made to (a) the General Partners, (b) any stockholder of the General Partners, (c) any member of the family of a stockholder of the General Partners or, (d) any Limited Partner or Partners.

3. The General Partner may pay on behalf of the Partnership commission in connection with the sale or exchange of said Property, but said commission shall not be in excess of five percent (5%) of the selling price, and said commission may be payable to any Limited Partner, who is a real estate licensee and who is the selling agent.

C. Exchange of Said Property

The General Partners shall exclusively determine if and the terms on which said Property may be exchanged solely for said like property pursuant to Section 1031(a) of the Code or for said like property and money pursuant to Section 1031, (b) of the Code; except that said Property shall not be exchanged for like property in which the following persons have any interest:

1. the General Partners,
2. any stockholder of the General Partners,
3. any member of the family of a stockholder of the General Partners,
4. any Limited Partner or Partners.

D. Sale of Said Like Property

1. In the event that said Property has been exchanged for said like property, which is to be improved and held, the General Partners shall exclusively determine the terms on which said like property shall be sold; except that the sale shall neither be made:

(a) to: (i) the General Partners, (ii) any stockholder of the General Partners, (iii) any member of the family of a stockholder of the General Partners or, (iv) any Limited Partner or Partners; nor

(b) unless the assets which shall be distributed immediately after the sale of said like property are sufficient to return to each Limited Partner cash in an amount equal to his initial contribution, less any prior cash distribution received by him.

2. In the event that the sale of said like property results in the Partnership's taking a promissory note secured by a deed of trust on the like property, said promissory note shall be due and payable not more than five (5) years from the date of said sale and shall bear interest at a rate of ten percent (10%). Further, in the event that the sale of said like property results in the Partnership's taking a promissory note secured by a deed of trust on the Property, the General Partner shall attempt to sell said promissory note at the best cash price obtainable; except that the sale shall not be made to: (a) the General Partner, (b) any partner of the General Partners, (c) any stockholder of the General Partners, (d) any member of the family of a stockholder the General Partners or, (e) any Limited Partner or Partners.

3. The General Partner may pay on behalf of the Partnership a commission in connection with the sale of said like property, but said commission shall not be in excess of five percent (5%) of the selling price, and said commission may be payable to any Limited Partner who is a real estate licensee and who is also the selling agent.

E. Refinance of Said Property

1. The General Partner shall exclusively determine the terms on which said Property shall be refinanced, except that the cash which shall be distributed immediately after the Property is refinanced shall be sufficient to return to each Limited Partner cash in an amount at least equal to his initial cash contribution, less any prior cash distribution received by him.

F. Distribution of Partnership Assets to Partners

The accounts of the Partners shall be entitled to payment in the following order:

1. To the Class A Limited Partners in respect to their contributions;
2. To the Class B Limited Partners in respect to their contributions;
3. To the General Partners in respect to any loans that the General Partners may make to the Partnership;
4. To the General Partner other than for profits and capital;
5. To all Limited Partners in respect of profits.

G. Miscellaneous Terms

This Agreement and Certificate of Limited Partnership constitutes the entire agreement between the parties hereto and supersedes all prior and contemporaneous agreements pertaining to the subject matter hereof and shall inure to the benefit of all the parties and their heirs, representatives, successors, and assigns.

GENERAL PARTNERS: LIMITED PARTNERS:

_____   _____

JOE BLOW for APEX, INC.   (NAME)   CLASS (A OR B)

_____

DAVE SMITH for APEX,
INC.

STATE OF CALIFORNIA   )
) ss.
COUNTY OF LOS ANGELES)

     On this _____ day of _____ , 19_____ , before
me personally appeared _____ , known to me to
be the person(s) whose name(s) _____ subscribed to the within AGREEMENT AND
CERTIFICATE OF LIMITED PARTNERSHIP, and acknowledged that _____
executed the same on this date.

                                           (SEAL)

_____

NOTARY PUBLIC IN AND FOR SAID STATE

Subscription Agreement

TO: APEX, INC.
General Partner
XYZ ASSOCIATES
A California Limited Partnership

FROM: _____

Enclosed is my personal check for $_____, made payable to XYZ ASSOCIATES for the purchase of _____ Limited Partnership unit(s) in XYZ ASSOCIATES at purchase price of $5,000.00 for each unit, and an executed and acknowledged signature page of the Agreement and Certificate of Limited Partnership of
The Limited Partnership interest is to appear in the following name(s): _____
_____.

In order to induce you to accept this subscription, I hereby acknowledge, represent and warrant that I:

1. am a California resident;
2. am over the age of 21 years;
3. have read the Offering Circular and Agreement and Certificate of Limited Partnership and that I understand the speculative nature of the proposed investment;
4. have received no representation or warranties concerning the investment;
5. have had unrestricted access to all information concerning the proposed investment;
6. have had the investment proposal reviewed by my _____
(investment counselor, C. P. A., or attorney);
7. have known the following partner of the General Partner personally or in business as follows:
_____
_____
_____ ;
8. have a projected adjusted gross income for the taxable year 19xx of at least $_____;
9. have an existing net worth of at least $_____ (net worth to be determined exclusive of home, furnishings and automobiles);
10. have had the following experience with investments similar to the proposed investment:
_____
_____
_____ ;
11. have had the following occupational experience:
_____
_____ ;
12. have achieved the following educational level:
_____
_____
_____ ;

I understand that subscriptions will be accepted subject to my suitability as an investor and at the discretion of the General Partners. If this subscription is rejected, the signature page enclosed and my funds forwarded herein will be returned promptly to me without deduction or cost.

DATED:_____   By _____
                                        Address _____
                                        _____
                                        Social Security Number:
                                        _____

SUBSCRIPTION INSTRUCTIONS
1. Have jurat notarized (sign in space provided in upper right corner).
2. Complete and sign subscription agreement.
3. Return items 1 and 2 above together with check.

Glossary
Key Real Estate Terms

Abatement of Nuisance: Extinction or termination of a nuisance.

Abstract of Judgement: A condensation of the essential provisions of a court judgment.

Abstract of Title: A summary or digest of the conveyances, transfers, and any other facts relied on as evidence of title, together with any other elements of record that may impair the title.

Abstraction: A method of valuing land; the indicated value of the improvement is deducted from the sale price.

Acceleration Clause: Clause in trust deed or mortgage giving lender right to call all sums owing him or her to be immediately due and payable upon the happening of a certain event.

Acceptance: When the seller or agent's principal agrees to the terms of the agreement of sale, and approves the negotiation on the part of the agent, and acknowledges receipt of the deposit in subscribing to the agreement of sale, that act is termed an acceptance.

Access Right: The right of an owner to have ingress and egress to and from his or her property.

Accretion: An addition to land from natural causes as, for example, from gradual action of the ocean or river waters.

Accrued Depreciation: The difference between the cost of replacement new as of the date of the appraisal and the present appraised value.

Acknowledgment: A formal declaration before a duly authorized officer by a person who has executed an instrument that such execution is his or her act and deed.

Acquisition: The act or process by which a person procures property.

Acre: A measure of land equaling 160 square rods, or 4,840 square yards, or 43,560 square feet, or a tract about 208.71 feet square.

Ad Valorom: According to valuation.

Administrator: A person appointed by the probate court to administer the estate of a person deceased.

Administrator C.T.A.: The representative of a decedent's estate where no one is named as executor, or where the named person is unable or unwilling to act.

Adverse Possession: The open and notorious possession and occupancy under an evident claim or right, in denial or opposition to the title of another claimant.

Affidavit: A statement or declaration in writing sworn to or affirmed before an officer who has authority to administer an oath or affirmation.

Affirm: To confirm, to aver, to ratify, to verify.

AFLB: Accredited Farm and Land Broker.

Agency: The relationship between principal and agent which arises out of a contract, either expressed or implied, written or oral, wherein the agent is employed by the principal to do certain acts dealing with a third party.

Agent: One who represents another from whom he or she has derived authority.

Agreement of Sale: A written agreement or contract between seller and purchaser in which they reach a meeting of minds on the terms and conditions of the sale.

Alienation: Transferring of property to another; transfer of property and possession of lands, or other things, from one person to another.

Alienation Clause: Specific type of acceleration clause that "accelerates" the note, making it due and payable on sale or transfer of the property.

Alluvion (alluvium): Soil deposited by accretion; increase of earth on shore or bank of a river.

A.L.T.A. Title Policy: A type of title insurance policy issued by title insurance companies, which expands risks normally insured against under the standard type policy.

Amenities: Satisfaction of enjoyable living to be derived from a home; conditions of agreeable living or beneficial influence arising from the location or improvements.

American Title Association (A.T.A.) Title Policy: A title insurance policy that has expanded coverage more than standard policy such that it includes unrecorded liens, easements, and other unrecorded instruments.

Amortization: The liquidation of a financial obligation on an installment basis; also, recovery, over a period, of cost or value.

Amortized Loan: A loan that is completely paid off, interest and principal, by a series of regular payments that are equal or nearly equal; also called Level Payments Loan.

Annuity: A series of assured equal or nearly equal payments to be made over a period of time or it may be a lump sum payment to be made in the future. The installment payments due to the landlord under a lease is an Annuity. So are the installment payments due to a lender.

Anticipation, (principle of): Affirms that value is created by anticipated benefits to be derived in the future.

Appraiser: One qualified by education, training, and experience, hired to estimate the value of real and personal property based on experience, judgment, facts, and use of formal appraisal processes.

Appurtenance: Something annexed to another thing which may be transferred incident to it. That which belongs to another thing, as a barn, dwelling, garage, or orchard is incident to the land to which it is attached.

Architectural Style: Generally the appearance and character of a building's design and construction.

Assessed Valuation: A valuation placed on property by a public officer or board, as a basis for taxation.

Assessed Value: Value placed on property as a basis for taxation.

Assessment: The valuation of property for the purpose of levying a tax or the amount of the tax levied.

Assessor: The official who has the responsibility of determining assessed values.

Assignment: A transfer or making over to another of the whole of any property, real or personal, in possession or in action, or of any estate or right therein.

Assignor: One who assigns or transfers property.

Assigns, Assignees: Those to whom property has been transferred.

Assumption Agreement: An undertaking or adoption of a debt or obligation primarily resting on another person.

Assumption Fee: A lender's charge for changing over and processing new records for a new owner who is assuming an existing loan.

Assumption of Mortgage: The taking of title to property by a grantee, wherein he assumes liability for payment of an existing note secured by a mortgage or deed of trust against the property; becoming a coguarantor for the payment of a mortgage or deed of trust note.

Attachment: Seizure of property by court order, usually to have it available in event a judgment is obtained in a pending suit.

Attest: To affirm to be true or genuine; an official act establishing authenticity.

Attorney in Fact: One who is authorized to perform certain acts for another under a power of attorney; power of attorney may be limited to a specific act or acts, or be general.

Avulsion: The sudden tearing away or removal of land by action of water flowing over or through it.

Balloon Payment: Where the final installment payment on a note is greater than the preceding installment payments and it pays the note in full, such final installment is termed a balloon payment.

Base and Meridian: Imaginary lines used by surveyors to find and describe the location of private or public lands.

Bearing Wall or Partition: A wall or partition supporting any vertical load in addition to its own weight.

Bench Marks: A location indicated on a durable marker by surveyors.

Beneficiary: (1) One entitled to the benefit of a trust; (2) One who receives profit from an estate, the title of which is vested in a trustee; (3) The lender on the security of a note and deed of trust.

Bequeath: To give or hand down by will; to leave by will.

Bequest: That which is given by the terms of a will.

Betterment: An improvement on property that increases property value and is considered as a capital asset, as distinguished from repairs or replacements where the original character or cost is unchanged.

Bilateral Contract: A document in which the promise of one party is given in exchange for the promise of the other party.

Bill of Sale: A written instrument given to pass title of personal property from vendor to vendee.

Binder: A notation of coverage on an insurance policy, issued by an agent, and given to the insured prior to issuing of the policy.

Blanket Mortgage: A single mortgage which covers more than one piece of real estate.

Blighted Area: A declining area in which real property values are seriously affected by destructive economic forces, such as encroaching inharmonious property usages, infiltration of poor-risk inhabitants, and/or rapidly depreciating buildings.

Board Foot: A unit of measurement of lumber, one foot wide, one foot long, one inch thick; 144 cubic inches.

Bona Fide: In good faith; without fraud.

Boot: Any cash, mortgage reduction, or other nonqualified property received by the taxpayer in a tax-free exchange.

Breach: The breaking of a law, or failure of duty, either by omission or commission.

Broker: A natural or legal person who, for a fee or commission, brings parties together and assists in negotiating contracts concerning real estate, securities, insurance, and the like.

Broker's Loan Statement: A document received by a borrower at the time of a loan transaction; indicates maximum costs, expenses, commissions, and the like to be paid by the borrower of the loan.

B.T.U. (British thermal unit): The quantity of heat required to raise the temperature of one pound of water one degree Fahrenheit.

Building Code: A city, county, or state law that requires minimum building construction standards.

Building Line: A line set by law a certain distance from a street line in front of which an owner cannot build on his or her lot (a setback line).

Building Residual Technique: The method of determining accrued depreciation of a building, used in appraising.

Building Restrictions: Ordinances or laws that require sound construction for protection of health and safety.

Bulk Sales Law: A state law for the protection of creditors that requires the sale of a business to be advertised beforehand.

Bundle of Rights: Beneficial interests or rights.

Cal-Vet Loan: California veterans farm and home purchase program for qualified native born veterans or veterans who entered service from this state.

Capital Assets: Assets of a permanent nature used in the production of an income, such as land, buildings, machinery, equipment.

Capitalization: In appraising, determining value of property by considering net income and percentage of reasonable return on the investment.

Capitalization Rate: The rate of interest which is considered a reasonable return on investment and used in the process of determining value based on net income.

Cash Flow: The net or spendable income from an investment, which is determined after deducting from the gross income all loan payments, operating expenses, and an allowance for the income tax related to the income.

Caveat Emptor (Let the buyer beware): The buyer must examine the goods or property and buy at his or her own risk.

Certificate of Eligibility: A certificate of eligibility for a Cal-Vet loan issued by California Department of Veteran Affairs.

Certificate of Reasonable Value (CRV): The federal Veterans Administration appraisal commitment of property value.

Certificate of Title: A document furnished by a title company, which certifies that according to the records a certain ownership is properly vested in the present owner.

Certification of Sale: A certificate issued to the buyer at a judicial sale.

CCIM: Certified Commercial Investment Member.

Chain of Title: A history of conveyances and encumbrances affecting the title from the time the original patent was granted, or as far back as records are available.

Change (principle of): Holds that the future, not the past, is of prime importance in estimating value.

Chattel Mortgage: A personal property mortgage (see Security Agreement and Security Interest).

Chattel Real: An estate related to real estate, such as a lease on real property.

Chattels: Goods or every species of property movable or immovable that are not real property.

Cloud on the Title: Any conditions revealed by a title search that affect the title to property; usually relatively unimportant items, but which cannot be removed without a quitclaim deed or court action.

Collateral: This is the property subject to the security interest (See definition of Security Interest).

Collateral Security: A separate obligation attached to contract to guarantee its performance; the transfer of property or of other contracts, or valuables, to insure the performance of a principal agreement.

Collusion: An agreement between two or more persons to defraud another of his or her rights by the forms of law, or to obtain an object forbidden by law.

Color of Title: That which appears to be good title, but which is not title in fact.

Commercial Acre: A term applied to the remainder of an acre of newly subdivided land after the area devoted to streets, sidewalks and curbs, and the like has been deducted from the acre.

Commercial Paper: Bills of exchange used in commercial trade.

Commission: An agent's compensation for performing the duties of his or her agency; in real estate practice, a percentage of the selling price of property, percentage of rentals, and the like.

Commitment: A pledge, promise, or firm agreement.

Common Law: The body of law that grew from customs and practices developed and used in England "since the memory of man runneth not to the contrary."

Community: A part of a metropolitan area that has a number of neighborhoods with a tendency toward common interests and problems.

Community Property: Property accumulated through joint efforts of husband and wife living together.

Compaction: Whenever extra soil is added to a lot to fill in low places or to raise the level of the lot, the added soil is often too loose and soft to sustain the weight of the buildings; therefore, it is necessary to compact the added soil so that it will carry the weight of buildings without the danger of their tilting, settling, or cracking.

Comparable Sales: Sales that have similar characteristics as the subject property and are used for analysis in the appraisal process.

Comparative Analysis: A method of appraising a lot or home by comparing it with others of similar qualities with recent sales prices, also known as Market Data Approach.

Competent: Legally qualified.

Competition (principle of): Holds that profits tend to breed competition and excess profits tend to breed ruinous competition.

Compound Interest: Interest paid on original principal and also on the accrued and unpaid interest that has accumulated.

Condemnation: Act of taking private property for public use by a political subdivision; declaration that a structure is unfit for use.

Conditional Commitment: A commitment of a definite loan amount for some future unknown purchaser of satisfactory credit standing.

Conditional Sales Contract: A contract for the sale of property stating that delivery is to be made to the buyer, title to remain vested in the seller until the conditions of the contract have been fulfilled.

Condominium: A system of individual fee ownership of units in a multifamily structure, combined with joint ownership of common areas of the structure and the land.

Confirmation of Sale: A court approval of the sale of property by an executor, administrator, guardian, or conservator.

Conformity (principle of): Holds that the maximum of value is realized when a reasonable degree of homogeneity of improvements is present.

Consideration: Anything of value given to induce entering into a contract; may be money, personal services, or even love and affection.

Construction Loans: Loans made for the construction of homes or commercial buildings; usually funds are disbursed to the contractor-builder during construction and after periodic inspections; disbursements are based on an agreement between borrower and lender.

Constructive eviction: When a tenant's possession is disturbed by the landlord to the extent that the premises are unfit, or the tenant is deprived of the benefit of the premises.

Constructive Notice: Notice given by the public records.

Contour: The surface configuration of land.

Contract: An agreement, either written or oral, to do or not to do certain things.

Contribution (principle of): Holds that maximum real property values are achieved when the improvements on the site produce the highest (net) return commensurate with the investment.

Consumer Goods: These are goods used or bought primarily for personal, family, or household purposes.

Conversion: Change from one character or use to another.

Conveyance: The transfer of the title of land from one to another; denotes an instrument that carries from one person to another an interest in land.

Corporation: A group or body of persons established and treated by law as an individual or unit with rights and liabilities or both, distinct and apart from those of the persons composing it.

Correlation: To bring the indicated values developed by the three approaches into mutual relationship with each other.

Cost Approach: One of three methods in the appraisal process; an analysis in which a value estimate of a property is derived by estimating the replacement cost of the improvements, deducting there from the estimated accrued depreciation, then adding the market value of the land.

Cost Basis: Used for income tax purposes; the original cost of a property plus acquisition expense.

Covenant: Agreements written into deeds and other instruments promising performance or nonperformance of certain acts, or stipulating certain uses or nonuses of the property.

CPM (Certified Property Manager): Member of the Institute of Real Estate Management (IREM) of the National Association of Realtors.

CREA: California Real Estate Association.

CRE (Counselor of Real Estate): Member of American Society of Real Estate Counselors.

Curable Depreciation: Items of physical deterioration and functional obsolescence that are customarily repaired or replaced by a prudent property owner.

Curtesy: The right that a husband has in a wife's estate at her death.

Damages: The indemnity recoverable by a person who has sustained an injury, either in person, property, or relative rights, through the act or default of another.

Debtor: This is the party who "owns" the property that is subject to the security interest, previously known as the mortgagor or pledgor.

Deciduous Trees: Lose their leaves in the autumn and winter.

Declining Balance: An accelerated method of depreciation used to determine the amount of nontaxable income for income tax purposes.

Dedication: An appropriation of land by its owner for some public use accepted for such use by authorized public officials on behalf of the public.

Deed: Written instrument that, when properly executed and delivered, conveys title.

Default: Failure to fulfill a duty or promise or to discharge an obligation; omission or failure to perform any act.

Defeasance Clause: The clause in a mortgage that gives the mortgagor the right to redeem property on the payment of his or her obligations to the mortgagee.

Deferred Maintenance: Existing but unfulfilled requirements for repairs and rehabilitation.

Deficiency Judgement: A judgement given when the security pledge for a loan does not satisfy the debt upon its default.

Deposit Receipt: A document used to secure a firm offer to purchase property and provide a receipt for the buyer for the "earnest money" used to show good faith in making the offer.

Depreciation: Loss of value in real property brought about by age, physical deterioration, or functional or economic obsolescence; broadly, a loss in value from any cause.

Desist and Refrain Order: The Real Estate Comissioner is empowered by law to issue an order directing a person to desist and refrain from committing an act in violation of the real estate law.

Deterioration: Impairment of condition; one of the causes of depreciation and reflecting the loss in value brought about by wear and tear, disintegration, use in service, and the action of the elements.

Devisee: One who receives a bequest made by will.

Devisor: One who bequeaths by will.

Directional Growth: The location or direction toward which the residential sections of a city are destined or determined to grow.

Discount: An amount deducted in advance from the principal before the borrower is given the use of the principal (see Points).

Donee: A person to whom a gift is made.

Donor: A person who makes a gift.

Dower: The right that a wife has in her husband's estate at his death.

Duress: Unlawful constraint exercised on a person whereby he or she is forced to do some act against his or her will.

Earnest Money: Money deposited and receipted for in order to bind an offer.

Easement: Created by grant or agreement for a specific purpose, an easement is the right, privilege or interest which one party has in the land of another. (Example: right of way).

Economic Life: The period over which a property will yield a return on the investment, over and above the economic or ground rent due to land.

Economic Obsolescence: A loss in value due to factors away from the subject property, but adversely affecting the value of the subject property.

Economic Rent: The reasonable rental expectancy if the property were available for renting at the time of its valuation.

Effective Age of Improvement: The number of years of age that is indicated by the condition of the structure.

Effective Interest Rate: The percentage of interest that is actually being paid by the borrower for the use of the money.

Eminent Domain: The right of the government to acquire property for necessary public or quasi-public use by condemnation; the owner must be fairly compensated.

Encroachment: Trespass; the building of a structure or construction of any improvements, partly or wholly on the property of another.

Encumbrance: Anything that affects or limits the fee simple title to property, such as mortgages, easements, or restrictions of any kind; liens are special encumbrances, which make the property security for the payment of a debt or obligation, such as mortgages and taxes.

Equity: The interest or value an owner has in real estate over and above the liens against it; branch of remedial justice by and through which relief is afforded to suitors in courts of equity.

Equity of Redemption: The right to redeem property during the foreclosure period, such as a mortgagor's right to redeem within a year after foreclosure sale.

Erosion: The wearing away of land by the action of water, wind, or glacial ice.

Escalation: The right reserved by the lender to increase the amount of the payments and/or interest upon the happening of a certain event.

Escalator Clause: A clause in a contract providing for the upward or downward adjustment of certain items to cover specified contingencies.

Escheat: The reverting of property to the state when heirs capable of inheriting are lacking.

Escrow: The deposit of instruments and funds with instructions to a third neutral party to carry out the provisions of an agreement or contract; when everything is deposited to enable carrying out the instructions, it is called a complete or perfect escrow.

Estate: As applied to the real estate practice, signifies the quantity of interest, share, right, equity, of which riches or fortune may consist, in real property. The degree, quantity, nature, and extent of interest a person has in real property.

Estate for Life: A freehold estate, not of inheritance, but which is held by the tenant for his or her own life or the life or lives of one or more other persons, or for an indefinite period may endure for the life or lives of persons in being and beyond the period of life.

Estate for Years: An interest in lands by virtue of a contract for the possession of them for a definite and limited period of time; a lease may be said to be an estate for years.

Estate of Inheritance: An estate that may descend to heirs; all freehold estates are estates of inheritance, except estates for life.

Estate of Will: The occupation of lands and tenements by a tenant for an indefinite period, terminable by one or both parties.

Estimate: To form a preliminary opinion of value.

Estimated Remaining Life: The period of time (years) it takes for the improvements to become valueless.

Estoppel: A doctrine that bars one from asserting rights which are inconsistent with a previous position or representation.

Ethics: That branch of moral science, idealism, justness, and fairness, which treats of the duties which a member of a profession or craft owes to the public, to clients or patron, and to professional brethren or members.

Exclusive Agency Listing: A written instrument giving one agent the right to sell property for a specified time, but reserving the right of the owner to sell the property without the payment of a commission.

Exclusive Right to Sell Listing: A written agreement between owner and agent giving agent the right to collect a commission if the property is sold by anyone during the term of agreement.

Execute: To complete, make, perform, do, or follow out; to execute a deed, to make a deed, including especially signing, sealing, and delivery; to execute a contract is to perform the contract, to follow out to the end, to complete.

Executor: A person named in a will to carry out its provisions as to the disposition of the estate of a person deceased.

Fee: An estate of inheritance in real property.

Fee Simple: In modern estates, the terms "Fee" and "Fee Simple" are substantially synonymous.

Fiduciary: A person in a position of trust and confidence, as between principal and broker; broker as fiduciary owes certain loyalty that cannot be breached under rules of agency.

Financing Statement: This is the instrument that is filed in order to give public notice of the security interest and thereby protect the interest of the secured parties in the collateral.

Fixtures: Appurtenances attached to land or improvements, which usually cannot be removed without agreement as they become real property (examples; plumbing fixtures, store fixtures built into the property).

Foreclosure: Procedure whereby property pledged as security for a debt is sold to pay the debt in event of default in payments or terms.

Forfeiture: Loss of money or anything of value due to failure to perform.

Fraud: The intentional and successful employment of any cunning, deception, collusion, or artifice, used to circumvent, cheat, or deceive another person, whereby that person acts upon it to the loss of his or her property and to his or her legal injury.

Front Foot: Property measurement for sale or valuation purposes; the property measures by the front foot on its street line—each front foot extending the depth of the lot.

Frontage: Land bordering a street.

Functional Obsolescence: A loss of value due to adverse factors from within the structure that affect the utility of the structure.

Future Benefits: The anticipated benefits the present owner will receive from his or her property in the future.

Gift Deed: A deed for which the consideration is love and affection and where there is no material consideration.

Graduated Lease: Lease that provides for a varying rental rate, often based on future determination; sometimes rent is based on result of periodical appraisals; used largely in long-term leases.

Grant: A technical term made use of in deeds of conveyance of lands to impart a transfer.

Grantee: The purchaser, a person to whom a grant is made.

Grantor: Seller of property, one who signs a deed.

GRI: Graduate, Realtors Institute.

Grid: A chart used in rating the borrower risk, property, and neighborhood.

Gross Income: Total income from property before any expenses are deducted.

Gross Rent Multiplier: A figure that, times the gross income of a property, produces an estimate of value of the property.

Ground Lease: An agreement for the use of the land only, sometimes secured by improvements placed on the land by the user.

Ground Rent: Earnings of improved property credited to earnings of the ground itself after allowance is made for earnings of improvements; often termed economic rent.

Guarantee of Title: Not the same as title insurance, an opinion on the condition of title made by a search of the official records at a specific time; opinion is backed by the assets of the company giving the opinion.

Highest and Best Use: An appraisal phrase meaning that use, at the time of appraisal, is most likely to produce the greatest net return to the land and/or buildings over a given period of time; use that will produce the greatest amount of amenities or profit.

Holder in Due Course: One who has taken a note, check, or bill of exchange in due course: before it was overdue; in good faith and for value; without knowledge that it has been previously dishonored and without notice of any defect at the time it was negotiated to him or her.

Homestead: A home upon which the owner or owners have recorded a Declaration of Homestead; protects home against judgements up to specified amounts.

Hundred Percent Location: A city retail business location that is considered the best available for attracting business.

Hypothecate: To give a thing as security without the necessity of giving up possession of it.

Impounds: A trust-type account established by lenders for the accumulation of funds to meet taxes, FHA mortgage insurance premiums, and/or future insurance policy premiums required to protect their security. Impounds are usually collected with the note payment.

Income Approach: One of the three methods in the appraisal process; an analysis in which the estimated gross income from the subject residence is used as a basis for estimating value along with gross rent multipliers derived.

Incompetent: One who is mentally incapable; any person who, though not insane, is, by reason of old age, disease, weakness of mind, or any other cause, unable, unassisted, to properly manage and take care of him-or herself or personal property and by reason thereof would be likely to be deceived or imposed upon by artful or designing persons.

Increment: An increase; most frequently used to refer to the increase of value of land that accompanies population growth and increasing wealth in the community; the term "unearned increment" is used in this connection since values are supposed to have increased without effort on the part of the owner.

Indorsement: The act of signing one's name on the back of a check or a note, with or without further qualification.

Injunction: A writ or order issued under the seal of a court to restrain one or more parties to a suit or proceeding from doing an act deemed inequitable or unjust in regard to the rights of some other party or parties in the suit or proceeding.

Installment Note: A note that provides for payments of a certain sum or amount to be paid on the dates specified in the instrument.

Installment Sale: An individual selling a piece of property on an installment sale may receive as much as 80 percent or more but not more than 100 percent within the first year. All that is received in the first year is taxable in that year. However, the seller may, if he wishes, take payments over a longer period of time.

Installment Sales Contract: Same as Conditional Sales Contract.

Instrument: A written legal document created to effect the rights of the parties.

Interest Rate: The percentage of a sum of money charged for its use.

Intestate: A person who dies having made no will, or is defective in form, in which case the estate descends to the heirs at law or next of kin.

Involuntary Lien: A lien imposed against property without consent of an owner; example, taxes, special assessments, federal income tax liens.

Irrevocable: Incapable of being recalled or revoked, unchangeable.

Irrigation Districts: Quasi-political districts created under special laws to provide for water services to property owners in the district; operation governed to a great extent by law.

Joint Note: A note signed by two or more persons who have equal liability for payment.

Joint Tenancy: Joint ownership by two or more persons with right of survivorship; all joint tenants own equal interest and have equal rights in the property.

Judgment: The final determination of a court of competent jurisdiction of a matter presented to it; money judgments provide for the payment of claims presented to the court, or are awarded as damages, etc.

Junior Lien: A subordinate lien.

Jurisdiction: The authority by which judicial officers take cognizance of and decide causes; the power to hear and determine a cause; the right and power which a judicial officer has to enter upon the inquiry.

Laches: Delay or negligence in asserting one's legal rights.

Land Contract: A contract ordinarily used in connection with the sale of property in cases where the seller does not wish to convey title until all of a certain part of the purchase price is paid by the buyer; often used when property is sold on small down payment.

Landowner's Royalty: The interest retained by the landlord in gas and oil rights when he or she transfers title or interest in the land.

Lateral Support: The support that the soil of an adjoining owner gives to his neighbor's land.

Lease: A contract between owner and tenant setting forth conditions upon which the tenant may occupy and use the property, and the term of the occupancy.

Legal Description: A description recognized by law, a description by which property can be definitely located by reference to government surveys or approved recorded maps.

Lessee: One who contracts to rent property under a lease contract.

Lessor: An owner who enters into a lease with a tenant.

Lien: A form of encumbrance that usually makes property security for the payment of a debt or discharge of an obligation, (example: judgments, taxes, mortgages, deeds of trust).

Limited Partnership: A partnership composed of some partners whose contribution and liability are limited.

Lis Pendens (Suit pending): Usually recorded so as to give constructive notice of pending litigation.

Listing: An employment contract between principal and agent authorizing the agent to perform services for the principal involving the latter's property; listing contracts are entered into for the purpose of securing persons to buy, lease, or rent property; employment of an agent by a prospective purchaser or lessee to locate property for purchase or lease may be considered a listing.

Loan Application: The loan application is a source of information on which the lender bases decision to make the loan, defines the terms of the loan contract, gives the name of the borrower, place of employment, salary, bank accounts, and credit references, and describes the real estate that is to be mortgaged; it also stipulates the amount of loan being applied for, and repayment terms.

Loan Closing: When all conditions have been met, the loan officer authorizes the recording of the trust deed or mortgage; the disbursal procedure of funds is similar to the closing of a real estate sales escrow; the borrower can expect to receive less than the amount of the loan, as title, recording, service, and other fees may be withheld, or can expect to deposit the cost of these items into the loan escrow. This process is sometimes called "funding" the loan.

Loan Commitment: Lender's contractual commitment to a loan based on the appraisal and underwriting.

Loan Value: The value an appraiser sets on real property to aid the lender in determining the amount of a new trust deed loan.

MAI (Member of the Appraisal Institute): Designates a person who is a member of the American Institute of Real Estate Appraisers of the National Association of Realtors.

Margin of Security: The difference between the amount of the mortgage loan(s) and appraised value of the property.

Marginal Land: Land that barely pays the cost of working or using.

Market Data Approach: One of the three methods in the appraisal process; a means of comparing similar type residential properties, which have recently sold, to the subject property.

Market Price: The price paid regardless of pressures, motives, or intelligence.

Market Value: (1) The price at which a willing seller would sell and a willing buyer would buy, neither being under abnormal pressure; (2) as defined by the courts, the highest price estimated in terms of money that a property will bring if exposed for sale in the open market, allowing a reasonable time to find a purchaser with knowledge of property's use and capabilities for use.

Marketable Title: Merchantable title; title free and clear of objectionable liens or encumbrances.

Material Fact: A fact is material if it is one that the agent should realize would be likely to affect the judgment of the principal in giving consent to the agent to enter into the particular transaction on the specified terms.

Mechanic's Lien: A statuatory lien whereby payment for labor or materials contributed to a specific work of improvement may be obtained.

Meridians: Imaginary north-south measuring lines that intersect base lines to form a starting point for the measurement of land.

Metes and Bounds: A term used in describing the boundary lines of land, setting forth all the boundary lines together with their terminal points and angles.

Minors: All persons under 18 years of age.

Misplaced Improvements: Improvements on land that do not conform to the most profitable use of the site.

Month-to-Month Tenancy: The usual arrangement for renting houses or apartments; rent is paid by the month.

Monument: A fixed object and point established by surveyors to establish land locations.

Moratorium: The temporary suspension, usually by statute, of the enforcement of liability for debt.

Mortgage: An instrument recognized by law by which property is hypothecated to secure the payment of a debt or obligation; procedure for foreclosure in event of default is established by statute.

Mortgage Guaranty Insurance: Insurance against financial loss available to mortgage lenders from a private company.

Mortgagee: One to whom a mortgagor gives a mortgage to secure a loan or performance of an obligation, a lender.

Mortgagor: One who gives a mortgage on his or her property to secure a loan or assure performance of an obligation, a borrower.

Multiple Listing: A listing, usually an exclusive right to sell, taken by a member of an organization composed of real estate brokers, with the provision that all members will have the opportunity to find an interested client; a cooperative listing.

Mutual Water Company: A water company organized by or for water users in a given district with the object of securing an ample water supply at a reasonable rate; stock issued to users.

NAR: National Association of Realtors.

Narrative Appraisal: A summary of all factual materials, techniques, and appraisal methods used by appraiser in setting forth value conclusion.

Negotiable: Capable of being negotiated; assignable or transferable in the ordinary course of business.

Net Listing: A listing which provides that the agent may retain as compensation for services all sums received over and above a net price to the owner.

Note: A signed written instrument acknowledging a debt and promising payment.

Notice of Abandonment: Notice filed when work on an unfinished building is discontinued.

Notice of Completion: Instrument filed to give public notice that a building job has been completed.

Notice of Default: Document filed by the owner of a trust deed indicating the borrower has defaulted and foreclosure proceedings may be started.

Notice of Nonresponsibility: A notice provided by law designed to relieve a property owner from responsibility for the cost of work done on the property or materials furnished therefore; notice must be verified, recorded, and posted.

Notice to Quit: A notice to a tenant to vacate rented property.

Obsolescence: Loss in value due to reduced desirability and usefulness of a structure because its design and construction become obsolete; loss because of becoming old-fashioned and not in keeping with modern needs, with consequent loss of income.

Offset Statement: Statement by owner of property or owner of lien against property setting forth the present status of liens against said property.

Open Listing: An authorization given by a property owner to a real estate agent wherein said agent is given the nonexclusive right to secure a purchaser; open listings may be given to any number of agents without liability to compensate any except the one who first secures a buyer ready, willing, and able to meet the terms of the listing, or secures the acceptance by the seller of a satisfactory offer.

Open-end Mortgage: A mortgage containing a clause that permits the mortgagor to borrow additional money after the loan has been reduced, without rewriting the mortgage.

Option: A right given for a consideration to purchase or lease a property on specified terms within a specified time.

Oral Contract: A verbal agreement, one that is not reduced to writing.

Orientation: Placing a house on its lot with regard to exposure to the rays of the sun, prevailing winds, privacy from the street, and protection from outside noises.

Over Improvement: An improvement that is not the highest and best use for the site on which it is placed by reason of excess size or cost.

Owner's Equity: The worth of a property over and above all liens against it.

Ownership: The right to use and enjoy property to the exclusion of others.

Overriding Royalty: That interest in gas and oil rights that a lessee may retain when executing a sublease.

Par Value: Market value, nominal value.

Partial Release Clause: A clause in a mortgage or trust deed whereby upon the payment of an agreed sum, certain property is removed from the effect of the "blanket lien."

Participation: In addition to base interest on mortgage loans on income properties, a small percentage of gross income is required, sometimes predicated on certain conditions being fulfilled, such as minimum occupancy or a percentage of net income after expenses, debt service, and taxes.

Partition Action: Court proceedings by which co-owners seek to sever joint ownership.

Partnership: A contract of two or more persons to unite property, labor, or skill, or some of them, in prosecution of some joint or lawful business, and to share the profits in certain proportions.

Party Wall: A wall erected on the line between adjoining properties, which are under different ownership, for the use of both properties.

Patent: Coveyance of title to government land.

Percentage Lease: Lease on property, the rental for which is determined by amount of business done by the lessee; usually a percentage of gross receipts from the business with provision for a minimum rental.

Personal Property: Any property that is not real property.

Physical Deterioration: Impairment of condition, loss in value brought about by wear and tear, disintegration, use and actions of the elements.

Plat Book: A book showing the legal subdivisions and lots of a specific area.

Pledge: The depositing of personal property by a debtor with a creditor as security for a debt or engagement.

Plottage Increment: The appreciation in unit value created by joining smaller ownerships into one large single ownership.

Points: A term commonly used in the loan business to denote one percent of the loan amount, usually paid to the lender in order to obtain the loan.

Police Power: The right of the state to enact laws and enforce them for the order, safety, health, morals, and general welfare of the public.

Power of Attorney: An instrument authorizing a person to act as the agent of the person granting it, and a general power authorizing the agent to act generally in behalf of the principal.

Prepayment: Provision can be made for the loan payments to be larger than those specified in the note; controlling language is usually "$____ a month or more"; if payments state a definite amount, one must look to the prepayment privilege provided in the trust deed.

Prepayment Penalty: Penalty for the payment of a mortgage or trust deed note before it actually becomes due.

Prescription: The securing of title to property by adverse possession; by occupying it for the period determined by law barring action for recovery.

Presumption: A rule of law that courts and judges shall draw a particular inference from a particular fact, or from particular evidence, unless and until the truth of such inference is disproved.

Prima Facie: Presumptive on its face.

Primary Financing: First in order, the note and trust deed having first priority.

Primary Mortgage Market: Where a loan is made to a borrower directly from the lender.

Principal: The employer of an agent.

Privity: Mutual relationship to the same rights of property, contractual relationship.

Procuring Cause: That cause originating from series of events that, without break in continuity, results in the prime object of an agent's employment producing a final buyer.

Progression (principle of): The worth of a lesser valued residence tends to be enhanced by association with many higher valued residences in the same area.

Promissory Note: Following a loan commitment from the lender, the borrower signs a note, promising to repay the loan under stipulated terms; the promissory note establishes personal liability for its repayment.

Proration of Taxes: To divide or prorate the taxes equally or proportionately to time of use.

Public Report (subdivision): A report prepared by the Real Estate Commissioner on the conditions attendant to a new subdivision.

Purchase and Installment Saleback: Involves purchase of the property upon completion of construction and immediate saleback on a long-term installment contract.

Purchase and Leaseback: Involves the purchase of property subject to an existing mortgage and immediate leaseback.

Purchase Contract and Receipt for Deposit: The formal name of the document used to make an offer to purchase property and receipt the deposit of any money given to bind the offer.

Purchase of Land, Leaseback, and Leasehold Mortgages: An arrangement whereby land is purchased by the lender and leased back to the developer with a mortgage negotiated on the resulting leasehold of the income property constructed; lender receives an annual ground rent, plus a percentage of income from the property.

Purchase Money Mortgage or Trust Deed: Trust deed or mortgage given as part or all of the purchase consideration for property.

Quantity Survey: A highly technical process in arriving at cost estimate of new construction; It is usually used by contractors and experienced estimators.

Quiet Enjoyment: Right of an owner to the use of property without interference of possession.

Quitclaim Deed: A deed to relinquish any interest in property that the grantor may have.

Quite Title: A court action brough to establish title; to remove a cloud on the title.

Range: A strip of land six miles wide determined by a government survey, running in a north-south direction.

Ratification: The adoption or approval of an act performed on behalf of a person without previous authorization.

Real Estate Board: An organization whose members consist primarily of real estate brokers and salespeople.

Real Estate Trust: A special arrangement under federal and state law whereby investors may pool funds for investments in real estate and mortgages and yet escape corporation taxes.

Real Property: Land, that which is affixed to the land, that which is incidental or appertenant to land, and that which is immovable. Everything else is Personal Property.

Realized Gain: That amount by which the sale or exchange price exceeds the adjusted cost basis.

Realtor: A real estate broker holding active membership in a real estate board affiliated with the National Association of Realtors.

Recapture: The rate of interest necessary to provide for the return of an investment, not to be confused with interest rate, which is a rate of interest on an investment.

Recision of Contract: The revocation or annulling of a contract by mutual consent of all parties to the contract, or for cause by any party to the contract.

Recognized Gain: That amount of gain subject to tax that is realized from the sale or exchange of property.

Reconveyance: The transfer of title of land from one person to the immediate preceding owner. This particular instrument or transfer is commonly used in California when the performance or debt is satisfied under the terms of a deed or trust, when the trustee conveys the title he has held on condition back to the owner. Check the law in your state.

Redemption: Buying back one's property after a judicial sale.

Regression: A principle used in appraising, which insists that when property of high value is placed in a neighborhood with property of lower value, it seeks the value level of the lower valued properties.

Rehabilitation: The restoration of a property to satisfactory condition without drastically changing the plan, form, or style of architecture.

Release Clause: This is a stipulation that upon payment of a specific sum of money to the holder of a trust deed or mortgage, the lien of the instrument as to a specific described lot or area shall be removed from the blanket lien on the whole area involved.

Remainder: An estate that takes effect after the termination of the prior estate, such as a life estate.

Replacement Cost: The cost to replace the structure with one having utility equivalent to that being appraised, but constructed with modern materials and according to current standards, design, and layout.

Reproduction Cost: The cost of replacing the subject improvement with one that is the exact replica, having the same quality of workmanship, design, and layout.

Rescission of Contract: The abrogation or annulling of contract; the revocation or repealing of contract by mutual consent by parties to the contract, or for cause by either party to the contract.

Reservation: A right retained by a grantor in conveying property.

Restriction: The term as used relating to real property means the owner of real property is restricted or prohibited from doing certain things relating to the property, or using the property for certain purposes.

Revenue Stamps: Stamps which are required under the U.S. Internal Revenue Act to be placed on all conveyances of real estate.

Reversion: The right to future possession or enjoyment by the person, or heirs, creating the preceding estate.

Reversionary Interest: The interest that a person has in lands or other property, upon the termination of the preceding estate.

Right of Survivorship: Right to acquire the interest of a deceased joint owner; distinguishing feature of a joint tenancy.

Right of Way: A privilege operating as an easement upon land, whereby the owner does by grant, or by agreement, give to another the right to pass over land, to construct a roadway, or use as a roadway, a specific part of land, or the right to construct through and over the land, telephone, telegraph, or electric power lines, or the right to place underground water mains, gas mains, or sewer mains.

Riparian Rights: The right of a landowner to water on, under, or adjacent to his or her land.

Sales Contract: A contract by which buyer and seller agree to terms of a sale.

Sale-leaseback: A situation where the owner of a piece of property wishes to sell the property and retain occupancy by leasing it from the buyer.

Sandwich Lease: A leasehold interest that lies between the primary lease and the operating lease.

Satisfaction: Discharge of mortgage or trust deed lien from the records upon payment of the evidenced debt.

Seal: An impression made to attest the execution of an instrument.

Second Trust Deed (also known as a 2ed TD): The second trust deed is subservient to the *first trust deed.* The instrument must be recorded. A request to be notified immediately in the event of a default on the first trust deed by the institution or individual holding the first trust deed is essentiral to protect your interest as the holder of the second trust deed.

Secondary Financing: A loan secured by a second mortgage or trust deed on real property.

Secondary Mortgage Market: The market where existing trust deeds and mortgages are traded.

Secured Party: This is the party having the security interest; thus the mortgagee, the conditional seller, the pledgee, etc., are all now referred to as the secured party.

Security Agreement: An agreement between the secured party and the debtor which creates the security interest.

Security Deposit: A deposit made to assure performance of an obligation.

Security Interest: A term designating the interest of the creditor in the property of the debtor in all types of credit transactions. It thus replaces such terms as the following: chattel mortgage, pledge, trust receipt, chattel trust, equipment trust, conditional sale, inventory lien.

Section: Section of land is established by government survey and contains 640 acres.

Separate Property: Property owned by a husband or wife that is not community property; property acquired by either spouse prior to marriage or by gift or devise after marriage.

Set-back Ordinance: An ordinance prohibiting the erection of a building or structure between the curb and the set-back line.

Severalty Ownership: Owned by one person only, sole ownership.

Sheriff's Deed: Deed given by court order in connection with sale of property to satisfy a judgment.

Short Rate: That amount of an insurance premium that is returned when one cancels his or her policy, less a minimum cancellation penalty.

Sinking Fund: Fund set aside from the income from property, which, with accrued interest, will eventually pay for replacement of the improvements.

SIR: Society of Industrial Realtors.

Special Assessment: Legal charge against real estate by a public authority to pay cost of public improvements, such as street lights, sidewalks, street improvements.

Specific Performance: An action to compel performance of an agreement, e.g., sale of land.

S.R.A.: Designates a person who is a member of the Society of Real Estate Appraisers.

Standard Depth: Generally the most typical lot depth in the neighborhood.

Standard Form: A basis title insurance policy usually issued to the buyer of real estate.

Standby Commitment: The mortgage banker frequently protects a builder by a "standby" agreement, under which he or she agrees to make mortgage loans at an agreed price for many months in the future; the builder deposits a "standby fee" with the mortgage banker for this service; frequently, the mortgage banker protects himself by securing a "standby" from a long-term investor for the same period of time, paying a fee for this privilege.

Statute of Frauds: State law that provides that certain contracts must be in writing in order to be enforceable at law (examples, real property lease for more than one year; agent's authorization to sell real estate).

Statutory Dedication: The act of surrendering land for public use when required by law.

Straight Line Depreciation: Definite sum set aside annually from income to pay cost of replacing improvements, without reference to interest it earns.

Subject to Mortgage: When grantee takes a title to real property subject to mortgage, he or she is not responsible to the holder of the promissory note for the payment of any portion of the amount due; the most he or she can lose in the event of a foreclosure is equity in the property (see Assumption of Mortgage); in neither case is the original maker of the note released from his responsibility.

Sublease: A lease given by a lessee.

Subordinate: To make subject to, or junior to.

Subordination Clause: A clause in a junior or a second lien permitting retention of priority for prior liens. A subordination clause may also be used in a first deed of trust, permitting it to be subordinated to subsequent liens as for example, the liens of construction loans.

Subpoena: A process to cause a witness to appear and give testimony.

Subrogation: The substitution of another person in place of the creditor, to whose rights he or she succeeds in relation to the debt; the doctrine is used very often where one person agrees to stand surety for the performance of a contract by another person.

Substitution (principle of): Affirms that the maximum value of a property tends to be set by the cost of acquiring an equally desirable and valuable substitute property, assuming no costly delay is encountered in making the substitution.

Sum of the Digits: A method of depreciation used only on new improvements for income tax purposes; it will give the largest cost recovery over the shortest period of time. Compute thus; a building has an expected economic life of 15 years; add all the digits from 1 through 15, and the total will be 120; form a ratio with these two figures— 15 (economic life years)/120 (the sum of the digits). This ratio is the first year's depreciation allowance; The second year ratio will be 14/120, third-year ratio 13/120, and so on); this ratio to cost of the improvement will determine the amount of depreciation allowed for each respective year.

Supply and Demand (principle of): Affirms that price or value varies directly, but not necessarily proportionally, with demand, and inversely, but not necessarily proportionally with supply.

Surety: One who guarantees the performance of another; Guarantor.

Surplus Productivity (principle of): Affirms that the net income that remains after the proper costs of labor, organization, and capital have been paid, which surplus is imputable to the land and tends to fix the value thereof.

Survey: The process by which a parcel of land is measured and its area is ascertained.

Take-out Loan: The loan arranged by the owner or builder developer for a buyer; the construction loan made for construction of the improvements is usually paid from the proceeds of this loan.

Tax Free Exchange: The act of exchanging one real property for another of like kind, for the purpose of deferring capital gains tax.

Tax Sale: Sale of property after a period of nonpayment of taxes.

Tenancy at Sufferance: A tenancy that results when a tenant holds over after a lease has been terminated.

Tenancy at Will: A tenancy that may be terminated at the will of either the lessor or the lessee.

Tenancy in Common: Ownership by two or more persons who hold undivided interest, without right of survivorship; interests need not be equal.

Tenancy in Partnership: The interest held by two or more persons who unite their property in order to form a partnership for business purposes.

Tenure in Land: The mode or manner by which an estate in lands is held.

Testator: One who leaves a will in force at death.

Third Trust Deed (see **Second Trust Deed**): The third trust deed is subservient to *second* and *first trust deed*. In this particular case it is necessary that you as a third trust deed holder be notified by the holder of the first and second trust deeds in the event of a default on either trust deed.

Time Is the Essence: One of the essential requirements to forming of a binding contract; contemplates a punctual performance.

Title: Evidence that owner of land is in lawful possession thereof, an instrument evidencing such ownership.

Title Insurance: Insurance written by a title company to protect property owner against loss if title is imperfect.

Topography: Nature of the surface of land; topography may be level, rolling, mountainous.

Tort: A wrongful act, wrong, injury, violation of a legal right.

Township: A territorial subdivision six miles long, six miles wide, and containing 36 sections, each one-mile square.

Trade Fixtures: Articles of personal property annexed to real property, but which are necessary to the carrying on of a trade and are removable by the owner.

Trade-in: An increasingly popular method of guaranteeing an owner a minimum amount of cash on sale of his or her present property to permit him or her to purchase another. If the property is not sold within a specified time at the listed price, the broker agrees to arrange financing to purchase the property at an agreed-upon discount.

Trust Deed: Deed given by borrower to trustee to be held pending fulfillment of an obligation, which is ordinarily repayment of a loan to a beneficiary.

Trustee: One who holds property in trust for another to secure the performance of an obligation.

Trustor: One who deeds property to a trustee to be held as security until he or she has performed obligation to a lender under terms of a deed of trust.

Under Improvement: An improvement that, because of deficiency in size or cost, is not the highest and best use of the site.

Underwriting: The technical analysis by a lender to determine the borrower's ability to repay a contemplated loan.

Undue Influence: Taking any fraudulent or unfair advantage of another's weakness of mind, or distress, or necessity.

Unearned Increment: An increase in value of real estate due to no effort on the part of the owner; often due to increase in population.

Uniform Commercial Code (Effective January 1, 1965): Establishes a unified and comprehensive scheme for regulation of security transactions in personal property, superseding existing statutes on chattel mortgages, conditional sales, trust receipts, assignment of accounts receivable, and others in this field.

Unit-in-place Method: The cost of erecting a building estimating the cost of each component part, such as foundations, floors, walls, windows, ceilings, roofs (including labor and overhead).

Urban Property: City property, closely settled property.

Usury: On a loan, claiming a rate of interest greater than that permitted by law.

Utilities: Refers to services rendered by public utility companies, such as water, gas electricity, telephone.

Utility: The ability to give satisfaction and/or excite desire for possession.

Valid: Having force, or binding force; legally sufficient and authorized by law.

Valuation: Estimated worth or price, estimation, act of valuing by appraisal.

Vendee: A purchaser, buyer.

Vendor: A seller, one who disposes of a thing in consideration of money.

Verification: Sworn statement before duly qualified officer to correctness of contents of an instrument.

Vested: Bestowed on someone, secured by someone, such as title to property.

Void: To have no force or effect; that which is unenforceable.

Voidable: That which is capable of being adjudged void, but is not void unless action is taken to make it so.

Voluntary Lien: Any lien placed on property with consent of, or as a result of, the voluntary act of the owner.

Waive: To relinquish or abandon; to forego a right to enforce or require anything.

Warranty Deed: A deed used to convey real property that contains warranties of title and quiet possession, and the grantor thus agrees to defend the premises against the lawful claims of third persons; it is commonly used in some states but not in California, where the grant deed has supplanted it. The modern practice of securing title insurance policies has reduced the importance of express and implied warranty in deeds.

Waste: The destruction, material alteration of, or injury to premises by a tenant for life or years.

Water Table: Distance from surface of ground to a depth at which natural groundwater is found.

Wrap Around Mortgage: Involves the borrower entering into a second mortgage; this arrangement represents the means by which the borrower can add to development without refinancing the first mortgage at substantially higher current rates.

Yield: The interest earned by an investor on his or her investment (or bank on the money it has lent); also, called return.

Zone: The area set off by the proper authorities for specific use, subject to certain restrictions or restraints.

Zoning: Act of city or county authorities specifiying type of use to which property may be put in specific areas.

Bibliography

BESTON, WILLIAM R., *Real Estate Finance*. Englewood Cliffs, N.J.: Prentice-Hall, Inc., 1975.

BENKE, WILLIAM, *Land Investor's Profit Guide and Negotiating Manual*. Englewood Cliffs, N.J.: Prentice-Hall, Inc., 1978.

CUMMINGS, JACK, *Complete Guide to Real Estate Financing*. Englewood Cliffs, N.J.: Prentice-Hall, Inc., 1978.

IBP RESEARCH AND EDITORIAL STAFF, *Business and Financial Table Desk Book*. Englewood Cliffs, N.J.: Institute for Business Planning, 1979.

_____. *Real Estate Tax Shelter Desk Book*. Englewood Cliffs, N.J.: Institute for Business Planning, 1979.

JOHNSON, IRVIN E., *Selling Real Estate by Mortgage Equity Analysis*. Lexington, MA: D.C. Heath, 1976.

MCKENZIE, DENNES J., AND RICHARD M. BELLS, *The Essentials of Real Estate Economics*. New York: John Wiley, 1976.

NIERENBERG, GERALD T., *Fundamentals of Negotiating*. New York: Hawthorne, 1978.

OWEN, BARRY, ED., *Crittenden Mortgage Directory*. Nevada City, CA: Crittenden Financing, 1980.

RINGER, ROBERT J., *Winning Through Intimidation*. Los Angeles: Los Angeles Book Publishing, 1976.

SUSSEX, MARGIE, AND JOHN F. STAPLETON, *The Complete Real Estate Math Book*. Englewood Cliffs, N.J.: Prentice-Hall, Inc., 1978.

SYLVESTER, RICHARD R., *Minimize Your Personal Income Tax*. Los Angeles: Richard R. Sylvester, 1978.

Thorndike Encyclopedia of Banking and Financial Tables. Boston, MA: Warren, Gorham, and Lamont, 1980.

Additional Management Forms

COMPLAINT

Wolcott 1022 Unlawful Detainer Kit (Complaint, Summons & Notice to Pay Rent or Quit)—Rev. 12-79

This standard form covers most usual problems in the field indicated. Before you sign, read it, fill in all blanks and make changes proper to your transaction. Consult a lawyer if you doubt the form's fitness for your purpose.

1   NAME:

2   ADDRESS:

3   TELEPHONE:

4

5   PLAINTIFF:

6

7

8   IN THE MUNICIPAL COURT OF THE   JUDICIAL DISTRICT

9   COUNTY OF   , STATE OF CALIFORNIA

10

11   )

12   )   NO.

13   Plaintiff,   )   COMPLAINT

14   vs.   )   (Unlawful Detainer)

15   )

16   )

17   DOE I through DOE III, Inclusive,   )

18   Defendants.   )

19   _____)

20   PLAINTIFF alleges:

21   1. That Plaintiff is entitled to the possession of, and is the Lessor of the real property described as

22   follows:

23

24

25   Said real property is located within the above-captioned Judicial District and County.

26   2. That on or about   , Plaintiff by an oral/written Lease,

27   leased, demised and let unto the Defendants on a   tenancy, the real property

28   described in Paragraph 1 above, to have and to hold said premises unto the Defendants at a monthly

The forms on page 258–272 were supplied by Wolcott, Inc. and are reprinted with permission. Wolcott forms are available in most stationery stores. Since laws frequently change, it is advisable when purchasing such forms to make sure they are current and reflect recent changes. They are updated constantly.

This standard form covers most usual problems in the field indicated. Before you sign, read it, fill in all blanks and make changes proper to your transaction. Consult a lawyer if you doubt the form's fitness for your purpose.

1   rental of $, payable in advance on the   day of each month.

2   Plaintiff received deposits from defendant(s) as follows:

3   a) cleaning deposit $_____;

4   b) key deposit $_____;

5   c) security deposit $_____;

6   d) other (   ) $_____.

7   3. By virtue of said agreement, the Defendants went into possession and occupation of said demised

8   premises actually due and owing as hereinabove set forth in Paragraph 6.

9   4. The true names or capacities, whether individual, corporate, associate, or otherwise of the Defen-

10   dants named herein as DOE I, DOE II, and DOE III are unknown to Plaintiff, who, therefore, sues

11   said Defendants by such fictitious names, and Plaintiff will amend this Complaint to show their true

12   names and capacities when same have been ascertained.

13   5. That pursuant to the terms of said Lease, $ was due and payable on

14   for the period of   to

15   and no part of said sum has been paid, and $

16   remains due, owing and unpaid to Plaintiff.

17   6. That on or about   , Plaintiff, by notice,

18   made demand, in writing, of said Defendants for and required the payment of the said rental then

19   due, amounting to $, or for the possession of said premises, all within three

20   days from service of said notice, a copy of which notice is attached hereto as Exhibit "A" and by this

21   reference, incorporated herein as if set forth in full.

22   7. Said Written Notice and demand was served upon the Defendants, and the Defendants have

23   neglected and refused for three days following its service upon them, and ever since, have neglected

24   and refused after service of said demand to pay said rent or surrender the possession of said premises.

25   8. Said Defendants unlawfully hold over and continue in possession of said premises after said default

26   in the payment of rent and after said demand and without permission of the Plaintiff and under no

27   claim of right.

28   9. By reason of the aforesaid acts, the Plaintiff has already sustained damages for rent of said prem-

—2—

This standard form covers most usual problems in the field indicated. Before you sign, read it, fill in all blanks and make changes proper to your transaction. Consult a lawyer if you doubt the form's fitness for your purpose.

1 ises actually due and owing as hereinabove set forth in Paragraph 6.

2   10. The reasonable value for the use and occupancy of the subject premises is $ per

3 day. Plaintiff seeks such sum as damages from   , and for each day

4 thereafter, until the date of Judgment herein, and for treble said sum.

5   11. That Plaintiff has performed all terms and conditions of said Lease on its part to be performed.

6   WHEREFORE, Plaintiff prays for Judgment as follows:

7   1. For restitution and possession of the subject premises;

8   2. For $, which is the unpaid rental and damages for the use and occupancy

9 of the subject premises for the period of time specified in Exhibit "A" hereto, and for the further

10 sum of $ per day for damages for the use and occupancy of the subject premises

11 from   , until rendition of Judgment herein, and for treble said total sum;

12 all recovery in excess of the jurisdiction of the Municipal Court being expressly waived;

13   3. For cost of suit herein incurred and such other relief as proper.

14   VERIFICATION   _____

15 STATE OF CALIFORNIA   } ss.   _____

16 COUNTY OF   PLAINTIFF

17 I am the plaintiff in the above entitled action; I have read the foregoing complaint and know the

18 contents thereof; and I certify that the same is true of my own knowledge.

19 I certify (or declare), under penalty of perjury, that the foregoing is true and correct.

20 Executed on _____ at _____ , California
                        (date)   (place)

21

22   _____
                              SIGNATURE

23

24

25

26

27

28

—3—

260

SUMMONS

NAME AND ADDRESS OF ATTORNEY:	TELEPHONE NO:	FOR COURT USE ONLY:

ATTORNEY FOR (Name):

Insert name of court, judicial district or branch court, if any, and post office and street address.

PLAINTIFF:

DEFENDANT:

SUMMONS **UNLAWFUL DETAINER** **STATE HOUSING LAW** ☐ 5 Day Response Time ☐ 10 Day Response Time	CASE NUMBER:

NOTICE! You have been sued. The court may decide against you without your being heard unless you respond within ☐ 5 ☐ 10 days. Read the information below.

If you wish to seek the advice of an attorney in this matter, you should do so promptly so that your written response, if any, may be filed on time.

¡AVISO! Usted ha sido demandado. El tribunal puede decidir contra Ud. sin audiencia a menos que Ud. responda dentro de ☐ 5 ☐ 10 días. Lea la información que sigue.

Si Usted desea solicitar el consejo de un abogado en este asunto, debería hacerlo inmediatamente, de esta manera, su respuesta escrita, si hay alguna, puede ser registrada a tiempo.

1. TO THE DEFENDANT: A civil complaint has been filed by the plaintiff against you. If you wish to defend this lawsuit, you must, within ☐ 5 ☐ 10 days after this summons is served on you, file with this court a written response to the complaint. Unless you do so, your default will be entered on application of the plaintiff, and this court may enter a judgment against you for the relief demanded in the complaint, which could result in garnishment of wages, taking of money or property or other relief requested in the complaint.

Dated: . . . . Clerk, By _____ , Deputy

(SEAL)

2. NOTICE TO THE PERSON SERVED: You are served
   a. ☐ As an individual defendant.
   b. ☐ As the person sued under the fictitious name of: . . . .
   c. ☐ On behalf of: . . . .

   Under: ☐ CCP 416.10 (Corporation)   ☐ CCP 416.60 (Minor)
           ☐ CCP 416.20 (Defunct Corporation)   ☐ CCP 416.70 (Incompetent)
           ☐ CCP 416.40 (Association or Partnership)   ☐ CCP 416.90 (Individual)
           ☐ Other:
   d. ☐ By personal delivery on (Date): . . . .

A written response must be in the form prescribed by the California Rules of Court. It must be filed in this court with the proper filing fee and proof of service of a copy on each plaintiff's attorney and on each plaintiff not represented by an attorney. The time when a summons is deemed served on a party may vary depending on the method of service. For example, see CCP 413.10 through 415.50. The word "complaint" includes cross-complaint, "plaintiff" includes cross-complainant, "defendant" includes cross-defendant, the singular includes the plural.

(See reverse for Proof of Service)

Form Adopted by Rule 982
Judicial Council California
Revised Effective January 1, 1979
WOLCOTTS FORM 982.11

SUMMONS
(UNLAWFUL DETAINER OR STATE HOUSING LAW)

CCP 412.20, 412.30,
415.10.

PROOF OF SERVICE
(Use separate proof of service for each person served)

1. I served the
   - a. ☐ summons ☐ complaint ☐ amended summons ☐ amended complaint

   - b. On defendant (Name):

   - c. By serving (1) ☐ Defendant (2) ☐ Other (Name and title or relationship to person served):

   - d. ☐ By delivery at ☐ home ☐ business (1) Date of:
     (2) Time of: (3) Address:

   - e. ☐ By mailing (1) Date of: (2) Place of:
2. Manner of service: (Check proper box)
   - a. ☐ **Personal service.** By personally delivering copies. (CCP 415.10)
   - b. ☐ **Substituted service on corporation, unincorporated association (including partnership), or public entity.** By leaving, during usual office hours, copies in the office of the person served with the person who apparently was in charge and thereafter mailing (by first-class mail, postage prepaid) copies to the person served at the place where the copies were left. (CCP 415.20(a))
   - c. ☐ **Substituted service on natural person, minor, incompetent, or candidate.** By leaving copies at the dwelling house, usual place of abode, or usual place of business of the person served in the presence of a competent member of the household or a person apparently in charge of the office or place of business, at least 18 years of age, who was informed of the general nature of the papers, and thereafter mailing (by first-class mail, postage prepaid) copies to the person served at the place where the copies were left. (CCP 415.20(b)) **(Attach separate declaration or affidavit stating acts relied on to establish reasonable diligence in first attempting personal service.)**
   - d. ☐ **Mail and acknowledgment service.** By mailing (by first-class mail or airmail) copies to the person served, together with two copies of the form of notice and acknowledgment and a return envelope, postage prepaid, addressed to the sender. (CCP 415.30) **(Attach completed acknowledgment of receipt.)**
   - e. ☐ **Certified or registered mail service.** By mailing to address outside California (by registered or certified airmail with return receipt requested) copies to the person served. (CCP 415.40) **(Attach signed return receipt or other evidence of actual delivery to the person served.)**
   - f. ☐ Other (Specify code section):
     ☐ Additional page is attached.
3. The notice to the person served (Item 2 on the copy of the summons served) was completed as follows (CCP 412.30, 415.10, and 474):
   - a. ☐ As an individual defendant
   - b. ☐ As the person sued under the fictitious name of: . . . .
   - c. ☐ On behalf of: . . . .
     Under: ☐ CCP 416 10 (Corporation) ☐ CCP 416.60 (Minor) ☐ Other:
     ☐ CCP 416.20 (Defunct corporation) ☐ CCP 416.70 (Incompetent)
     ☐ CCP 416.40 (Association or partnership) ☐ CCP 416.90 (Individual)
   - d. ☐ By personal delivery on (Date): . . . .
4. At the time of service I was at least 18 years of age and not a party to this action.
5. Fee for service: $ . . . . . .
6. Person serving
   - a. ☐ Not a registered California process server.
   - b. ☐ Registered California process server.
   - c. ☐ Employee or independent contractor of a registered California process server.
   - d. ☐ Exempt from registration under Bus. & Prof. Code 22350(b)
   - e. ☐ California sheriff, marshal, or constable.
   - f. Name, address and telephone number and if applicable, county of registration and number:

I declare under penalty of perjury that the foregoing is true and correct and that this declaration is executed on (Date): . . . . at (Place): . . . ., California.

(For California sheriff, marshal or constable use only)
I certify that the foregoing is true and correct and that this certificate is executed on (Date): . . . . at (Place): . . . ., California.

_____
(Signature)

_____
(Signature)

A declaration under penalty of perjury must be signed in California or in a state that authorizes use of a declaration in place of an affidavit; otherwise an affidavit is required.

BUILDING CONSTRUCTION CONTRACT

THIS AGREEMENT, made this _____ day of _____, 19_____,

between _____, hereinafter

called Owner, whose address is _____,

and _____, hereinafter

called Contractor, License No. _____, whose address is _____

_____

In consideration of the covenants and agreements herein contained, the parties hereto agree as follows:

1. Contractor agrees to construct and complete in a good, workmanlike and substantial manner, upon the real property hereinafter described, furnishing all labor, materials, tools and equipment therefore, a

_____

(hereinafter called the structure, whether one or more buildings or improvements), upon the following described real property:

_____

_____

2. The structure is to be constructed and completed in strict conformance with plans and specifications for the same signed by the parties hereto, a copy of which plans and specifications have been filed with

_____

hereinafter referred to as Lien Holder. If no Lien Holder is named herein all reference to same in this contract is to be disregarded.

The structure is also to be constructed and completed in strict compliance with all laws, ordinances, rules and regulations of competent public authority, and Contractor is to apply for and obtain all required permits, paying all fees therefore, and all other fees required by such public authority.

3. In consideration of the covenants and agreements hereof being strictly performed and kept by Contractor, including the supplying of all labor, materials and services required by this Contract, and the construction and completion of the structure, Owner agrees to pay to Contractor the sum of $ _____, in installments as follows:

4. The Contractor agrees to commence work hereunder within _____ days after receipt of written notice from the Owner and Lien Holder so to do, to prosecute said work thereafter diligently and continuously to completion, and in any and all events to complete the same within _____ days after commencement of work as aforesaid, subject to such delays as are permissible under paragraph 10 hereinbelow. In no event shall the Contractor commence said work or place any materials on the site thereof prior to receipt of such notice from the owner.

5. Contractor shall pay promptly all valid bills and charges for material, labor or otherwise in connection with or arising out of the construction of said structure and will hold Owner of the property free and harmless against all liens and claims of lien for labor and material, or either of them, filed against the property or any part thereof, and from and against all expense and liability in connection therewith, including, but not limited to, court costs and attorney's fees resulting or arising therefrom. Should any liens or claims of lien be filed for record against the property, or should Owner receive notice of any unpaid bill or charge in connection with the construction, Contractor shall forthwith either pay and discharge the same and cause the same to be released of record, or shall furnish Owner with proper indemnity either by satisfactory corporate surety bond or satisfactory title policy, which indemnity shall also be subject to approval of Lien Holder.

6. Contractor shall, if requested, before being entitled to receive the second or any subsequent payment herewith, furnish to Owner all bills paid to that date, properly receipted and identified, covering work done upon and materials furnished for said structure and showing an expenditure of an amount not less than the total of all previous payments made hereunder by Owner to Contractor.

7. The plans and specifications are intended to supplement each other, so that any works exhibited in either and not mentioned in the other are to be executed the same as if they were mentioned and set forth in both.

8. Should the Owner at any time during the progress of the work request any modification, alterations or deviations in, additions to, or omissions from, this contract or the plans or specifications, he shall be at liberty to do so, and the same shall in no way affect or make void this contract; but the amount thereof shall be added to or deducted from the amount of the contract price aforesaid, as the case may be, by a fair and reasonable valuation, based upon the actual cost of labor and materials plus 10% profit to the Contractor. And this contract shall be held to be completed when the work is finished in accordance with the original plans as amended or modified by such changes, whatever may be the nature or extent thereof. The rule of practice to be observed in fulfillment of this paragraph shall be that upon the demand of either the Owner or the Contractor, the character and valuation of any or all changes, omissions or extra work shall be agreed upon and fixed in writing, signed by the Owner and the Contractor, prior to execution. Where the alterations, deviations, additions, or omissions from the said plans or specifications require the written approval of the Lien Holder the Owner will secure said written approval. Provided however that the Contractor is not deemed to have waived his right to compensation for extra work if the same is not provided for in writing.

9. Should Contractor, at any time during the progress of the work, refuse or neglect to supply sufficient material or workmen for the expeditious progress of said work, Owner may, upon giving three days' notice in writing to Contractor, by registered mail, (a copy of which shall be furnished to aforesaid Lien Holder), provide the necessary material and workmen to finish the said work and may enter upon the premises for such purpose and complete said work, the expense thereof shall be deducted from the said contract price, or if the total cost of the work to Owner exceeds the contract price, Contractor shall pay to Owner upon demand the amount of such excess in addition to any and all other damages to which Owner may be entitled. In such event Owner may take possession of all materials and appliances belonging to Contractor upon or adjacent to the premises upon which said work is being performed and may use the same in the completion of said work.

10. The time during which the contractor is delayed in said work by (a) the acts of Owner or his agents or employees or those claiming under agreement with or grant from Owner, or by (b) the Acts of God which Contractor could not have reasonably foreseen and provided against, or by (c) stormy or inclement weather which necessarily delays the work or by (d) any strikes, boycotts or like obstructive actions by employees or labor organizations and which are beyond the control of Contractor and which he cannot reasonably overcome, shall be added to the time for completion by a fair and reasonable allowance.

11. The Contractor shall not be responsible for any damage occasioned by the Owner or Owner's agent, Acts of God, earthquake, or other causes beyond the control of Contractor, unless otherwise herein provided or unless he is obligated by the terms hereof to provide insurance against such hazard or hazards. It is understood and agreed that Contractor, before incurring any other expense or purchasing any other materials for this work, shall proceed with the foundation work and that if, at the time of excavation therefor, the Contractor finds that extra

foundation work is required he shall so notify the Owner, and Owner shall at that time have the right and option to immediately cancel and terminate the within contract or to deposit the estimated cost of the required extra foundation work with the Lien Holder if there be one named herein, or add such amount to the contract funds wherever same are at that time deposited; it being agreed that in the event of a cancellation the Contractor shall be paid his actual costs of the work done to the time of cancellation. In computing said costs building permit fees, insurance and such financing and title charges as are not refundable shall be included; but supervision time, office overhead and profit are not to be included.

12. No payment hereunder nor occupancy of said improvements or any part thereof shall be construed as an acceptance of any work done up to the time of such payment or occupancy, except such items as are plainly evident to anyone not experienced in construction work, but the entire work is to be subject to the inspection and approval of Owner at the time when it shall be claimed by Contractor that the work has been completed. At the completion of the work should there be any minor items in question, or to be adjusted, i.e., items not of a substantial nature, Owner may withhold from the payment then due a sum equal to twice the fairly estimated amount of money required to cover said items or involved by such adjustments, and shall pay the difference to the Contractor. It is understood and agreed that the acceptance of any works by the Owner shall not be an acceptance by aforesaid Lien Holder who is not a party hereto.

13. Owner agrees to sign and file for record within ten days after the completion and acceptance of said work a notice of completion (a copy thereof to be deposited with aforesaid Lien Holder at least forty-eight hours prior to such recording), and Contractor agrees upon receipt of final payment, to release the said work and property from any and all claims that may have accrued against same by reason of said construction. If the Contractor faithfully performs the obligations of this Contract on his part to be performed, he shall have the right to refuse to permit occupancy of the structure by the Owner or Owner's agent until Contractor has received the payment, if any, due hereunder at completion of construction, less such amounts as may be retained pursuant to mutual agreement of the Owner and Contractor under the provisions of the preceding paragraph hereof. Said Lien Holder has the right to make its own decisions as to the completion of any work, independent of the parties hereto.

14. Owner agrees to procure at its own expense and prior to the commencement of any work hereunder, fire insurance with course of construction clause and waiver of fallen building clause attached in a sum equal to the total cost of said improvements as set forth in paragraph 3 hereof, with loss, if any, payable to any mortgagee or beneficiary, such insurance to be written to protect the Owner and the Contractor; as their interests may appear, and should Owner fail so to do, Contractor may procure such insurance, but is not required to do so, and Owner agrees on demand to reimburse Contractor in cash for the cost thereof.

15. Contractor shall at this own expense carry all workmen's compensation insurance and public liability insurance necessary for the full protection of Contractor and Owner during the progress of the work. Certificates of such insurance shall be filed with Owner and with said Lien Holder if Owner so requires, and shall be subject to the approval of both of them as to adequacy of protection.

16. Any controversy or claim arising out of or relating to this contract, or the breach thereof shall be settled by arbitration in accordance with the Rules of the American Arbitration Association, and judgment upon the award rendered by the Arbitrator(s) may be entered in any Court having jurisdiction thereof. Any such award may include costs and reasonable attorney's fees as may be directed by the Arbitrator(s).

17. Should either party hereto bring suit in court to enforce the terms hereof any judgment awarded shall include court costs and reasonable attorney's fees to the successful party.

18. Upon the completion of the work the Contractor agrees to remove all debris and surplus materials from Owner's said property (including underarea of structure) and leave said property in a neat and broom clean condition.

19. The Contractor shall not assign or transfer this contract without first obtaining Owner's consent in writing.

20. The aforesaid Lien Holder is not a party to this Contract and is not bound or obligated by or under any of the terms hereof.

21. Time is of the essence of this Contract as to both parties hereto.

IN WITNESS WHEREOF, the said parties hereunto set their hands the day and year first above written.

Contractors are required by law to be licensed and regulated by the Contractors' State License Board. Any question concerning a contractor may be referred to the registrar of the board whose address is:

Contractors' State License Board
1020 N. Street
Sacramento, California 95814

_____

_____

_____

_____

NOTICE TO OWNER
(Section 7018.5—Contractors License Law)

THE LAW REQUIRES THAT, BEFORE A LICENSED CONTRACTOR CAN ENTER INTO A CONTRACT WITH YOU FOR A WORK OF IMPROVEMENT ON YOUR PROPERTY, HE MUST GIVE YOU A COPY OF THIS NOTICE.

Under the mechanics' lien laws of the State of California, persons who help to improve your property and are not paid have a right to enforce their claims against your property. This "claim" is known as a mechanics' lien. Basically, when somebody files a mechanics' lien, they are making claim on your property as security against payment of a just debt.

In other words, this law allows contractors, subcontractors, laborers, material men or certain others who may have provided goods or services to place a lien on your home or the structure they built or improved for you for any unpaid portion of the goods and services they furnish. For example, if you fail to pay your contractor, of if your contractor fails to pay his subcontractors or laborers, or neglects to make required contributions to a trust and/or other funds (where applicable), then those people can look to your property for payment, **EVEN IF YOU HAVE PAID YOUR CONTRACTOR IN FULL.**

There are a number of ways to protect yourself and your property at the onset of contracting and throughout the construction project. You might, for instance, request that the contractor furnish you with a payment and performance bond. (This is a different bond than the one currently required by Contractors License Law.) The additional cost is usually minimal and is a certain guarantee that the project will be completed and the bills paid. You may also wish to record this payment or performance bond and file the contract with the County Recorder to further protect yourself from anyone liening your property. If you do have a contractor provide a special bond on your project and the bonding company does not honor your claim promptly in the event the contractor defaults, you may wish to contact the California Insurance Commission to see if the bonding company is engaging in an unfair claims practice.

Another avenue available to you is to use a funding control company. The control company acts as a third party, disbursing all funds for payment and usually securing all the necessary releases of liens. A funding control company is a specialized construction escrow which makes payment directly to subcontractors and suppliers. By doing this, it affords additional protection against valid liens.

Should you choose not to use the above, the following are some of the important time requirements you should be aware of regarding the mechanics' lien law:

1. Preliminary Notice.
A claimant, contractor, subcontractor, or materialman is entitled to enforce a lien only if he gives the preliminary twenty (20) days notice, if applicable. All claimants, other than the original contractor (the person you contracted with), or a laborer performing actual labor for wages, must give this notice. Therefore, people who you may not even know, such as a subcontractor, or a material supplier, must notify you that they are providing supplies or services to your property which may later create a lien. This Preliminary Notice must be given no later than twenty (20) days after the claimant has first furnished labor, services, equipment or material to the job site.

If you get such a Preliminary Notice, do not be alarmed. The notice is intended for your protection so that you may then require your contractor to furnish you with a lien release prior to or concurrently with payment to him.

2. Notice of Mechanics' Lien.
Usually claimants must record the Notice and Claim of Lien within ninety (90) days of the completion of the work. If a Notice of Completion, or a Notice of Cessation of Labor has been recorded, then the Claim of Lien must be recorded within sixty (60) days by the original contractor and within thirty (30) days by all other claimants such as subcontractors, materialmen, etc. The claimants must indicate on the notice what is owed to them. This lien will now bind your property like a mortgage or trust deed.

3. Complaint to Foreclose a Mechanics' Lien.
If the claimants' demands are not satisfied, then they must usually file suit within ninety (90) days after the recordation of a Notice of Mechanics' Lien. The complaint to foreclose the lien is filed in a regular court proceeding and follows in a similar manner. **YOU SHOULD BE AWARE THAT YOUR PROPERTY COULD BE SOLD AND THE PROCEEDS FROM THE SALE USED TO SATISFY THE CLAIM.**

4. Notice of Non-Responsiblity.
You can protect yourself and your property from a valid claim of a contactor, or subcontractor who is doing work on your property, but not at your request (for example if you have a tenant who has contracted for work to be done). You can do this by posting and recording a Notice of Non-Responsibility. The notice must be posted in a conspicuous place within ten (10) days after you have obtained knowledge of the work. You must then record the notice at the County Recorder's office. You can usually purchase this form from various sources.

5. Unconditional Lien Release.
You may also require that the original contractor provide you with unconditional lien releases signed by each and every person who has performed any work or labor as well as every person who has delivered any materials to your job. Be sure to get releases from each person who gave you a Preliminary Notice.

6. Notice of Completion.
The owner of the property or his agent (sometimes the general contractor) can record a Notice of Completion within ten (10) days following the actual completion of the work of improvement. The effect of the Notice of Completion is to shorten the time period within which the contractors or subcontractors may file their Mechanics' Lien.

The above is not meant to be an exhaustive review of mechanics' liens. It is intended that you understand that you are entering into a contract which may bind your property and it is intended that you understand how to act to protect your property.

Read and acknowledged.

Signature _____

Dated _____

This standard form covers many areas in the field indicated. No form can cover every possible item which the parties may wish to include in an agreement. You may wish to consult a lawyer concerning the addition or deletion of provisions contained in this form.

(This form is not applicable to home improvement contracts. See Wolcotts Form 564 for a "Home Improvement Contract.")

NOTICE TO OWNER

(Section 7018.5—Contractors License Law)

THE LAW REQUIRES THAT, BEFORE A LICENSED CONTRACTOR CAN ENTER INTO A CONTRACT WITH YOU FOR A WORK OF IMPROVEMENT ON YOUR PROPERTY, HE MUST GIVE YOU A COPY OF THIS NOTICE.

Under the mechanics' lien laws of the State of California, persons who help to improve your property and are not paid have a right to enforce their claims against your property. This "claim" is known as a mechanics' lien. Basically, when somebody files a mechanics' lien, they are making claim on your property as security against payment of a just debt.

In other words, this law allows contractors, subcontractors, laborers, material men or certain others who may have provided goods or services to place a lien on your home or the structure they built or improved for you for any unpaid portion of the goods and services they furnish. For example, if you fail to pay your contractor, of if your contractor fails to pay his subcontractors or laborers, or neglects to make required contributions to a trust and/or other funds (where applicable), then those people can look to your property for payment, **EVEN IF YOU HAVE PAID YOUR CONTRACTOR IN FULL.**

There are a number of ways to protect yourself and your property at the onset of contracting and throughout the construction project. You might, for instance, request that the contractor furnish you with a payment and performance bond. (This is a different bond than the one currently required by Contractors License Law.) The additional cost is usually minimal and is a certain guarantee that the project will be completed and the bills paid. You may also wish to record this payment or performance bond and file the contract with the County Recorder to further protect yourself from anyone liening your property. If you do have a contractor provide a special bond on your project and the bonding company does not honor your claim promptly in the event the contractor defaults, you may wish to contact the California Insurance Commission to see if the bonding company is engaging in an unfair claims practice.

Another avenue available to you is to use a funding control company. The control company acts as a third party, disbursing all funds for payment and usually securing all the necessary releases of liens. A funding control company is a specialized construction escrow which makes payment directly to subcontractors and suppliers. By doing this, it affords additional protection against valid liens.

Should you choose not to use the above, the following are some of the important time requirements you should be aware of regarding the mechanics' lien law:

1. Preliminary Notice.
A claimant, contractor, subcontractor, or materialman is entitled to enforce a lien only if he gives the preliminary twenty (20) days notice, if applicable. All claimants, other than the original contractor (the person you contracted with), or a laborer performing actual labor for wages, must give this notice. Therefore, people who you may not even know, such as a subcontractor, or a material supplier, must notify you that they are providing supplies or services to your property which may later create a lien. This Preliminary Notice must be given no later than twenty (20) days after the claimant has first furnished labor, services, equipment or material to the job site.

If you get such a Preliminary Notice, do not be alarmed. The notice is intended for your protection so that you may then require your contractor to furnish you with a lien release prior to or concurrently with payment to him.

2. Notice of Mechanics' Lien.
Usually claimants must record the Notice and Claim of Lien within ninety (90) days of the completion of the work. If a Notice of Completion, or a Notice of Cessation of Labor has been recorded, then the Claim of Lien must be recorded within sixty (60) days by the original contractor and within thirty (30) days by all other claimants such as subcontractors, materialmen, etc. The claimants must indicate on the notice what is owed to them. This lien will now bind your property like a mortgage or trust deed.

3. Complaint to Foreclose a Mechanics' Lien.
If the claimants' demands are not satisfied, then they must usually file suit within ninety (90) days after the recordation of a Notice of Mechanics' Lien. The complaint to foreclose the lien is filed in a regular court proceeding and follows in a similar manner. **YOU SHOULD BE AWARE THAT YOUR PROPERTY COULD BE SOLD AND THE PROCEEDS FROM THE SALE USED TO SATISFY THE CLAIM.**

4. Notice of Non-Responsiblity.
You can protect yourself and your property from a valid claim of a contactor, or subcontractor who is doing work on your property, but not at your request (for example if you have a tenant who has contracted for work to be done). You can do this by posting and recording a Notice of Non-Responsibility. The notice must be posted in a conspicuous place within ten (10) days after you have obtained knowledge of the work. You must then record the notice at the County Recorder's office. You can usually purchase this form from various sources.

5. Unconditional Lien Release.
You may also require that the original contractor provide you with unconditional lien releases signed by each and every person who has performed any work or labor as well as every person who has delivered any materials to your job. Be sure to get releases from each person who gave you a Preliminary Notice.

6. Notice of Completion.
The owner of the property or his agent (sometimes the general contractor) can record a Notice of Completion within ten (10) days following the actual completion of the work of improvement. The effect of the Notice of Completion is to shorten the time period within which the contractors or subcontractors may file their Mechanics' Lien.

The above is not meant to be an exhaustive review of mechanics' liens. It is intended that you understand that you are entering into a contract which may bind your property and it is intended that you understand how to act to protect your property.

Read and acknowledged.

Signature _____ Dated _____

WOLCOTTS FORM 540—Rev. 9-80

PROPOSAL AND CONTRACT FOR HOME IMPROVEMENT

Date: _____, 19_____ TO_____

_____, (hereinafter "Owner"), Telephone no._____

_____(hereinafter "Contractor")

propose(s) to furnish all materials and perform all labor necessary to complete the following: [Insert a description of the work to be done and a description of the materials to be used and the equipment to be used or installed.]

All of the above work is to be completed in a substantial and workmanlike manner according to standard practices for the sum of _____

_____ Dollars ($ _____).

Progress payments to be made as follows and in accordance with the terms and conditions of paragraph 1 on the reverse side:

Amount of Work or Services to be performed or Description of any Materials or Equipment to be Supplied	Amount of Payment (Must be shown as a sum in dollars and cents)

The entire amount of the contract is to be paid within _____ days after completion.

This proposal is valid until _____ and if accepted by that time work will commence _____ days after acceptance and will be substantially completed approximately_____ working days thereafter subject to delays caused by acts of God, stormy weather, uncontrollable labor trouble, or unforeseen contingencies.

The following constitutes substantial commencement of work pursuant to this proposal and contract: [Specify]

FAILURE BY CONTRACTOR WITHOUT LAWFUL EXCUSE TO SUBSTANTIALLY COMMENCE WORK WITHIN TWENTY (20) DAYS FROM THE APPROXIMATE DATE SPECIFIED IN THIS PROPOSAL AND CONTRACT WHEN WORK WILL BEGIN IS A VIOLATION OF THE CONTRACTORS LICENSE LAW.

Any alteration or deviation from the above specifications involving extra cost of material or labor will be executed only upon written orders for same, and will become an extra charge over the sum mentioned in this contract. All agreements must be in writing.

FURTHER NOTICE TO OWNER OR TENANT: You have the right to require the Contractor to have a performance and payment bond or funding control.

THIS CONTRACT IS NOT VALID UNLESS THE "NOTICE TO OWNER" ACKNOWLEDGMENT IS SIGNED AND DATED ON THE REVERSE SIDE.

Respectfully submitted,

By _____

_____
Address

_____
Telephone

Name and Registration No. of any Salesperson who solicited or negotiated this contract:

Name: _____ No. _____

_____
Contractor's State License No.

ACCEPTANCE

You are hereby authorized to furnish all materials and labor required to complete the work mentioned in the above Proposal, for which _____ agree to pay the amount mentioned in said Proposal, and according to the terms thereof. I have read and agree to the provisions contained herein, and in any attachments hereto.

_____
Owner's Name

_____
Street Address

_____
City   State   Zip

_____
Place of Business

ACCEPTED: _____
(Owner's Signature)   (Date)

Contractors are required by law to be licensed and regulated by the Contractors' State License Board. Any questions concerning a contractor may be referred to the registrar of the board whose address is:

**Contractor State License Board
1020 N Street
Sacramento, CA 95814**

If either the proposal and/or the acceptance of this Proposal and Contract is made at other than the premises at which Contractor or Owner normally carries on a business, then you, the Buyer, may cancel this transaction at any time prior to midnight of the third business day after the date of this transaction. See the attached Notice of Cancellation form (Wolcotts Form 560) for an explanation of this right.

The provision that Owner may cancel this transaction within three working days shall not apply to a contract in which Owner has initiated the Contract and which is executed in connection with the making of emergency repairs or services which are necessary for the immediate protection of persons or real or personal property, provided that the Owner furnishes the Contractor with a separate dated and signed personal statement describing the situation requiring immediate remedy and expressly acknowledging and waiving the right to cancel the sale within three business days (Wolcotts Form 570).

WOLCOTTS FORM 564—PROPOSAL AND CONTRACT FOR HOME IMPROVEMENT—Rev. 10-80   IMPORTANT: SEE REVERSE SIDE FOR IMPORTANT INFORMATION   ©1980 WOLCOTTS, INC.

TERMS AND CONDITIONS (Continued)

1. The following terms and conditions apply to the payment schedule on the reverse side:

a. If the payment schedule contained in the contract provides for a downpayment to be paid to Contractor by Owner before the commencement of work, such downpayment shall not exceed One Thousand Dollars (1,000) or 10% of the contract price, excluding finance charges, whichever is the lesser.

b. In no event shall the payment schedule provide for Contractor to receive, nor shall Contractor actually receive, payment in excess of 100% of the value of the work performed on the project at any time, excluding finance charges, except that Contractor may receive an initial downpayment authorized by condition (a), above.

c. A failure by Contractor without lawful excuse to substantially commence work within twenty (20) days of the approximate date specified in this Proposal and Contract when work will begin shall postpone the next succeeding payment to Contractor for that period of time equivalent to the time between when substantial commencement was to have occurred and when it did occur.

d. Conditions (a), (b), and (c) pertaining to the payment schedule shall not apply when the contract provides for Contractor to furnish performance and payment bond, lien and completion bond, a bond equivalent, or a funding control approved by the Registrar of Contractors covering full performance and completion of the contract and such bonds are furnished by Contractor, or when the parties agree for full payment to be made upon satisfactory completion of the project.

2. **WARNING:** a. Do not use this form if the owner is going to pay interest or any finance charge. A Home Improvement Contract with finance charges must comply both with the California Retail Installment Sales (Unruh) Act and the Federal Truth in Lending Law. The Federal Truth in Lending Law also applies if the contract price is payable in more than four installments even if there is no interest or finance charges. (Note: Progress payments are not installment payments.)

b. Do not use this form if this is a contract for construction of a swimming pool.

3. For your assistance the complete text of Sections 7151, 7151.2 and 7159 of the California Business and Professions Code are quoted below under the ''Notice to Owner.'' Should you have any doubt as to the usefulness of this form for your purposes, you are urged to consult your own attorney.

NOTICE TO OWNER

(Section 7018.5—Contractors License Law)

THE LAW REQUIRES THAT, BEFORE A LICENSED CONTRACTOR CAN ENTER INTO A CONTRACT WITH YOU FOR A WORK OF IMPROVEMENT ON YOUR PROPERTY, HE MUST GIVE YOU A COPY OF THIS NOTICE.

Under the mechanics' lien laws of the State of California, persons who help to improve your property and are not paid have a right to enforce their claims against your property. This ''claim'' is known as a mechanics' lien. Basically, when somebody files a mechanics' lien, they are making claim on your property as security against payment of a just debt.

In other words, this law allows contractors, subcontractors, laborers, material men or certain others who may have provided goods or services to place a lien on your home or the structure they built or improved for you for any unpaid portion of the goods and services they furnish. For example, if you fail to pay your contractor, of if your contractor fails to pay his subcontractors or laborers, or neglects to make required contributions to a trust and/or other funds (where applicable), then those people can look to your property for payment, **EVEN IF YOU HAVE PAID YOUR CONTRACTOR IN FULL.**

There are a number of ways to protect yourself and your property at the onset of contracting and throughout the construction project. You might, for instance, request that the contractor furnish you with a payment and performance bond. (This is a different bond than the one currently required by Contractors License Law.) The additional cost is usually minimal and is a certain guarantee that the project will be completed and the bills paid. You may also wish to record this payment or performance bond and file the contract with the County Recorder to further protect yourself from anyone liening your property. If you do have a contractor provide a special bond on your project and the bonding company does not honor your claim promptly in the event the contractor defaults, you may wish to contact the California Insurance Commission to see if the bonding company is engaging in an unfair claims practice.

Another avenue available to you is to use a funding control company. The control company acts as a third party, disbursing all funds for payment and usually securing all the necessary releases of liens. A funding control company is a specialized construction escrow which makes payment directly to subcontractors and suppliers. By doing this, it affords additional protection against valid liens.

Should you choose not to use the above, the following are some of the important time requirements you should be aware of regarding the mechanics' lien law:

1. Preliminary Notice.
A claimant, contractor, subcontractor, or materialman is entitled to enforce a lien only if he gives the preliminary twenty (20) days notice, if applicable. All claimants, other than the original contractor (the person you contracted with), or a laborer performing actual labor for wages, must give this notice. Therefore, people who you may not even know, such as a subcontractor, or a material supplier, must notify you that they are providing supplies or services to your property which may later create a lien. This Preliminary Notice must be given no later than twenty (20) days after the claimant has first furnished labor, services, equipment or material to the job site.

If you get such a Preliminary Notice, do not be alarmed. The notice is intended for your protection so that you may then require your contractor to furnish you with a lien release prior to or concurrently with payment to him.

2. Notice of Mechanics' Lien.
Usually claimants must record the Notice and Claim of Lien within ninety (90) days of the completion of the work. If a Notice of Completion, or a Notice of Cessation of Labor has been recorded, then the Claim of Lien must be recorded within sixty (60) days by the original contractor and within thirty (30) days by all other claimants such as subcontractors, materialmen, etc. The claimants must indicate on the notice what is owed to them. This lien will now bind your property like a mortgage or trust deed.

3. Complaint to Foreclose a Mechanics' Lien.
If the claimants' demands are not satisfied, then they must usually file suit within ninety (90) days after the recordation of a Notice of Mechanics' Lien. The complaint to foreclose the lien is filed in a regular court proceeding and follows in a similar manner. **YOU SHOULD BE AWARE THAT YOUR PROPERTY COULD BE SOLD AND THE PROCEEDS FROM THE SALE USED TO SATISFY THE CLAIM.**

4. Notice of Non-Responsibility.
You can protect yourself and your property from a valid claim of a contactor, or subcontractor who is doing work on your property, but not at your request (for example if you have a tenant who has contracted for work to be done). You can do this by posting and recording a Notice of Non-Responsibility. The notice must be posted in a conspicuous place within ten (10) days after you have obtained knowledge of the work. You must then record the notice at the County Recorder's office. You can usually purchase this form from various sources.

5. Unconditional Lien Release.
You may also require that the original contractor provide you with unconditional lien releases signed by each and every person who has performed any work or labor as well as every person who has delivered any materials to your job. Be sure to get releases from each person who gave you a Preliminary Notice.

6. Notice of Completion.
The owner of the property or his agent (sometimes the general contractor) can record a Notice of Completion within ten (10) days following the actual completion of the work of improvement. The effect of the Notice of Completion is to shorten the time period within which the contractors or subcontractors may file their Mechanics' Lien.

The above is not meant to be an exhaustive review of mechanics' liens. It is intended that you understand that you are entering into a contract which may bind your property and it is intended that you understand how to act to protect your property.

Read and acknowledged.

Signature ____

Dated ____

CALIFORNIA BUSINESS AND PROFESSIONS CODE

§ 7151 Home Improvement; home improvement goods or services; definitions

''Home improvement'' means the repairing, remodeling, altering, converting, of modernizing of, or adding to, residential property and shall include, but not be limited to, the construction, erection, replacement, or improvement of driveways, swimming pools, terraces, patios, landscaping, fences, porches, garages, fallout shelters, basements, and other improvements of the structures or land which is adjacent to a dwelling house. ''Home improvement'' shall also mean the installation of home improvement goods or the furnishings of home improvement services.

For purposes of this chapter, ''home improvement goods or services'' means goods and services, as defined in Section 1689.5 of Civil Code, which are bought in connection with the improvement of real property. Such home improvement goods and services include, but are not limited to, burglar alarms, carpeting, texture coation, fencing, air conditioning or heating equipment, and termite extermination. Home improvement goods include goods which, at the time of sale or subsequently, are to be so affixed to real property as to become a part of real property whether or not severable therefrom.

§ 7152.2. Home improvement contract defined

''Home improvement contract'' means an agreement, whether oral or written, or contained in one or more documents, between a contractor and an owner or between a contractor and a tenant, regardless of the number of residence or dwelling units contained in the building in which the tenant resides, if the work is to be performed in, to, or upon the residence or dwelling unit of such tenant, for the performance of a home improvement and includes all labor, services, and materials to be furnished and performed thereunder ''Home improvement contract'' also means an agreement, whether oral or written, or contained in one or more documents, between a salesman, whether or not he is a home improvement salesman, and (a) an owner or (b) a tenant, regardless of the number of residence or dwelling units contained in the building in which the tenant resides, which provides for the sale, installation, or furnishing of home improvement goods or services.

§ 7159 Contract requirements; effect of noncompliance; violations

This section shall apply only to home improvement contracts as defined in Section 7151.2, between contractor, whether a general contractor or a specialty contractor, who is licensed or subject to be licensed pursuant to this chapter with regard to such transaction and who contracts with an owner or tenant for work upon a building or structure for purposed repairing, remodeling, alterina, converting, or modernizing such building or structure and where the aggregate contract price specified in one or more improvement contracts, including all labor, servies, and materials to be furnished by the contractor, exceeds five hundred dollars ($500).

Every home improvement contract and any changes in the contract subject to the provisions of this section shall be evidenced by a writing and shall be signed by all the parties to the contract thereto. The writing shall contain the following:

(a) The name, address, and license number of the contractor, and the name and registration number of any salesman who solicited or negotiated the contract.

(b) The approximate dates when the work will begin and be substantially completed.

(c) A description of the work to be done and description of the materials to be used and the equipment to be used or installed and the agreed consideration for the work.

(d) A schedule of payment showing the amount of each payment as a sum in dollars and cents. The schedule of payments shall be referenced to the amount of work or services to be performed or to any materials or equipment to be supplied.

(e) If the payment schedule contained in the contract provides for a downpayment to be paid to the contractor by the owner or the tenant before the commencement of work, such downpayment shall not exceed one thousand dollars ($1,000) or 10 percent of the contract price, excluding finance charges, whichever is the lesser.

(f) In no event shall the payment schedule provide for the contractor to receive, or shall the contractor actually receive, payment in excess of 100 percent of the value of the work performed on the project at any time, excluding finance charges, except that the contractor may receive an initial downpayment authorized by subdivision (e). A failure by the contractor without lawful excuse to substantially commence work within twenty (20) days the approximate date specified in the contract when work will begin shall postpone the next succeeding payment to the contractor for that period of time equivalent to the time between when subtantial commencement was to have occurred and when it did occur.

(g) The requirements of subdivisions (d), (e), and (f) pertaining to the payment schedule shall not apply when the contract provides for the contractor to furnish performance and payment bond, lien and completion bond, a bond equivalent, or a funding control approved by the Registrar of Contractors covering full performance and completion of the contract and such bonds are furnished by the contractor, or when the parties agree for full payment to be made upon satisfactory completion of the project. The contract shall contain in close proximity to the signatures of the owner and contractor in at least 10-point type a notice to the owner or tenent stating that such owner or tenant has the right to require the contractor to have a performance and payment bond or funding control.

(h) If the contract provides for a payment of a salesman's commission out of the contract price, such payment shall be made on a pro rata basis in proportion to the schedule of payments made in accordance with subdivision (d).

(i) The language of the notice required pursuant to Section 7018.5.

(j) What constitutes substantial commencement of work pursuant to the contract.

(k) A notice that failure by the contractor without lawful excuse to substantially commence work within twenty (20) days from the approximate date specified in the contract when work will begin is a violation of the Contractors License Law.

A failure by the contractor without lawful excuse to substantially commence work within twenty (20) days from the approximate date specified in the contract when work will begin is a violation of this section.

This section shall not be construed to prohibit the parties to a home improvement contract from agreeing to a contract or account subject to Chapter 1 (commencing with Section 1801) of the Title 2 of Party 4 of Division 3 of the Civil Code.

The writing may also contain other matters agreed to by the parties to the contract.

The writing shall be legible and shall be in such form as to clearly describe any other document which is to be incorporated into the contract, and before any work is done, the owner shall be furnished a copy of the written agreement, signed by the contractor.

For purposes of this section, the board shall, by regulation, determine what constitutes ''without lawful excuse.''

The provisions of this section are not exclusive and do not relieve the contractor or any contract subject to it from compliance with all other applicable provisions of law.

A violation of this section by a licensee, or a person subject to be licensed, under this chapter, his agent, or salesman is a misdemeanor punishable by a fine of not less than one hundred dollars ($100) nor more than five thousand dollars ($5,000) or by imprisonment in the county jail not exceeding one year, or by both such fine and imprisonment.

GENERAL COMMERCIAL LEASE

THIS LEASE, executed in duplicate at _____ , California, this

_____ day of _____ , 19 _____ , by and between

and

hereinafter called respectively lessor and lessee, without regard to number or gender,

WITNESSETH: That lessor hereby leases to lessee, and lessee hires from lessor, for the purpose of conducting therein

and for no other purpose, those certain premises with the appurtenances, situated in

_____ , State of California, and more particularly described as follows, to-wit:

The term shall be for _____ years, commencing on the

_____ day of _____ , 19 _____ , and ending on the

_____ day of _____ , 19 _____ , at the total rent or sum of

($ _____) Dollars,

lawful money of the United States of America, which lessee agrees to pay to lessor, without deduction or offset, prior notice or demand, at such place or places as may be designated from time to time by lessor, in installments as follows:

Lessor acknowledges receipt from lessee of the sum of $ _____ , placed with lessor to secure the faithful performance by lessee of each and every covenant and condition herein required to be performed by lessee, including but not limited to, at lessor's options, lessee's defaults in the payment of rent or other sums due herein, repair of damages to the premises caused by lessee, or cleaning of the premises upon termination of the premises. Lessor may use such funds and shall have no obligation to credit lessee's account with any interest thereon.

It is further mutually agreed between the parties as follows:

1. If lessor, for any reason, cannot deliver possession of said premises to lessee at the commencement of said term, this lease shall not be void or voidable, nor shall lessor be liable to lessee for any loss or damage resulting therefrom; but there shall be a proportionate deduction of rent covering the period between the commencement of said term and the time when lessor can deliver possession.

2. Lessee shall not use, or permit said premises, or any part thereof, to be used, for any purpose or purposes other than the purpose or purposes for which said premises are hereby leased; and no use shall be made or permitted to be made of said premises, nor acts done, which will increase the existing rate of insurance upon the building in which said premises may be located, or cause a cancellation of any insurance policy covering said building, or any part thereof, nor shall lessee sell, or permit to be kept, used, or sold, in or about said premises, any article which may be prohibited by standard form of fire insurance policies. Lessee shall, at his sole cost, comply with any and all requirements, pertaining to the use of said premises, of any insurance organization or company, necessary for maintenance of reasonable fire and public liability insurance, covering said building and appurtenances.

WOLCOTTS FORM 973, REV. 7-80   ©WOLCOTTS, INC., 1980   8 pt. type or larger
GENERAL COMMERCIAL LEASE

270

3. Lessee shall not commit, or suffer to be committed, any waste upon said premises, or any nuisance, or other act or thing which may disturb the quiet enjoyment of any other tenant in the building in which the demised premises may be located. Lessee shall not make, or suffer to be made, any alterations of the said premises, or any part thereof, without the written consent of lessor first had and obtained, and any additions to, or alterations of, said premises, except movable furniture and trade fixtures, shall become at once a part of the realty and belong to lessor.

4. Lessee shall not vacate or abandon the premises at any time during the term; and if lessee shall abandon, vacate or surrender said premises or be dispossessed by process of law, or otherwise, any personal property belonging to lessee and left on the premises may be removed, and the lessor shall have a lien upon all such property not exempt from a lien by California Civil Code Section 1861, Notice of Sale, and the sale to enforce said lien, shall be governed by California Civil Code. The proceeds realized from any such sale shall be applied first to the payment of the expenses of sale, reimbursement of costs to remove the property from the premises, costs of storage pending sale, and reasonable attorney's fees incurred in connection therewith; any balance remaining shall be applied to the payment of any other sums which may then or thereafter be legally due lessor from lessee; after satisfying all of the obligations previously enumerated, the balance, if any, shall be paid over to the lessee.

5. As part of the consideration for rental, lessee shall, at his sole cost, keep and maintain said premises and appurtenances and every part thereof (excepting exterior walls and roof which lessor agrees to repair), including sidewalks adjacent to said premises, any store front and interior of the premises, in good and sanitary order, condition and repair, and replace broken glazing. By entry hereunder, lessee accepts the premises as being in good and sanitary order, condition and repair and agrees on the last day of said term, or sooner termination of this lease, to surrender unto lessor all and singular said premises with said appurtenances in the same condition as when received, reasonable use and wear thereof and damage by fire, act of God, or by the elements excepted, and to remove all of the lessee's signs, from said premises.

6. Lessee shall, at his sole cost, comply with all of the requirements of all Municipal, State and Federal authorities now in force, or which may hereafter be in force, pertaining to the use of said premises, and shall faithfully observe in said use all Municipal ordinances and State and Federal statutes now in force or which may hereafter be in force. The judgment of any court of competent jurisdiction, or the admission of lessee in any action or proceeding against lessee, whether lessor be a party thereto or not, that lessee has violated any such ordinance or statute in said use, shall be conclusive of that fact as between lessor and lessee.

7. Lessee as a material part of the consideration to be rendered to lessor, hereby waives all claims against lessor for damages to goods, wares and merchandise, in, upon, or about said premises and for injuries to persons, in, upon, or about said premises, from any cause whatsoever arising at any time, and lessee will hold lessor exempt and harmless from any liability, loss, cost and obligation on account of any damage or injury to any person, or to the goods, wares and merchandise of any person, arising in any manner from the use or occupancy of the premises by the lessee.

8. Lessee shall not conduct or permit to be conducted any sale by auction on said premises. Lessee shall not place or permit to be placed any sign, marquee or awning on the front of said premises without the written consent of lessor; lessee upon request of lessor, shall immediately remove any sign or decoration which lessee has placed or permitted to be placed in, on, or about the front of the premises which, in the opinion of lessor, is objectionable or offensive, and if lessee fails so to do, lessor may enter said premises and remove the same. Lessor has reserved the exclusive right to the exterior sidewalls, rear wall and roof of said premises, and lessee shall not place or permit to be placed upon said sidewalls, rear wall or roof, any sign, advertisement or notice without the written consent of lessor.

9. Lessee shall pay for all water, gas, heat, light, power, telephone service and all other services and utilities supplied to said premises.

10. Lessee shall permit lessor and his agents to enter into and upon said premises at all reasonable times after giving notice for the purpose of inspecting the same or for the purpose of maintaining the building in which said premises are situated, or for the purpose of making repairs, alterations or additions to any other portion of said building, including the erection and maintenance of such scaffolding, canopies, fences and props as may be required, or for the purpose of posting notices of non-liability for alterations, additions, or repairs or for the purpose of placing upon the property in which the said premises are located any usual or ordinary "for sale" signs, without any rebate of rent and without any liability to lessee for any loss of occupation or quiet enjoyment of the premises thereby occasioned; and shall permit lessor, at any time within thirty days prior to the expiration date of this lease, to place upon said premises any usual or ordinary "to let" or "to lease" signs.

11. In the event of (a) a partial destruction of said premises or the building containing same during said term which requires repairs to either said premises or said building, or (b) said premises or said building being declared unsafe or unfit for occupancy by any authorized public authority for any reason other than lessee's act, use or occupation which declaration requires repairs to either said premises or said building, lessor shall forthwith make such repairs, provided such repairs can be made within sixty (60) days under the laws and regulations of authorized public authorities, but such partial destruction (including any destruction necessary in order to make repairs required by any such declaration) shall in no wise annul or void this lease, except that lessee shall be entitled to a proportionate deduction of rent while such repairs are being made, such proportionate deduction to be based upon the extent to which the making of such repairs shall interfere with the business carried on by lessee in said premises. If such repairs cannot be made within sixty (60) days, lessor may, at his option, make same within a reasonable time, this lease continuing in full force and effect and the rent to be proportionately rebated, as in this paragraph provided. In the event that lessor does not so elect to make such repairs which cannot be made within sixty (60) days, or such repairs cannot be made under such laws and regulations, this lease may be terminated at the option of either party. In respect to any partial destruction (including any destruction necessary in order to make repairs required by any such declaration) which lessor is obligated to repair or may elect to repair under the terms of this paragraph, the provisions of Section 1932, Subdivision (2), and Section 1933, Subdivision (4), of the Civil Code of the State of California are waived by lessee. A total destruction (including any destruction required by any authorized public authority) of either said premises or said building shall terminate this lease. In the event of any dispute between lessor and lessee relative to the provisions of this paragraph, they shall each select an arbitrator, the two arbitrators so selected shall select a third arbitrator and the three arbitrators so selected shall hear and determine the controversy and their decision thereof shall be final and binding on both lessor and lessee who shall bear the cost of such arbitration equally between them.

12. Lessee shall not assign this lease, or any interest therein, and shall not sublet said premises or any part thereof, or any right or privilege appurtenant thereto, or suffer any other person (the agents and servants of lessee excepted) to occupy or use said premises, or any portion thereof, without the written consent of lessor first had and obtained. Furthermore, this lease shall not, nor shall any interest therein, be assignable, as to the interest of lessee, by operation of law, without the written consent of lessor first had and obtained. A consent by lessor to one assignment, subletting, occupation or use by any other person, whether by operation of law or otherwise, shall not be deemed to be a consent to any subsequent assignment, subletting occupation or use by any other person. Any such assignment or subletting, whether by operation of law or otherwise, without such written consent first had and obtained shall be void, and shall, at the option of lessor, terminate this lease.

13. It is expressly understood and agreed that the lessor is relying on the personal integrity, experience, and knowledge of the individuals operating the lessee enterprise and has relied upon their personal ability to maintain the commercial viability of the premises and the lessor's interest in the property, and therefore either (a) the appointment of a receiver to take possession of all or substantially all of the assets of lessee, or (b) a general assignment by lessee for the benefit of creditors, or (c) any action taken or suffered by lessee under any insolvency or bankruptcy act shall constitute a breach of this lease by lessee, and shall, at the option of lessor, terminate this lease.

14.A In the event lessee breaches the lease and abandons the property before the end of the term or, if his right to possession is terminated by the lessor because of a breach of the lease, this lease shall thereupon terminate. Upon such termination, lessor may recover from lessee: (a) the worth at the time of award of judgment of the unpaid rent which had been earned at the time of termination, together with interest thereon at the rate of nine (9%) percent per annum; and (b) the worth at the time of award of judgment by which the unpaid rent which would have been earned after termination until the time of judgment exceeds the amount of such rental loss that the lessee proves could have been reasonably avoided, together with interest thereon at the rate of nine (9%) percent per annum, and (c) the worth at the time of award of judgment of the amount by which the unpaid rent for the balance of the term after the time of award exceeds the amount of such rental loss that the lessee proves could be reasonably avoided discounted by the discount rate of Federal Reserve Bank of San Francisco at the time of award of judgment plus one (1%) percent; and (d) any other amount necessary to compensate the lessor for all the detriment proximately caused by the lessee's failure to perform his obligations under the lease or which in the ordinary course of things would be likely to result therefrom, together with costs of suit and reasonable attorney's fees.

14.B If default be made by lessee in payment of rent or in the observance, payment or performance of any of the other provisions, terms or conditions of this lease, or if any conduct of the lessee, his family, servants, employees, agents, invitees or licensees shall obstruct or interfere with the rights of other occupants, or annoy them by unreasonable noises or otherwise, or should they commit or perform any nuisance on the premises or commit or suffer any illegal or immoral act to be committed thereon, the lessor may, at its option, terminate this lease and, any holding over thereafter by lessee shall be construed to be a tenancy from month to month only, for the same rental rate and payable in the same manner as herein specified.

15. The voluntary or other surrender of this lease by lessee, or a mutual cancellation thereof, shall not work a merger, and shall, at the option of lessor, terminate all or any existing subleases or subtenancies or may, at the option of lessor, operate as an assignment to him of any or all of such subleases of subtenancies.

16. If lessor is made a party defendant to any litigation concerning this lease or the leased premises or the occupancy thereof by lessee, then lessee shall hold harmless lessor from all liability by reason of said litigation, including reasonable attorneys fees and expenses incurred by lessor in any such litigation, whether or not any such litigation is prosecuted to judgment. If lessor commences an action against lessee to enforce any of the terms hereof or because of the breach by lessee of any of the terms hereof, or for the recovery of any rent due hereunder, or for any unlawful detainer of said premises, lessee shall pay to lessor reasonable attorneys fees and expenses, and the right to such attorneys fees and expenses shall be deemed to have accrued on the commencement of such action, and shall be enforceable whether or not such action is prosecuted to judgment. If lessee breaches any term of this lease, lessor may employ an attorney or attorneys to protect lessor's rights hereunder, and in the event of such employment following any breach by lessee, lessee shall pay lessor reasonable attorneys fees and expenses incurred by lessor, whether or not an action is actually commenced against lessee by reason of said breach.

17. All notices to be given to lessee shall be given in writing personally or by depositing the same in the United States mail, postage prepaid, and addressed to lessee at said premises, whether or not lessee has departed from, abandoned or vacated the premises. All notices to be given to lessor shall be given in writing personally or by depositing the same in the United States mail, postage prepaid, and addressed to the lessor at the place designated by lessor for the payment of rent, or at such other place or places as may be designated from time to time by lessor.

18. If any security be given by lessee to secure the faithful performance of all or any of the covenants of this lease on the part of lessee, lessor may transfer and/or deliver the security, as such, to the purchaser of the reversion, in the event that the reversion be sold, and thereupon lessor shall be discharged from any further liability in reference thereto. Lessee hereby waives notice in the event of lessor's transfer of its interest in the leased premises.

19. The waiver by lessor of any breach of any term, covenant or condition herein contained shall not be deemed to be a waiver of such term, covenant or condition or any subsequent breach of the same or any other term, covenant or condition herein contained.

20. Any holding over after the expiration of the said term, with the consent of lessor, shall be construed to be a tenancy from month to month, at a rental of
($) Dollars a month, and shall otherwise be on the terms and conditions herein specified, so far as applicable.

21. ESCALATION CLAUSE: The lessee agrees that should the leased premises be taxed at a higher rate than the rate for the "present" tax year, then said increase shall be paid by the lessee monthly and shall be prorated over the twelve month period to which said tax is attributable and shall be due and payable as rent.
The "present" tax year heretofore referred to is the fiscal year 19____ ____. The tax bill for the leased premises for the "present" tax year is $

22. SUBORDINATION CLAUSE: This lease is subject and subordinate to all existing leases and to all mortgages and deeds of trust which may now or hereafter affect the real property of which the leased premises form a part, and to all renewals, modifications, replacements and extensions thereof. The lessee hereby agrees to execute any instruments for the benefit of the lessor as may be necessary to effectuate this provision of the lease.

23. TAKING BY EMINENT DOMAIN: In case the whole of the leased premises are taken by right of eminent domain or other authority of law during the period of this lease, or any extension thereof, this lease shall terminate. In case a part of the leased premises are taken by right of eminent domain or other authority of law, this lease may, at the election of the lessor, be terminated.
If a part of the premises are taken by the right of eminent domain and the lessor does not elect to terminate the lease the rent herein stipulated shall be decreased proportionately according to the value of that part of the premises taken. If the entire premises are taken or if a part of the leased premises are taken and the lessor elects to terminate the lease, then all compensation paid for the taking shall belong to the lessor.

24. The covenants and conditions herein contained shall, subject to the provisions as to assignment, apply to and bind the heirs, successors, executors, administrators and assigns of all the parties hereto; and all of the parties hereto shall be jointly and severally liable hereunder.

25. Time is of the essence of this lease.

IN WITNESS WHEREOF, lessor and lessee have executed these presents, the day and year first above written.

_____ (Seal)   _____ (Seal)

_____ (Seal)   _____ (Seal)

_____ (Seal)   _____ (Seal)

                    LESSOR   LESSEE

Index